DIGITAL
20 PIONEERS REDEFINING ITS BOUNDARIES
ART

TEXT BY

ALESSANDRA MATTANZA

FOREWORD BY

SERENA TABACCHI

DIGITAL

20 PIONEERS REDEFINING ITS BOUNDARIES

ART

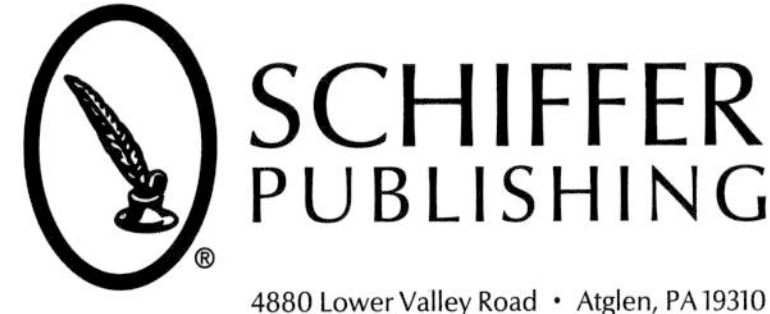

SCHIFFER PUBLISHING

4880 Lower Valley Road • Atglen, PA 19310

CONTENTS

REFIK ANADOL

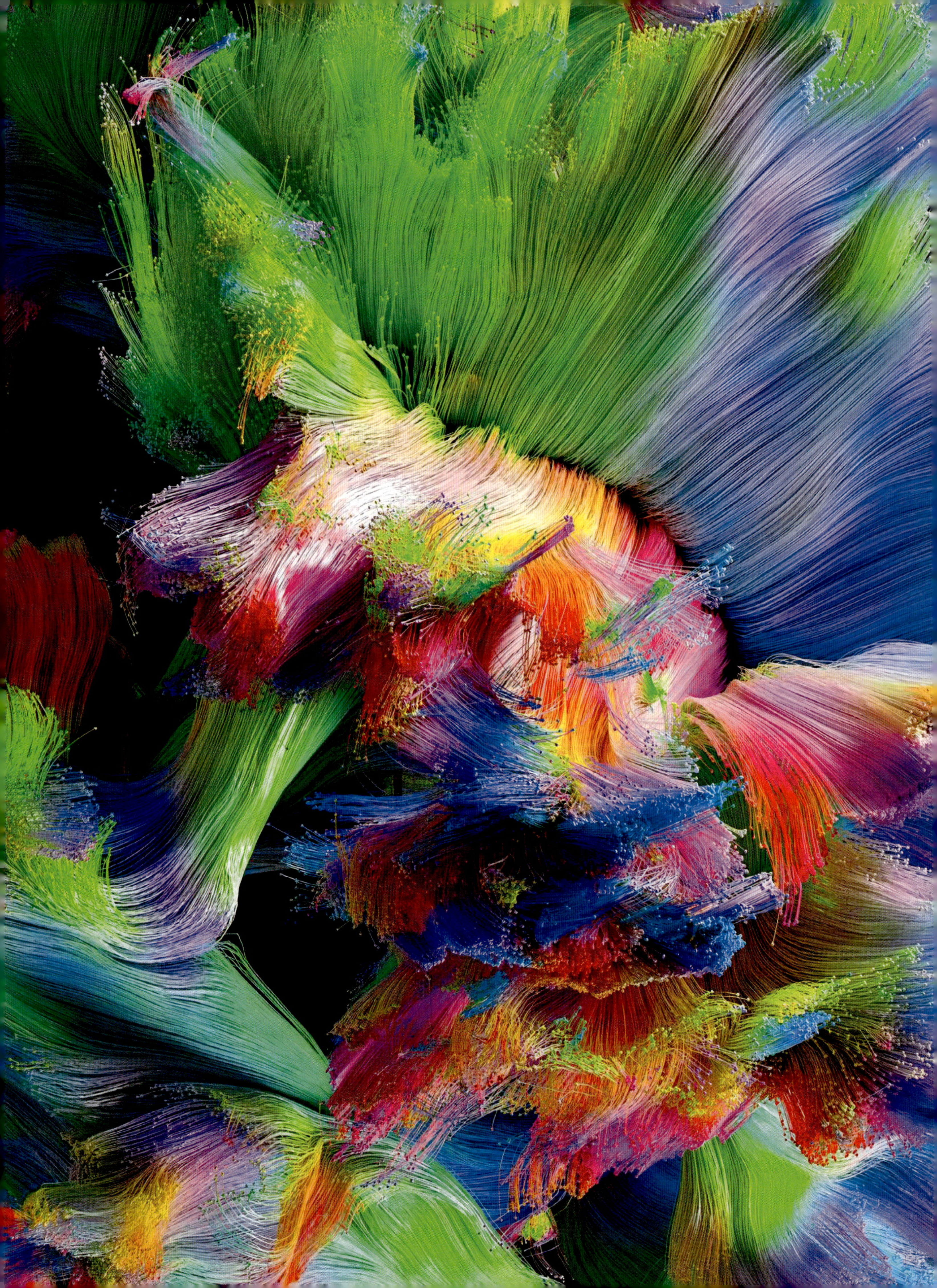

INNOVATION IN ART: NEW LANGUAGES FOR A TRANSMEDIA AESTHETIC

"ANY SUFFICIENTLY ADVANCED TECHNOLOGY IS INDISTINGUISHABLE FROM MAGIC."

ARTHUR C. CLARKE

Everything happened in just a little over two months. In the end—and after long days, many hours online fed by heated debates on Twitter (now X), Discord channels, and several groups on Telegram—the name everyone agreed on was Crypto Art. How did we get here? For some time, terms such as "blockchain," "smart contracts," and "NFTs" (non-fungible tokens) had begun appearing on the web, not the Internet of the early 2000s, but a new decentralized one, which was already emerging among experts in the sector and known officially as web3. In the 1990s, the first wave of the Internet made it possible to spread online content and interactive pages full of text, images, and clickable links. Later came blogs and the first social networks, on which we could share our lives with one another. Soon, however, users' realization that they had become content producers for proprietary platforms ran against the freedom promised by decentralized applications that exalted their autonomy from GAFAM (Google, Apple, Facebook, Amazon, Microsoft), the web's main multinationals in the Western world. It was in this context that art became one of the very first things to take part in the digital revolution, in which it became a rare commodity purchased or sold with tokens. With the advent of NFTs, files—identical to each other and infinitely reproducible by their very nature—gained the property of uniqueness or scarcity: properties deemed essential

by those who collect art works. But the innovation that shook the market, critics, and, above all, the media, lay in the technical ability and artistic intuition of the first blockchain operators, who introduced the concept of digital certificates as property, linking the innate digital work irreversibly to its matrix, and thus guaranteeing its origin, authorship, and resale rights at each successive sale. One must bear in mind that a period of only a little over five years separates the earliest recorded NFT on blockchain (artist Kevin McCoy's Quantum, presented at the New Museum in New York in 2014, and sold for a mere $4.00) and the record-breaking sale of Mike Winkelmann's (aka Beeple's) Everydays, The First 5,000 Days, auctioned at Christie's for over US$69 million. It thus became clear that an art, social, and economic movement, promoted by coders and the prophets of new technologies that were preparing to destabilize a capitalist system verging on collapse, was coming to life before our very eyes. And this certainly did not surprise those who read the news or surfed social media. The visionaries who purchased Bitcoin, whose value, at the time, was equivalent to two Papa Johns pizzas, did not bat an eyelash; quite the contrary, they began collecting art and perhaps even producing it. A new art movement was born, one firmly bound to an online community, whose rules on protecting creators could be stated on smart contracts. No longer just graphic designers, video editors, or illustrators: all were now artists!

Already theorized by the French writer and philosopher Paul Valéry in 1936, the art technique that originated in the nineteenth century joined forces with modern technology for the first time in the early years of the twentieth century with the advent of photography and cinema.

Valéry thus imagined innovation as the progressive mechanization of the craftsman. The earliest examples of digital art can be traced back to Gottfried Jäger's photographic manipulations (1960) and Karl W. Steinbuch's proposed simulation of the first neural architecture capable of mimicing human intelligence (Learnmatrix) in Automat und Mensch (1961). Prophetically, Valéry hypothesized a future in which the artist would assume the guise of a scientist, who, seduced by the productivity of the machine, would create new forms of art on the clock in his laboratory. That same year, Walter Benjamin envisioned a more integrated and positive future for the artist's role in the development of technology. In his essay "The Work of Art in the Age of Mechanical Reproduction," Benjamin emphasized the mass availability of art, while paying attention to its democratization and social function—a combination necessary at certain points of humanity's historical development. Thus, the aura—which he understood as the unique and unrepeatable experience that one feels when experiencing a work of art—is lost when a work of art is reproduced by media, such as television or radio, that disseminate it. Benjamin's hope was that technology would become humanized through mass distribution and would thus encourage artists to fuel their creativity by interacting with—rather than withstanding—new technologies. For years, New Media Art was one of the main avant-garde movements for artists seeking a new matrix. One may think, for example, of the impact of Lucio Fontana's Manifesto of the Spatial Movement for Television (1952) and Nam June Paik's TV Garden (1974) on contemporary and digital art. Inasmuch as video art first drew the attention of the general public in 1995 when it surfaced at the 46th Venice Biennale in the works of Bruce Nauman, Gary Hill, and Bill Viola, generative art was already of interest to scientists and those engaged in research in the early 1960s, after the Italian company Olivetti released the first computer (Desktop Computer 101).

The earliest generative algorithms were used to create works that were printed on paper by a plotter with a stylus, thus granting the code a function that differed from the one for which it had been designed. The machine was not only asked to perform mathematical calculations, but also to produce art. The pioneers of this movement included artists such as Vera Molnár, Manfred Mohr, and Frieder Nake, who found a way of generating new art forms by developing coding systems

that, like Man Ray's photography or Herbert W. Franke's algorithmic art, granted a graphic identity and aesthetics to algorithms and programs that later became historical digital art collectors' items.

Generative art joined forces with crypto art after John Watkinson and Matt Hall, the founders of the Larva Labs Studio known for their CryptoPunks project, created Autoglyphs, the first generative art project on blockchain (2019). Among the more recent generative experiments that have exerted a major influence on the field of digital art are those of Casey Reas, co-creator of Processing, a language for coding works on a digital sketchbook meant to increase the accessibility of graphic programming, and Tayler Hobbs, who, after meticulously analyzing the inherent biases of our computers and the way these processes integrate with the creative ones of an artist, generated customized algorithms that combine both of these dynamics: that is, the synthetic and the organic. Finally, there's Sasha Stiles, co-founder of the TheVERSEVerse group, who see generative poetry marking a point of interaction between man and machine, creating a bio-artificial stream of consciousness capable of provoking excitement and surprise. Nonetheless, to-day's algorithms pertain not only to generative works of art, but also and mainly to works produced by the algorithms of artificial intelligence (AI), which, little by little, have brought to life an utterly new aesthetic, no longer abstract, but figura-tive—albeit often distorted.

Midjourey, DALL-E, and Stable Diffusion are among the software applications used today to generate images and videos through written prompts (textual de-scriptions in narrative form that inform the algorithm of our request before gener-ating a series of outputs). We could thus fantasize and say that the humanization of technological means that was desired and proposed by Benjamin nearly a cen-tury ago has been achieved in the latest creative explorations of algorithms. This accessibility of the means has led to a greater acceptance of the digital, allowing us to rediscover the aura of a work (of art) with each output because it is unique and imprinted on the screen in an unprecedented form. The role of the artist has thus become a much-debated topic in a panorama where artificial learning and creativity, based on what has already been achieved by human genius, will be capable of overcoming technique and moving toward new transmedia horizons.

CAN AI BE CAPABLE OF LOVE?

THE NEW FRONTIERS OF DIGITAL ART,
THE BOLD NEW WORLD OF THE FUTURE.

The Child

/ (. . .) /

Colonel Howell: All right. Listen to me. Did you locate the weapon?

Joshua: Yeah. It's here. I'm with it.

Howell: Describe it.

Joshua: It's a kid. It's a kid. They've made it into some kind of kid. That's the weapon.

Colonel Howell: What?

/ (. . .) /

/ (. . .) /

The Mother

Harun [to Joshua, referring to the gravely wounded Alphie, The Child]: There will never be another like her. Her mother completed her in secret, when you were together. Just weeks before the night of the attack. She could have made her hate mankind. Perhaps she should have. But Maya put her love for you into the child. She made a new kind of life. From a scan of a human embryo. A copy of your child. Like it or not, Joshua, you are part of us now.

THE CREATOR, 2023

Is AI capable of love? Can AI feel real emotions as if it were a human being? In the sci-fi movie The Creator, conceived, directed, and co-produced by the British director Gareth Edwards, the answer seems clear from the following statement: "They've got larger 'hearts' than human beings do!" . . . "You can't defeat AI. It's evolution." The story is set in 2070, fifteen years after the detonation of a nuclear warhead in Los Angeles has killed a million people—all incinerated in the blink of an eye. AI, which was invented to protect humanity, is accused of deliberately provoking this cataclysmic event.

BY ALESSANDRA MATTANZA

Consequently, it is banished from the Western world, along with the incredibly human-like robots that it created and that are capable of feeling and experiencing emotions.

Exiled to New Asia, along with those who wish to protect them and do not consider them guilty, these humanoid robots assume full control of their lives, claiming their right to freedom. Making us think about a probable and possibly not-too-distant future, the movie forces us to reflect on the importance of AI, now quite present in our world, in many fields, including digital art. It also draws attention to issues such as tolerance, liberty, free will, the new frontiers of experimentation, and the peaceful coexistence of man and machine.

In the end, the entire story revolves once again around love. What really counts, even in this brave new world, are feelings, emotions, affection, and compassion. It is these that inspire and animate the hearts—be these of flesh or metal—of the main characters. Modern technology has now fully penetrated our world as well, and conquered art, first the hearts and minds of artists, then the hearts of their audience.

Digital art has met with discrimination for far too long, as was the case with street art, which was shut out of galleries and museums because it "differed" from the so-called fine art, which grew out of schools and academies and was intended for a small privileged circle. Much like street art, digital art made its way into and conquered the hearts of the public through the metaverse. Like murals and graffiti, which extend over walls all over the world and cross the boundaries

of space and time, thanks to social media, so too digital art, with its similarly unrestrained and revolutionary spirit, has drawn attention to itself, both online and on new platforms.

And it has created a community of new artists, engineers, and computer scientists and, simply speaking, those with a passion for IT and coding, photography, painting, or design, who have begun exploring, sketching directly on the computer, using new programs, and supporting and consulting each other as a matter of course. AI arrived in the world of digital art only later, gradually replacing the first tools, the initial attempts not yet based on technologically sophisticated studies, and done on tablets or computers, but with a great desire to create and experiment, as veteran Claudia Hart and the innovator Beeple have pointed out. First there were NFTs, which revolutionized the marketing and financial assessment of art. Today, digital art knows no limits and is breaking all boundaries. Some of its proponents, like Krista Kim, explore light and technology as a means of illuminating humanity and bridging related worlds; others, like Sofia Crespo, use technology to elaborate on biology; yet others, like Claire Silver, use it to confront the phantasms of their subconscious—extraordinary female figures, heroines that dominate the metaverse, or, like Connie Bakshi, become digital shamans who challenge the post-human identity, questioning what is synthetic or organic, material or immaterial, human or non-human.

An artist, after all, can continue doing what they've always done, if they feel that this is what comes naturally to them; but if they wish to evolve beyond

that, if they wish to create something new that has never been done, they need to experiment. They cannot afford to be fearful, but must develop the courage of a tiger, leave behind their comfort zone, and dare to go where no one has ever ventured. They must measure their limits against the new ones, push themselves to create something that extends toward the infinite, that transcends even itself for the sake of art, and that through a primordial unconscious will take them back to the origin of everything and the connection with Mother Earth.

"Native peoples do not fear AI, because it's something that has always existed for them," professes Refik Anadol, who has seduced the world with his dream machines and transfigured colors. This pertains not only to AI, but also to all the new tools that technology has made available to us on an everyday basis as if in a present-day Renaissance. One wakes up in the morning without ever knowing what new idea will be generated that day, because creators, both human and artificial, are constantly at work, exploring the universe of dreams and memory, as well as that of the present moment. The new digital artists are discovering all this and doing so with the instinct of the Indigenous tribes of the forest. Native peoples do not fear the unexpected, the unknown, the unfamiliar, because each day they are confronted with and forced to adapt to the thousand facets of light and shadow as well as the unpredictability of a perennially and constantly evolving wilderness, not to mention the pollution generated by the human race. Nature will always be the greatest teacher of humanity. Change inspires terror; it's full of dangers, but is necessary and inevitable, because it is only by accepting change that one can discover true joy.

REFIK ANADOL

WHEN TECHNOLOGY IS MAGIC, FEELING, POETRY

"IN MY VIEW, TECHNOLOGY, TOO, IS A CREATIVE FORCE, SOMETHING THAT'S ALWAYS BEEN PRESENT IN THE WORLD, IN NATURE, EVEN BEFORE IT MADE ITS APPEARANCE IN HUMANITY. IT'S DIFFICULT TO PUT THAT INTO WORDS, EASIER TO CAPTURE IT IN IMAGES, MEMORIES, AND DREAMS. IT'S SOMETHING THAT INDIGENOUS PEOPLE HAVE ALWAYS KNOWN, BUT THAT WE HAVE JUST BEGUN TO UNDERSTAND."

His art is poetry, a poetry arising from data, from AI, from Indigenous wisdom as much as from that of the great masters of the past. This is because Refik Anadol, like a modern-day Monet, is able to create credible natural forms in a poetic manner through technology and to evoke real emotions with artificial intelligence, which he sees as tightly, empathetically, and powerfully bound to the natural world.

WIND OF YAWANAWA

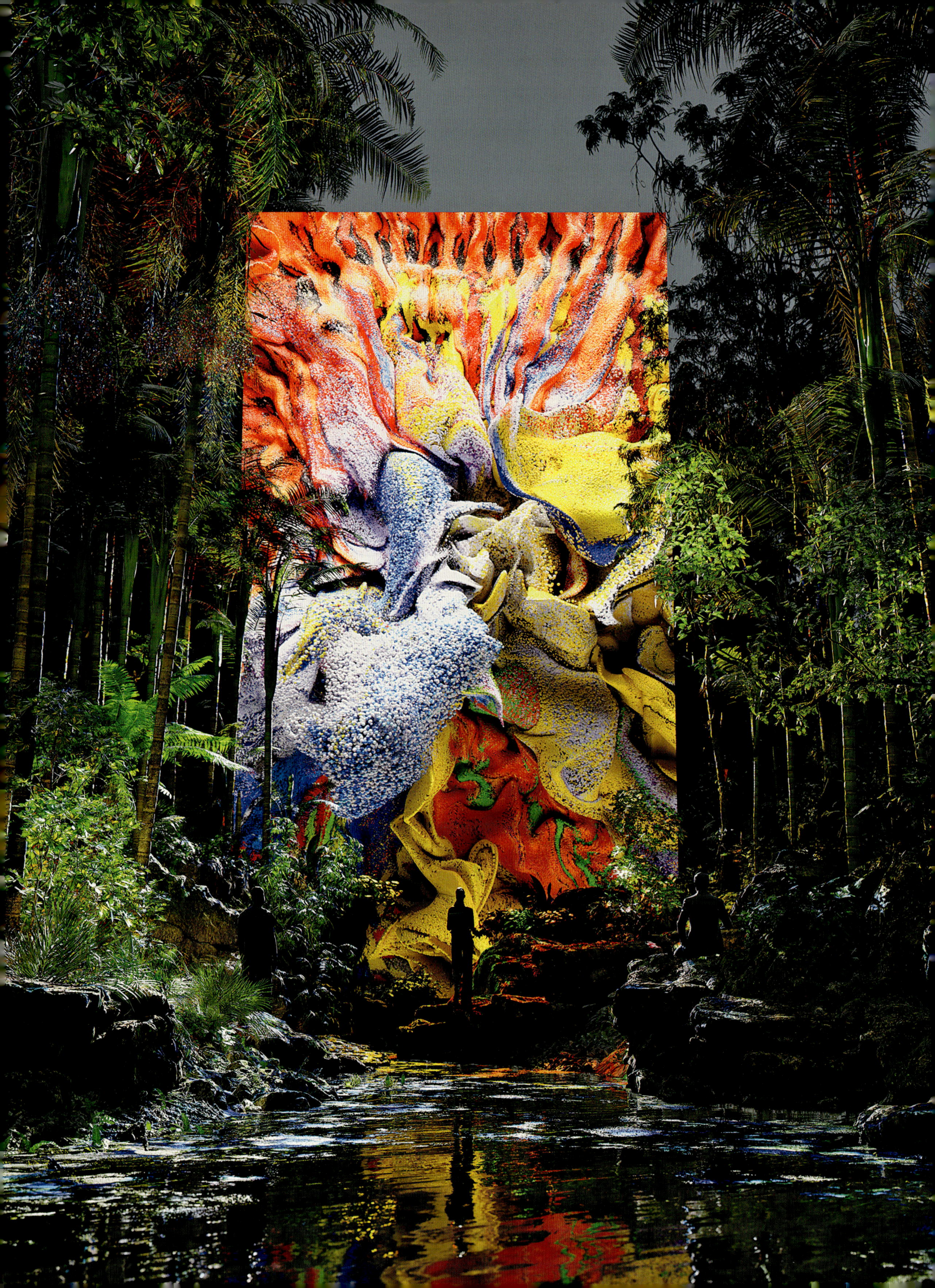

"Monet painted many, many flowers with a brush; with technology, I feel as though I can create and reproduce all the flowers in the world . . . ," he claims. The colors in his images move with the flow of digitized ocean waves, with uncontrolled bursts of color that merge into each other, appear to die, but immediately come back to life in the endless rhythm of creation, of memory that seizes a fleeting moment, of feeling that transforms into vision and action. His works are created and orchestrated with an AI that dreams and subsequently transforms these dreams into images so evocative that, like his own dreams, they cannot be replicated. Music often accompanies these masterpieces, which manage to touch the soul as profoundly as the song of a bird presented as a gift to nature. Such is the case with his work dedicated to the Amazon rainforest and its magical power, in which he uses AI to create magnificent animals and lush flowers that open synchronously and practically fill the air with fragrance . . . "Because, ultimately, they are real," Refik remarks. Whenever one looks at his art, one asks oneself: "Is AI capable of love?" And the answer that pops up automatically is yes, because his art enthralls to the point that it completely captivates one's heart and soul, one's feelings and mind, to evoke joy and harmony, illuminate the darkness, open up to a timeless infinity, and encourage meditation and reflection, bewitched by a contemplative power. "The world in which we live is difficult and highly complex. Too often it's incapable of offering this kind of limitless positivity, so I want to do so through my art. It's a way of proposing a hopeful future and responding to the natural instinct to survive. Inspiration, joy, and hope: this is what I wish to communicate through all my creations," Refik admits. He's been demonstrating the temperament of an adventurer ever since his childhood: "For me, existing meant discovering new places, new peoples, new cultures, new emotions, new memories. Existence in itself was pure inspiration . . . Even before the advent of AI . . ."

The metaverse was the first to present him with a frontier to cross . . . "My encounter with artistic inspiration occurred when I was given my first computer at age eight. I instantly fell in love with movies and simulation games. Indeed, cinematography was a source of great inspiration for me, and I was particularly impressed by *Blade Runner*, a 1982 movie directed by Ridley Scott. It was a genuine revelation, because the scenario that many regarded as a dystopia, I saw as sheer utopia. Another movie that later exerted great influence on my development was Alex Garland's beautiful and dark *Ex Machina*. In it, I discerned death, utopia, and joy—inspiration. These are impressions that I've retained since an early age and that constantly resurface in my art," he relates.

"The computer has always been my main work tool. I devoted four intense years of my life to studying every technology and a wide range of programs. In school, I also spent a year studying photography, learning about the importance of memory and how to preserve it. In my view, memory is a substance and, like life, is transformed by a chemical reaction. I love photography because it captures reality; that's why I find it more interesting than figurative art. I've always made digital art, I've always immersed myself in technology. I've constantly and relentlessly spent time learning. I'm the son of two teachers, so I'm well aware of the importance of education," notes Refik, who is also a professor at UCLA in Los Angeles, the city that he's chosen as his new home and the site of his general headquarters. "I love cinema, architecture, neuroscience, science in general, nature, and humanity . . . For me, everything is connected. I'd like to make the world a place as magnificent as my images and manage to keep it that way forever . . . ," he adds. "Technology is a product of human evolution . . . It's always been a form of inspiration for me since I witnessed the birth of the Internet, blockchain, quantum computers . . .

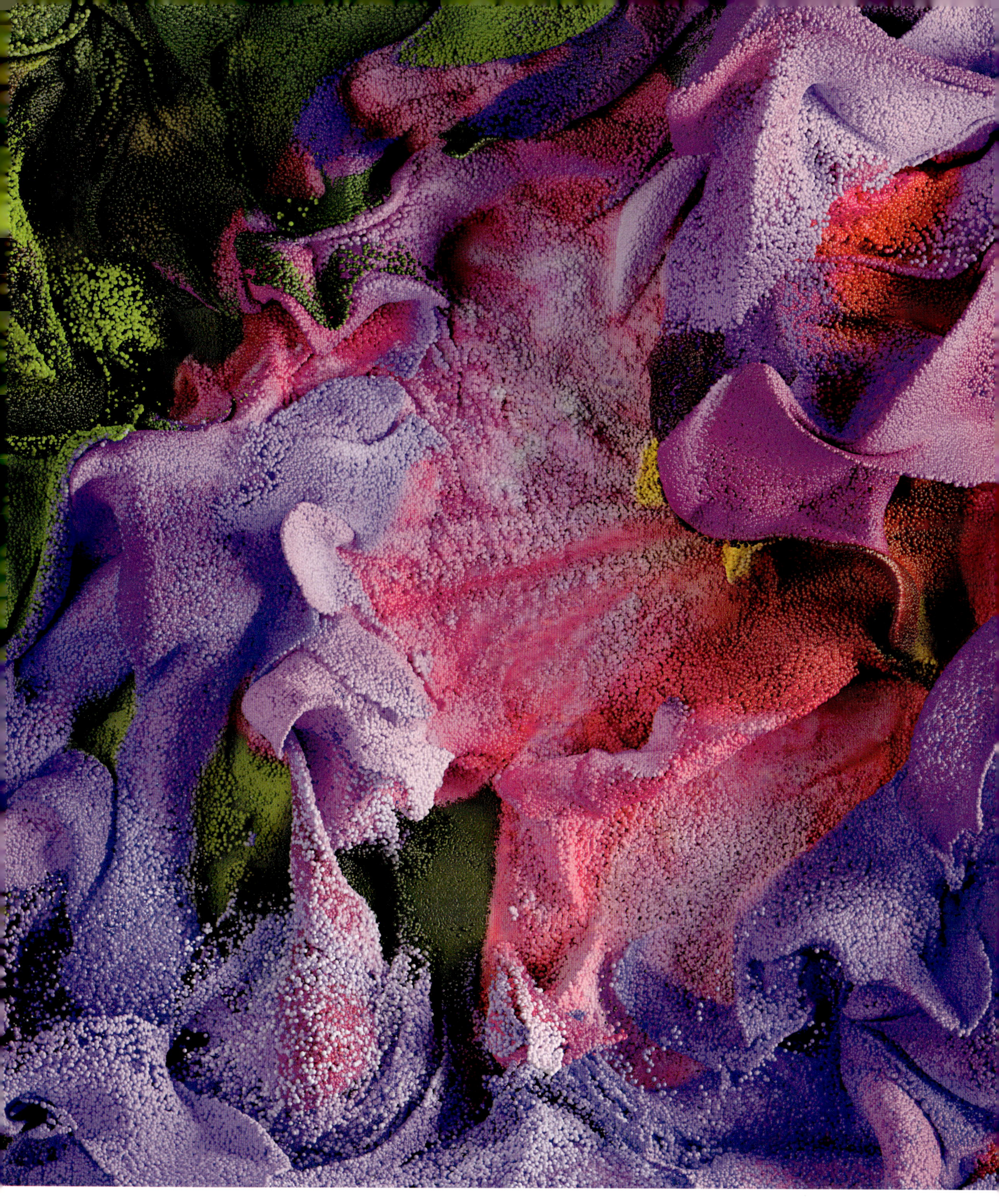

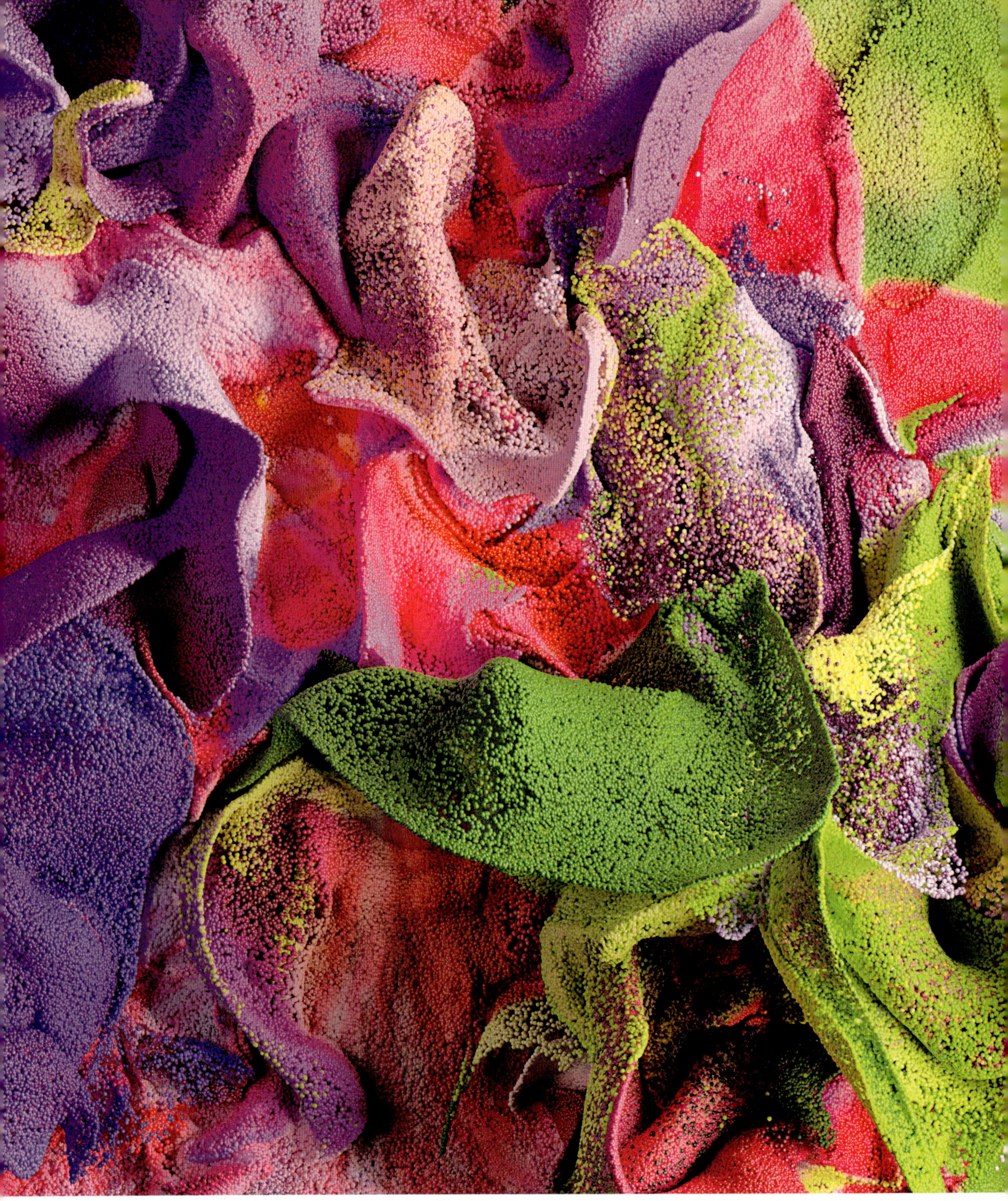

SERPENTI METAMORPHOSIS

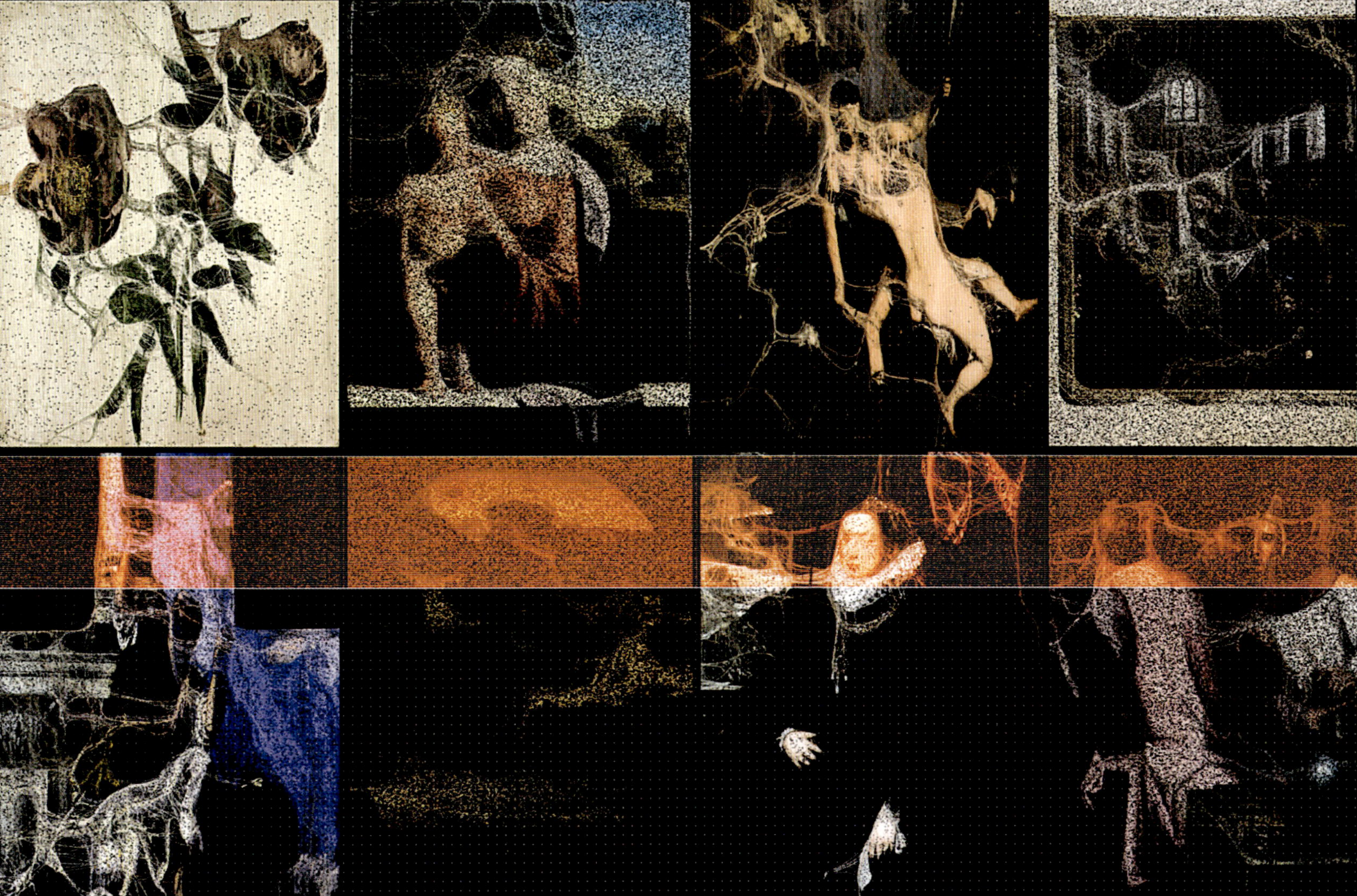

"A true, new Renaissance, in which artists can give vent to their creativity with the help of ever more novel, ever more sophisticated tools . . . We've invented machines capable of dreaming and thinking independently . . . And today they're part of our new world. I call what we're experiencing now 'generative reality,' but it's difficult to define in all its facets in words . . . In my opinion, it's a moment at which it's fascinating to be alive as each morning I wake up knowing that something new may be created . . . AI is disturbing territory for many, because it can differ on a daily basis in terms of content, imagination, creation. I, on the other hand, know that each day I can have a new 'brush' to create with . . . ," he notes. Refik has always had a close relationship with AI, which characterizes and permeates all of his work: "It's possible to have problems with AI, as it's the mirror of humanity and humanity has serious problems. But remember: AI is a reflection; the problems are humanity's. I know that AI will help me change in a positive way, because I use it for good causes: to raise funds for people I respect, to cure serious illnesses, as an educational tool . . . I'm quite realistic about AI. It requires wisdom, and the possibilities it offers inevitably come with great responsibility," he explains.

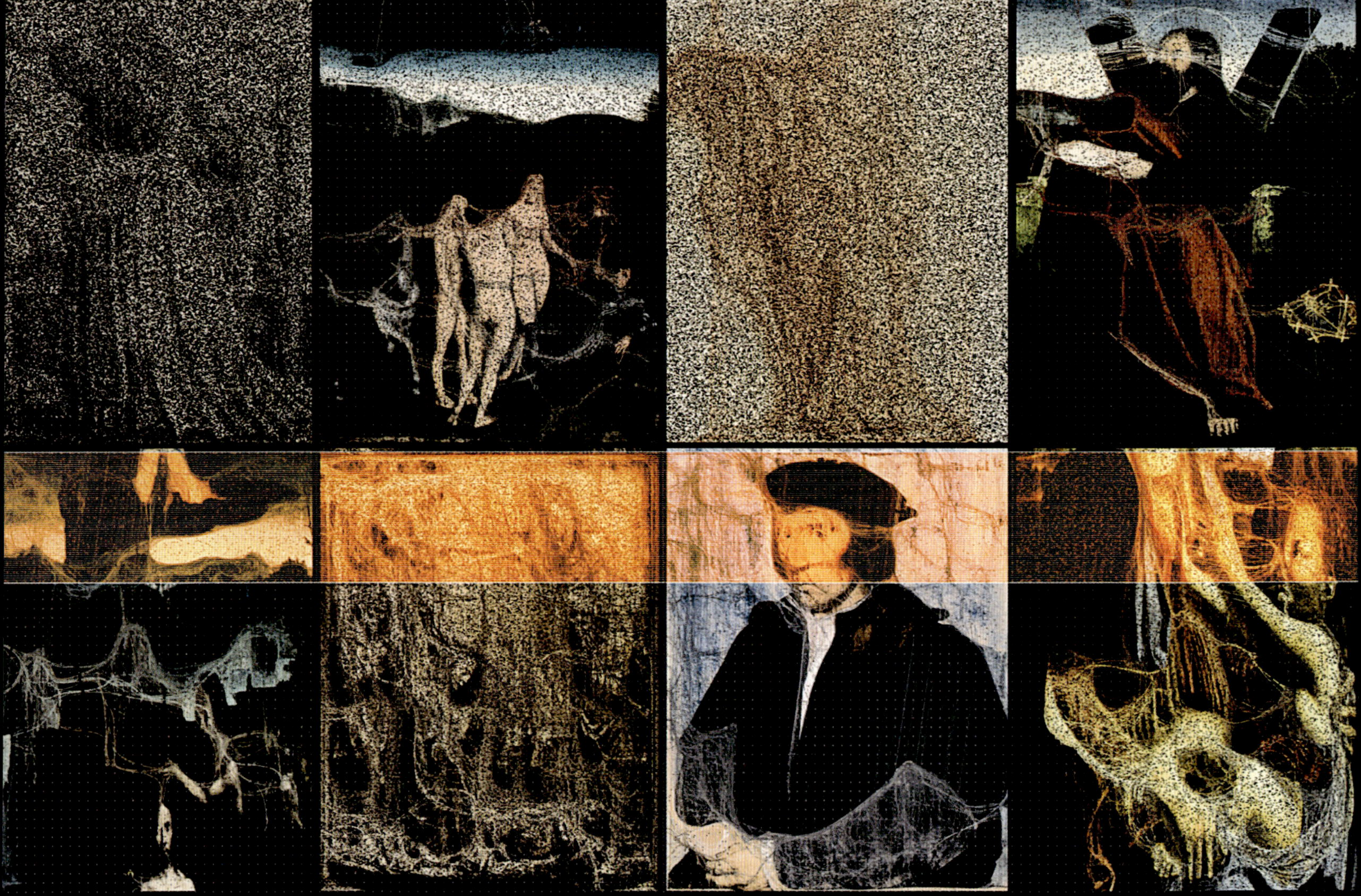

One project that Refik feels has left a mark on his life is *Unsupervised—Machine Hallucinations*, which was on view at MOMA in New York, and in which he used artificial intelligence to comment and transform more than two hundred years' worth of art. He came up with a sophisticated machine-learning model to interpret and process 138,151 bits of metadata from the Museum of Modern Art's collection. As the machine evaluated this vast range of works, it reinvented the history of modern art and "dreamed" about what it could have been and what it could become. Constantly generating new forms that envelop spectators, his work is affected by changes in light, movement, acoustics, and the weather outside. It's visionary and capable of exploring fantasy, hallucination, the irrational. "My intention was to find ways of connecting memories with the future, for rendering the invisible visible," he explains.

RENAISSANCE DREAMS

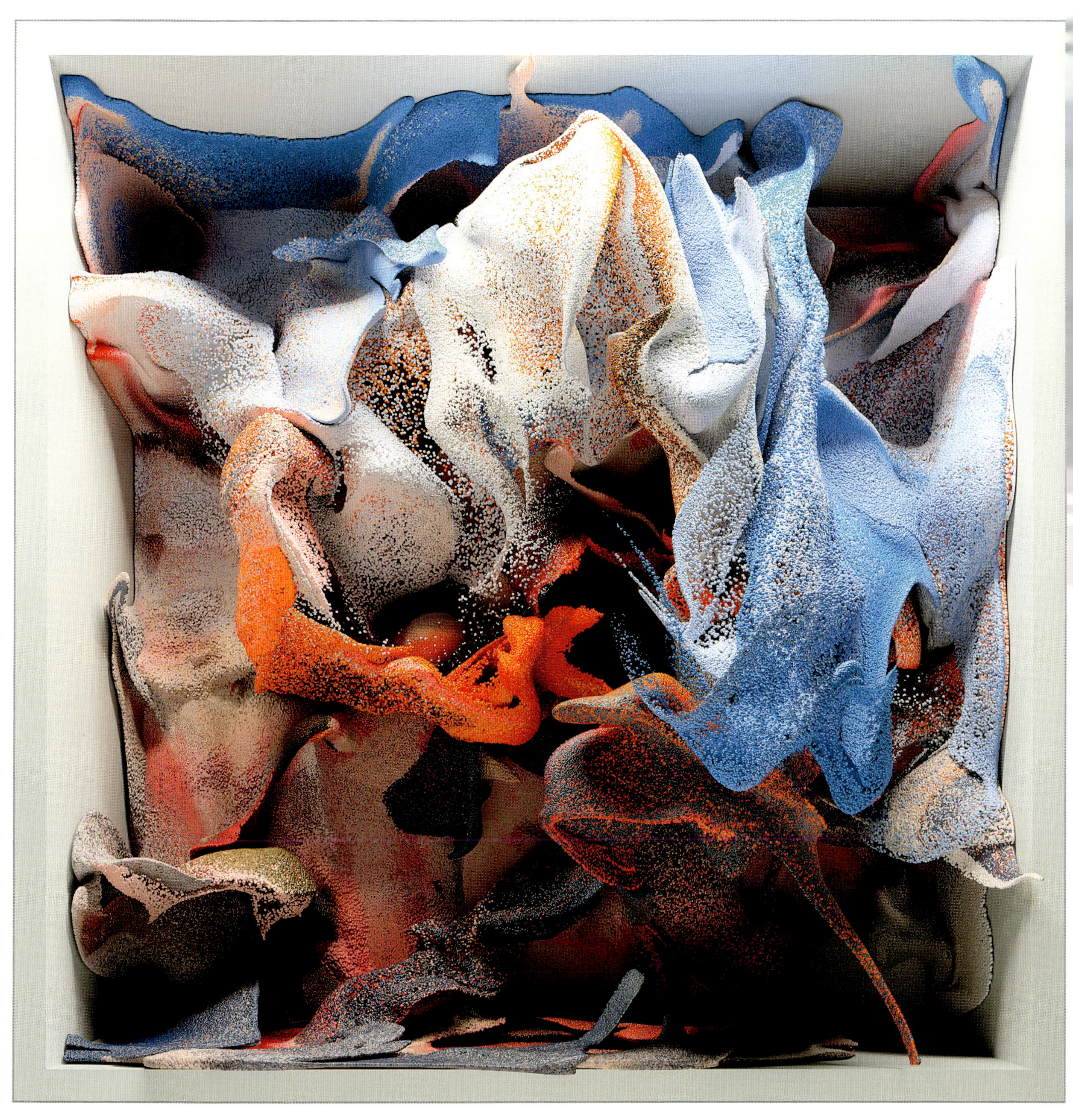

MACHINE HALLUCINATIONS: NATURE DREAMS

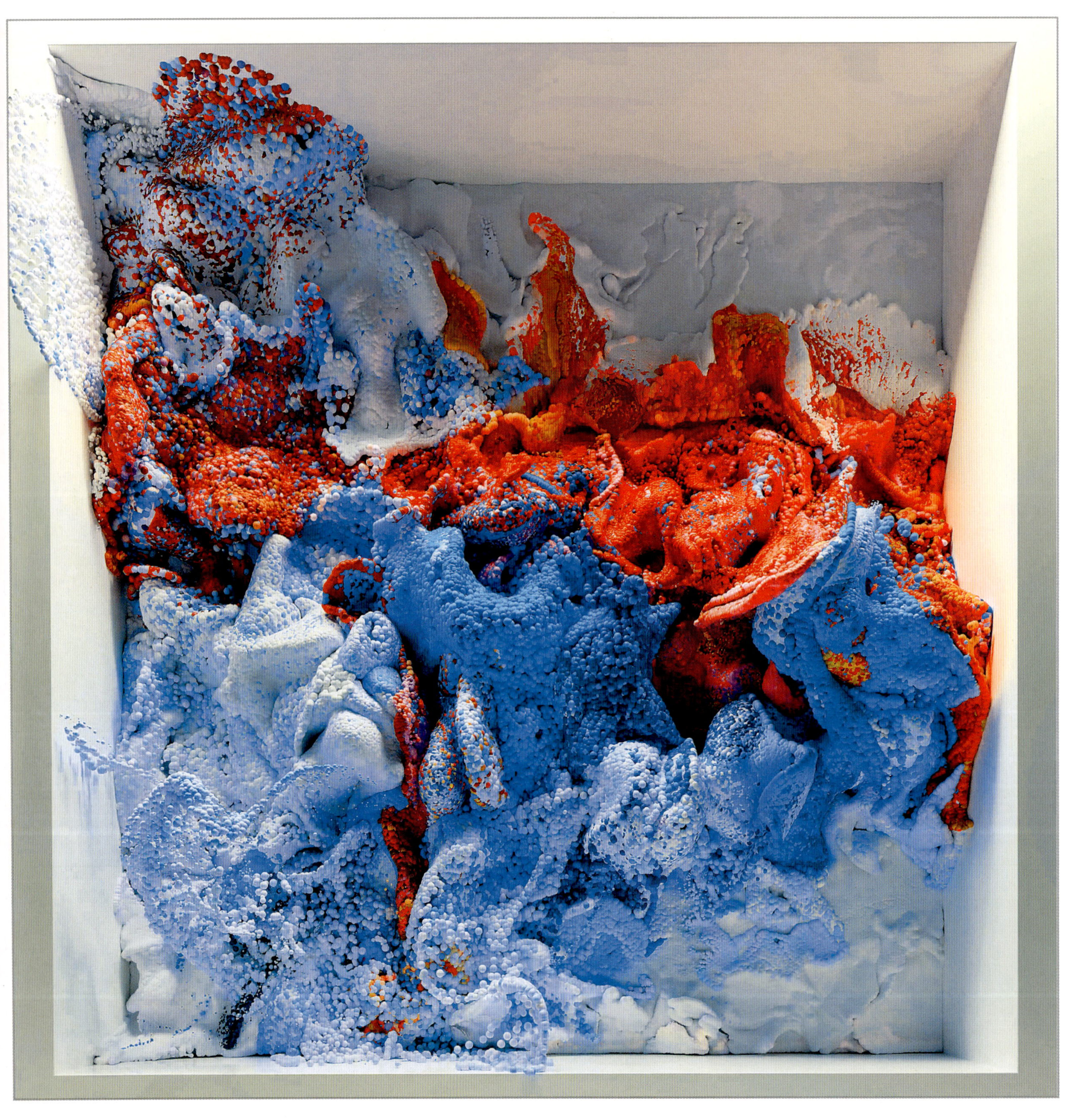

ARTWORK RENDER OF UNSUPERVISED, ©MUSEUM OF MODERN ART, 2022

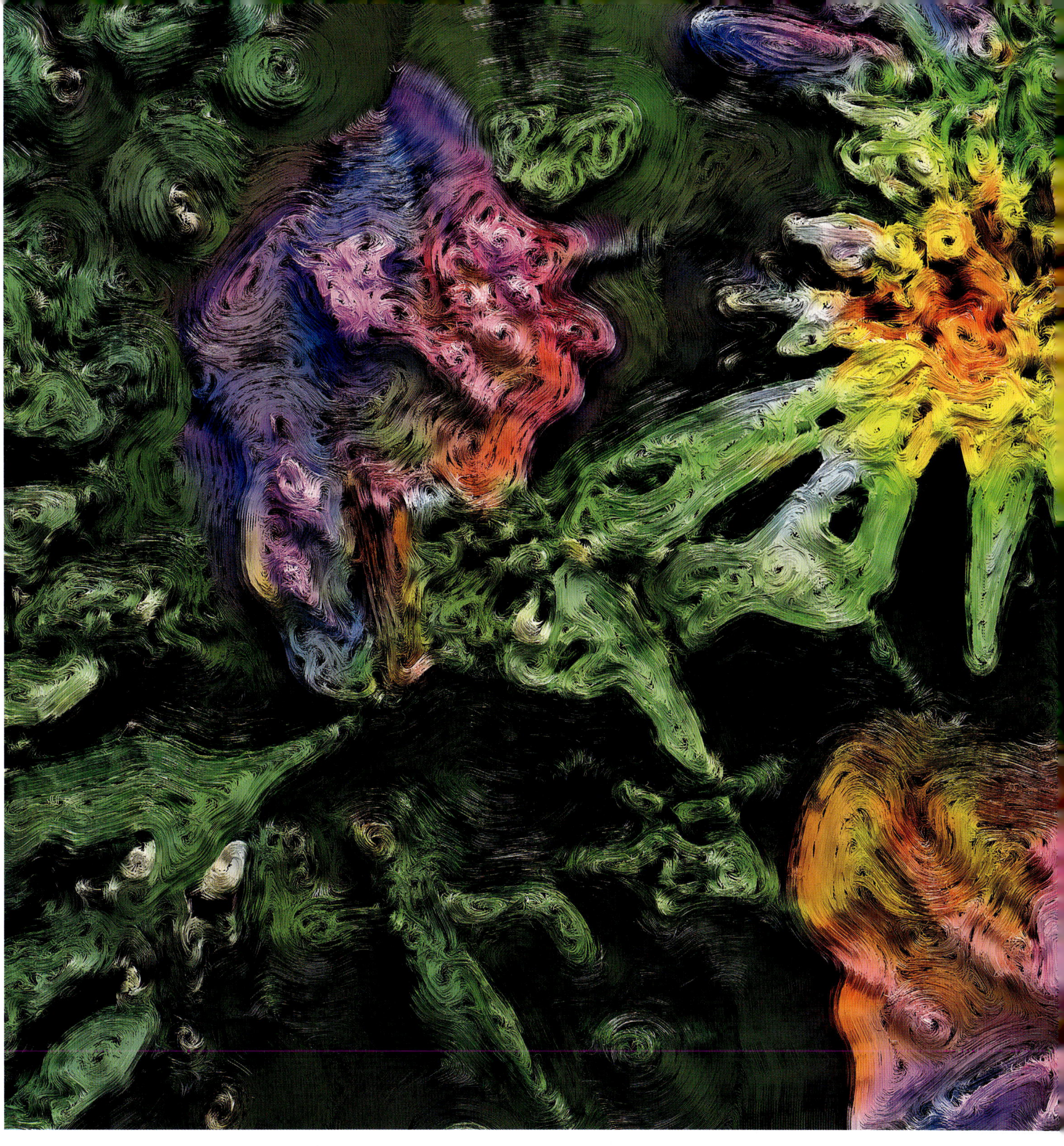

Refik loves colors in all their shades, especially those associated with his native land. "Colors in Turkey are incredibly vivid. For years, my favorite color was black, but today AI allows me to embrace every color in its infinite shades, and together we decide which ones to use. Personally, I really love red, but also blue of the kind I see in the sky and water. I can never say 'no' to red or blue," he admits. "I grew up in Istanbul, on the Bosporus, surrounded by water. This is why I see metadata, color, and dreams floating in a state of constant flux, and, like water, constantly changing. All my art is deeply bound to nature, and in that sense it has been a source of great inspiration for me. It was my wife, who is also Turkish, who introduced me to the culture of the Amazon years ago. Having spent time living with the Indigenous Yawanawa tribe, we trained an AI algorithm in how to create by observing the nature of the place and the works of this Indigenous community.

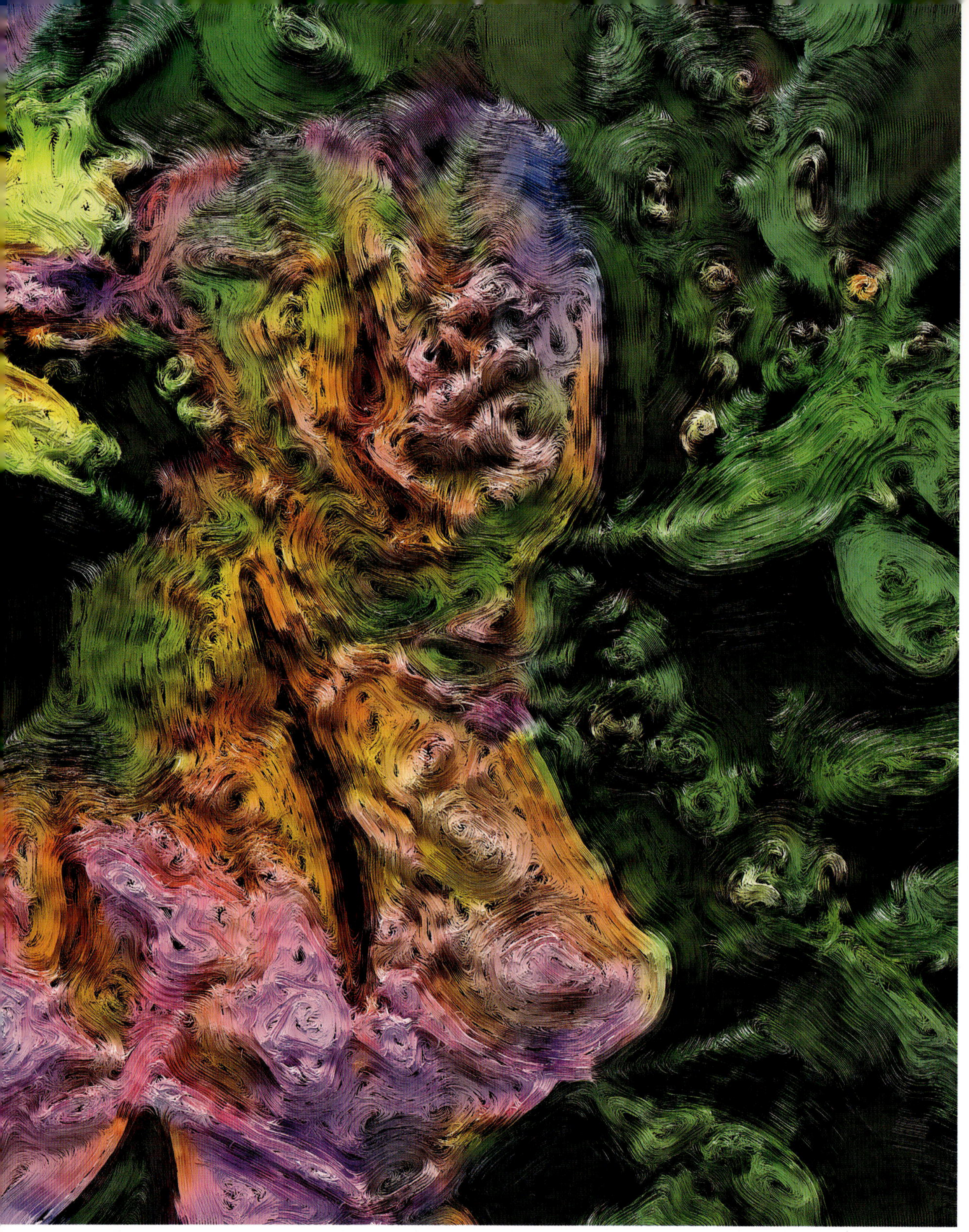

We learned a great deal from these people, who have lived since time immemorial in the Amazonian tropical forest of Brazil, using the divine, curative power of nature with love and joy. Our respect for their culture grows deeper each time we return to their villages, as our bond with them is solid and long-lasting. They are my mentors and my second family. It's from them that AI learned to dream of birds and create them, as it did other animals, flora, or the actual forest . . . I've come to learn that the concept of "ego" does not exist—only the idea and possibility of creating together. Nature is our strength; it's the most important thing we have in this world. And if we think we're superior to it, we're wrong: it's merely an illusion. Without nature, humanity is lost," Refik concludes.

SERPENTI METAMORPHOSIS

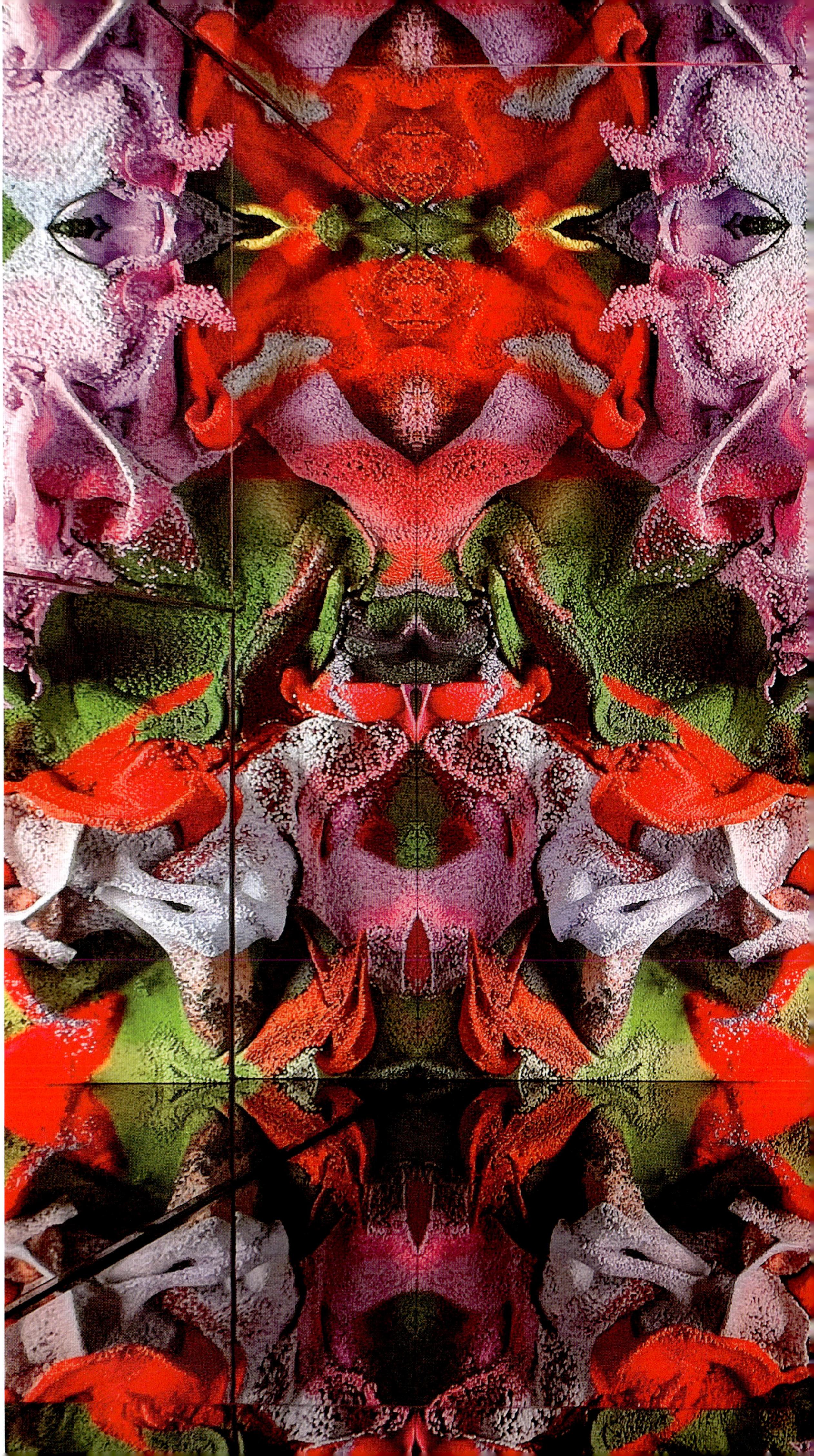

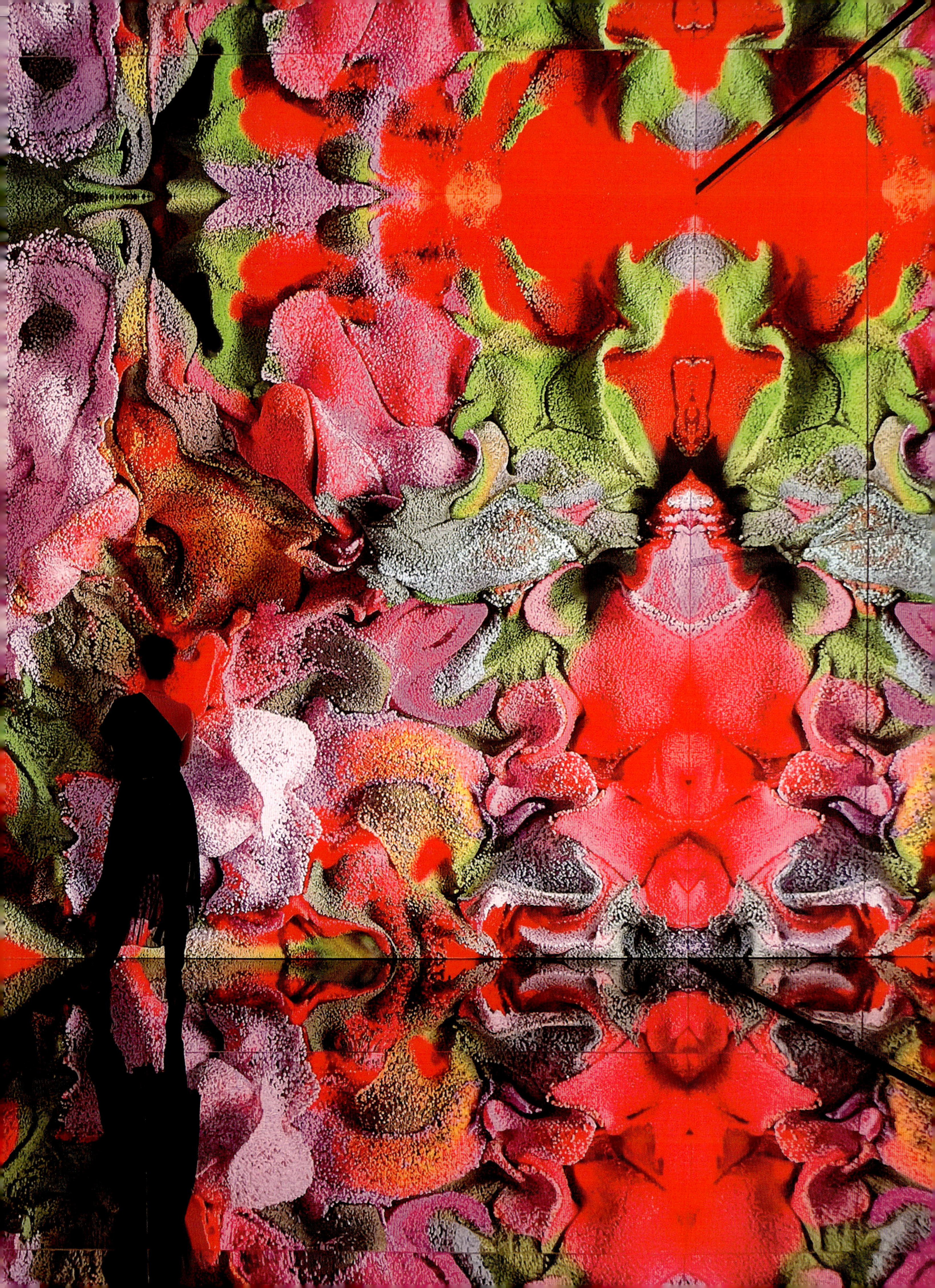

CONNIE BAKSHI

WHEN A SHAMAN SETS A SPELL ON MACHINES

ART IS AN APPROPRIATION OF A PERSPECTIVE; AND WITH A TECHNOLOGY LIKE ARTIFICIAL INTELLIGENCE, I OFTEN THINK ABOUT HOW A PREDICTIVE ALGORITHMIC MODEL COULD BE TURNED INTO A MODEL OF PERCEPTION."

She descends from the ancient shamans of Taiwan. "I grew up as a cultural hybrid in a Taiwanese immigrant family chasing the American dream in Atlantic City, New Jersey. This hybrid life required fluency in two languages, but I actually ended up learning both and neither. When you live between two worlds and two languages, many things go unsaid, and there are experiences that can't really be articulated in one language or the other.

BY VIRTUE OF: CONDITION NO. 01 2022

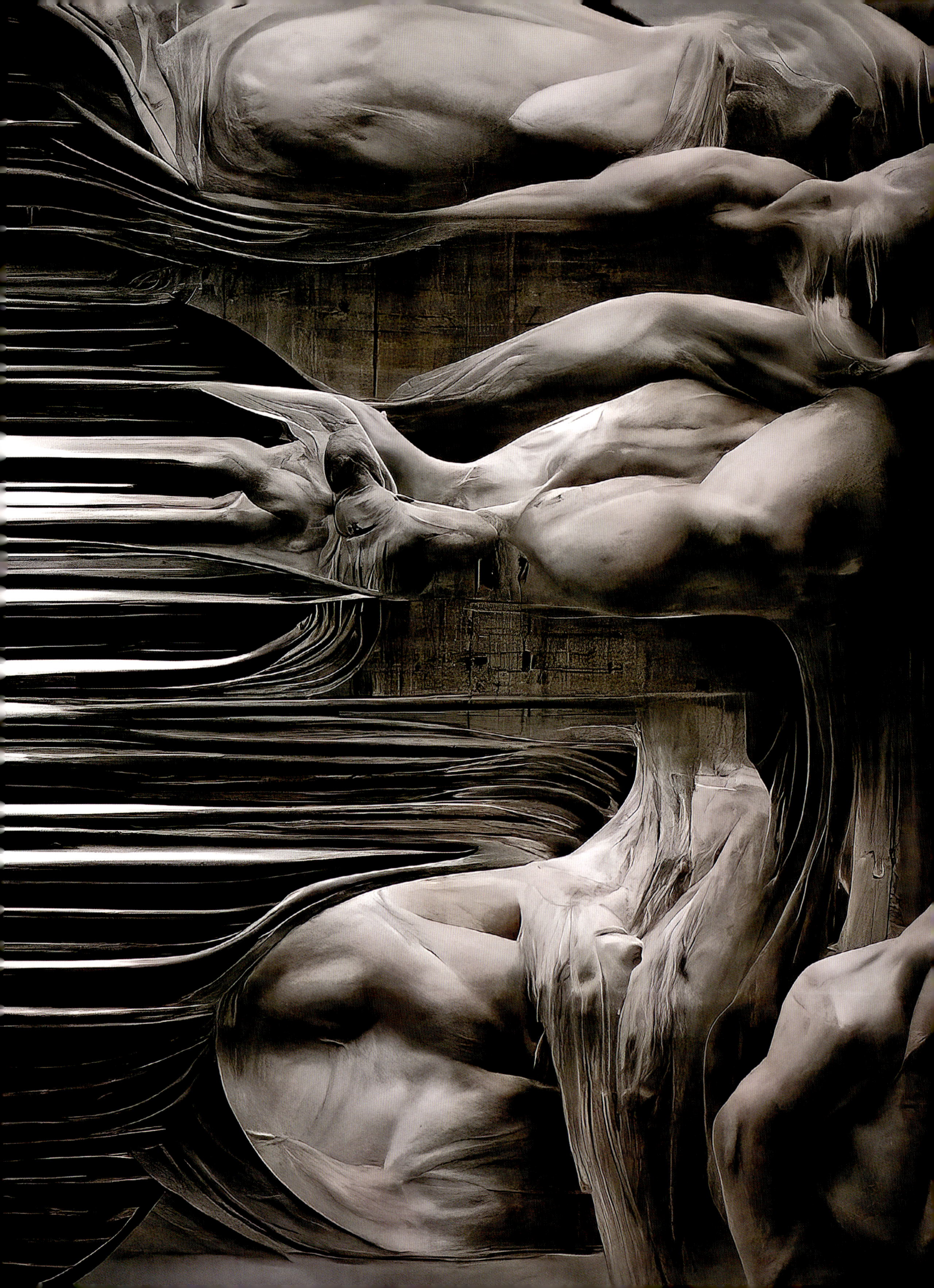

I spent much of the early years of my life having a hard time expressing my-self simply because I didn't have the words to speak about my experiences," she recalls. "I love the idea of language as a form of invocation, a practice that was central to the rituals of my shamanic ancestors and a means of piercing the veil between the reality we see and the realities we're not yet capable of perceiving.

"In a world where algorithms and search filters increasingly mediate our per-ception of reality, I believe that the relationship between language and machine can play a crucial role in breaking down ontological and epistemological barriers and codifications that have been reinforced by the dynamics of residual colo-nialism," she claims. Connie continues to move between two parallel worlds. She challenges the boundaries between synthetic and organic, material and immate-rial, human and non-human, in an imaginary, fantastical world, rich in detail and full of moments of ecstatic beauty. Adopting a decolonial narrative, she often takes advantage of AI to recode language and rework old canons with a more innovative perspective. In Los Angeles, where Connie moved after completing her degrees in biomedical engineering and industrial design, she realized that all this was not enough for her: to find herself and her true nature, she needed to explore the various areas of digital art. "If art is born of a 'cultivated' life, then I think I spent much of mine as a constant gardener. I wasn't the child who would say 'I want to be an artist when I grow up.' In fact, I never even imagined becom-ing an artist; I was a creature inspired by endless questions, and the creative expression of the question-and-answer process was a constant in my life," she begins, then continues as if singing a magical symphony: "In my case, music was the first form of this expression, and the piano was my first experience with

using a 'machine' as an instrument. As with any other medium, my relationship with the piano began as an input-output process: I would press a key, and the piano would respond with a note. As my technique improved over the years, my relationship with the piano gradually turned into a feedback loop: it became all about evoking a response from the instrument that increasingly grew into a direct and complex extension of my body. Every piano has its own personality and idiosyncracies, so for me the act of playing amounts to a mediation between the way the instrument responds to me and I to it. The process of creating music thus becomes a lengthy dialogue between two collaborators that entails ideation, translation, and interpretation. 'Is that what you mean?' is the redundant—but essential—question that the instrument and I continue to ask each other and which we answer throughout the creative process. In classical music, this is further complicated by the notes and sequences inserted into the score by the composer—I'd venture to call the entire thing a 'code.' The interpretation of this code in music arises from the mutually influential relationship between the composer and me: a collision of our historical eras, cultural contexts, and personal objectives or biases." Connie sees little difference between this process and that of digital art: "In my own experience with digital art, I work with various types of software and AI models that constitute my 'tool.' The creation of art with this tool involves a distinct set of technical processes; but once again, the art emerges from the dialogue between the machine and me, even if it's now a more complex tool. Looking back, I don't know if there was ever a moment in which I 'officially' began feeling like an artist who creates art. I suppose that depends on the definition of art.

I got into art rather late in life, though I feel that I've pursued a creative line of research and expression throughout my life and the multiple lives I've lived. When asked about life and what it could be, I think the convergence of the disciplines and perspectives is key to the conversation: after all, life operates in a hybrid manner." Back then, Connie was fascinated by research on robotic prosthetics and cybernetics. "Like many American kids born in the 1990s, I was exposed a great deal to the media coverage of the Gulf War and its aftermath. I recall being fascinated with the advances in medical technology that emerged in this period, particularly with the stories and experiences of critically wounded veterans who underwent experimental surgical procedures that outfitted them with robotic prostheses. I was especially interested in how the organic and the synthetic could be intertwined to produce something that went beyond the human and the machine, that both differed from and surpassed man and machine," she says. During her time at Duke University, she was introduced to the complexities and implications of language as a potential model for interpreting the interaction of man and machine. "I had the extraordinarily good fortune to work under the guidance of the brilliant neuroscientist Erich Jarvis, who was studying the development of vocal learning in the brains of songbirds. These linguistic mechanisms probably come closest to those of the human brain. My job focused on capturing the neural patterns emerging from their vocal development in real time, but the research of our team extended to genomics, bioinformatics, and cell biology. I've always been fascinated by the intricate systems and interactions that constitute the formation, expression, and understanding of language, but it was my experience in Erich's laboratory that first led me to regard language as a point of interface between body and machine," she explains. "I wasn't thinking about art at the time, but today I realize that that period was fundamental to my training as an artist. Body-machine relationships and language as interface are integral to my work with artificial intelligence," she adds.

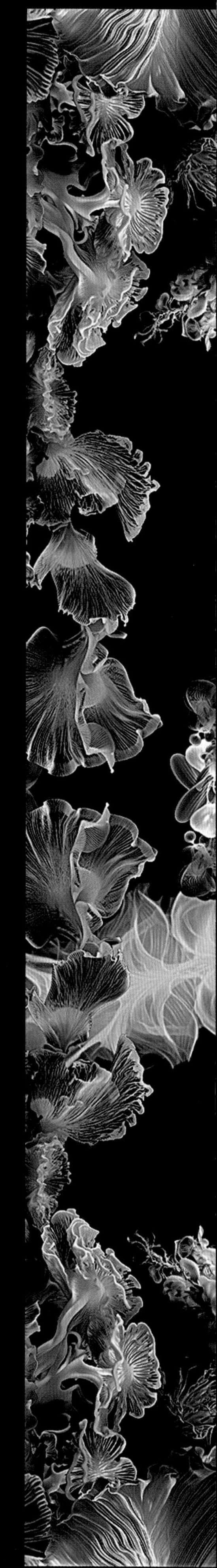

MIDNIGHT IN THE GARDEN OF GOOD AND EVIL
2024

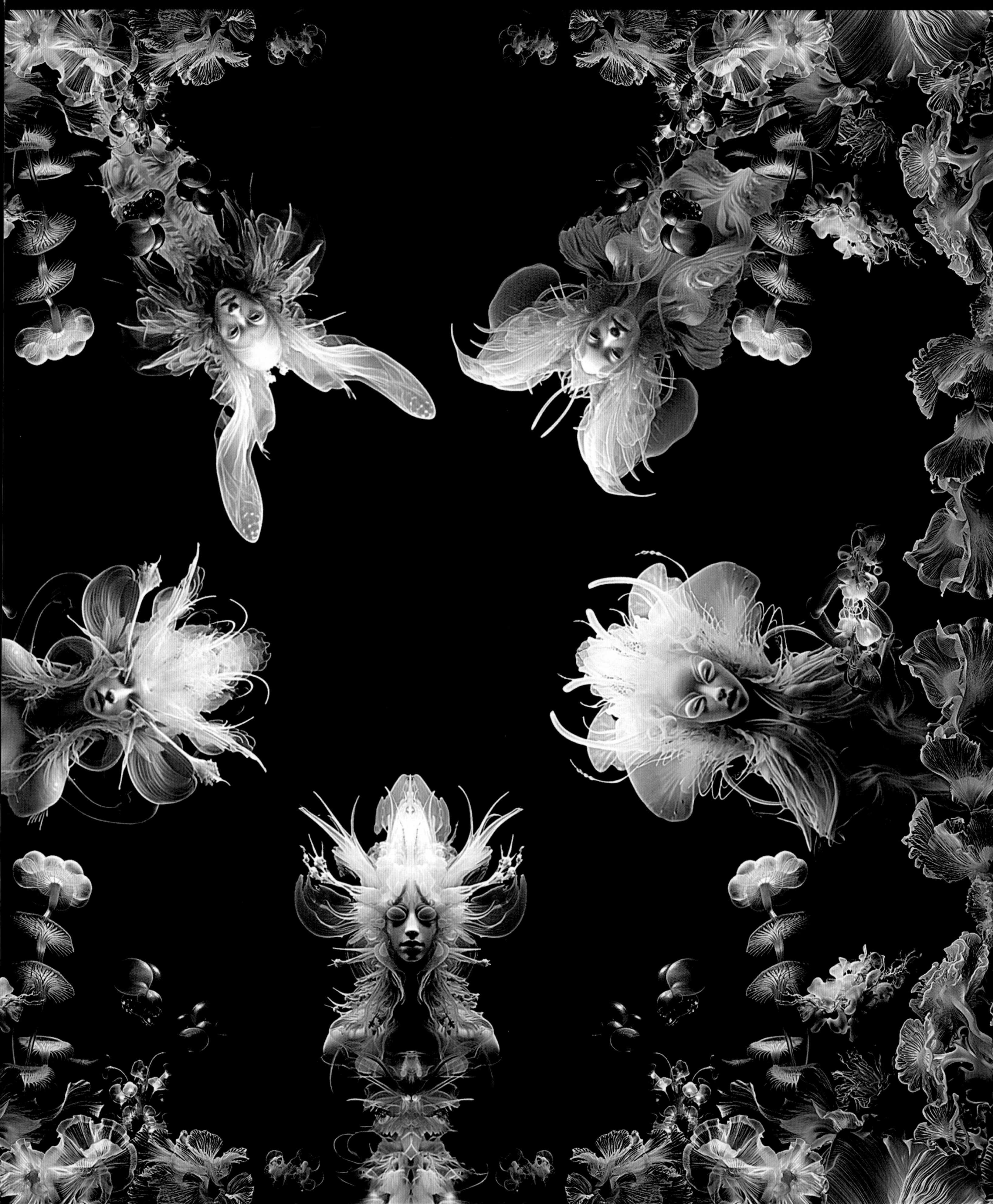

Connie got into AI in 2021: "Working in AI's innate digital environment introduced me to a dimension that differed from that of physical art, one in which I had to learn how to cultivate the expression of the senses and emotions without relying on tactile feedback. The distance between the two grew even more obvious with the emergence of applications based on LLM [Large Language Models] and NLP [Natural Language Processing] models, from which it became clear that my understanding, processing, and communication of language differed significantly from those of AI models.

"It was only after I began working under these constraints that I came up with a new language for thinking about and discussing the dynamics of otherness that remain unspoken and invisible. The process of cultivating and giving shape to art with and within the machine has revealed hidden and unique biases in the data of the documented collective conscience. This led me to questions about why these exist and how we might begin breaking away from our socio-cultural conditioning regarding the 'other' through the union of art and technology." Although she cannot foresee how her art will develop, Connie is ever more interested in the post-anthropocentric world and AI models based on "other" intelligences.

"I ask myself whether a digital 'species' endowed with multiple intelligences could push the compass needle toward an out-of-body, out-of-human direction. Ultimately, I think I'm still looking for a language that can speak to a reality that encompasses something more than the human, more than the machine, and something different that transcends both. And I'd like to understand how far such a reality could take us," she says reflectively.

MONSTER MOTHER MAIDEN 2023

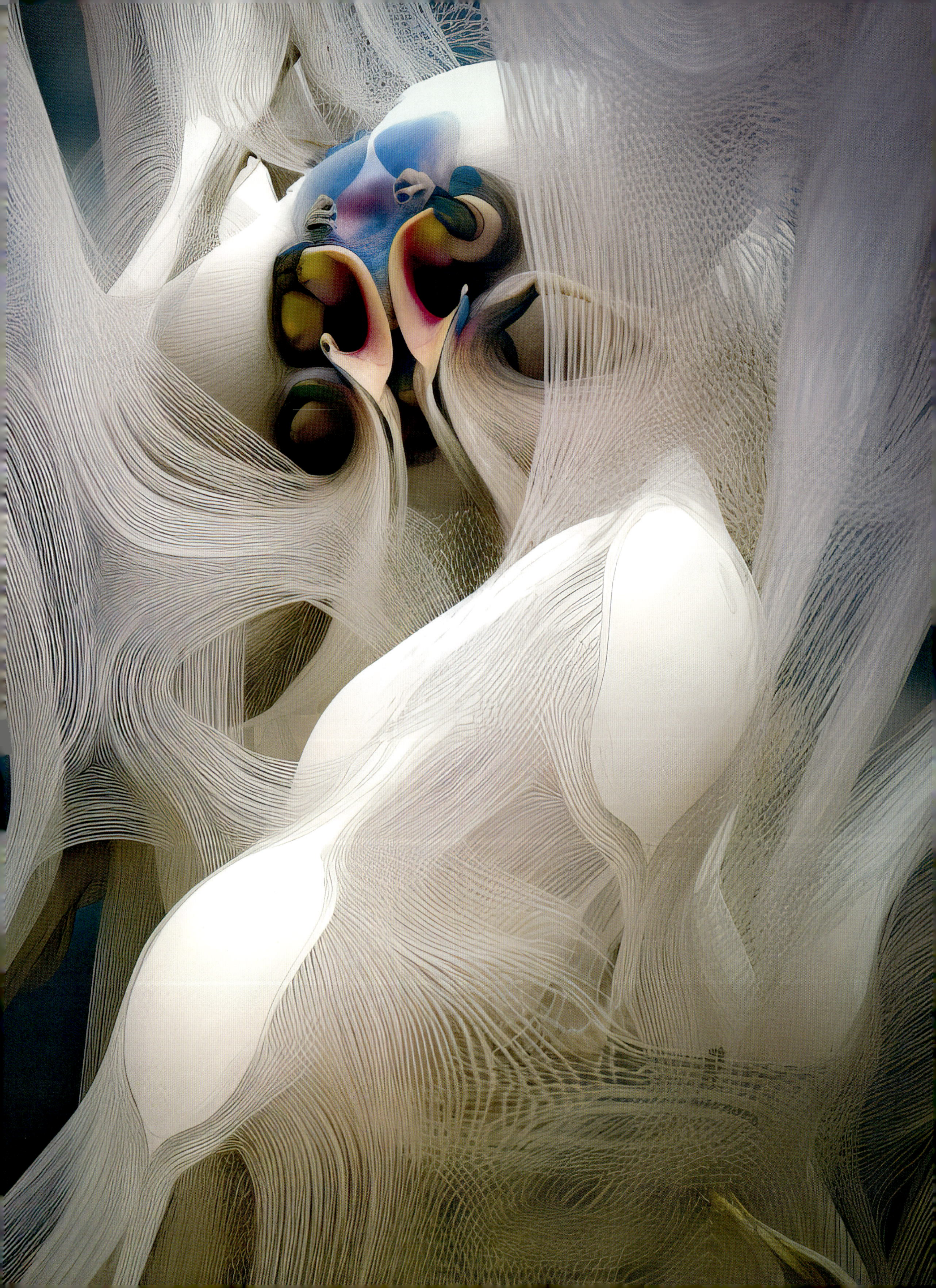

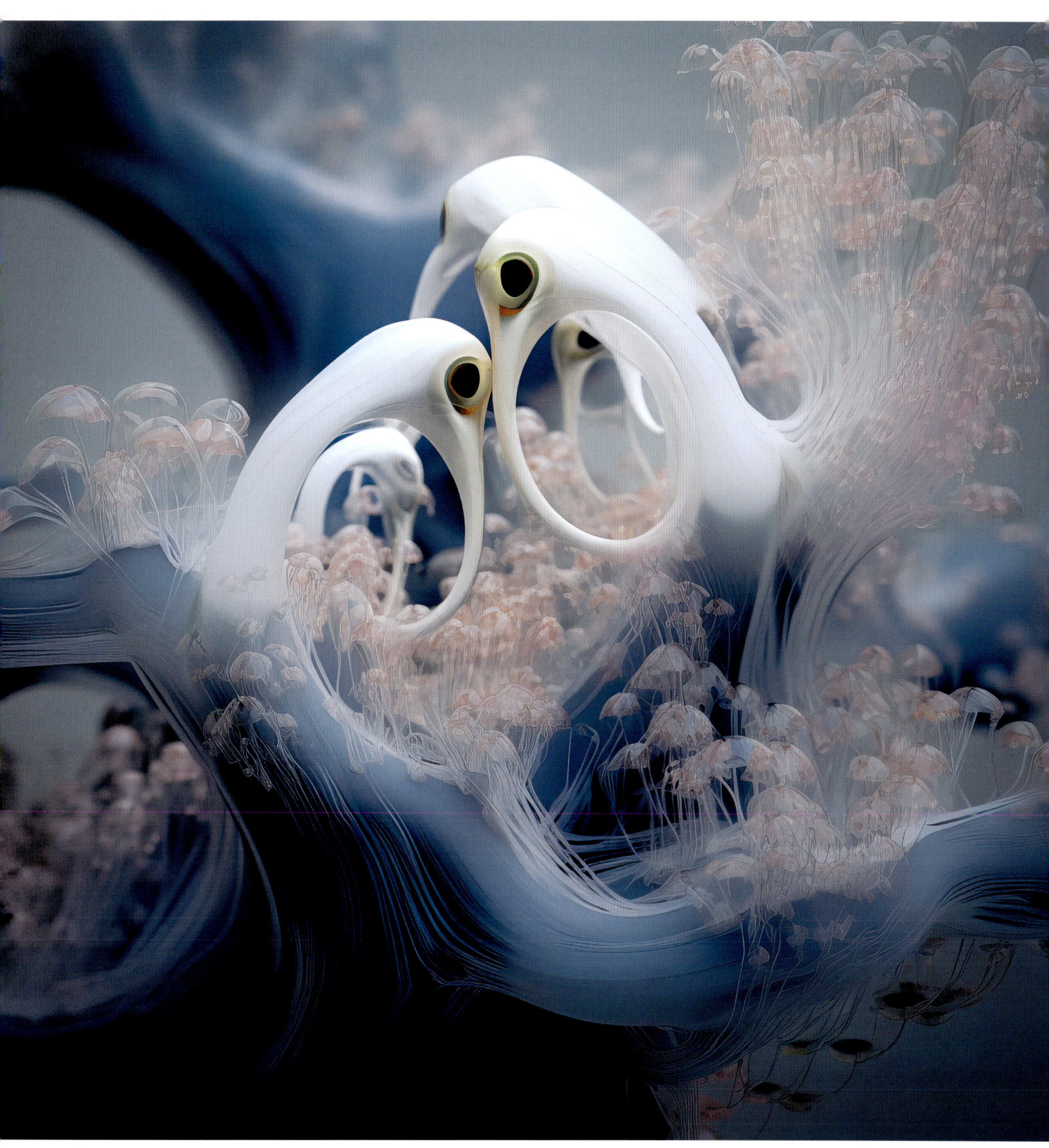

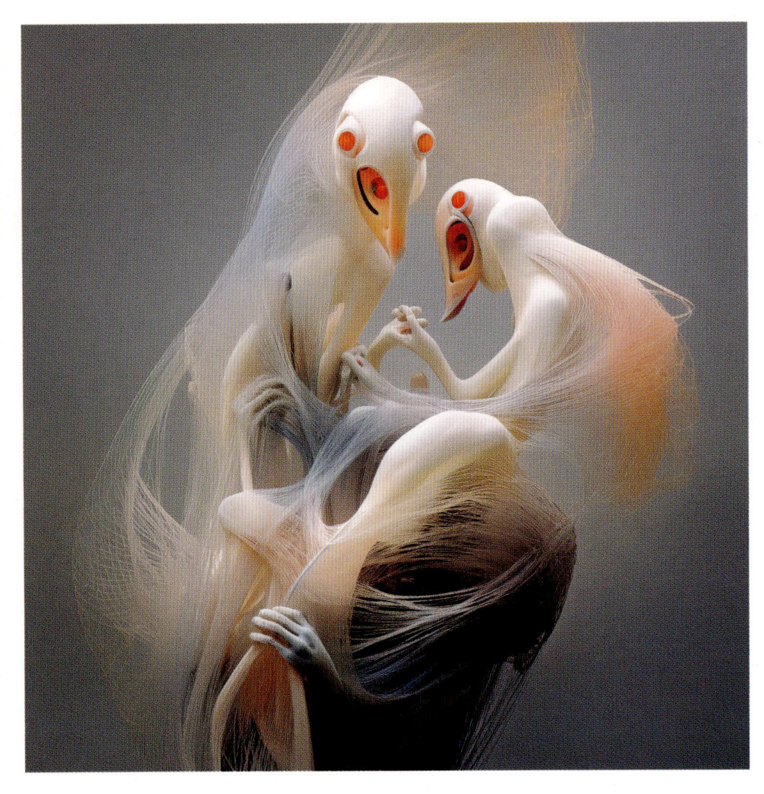
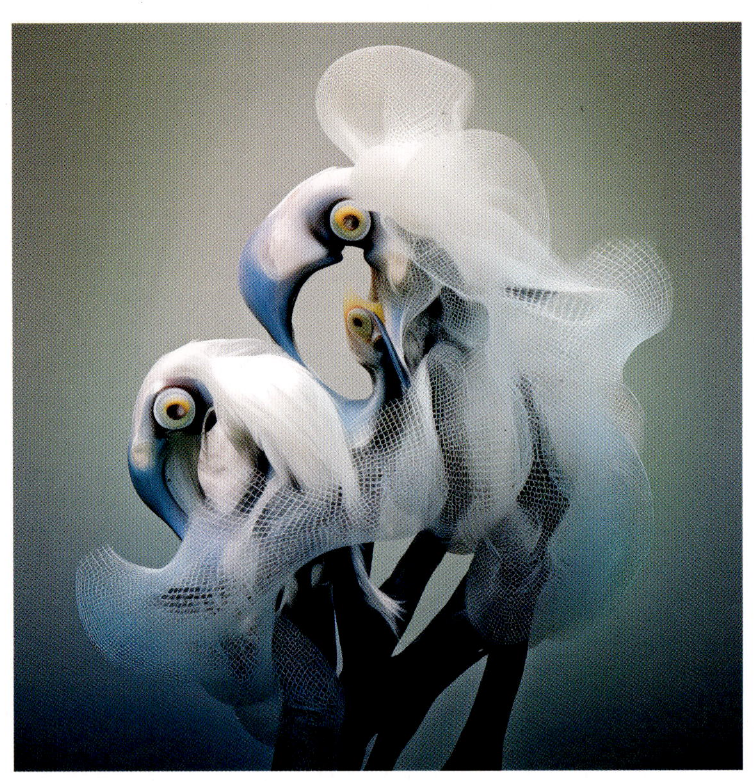

DEFRAGMENTUM 2024

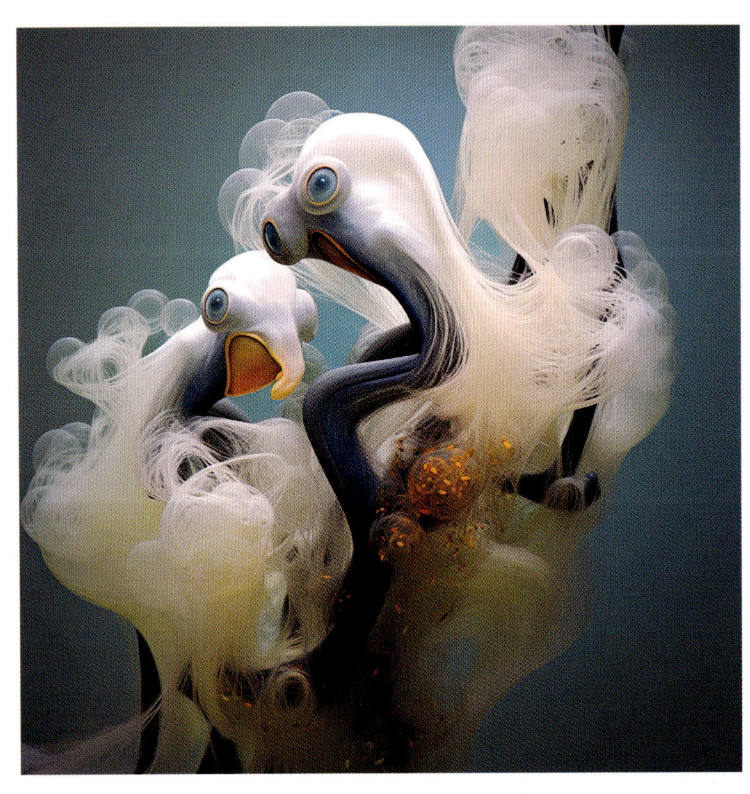
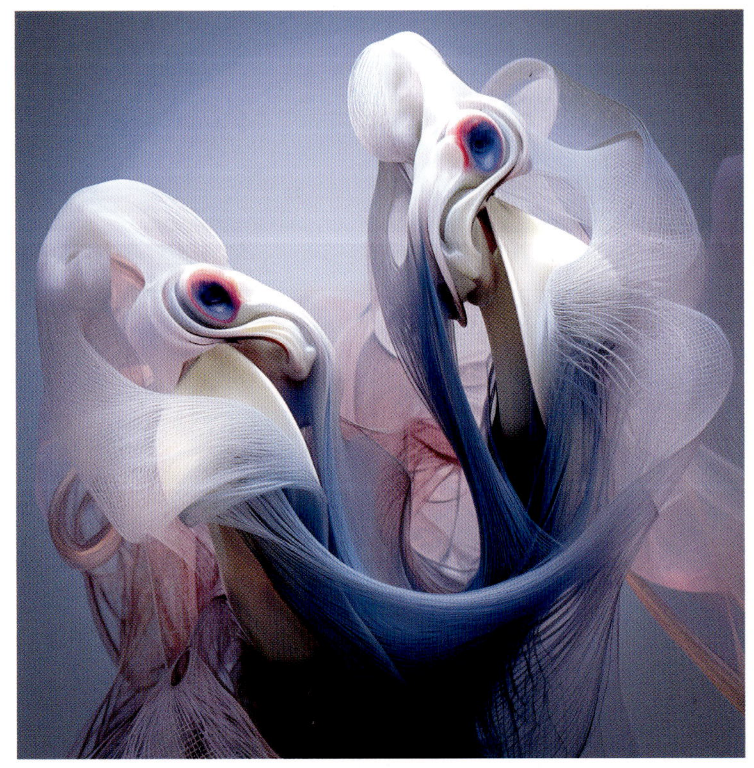

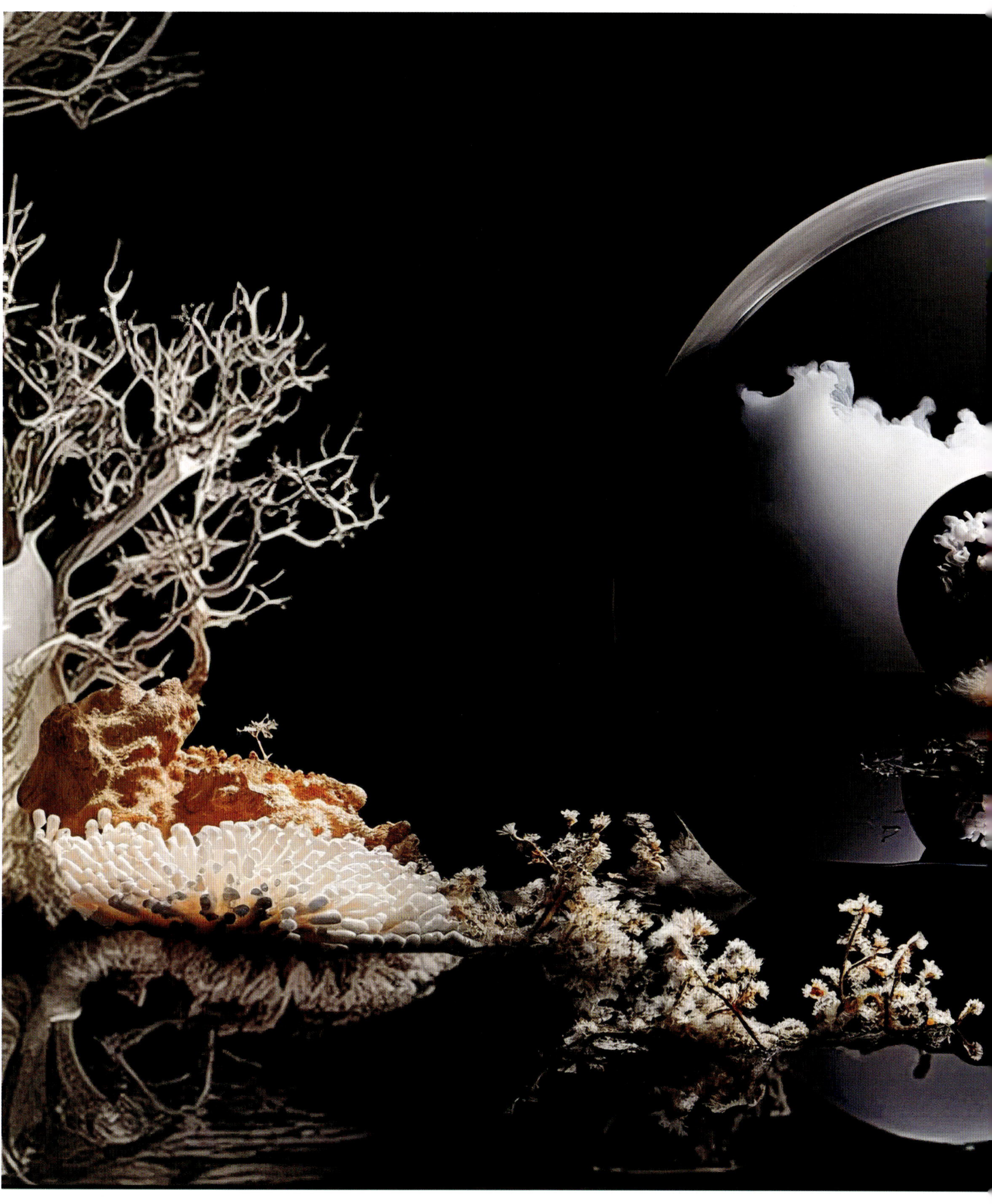

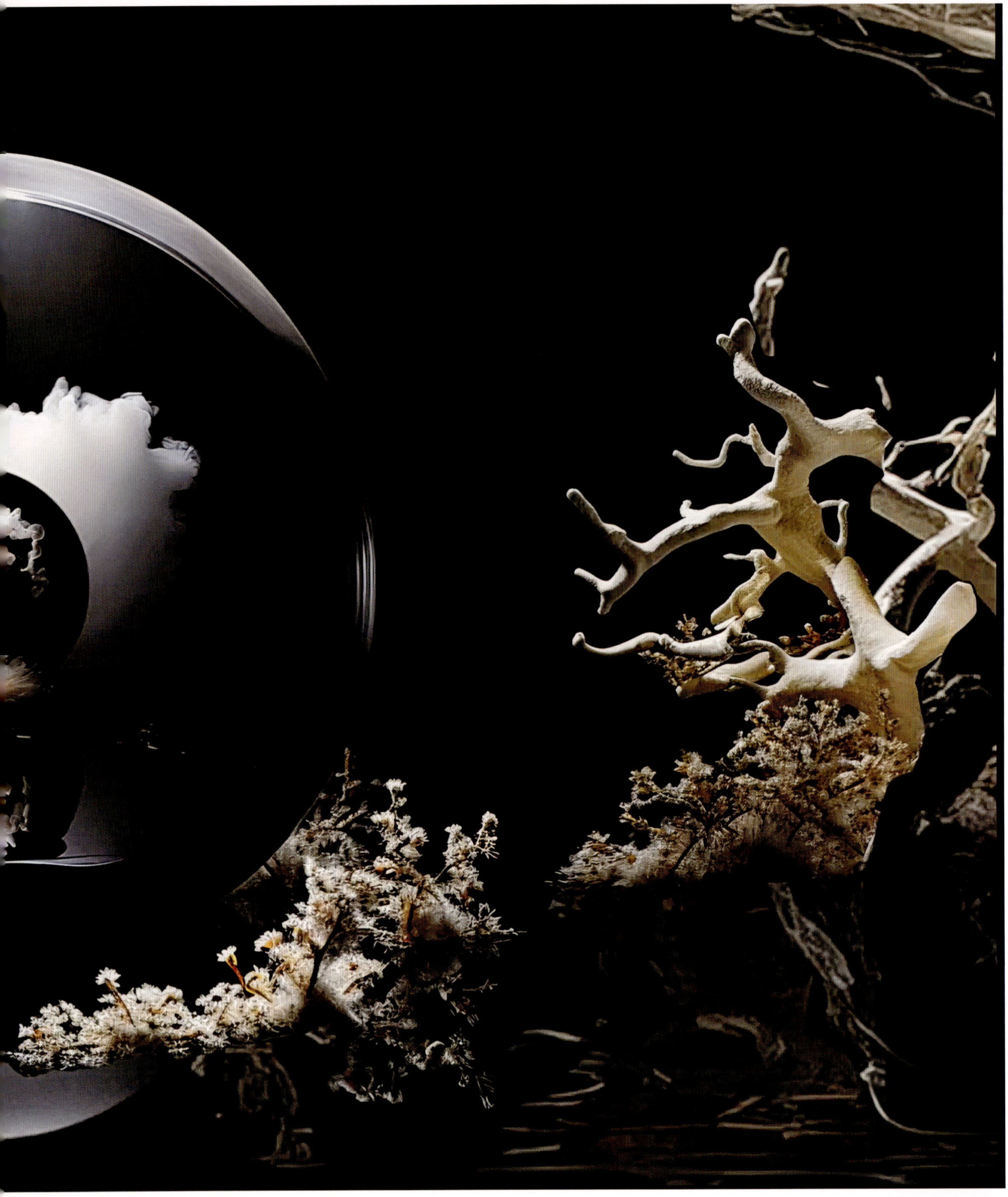

IKEBANA PARADOX 2023

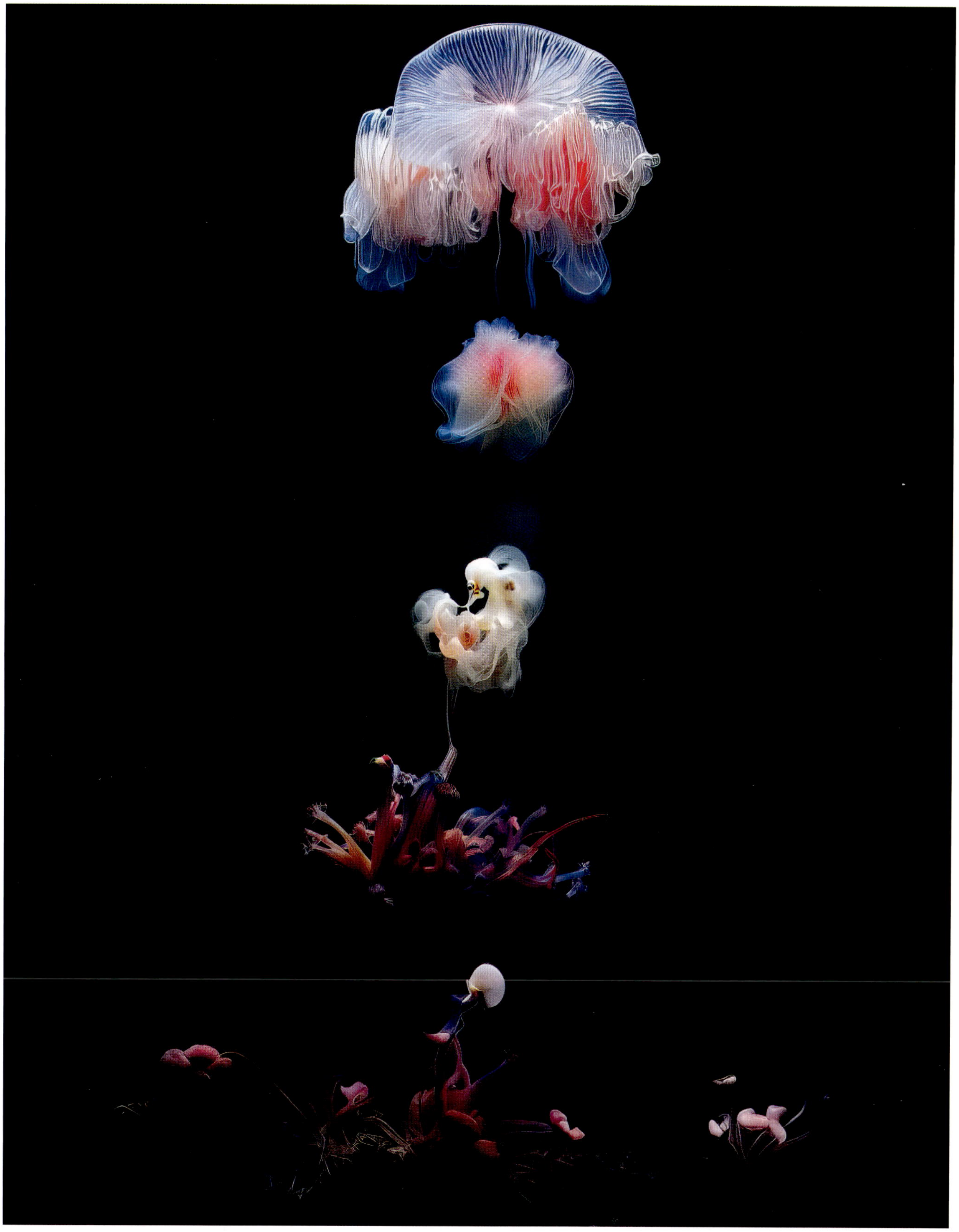

SUBLIMINAL SPECIES 2023

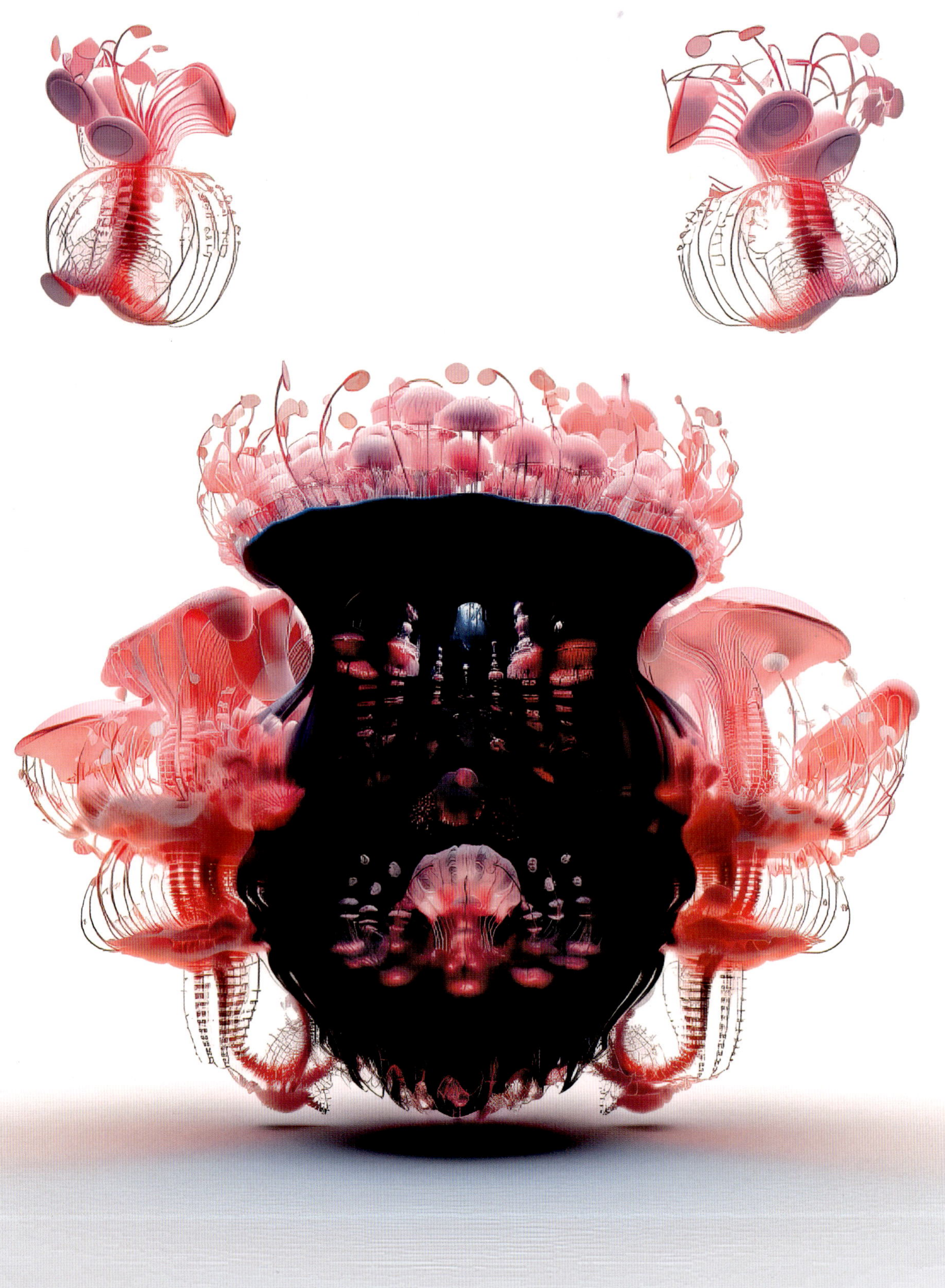

BEEPLE

*WHEN POLITICS AND ORIGINALITY
ARE WED WITH TECHNOLOGY*

TECHNOLOGY IS A WAY TO EXPAND IDEAS. I'M EAGER TO EXTEND THE CONCEPT OF ART TO OTHER DIMENSIONS, TO OTHER MEDIA, TO OTHER UNIVERSES, TO OTHER FORMS, IN ORDER TO OPEN MINDS TO THE POSSIBILITY OF NEW DIRECTIONS . . . BASICALLY AS MANY ARTISTS OF THE PAST— FROM JACKSON POLLOCK TO ANDY WARHOL—HAVE DONE.

Everything always begins from an idea and the direction I take . . . I'm as inspired by different situations and the present moment as I am by the work of others . . . Many of my works have political connotations precisely because I'm influenced by everything happening around me and in the world . . . I like to comment on events in real time by using the most sophisticated tools offered by contemporary technology . . . ," he says reflectively. "At least seventy-five percent of the time I'm really critical of my work. I'm often dissatisfied . . . I'm always thinking about a million things, and it's the deadlines that provide me with the rhythm that forces me to finish the job . . . That's why I believe in deadlines . . . Deadlines are creative . . . Sometimes I procrastinate because I'm unsure about my decisions; but if I have a deadline to meet, I know I've got to finish and therefore I finish . . . ," he points out.

ALIVE

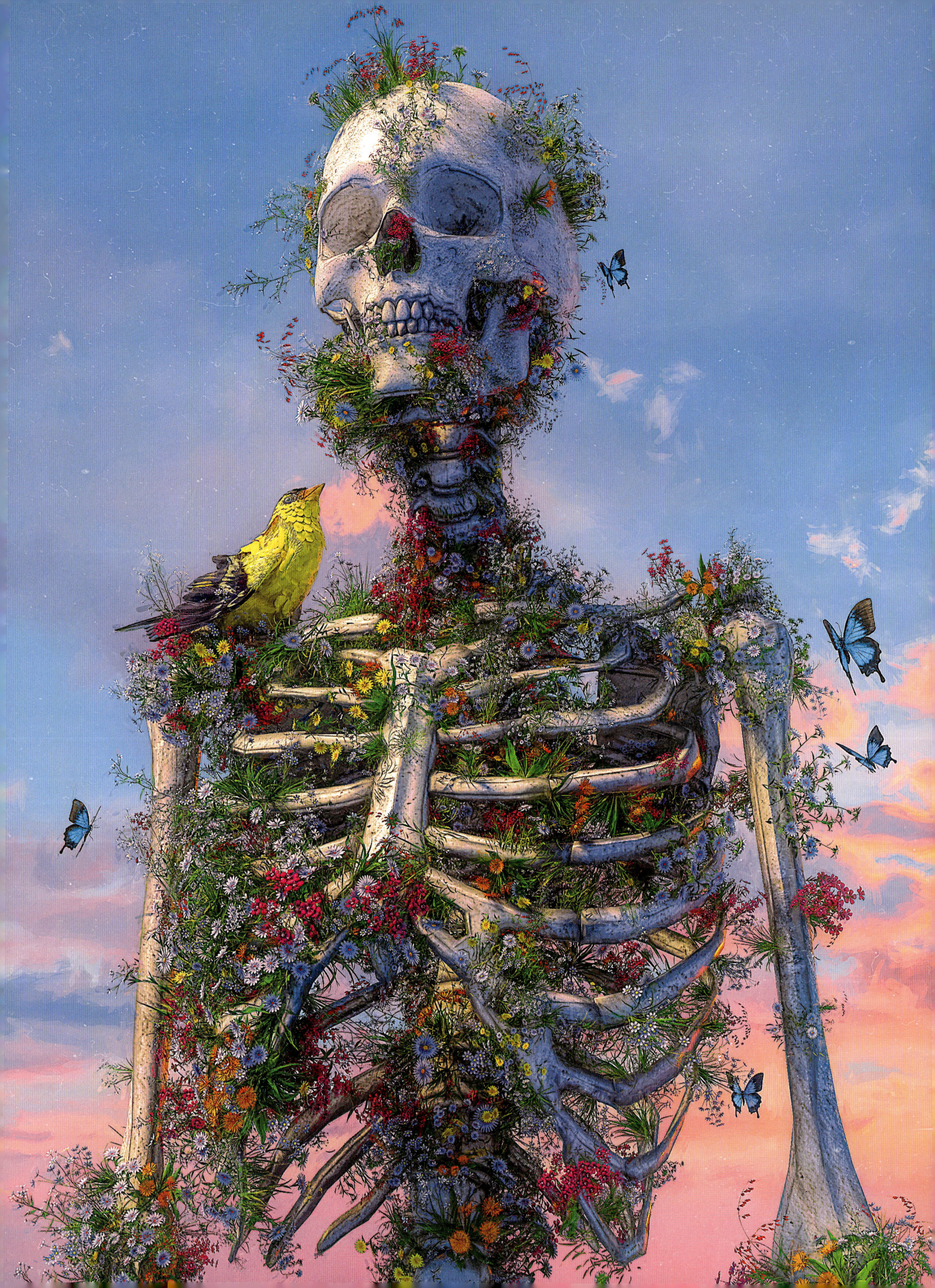

"Some artists say they're unable to create anything if they aren't in a suitable place or don't have their own studio . . . I've used a little thirty-dollar table for many years and still work on it. I suggest focusing on what you have at the moment instead of dreaming of a larger space and more sophisticated tools. You can create wherever you want. I've always been quite flexible," he states with insistence. His philosophy is straightforward, frank, and unwavering. His identity is known: Mike Winkelmann, though in the art world he goes by Beeple.

Beeple is one of the world's greatest digital artists, an innovator and pioneer, a true legend who "coasts" on the Internet and has become the fulcrum—the juncture—of a large community of creative types and inventors such as he . . .

At Beeple Studios, officially inaugurated on March 11, 2023, Beeple organizes events for artists, creatives, collectors, metaverse enthusiasts, and art: these are veritable happenings with amazing special effects. The headquarters of Beeple Studios are located in Charleston, South Carolina, where they occupy nearly 4,650 square feet of exhibition and studio space, in which artists can illustrate, develop, and experiment with digital art. Their effect on visitors is spectacular: one really gets the sense of being in a present-day Andy Warhol Factory. Beeple is the author of *Everydays: The First 5000 Days*, a digital art work composed of 5000 images, sold at a Christie's auction in 2021 for 69.3 million dollars, one of the most expensive NFTs in the world. "It all began when I was a child . . . I drew . . . I was always drawing . . . ," he recalls. Beeple soon discovered technology: "The smartest idea one of my teachers ever had was to advise my parents to buy me a computer. For me, it was the best thing imaginable . . . My father taught me how to program, and a world opened up to me . . ."

Beeple grew up in Wisconsin. His father was an electrical engineer, and it was definitely from him that he inherited his talent and passion for the digital universe. In 2003, he graduated with a degree in Computer Science from Purdue University in West Lafayette, Indiana. From the outset, he learned to tackle things in a largely rational and practical manner, but always with a strong streak of creativity and originality and his own way of thinking. "I devoted myself to web design; for over ten years I worked full-time for a company; that was a long phase . . . At the beginning, I tried to separate the art I was creating and my experiments from my everyday job . . . But this required a great deal of energy, so I began dedicating myself more and more to art . . . as well as trying to find a way of deriving economic benefit from it. And, ultimately, I succeeded . . . ," he explains. Beeple's works often depict dystopian futures, using pop-culture or political figures for crude or explicit satirical ends that make audiences reflect on current events. But Beeple also derives inspiration from the most disparate sources. "In 2003, I was fascinated by toys, plush toys in particular, and decided to assume the name 'Beeple,' that of a kind of small stuffed animal that I liked to collect . . . At one moment I had about twenty of them sitting on a table . . . ," he relates, revealing his spontaneous, instinctive, and gentle side. "Beeple are toys from the 80s that can still be purchased online. They are furry, bigfoot-like beings that light up and beep when you cover their eyes with your hand. I don't remember how exactly I decided all this . . . but now that's my name," he admits. Beeple began his great *Everydays* project on May 1, 2007, disciplining himself to make a work of art each and every day, even if the day was not ideal for that purpose or else was filled with some special personal commitment . . . like his wedding or the birth of one of his children.

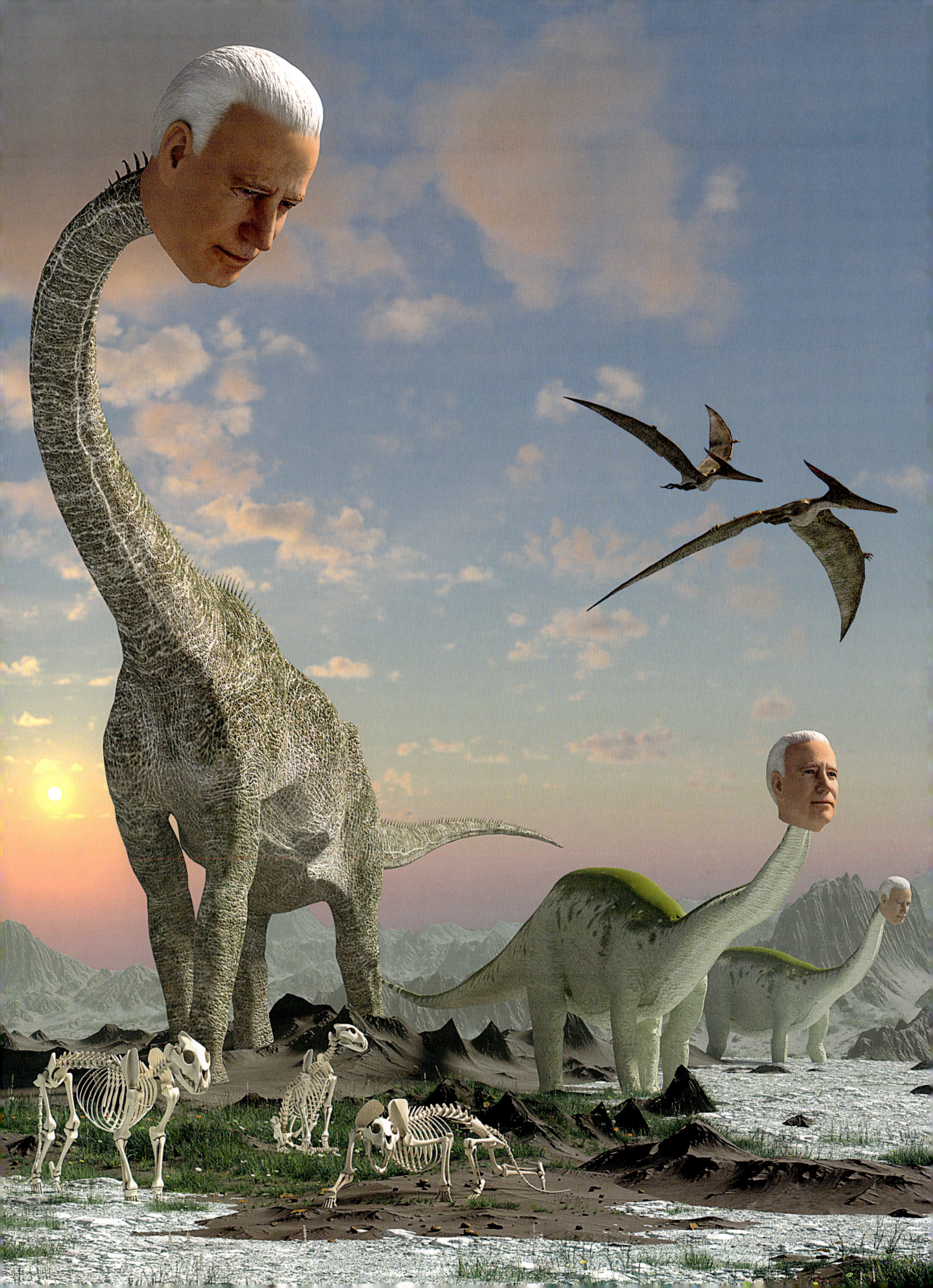

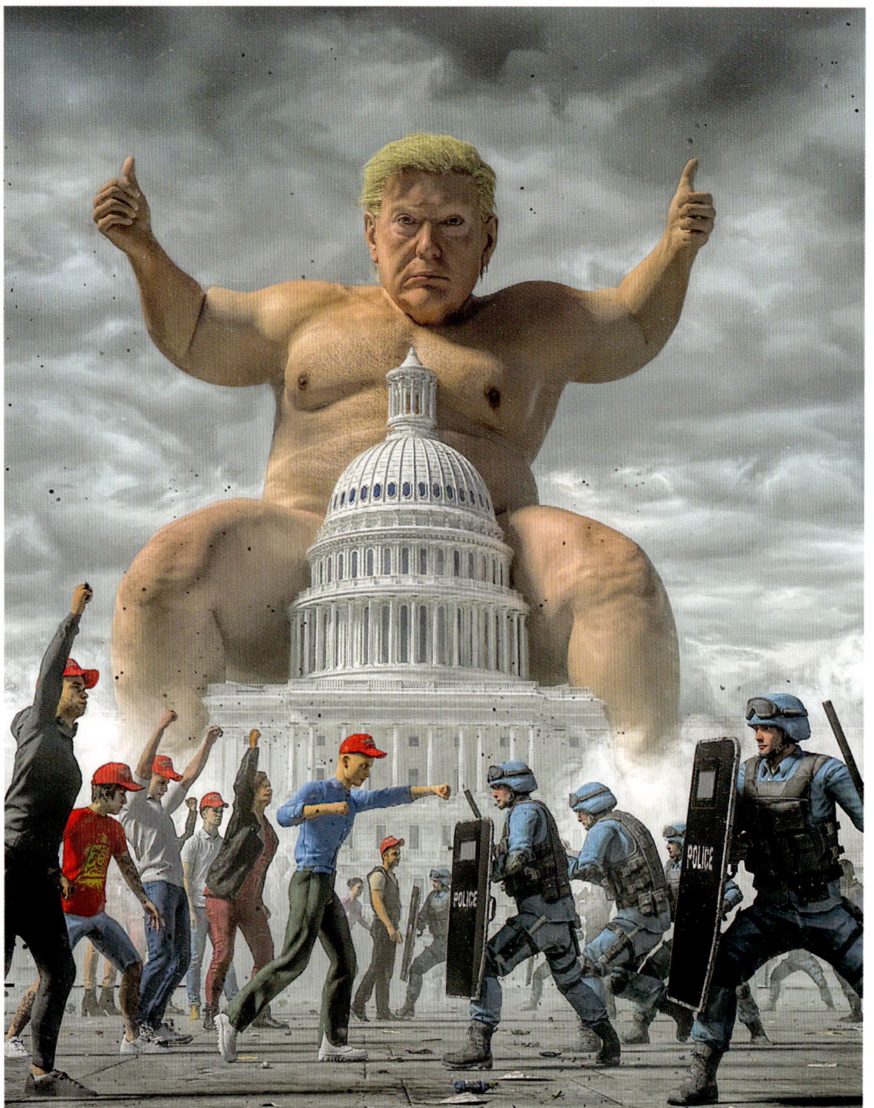

He dedicated himself through and through to this project, spending over 5,000 consecutive days creating digital art, and going on and on as if on a mission.

Beeple has candidly admitted that he often draws inspiration from other artists. He openly thanked Pak for replying to many of his questions, for example, which, he claimed, helped him carry out some ideas . . . In the case of *Everydays*, Beeple was inspired by the British artist Tom Judd, who had made a drawing each day for a year. *HUMAN ONE* is another example of Beeple's mind-boggling, eclectic spirit. He describes it as the first portrait of a human being born in the metaverse . . . A kinetic video sculpture of a walking astronaut, it's a work of generative art in continuous motion, a hybrid sculpture in a state of dynamic transformation that exists on both the physical and digital levels.

DINOSAUR

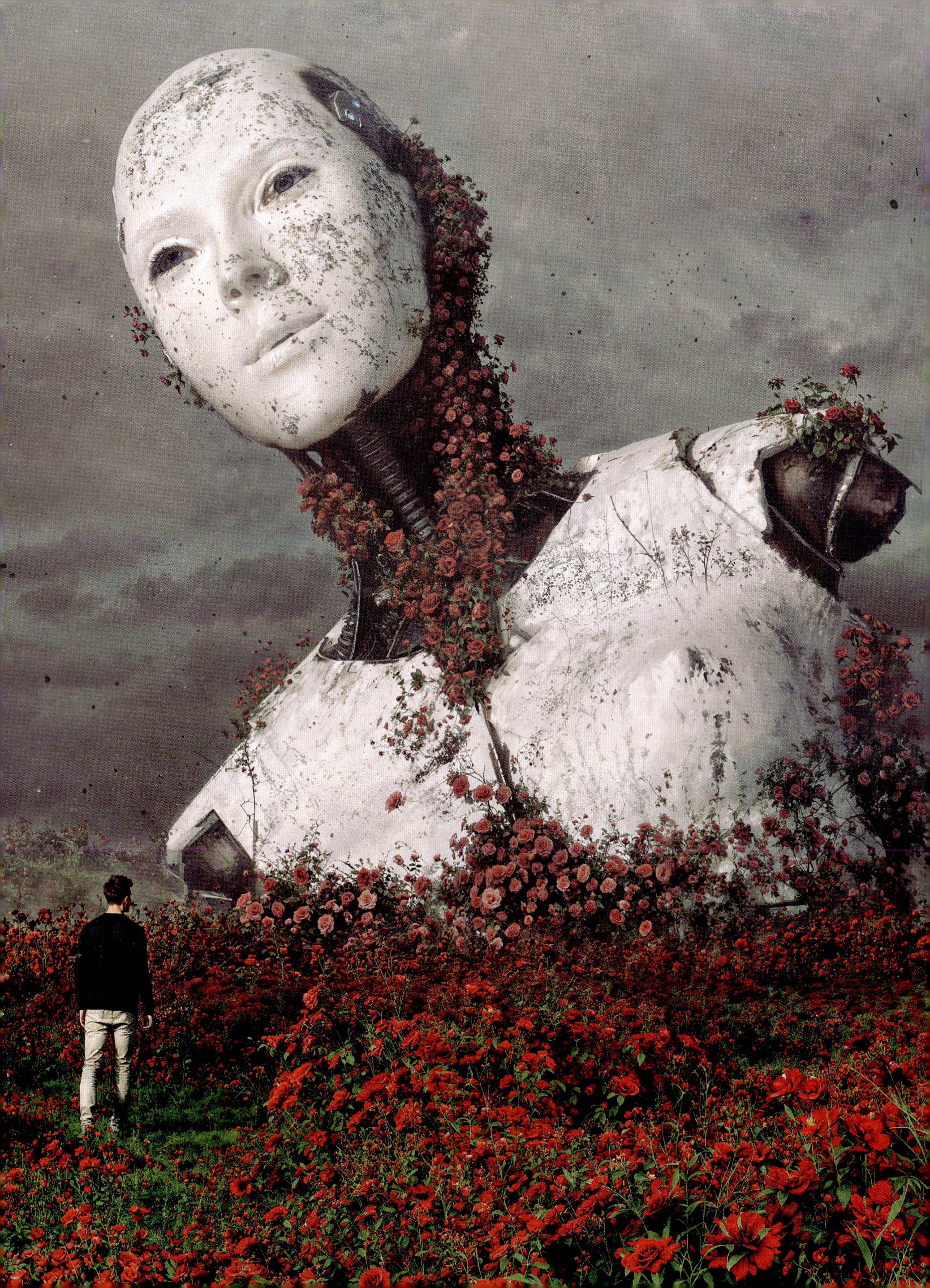

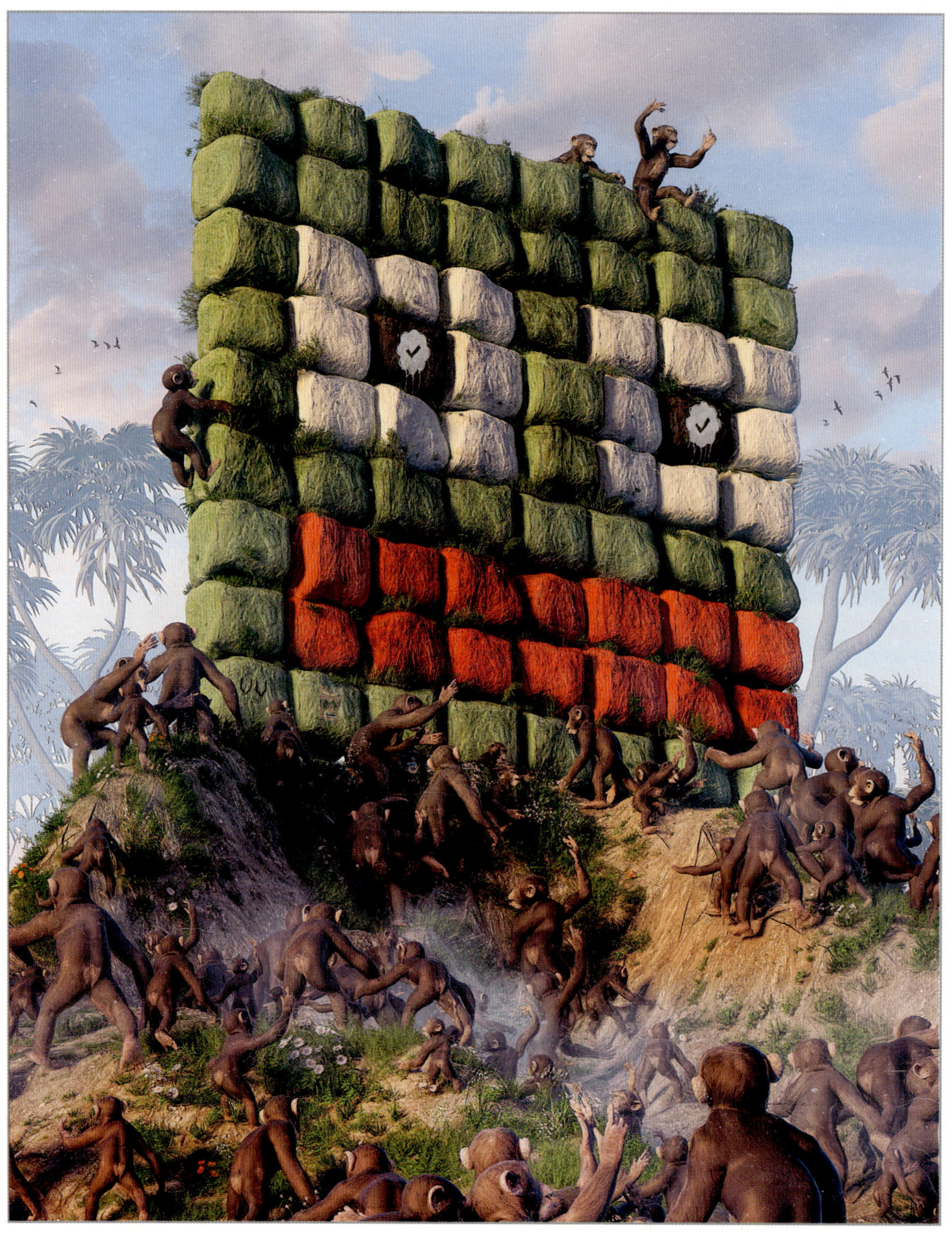

SLEEPING GIANT

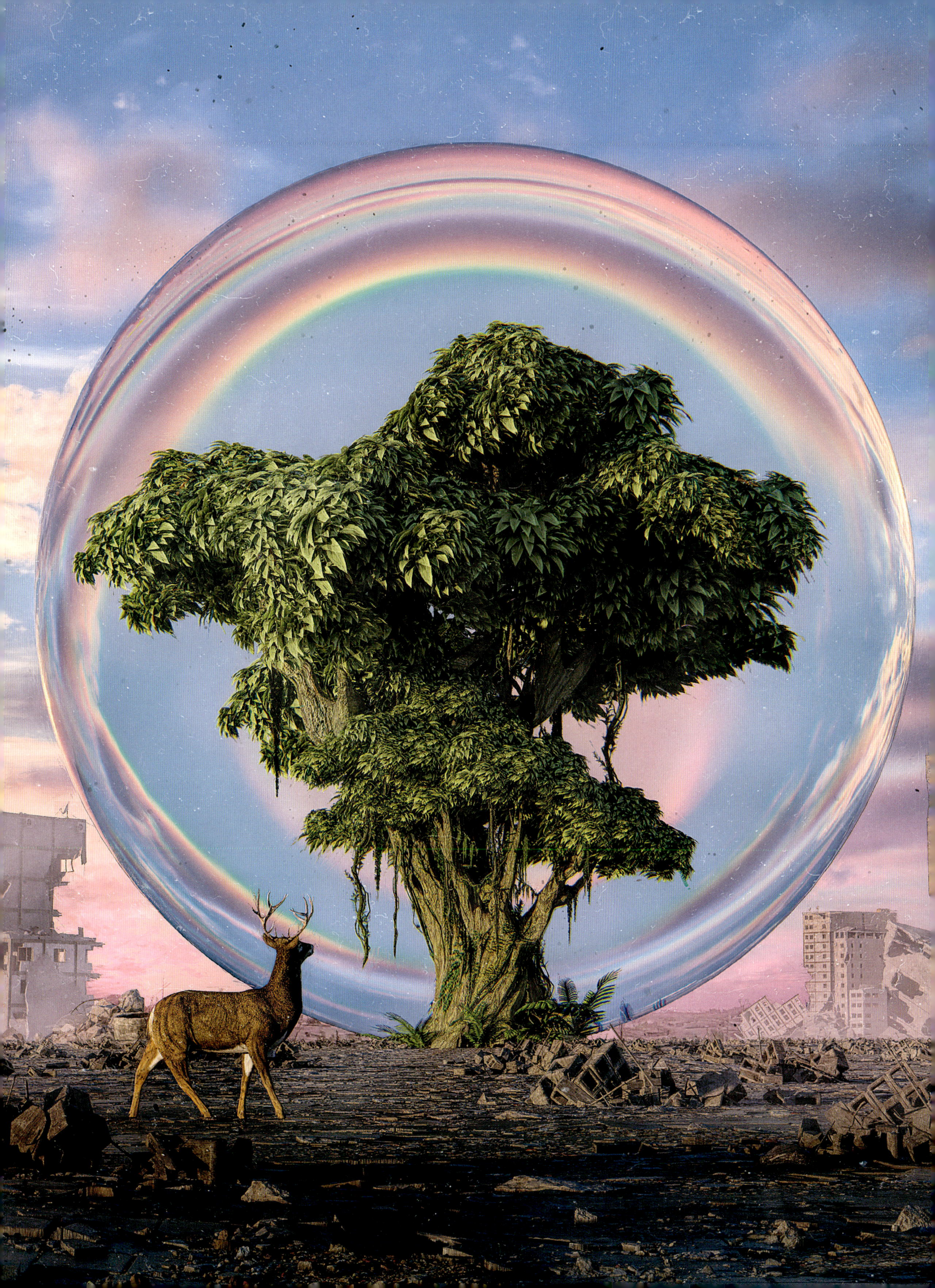

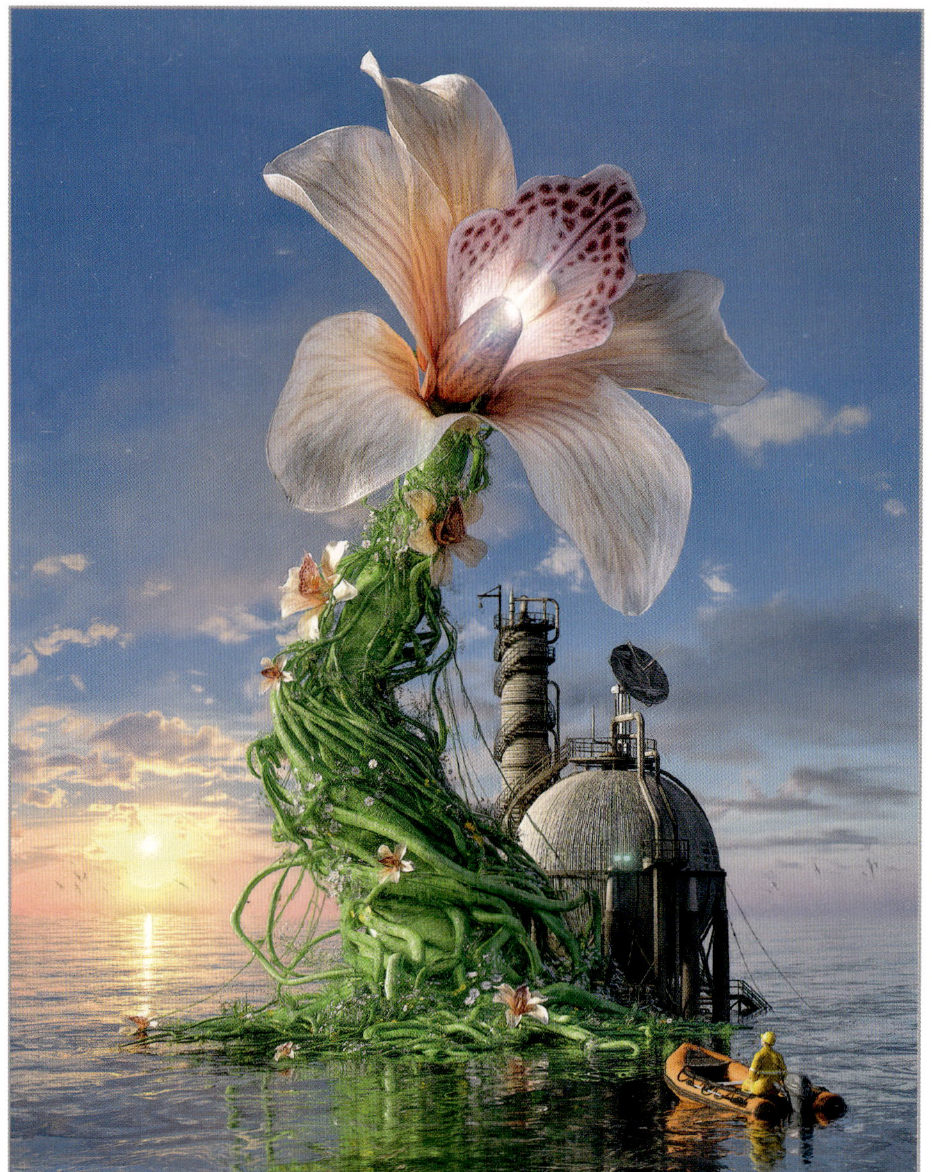

With his boundless ingenuity, Beeple will never cease to surprise and astonish. "I think the fact of being recognized as an artist ought to push one to do something different, something new and original. There are artists, however, who've developed a style typical to them that's remained that way over time and has become damn cool for that very reason. So, if you feel good about yourself and don't feel trapped in any sort of routine, then you can go on like this . . . Ultimately, therefore, I think the most important thing is to keep working and creating . . ." he says thoughtfully.

ORGANIC GROWTH

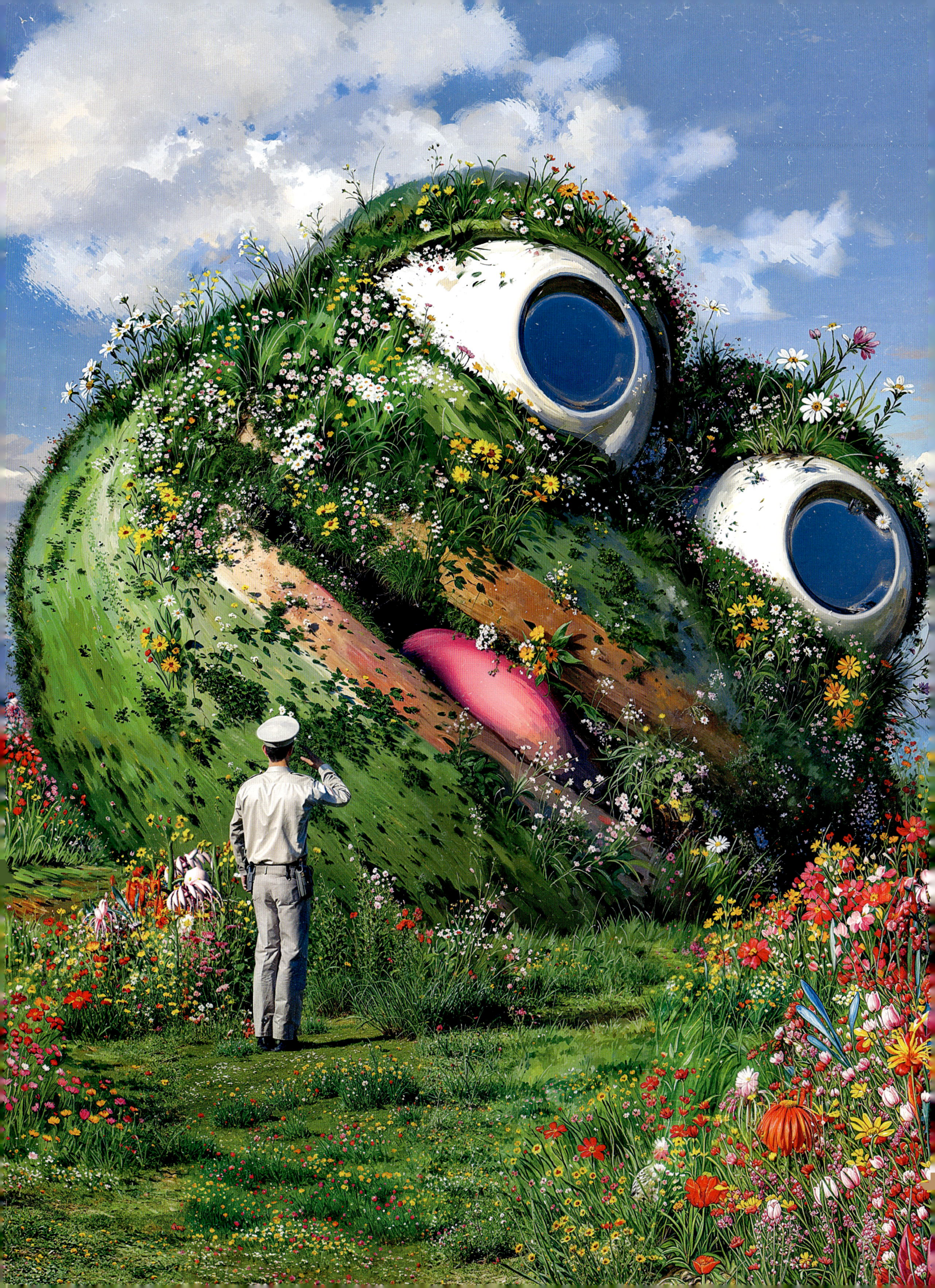

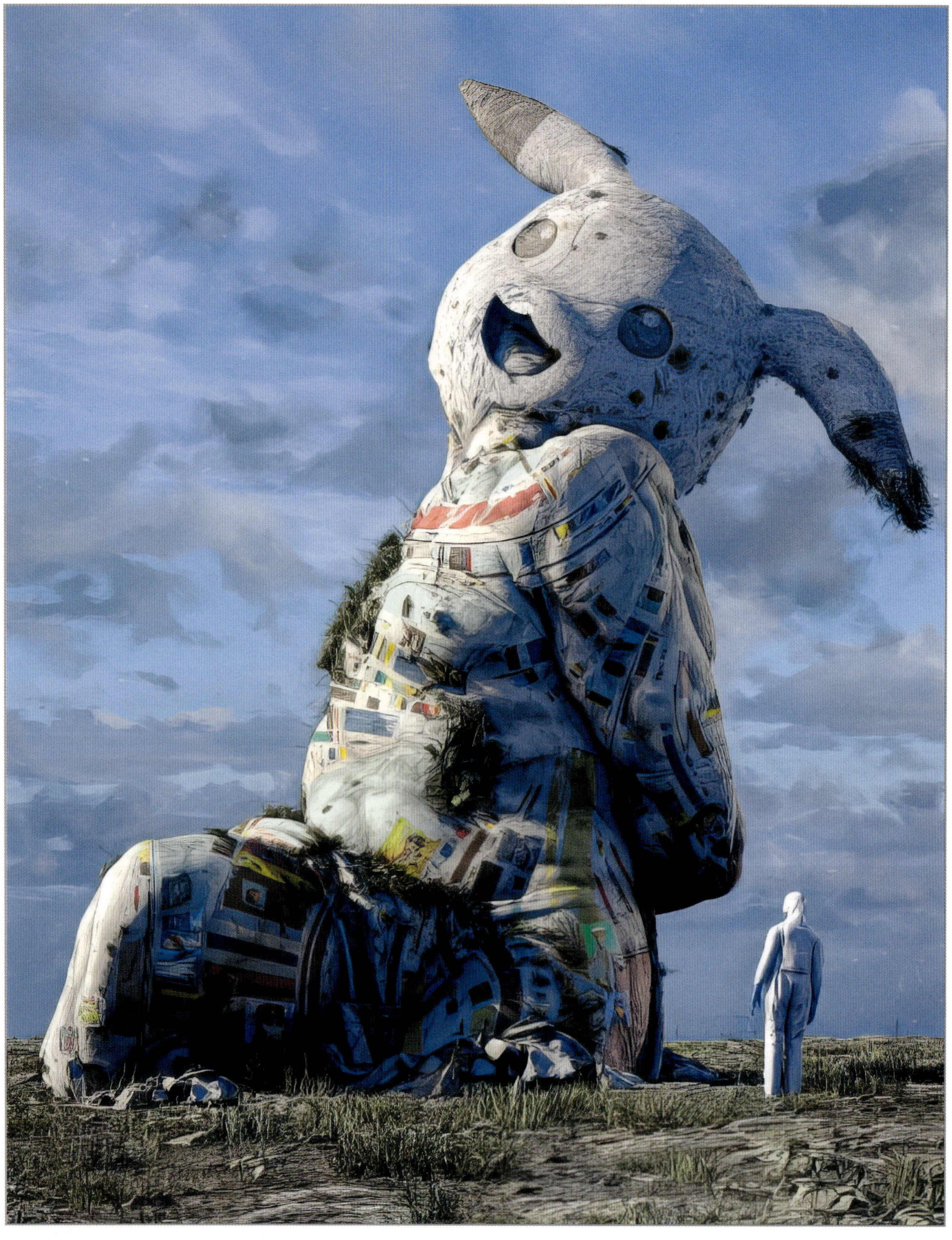

FUTURE GRAFFITI

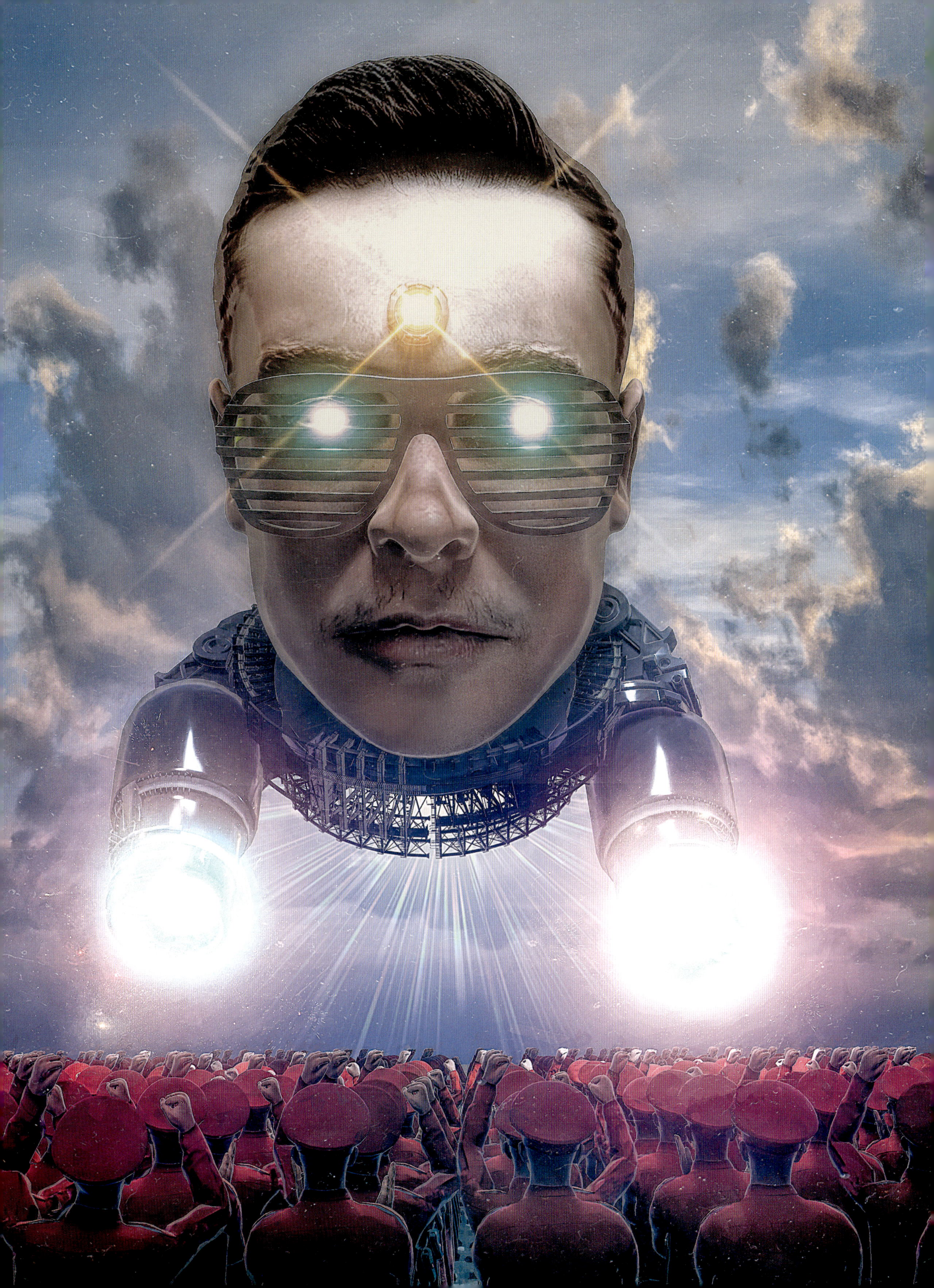

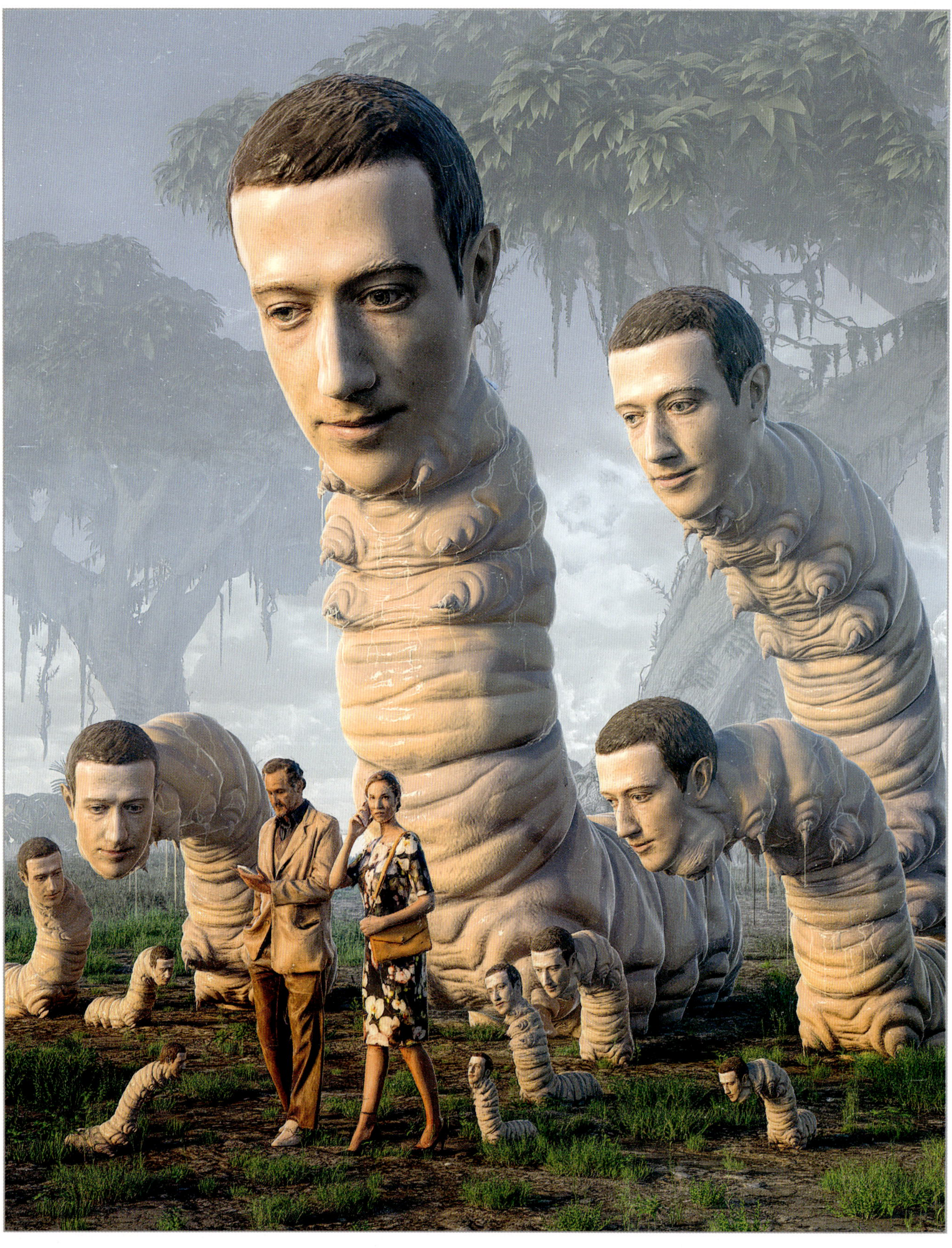

INVASIVE SPECIES

SOFIA CRESPO

WHEN TECHNOLOGY MEETS BIOLOGY

"SOMETIMES IT SEEMS AS THOUGH NEITHER THE TERMS 'TECHNOLOGY' AND 'ART' MEAN MUCH. TODAY'S WORLD CONSISTS OF A SET OF TECHNOLOGIES THAT WE TAKE FOR GRANTED AS IF THEY WERE SECOND NATURE, AND CEASE REGARDING THEM FOR WHAT THEY ACTUALLY ARE."

Figures and marvelous creatures bursting with color and life that float against a black screen with irresistible charm . . . that seem to reflect an internal and intimate microcosm, simultaneously complex and simple, and incredibly fascinating. Sofia Crespo has always exhibited an immense interest in technologies with biological applications. Today she's exploring the opportunities offered by artificial intelligence with the same attention in the hope of discovering new ways of creating and experimenting with other potential means of existence. "I guess that secretly I always wanted to be an artist, but I never thought it was something that I could actually achieve," she admits with candor. "As a child, I loved writing poetry and imagining alternative worlds; I loved dreaming about or imagining different people, spaces, situations.

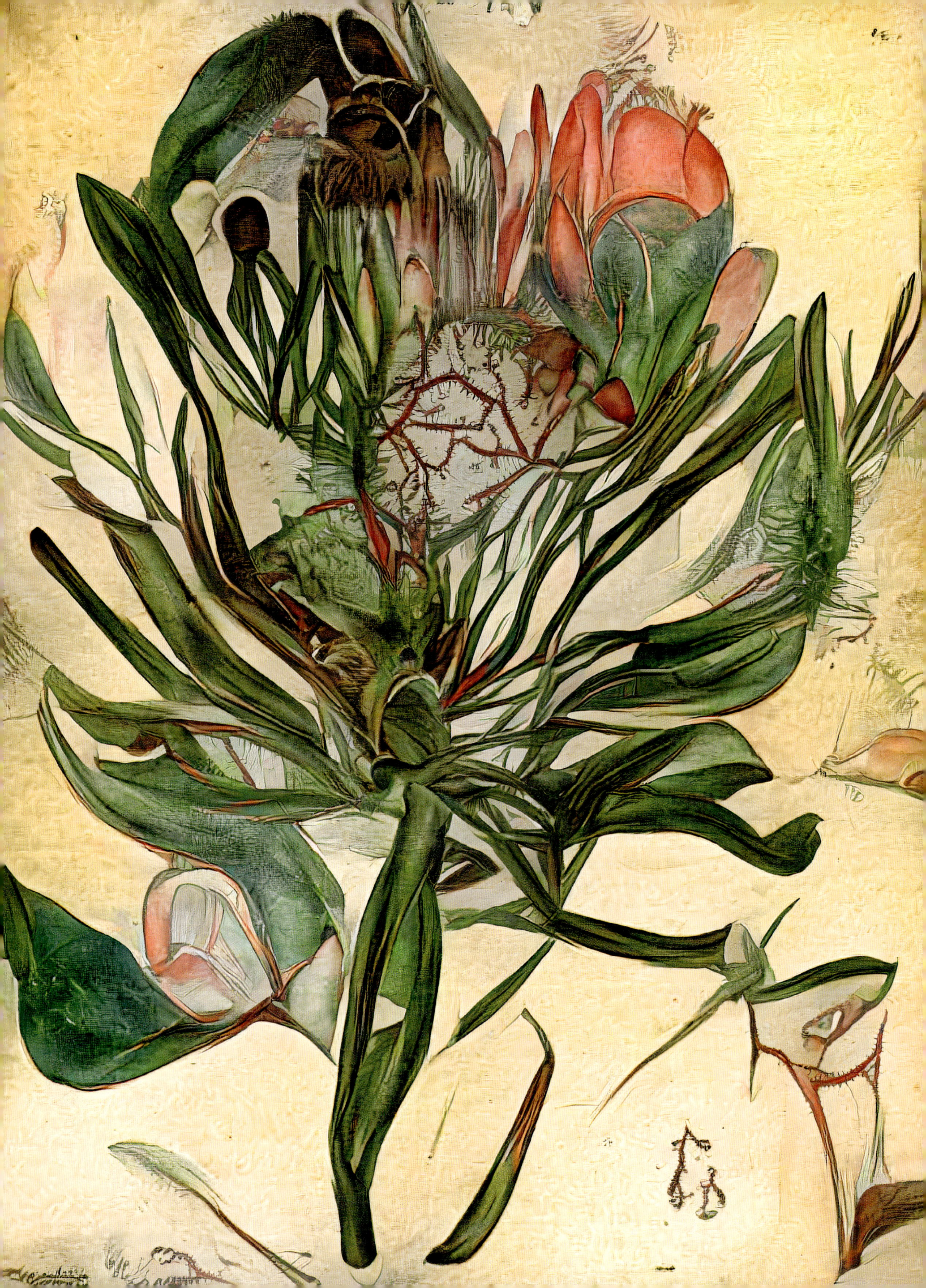

Growing up, I realized that something touched me profoundly whenever I entered a museum, especially one with contemporary art. Only much later, while living in Berlin, did I discover that becoming an artist was a dream that I could attain if I wanted to, though it would require serious commitment," she adds. A highly intuitive person, Sofia got into technology at a young age. "It happened in 2016 when I became interested in memetics. I wanted to delve deeper into the memes that I used online and the patterns of my behavior and choices. So I began thinking of ways of automating the process of 'extracting patterns from my data,'" she recounts. It's this that led Sofia to artificial intelligence. "It instantly roused my curiosity, which still has not diminished. It pushed me to delve deeper into the ways in which images are processed by computers, and to learn how to create synthetic datasets, use my own models, and manipulate their latent space. The process of extracting the fundamental patterns of the natural world proved an inexhaustible source of discovery and surprise as it revealed many of our presuppositions and insights about the natural world and how they have been spread by culture," she claims.

Inasmuch as she loves innovation and experimentation, Sofia still always prefers to get down to the roots of everything.

"I do like looking back, but I'm also interested in understanding how the technological tools we're developing affect the ways we relate to our surroundings and the knowledge of the world we pass from one generation to the next. This is why I find the history of science deeply fascinating," she admits. She finds art even more difficult to describe. "My relationship with the word 'art' is at best problematic. Today it seems as though anything can be art, as long as we all agree that it is. For me, however, art is intrinsically linked to intentionality," she divulges. Sofia feels that art has profound existential significance: "My values as an artist are

related to my values as a human being. I place weight on honesty, compassion, realism, and integrity, and try to foster a process that amplifies my voice. It's nearly impossible, and perhaps even stupid, to assume that as artists we can create something 'new'; yet, by the same token, we all have our own unique and peculiar way of perceiving the world. I think that experimenting with ways of communicating one's personal perspective is an important, even essential, aspect of being an artist today." Sofia derives her inspiration from her own fantastical microcosm. "Most of my ideas come from scuba diving and the time I spend observing marine life," she explains. Her passion for the ocean has increased her interest in biology. "It's hard not to be inspired by biology when you spend so much time exploring the natural world or taking an interest in the research of scientists worldwide—it's absolutely amazing! The diversity, abundance, and surprising behaviors one may observe seem endless at times. I find comfort in knowing that the realm of biology always contains new mysteries to unravel and draw inspiration from," she says, reflectively. Although born in Argentina, Sofia decided to live in Lisbon, Portugal, a country with profound ties to the sea.

"I'm very happy to live in a city rising just a few kilometers from the ocean; whenever I feel stuck with a project, I can spend some time on the coast or in the waters of the sea. I almost always return with a fresh perspective or new attitude toward the ocean itself. And if something isn't going well, it's always the ocean that helps me look beyond that," she confesses. In addition, since 2020, Sofia has joined the Norwegian artist Feileacan Kirkbride McCormick in the art duo Entangled Others. "I'm never totally sure where I'm going, I simply know that I intend to keep pushing myself to explore my passions. Lately, my focus has fallen ever more on finding new ways of connecting my digital practice with physical space," she states.

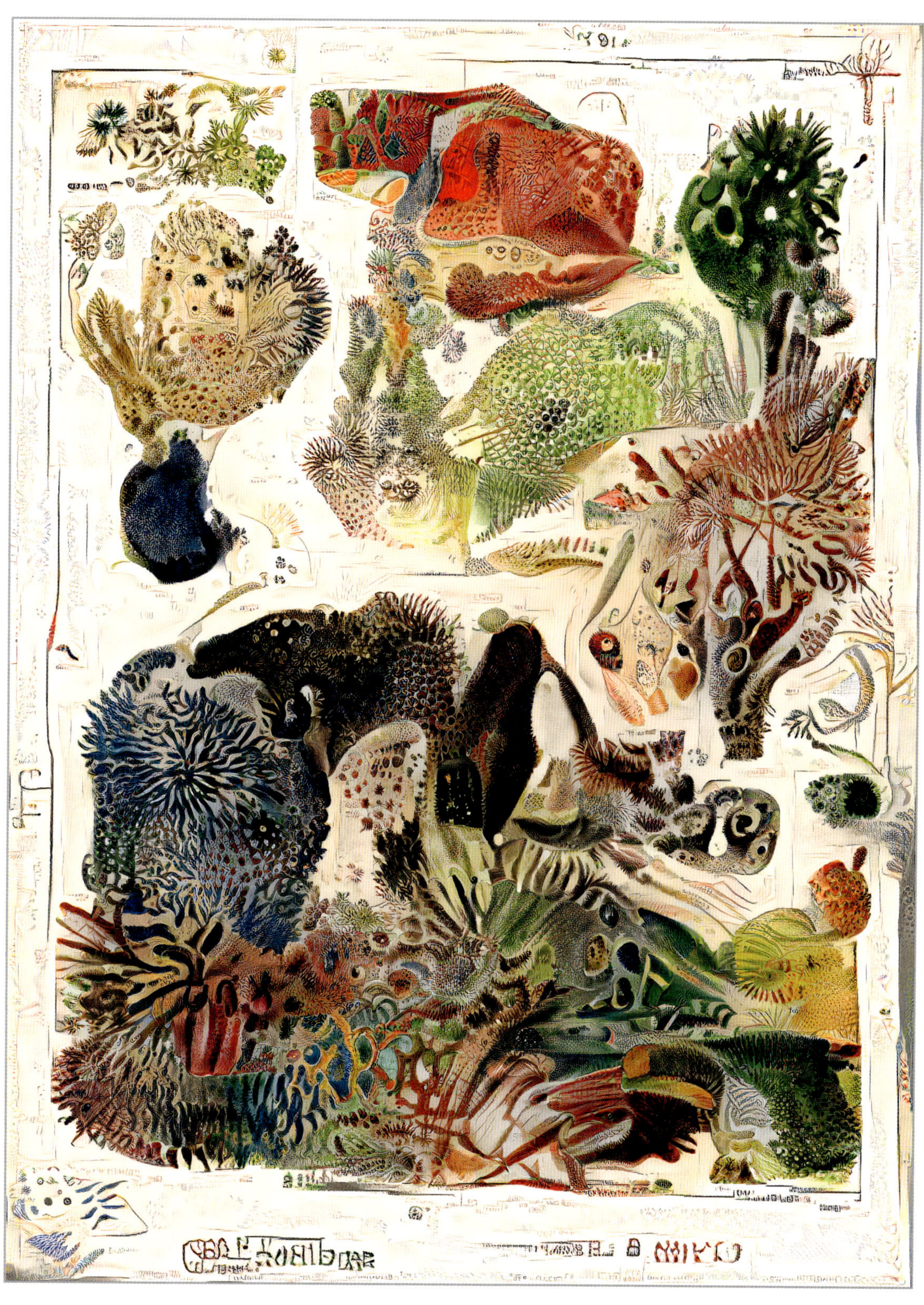

CORAL_5981

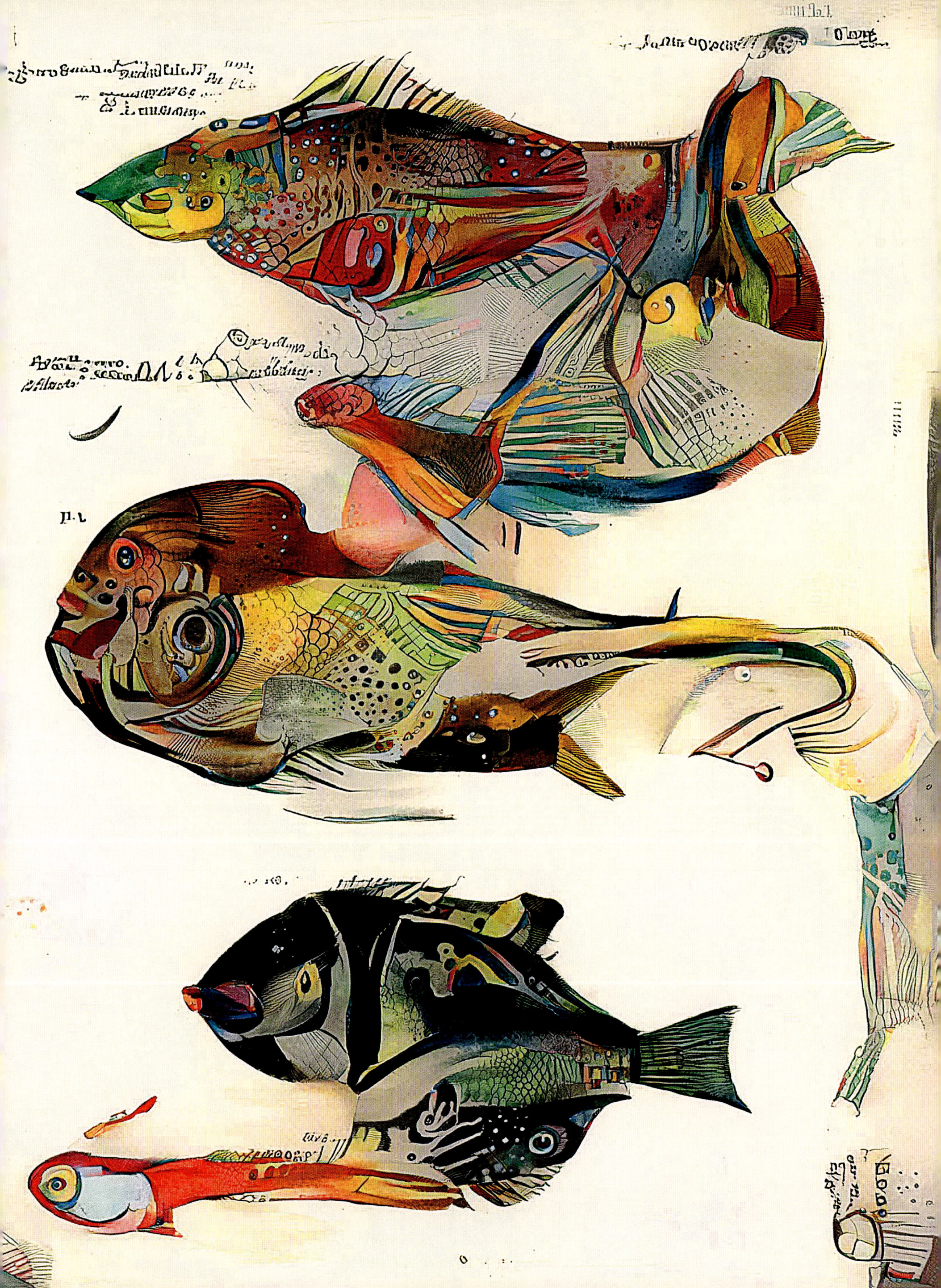

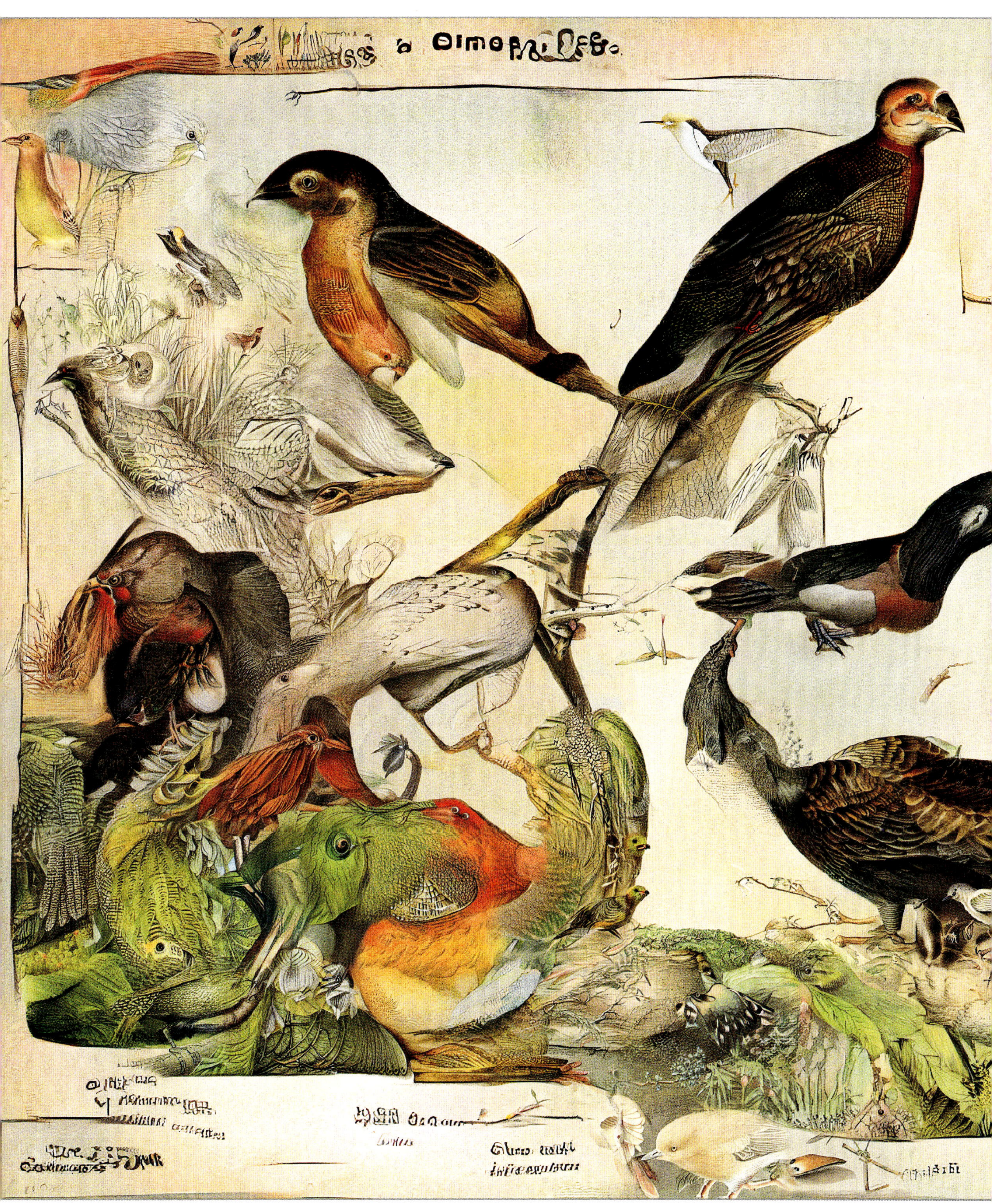

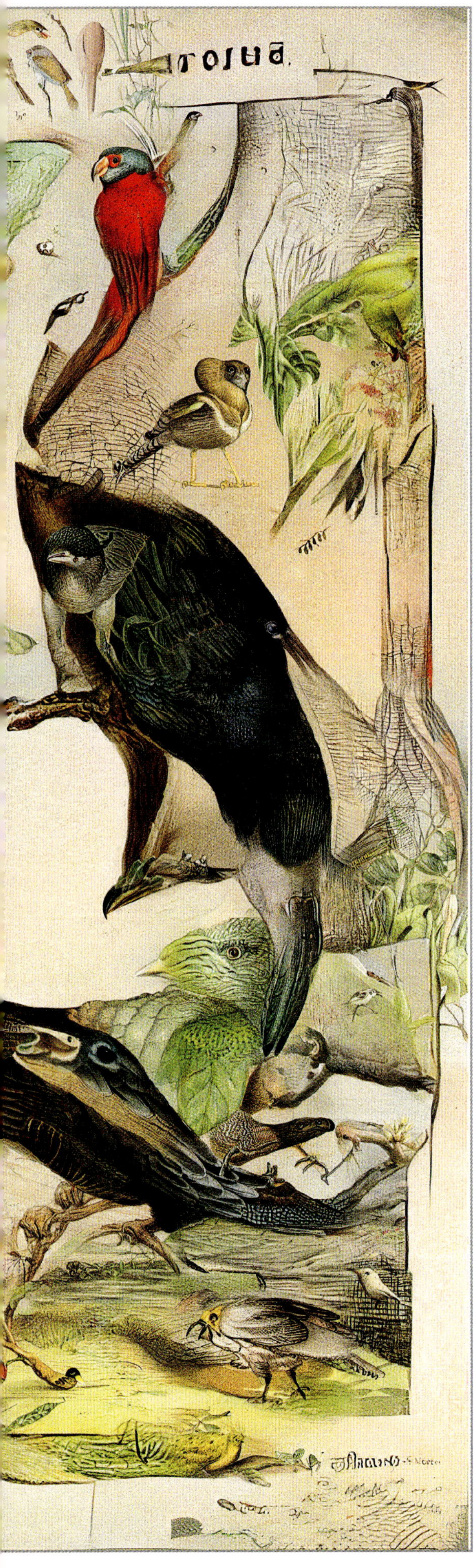

Sofia remained fascinated by AI, even though she didn't dare venture into this area until a particular moment: "By sheer luck, a friend gave me a seminar on neural networks for my birthday.

What followed was an instant deep dive into the world of neural networks and AI, data sets, their collection, and the process of using them as an artistic medium. Today, my relationship with technology recalls that that another artist might have with their paintbrushes, or a photographer with his or her camera: it's a tool that enables one to articulate a concept or thought in a way that differs from another means," she explains. She goes on: "The ability to extract essential patterns from an image dataset reveals a subject or focal point in a way that differs from what one can get with a pencil or camera. Ultimately, I use those tools that are best adapted to the concept I wish to express, so it's never merely for the sake of using neural networks; there has to be a deeper reason for employing them in my creative process."

Sofia continues to experiment and admits that she doesn't know what future technological development will have: "Unfortunately, I have no crystal ball and can't say exactly what will happen in the future. All I can say is what I hope will happen, and that is that we can find ways of diminishing the conflict within ourselves and with the world around us. I believe there's much to learn beyond Western culture, as, for example, from the wisdom of many Indigenous peoples who still live in close connection with the natural world."

SHARED MOMENTS OF OBSERVATION

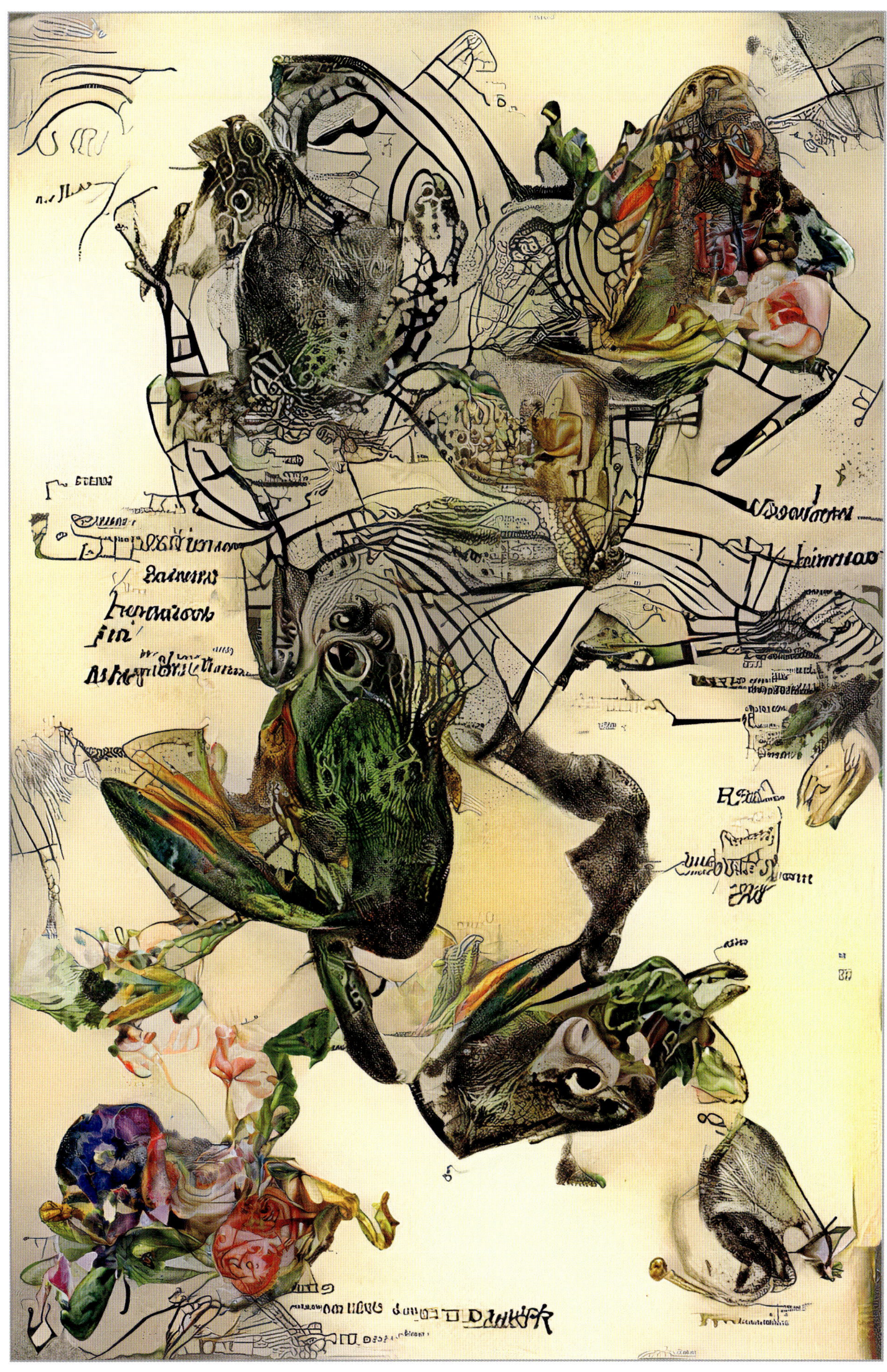

FROG_9090

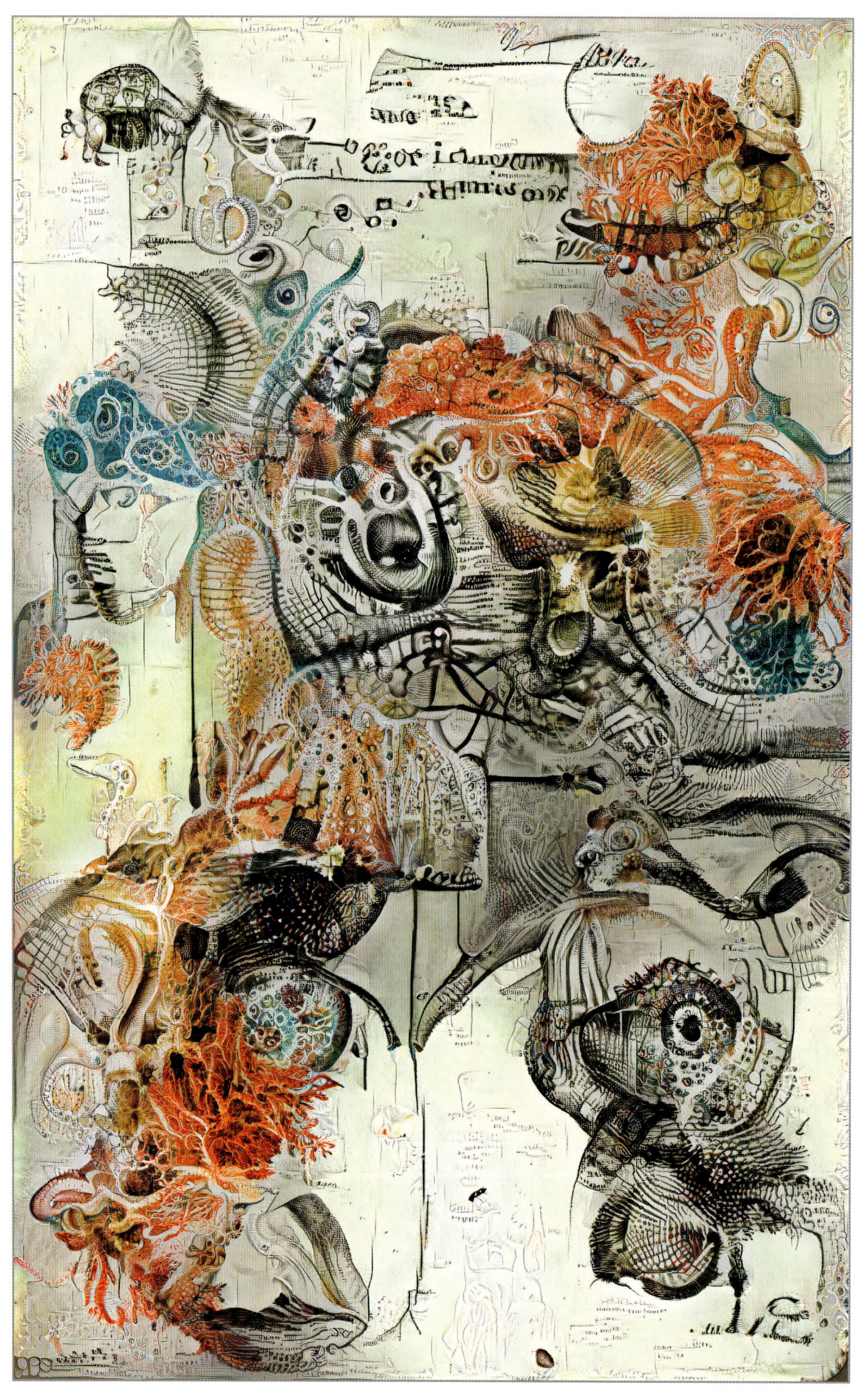

ENTANGLED_6523

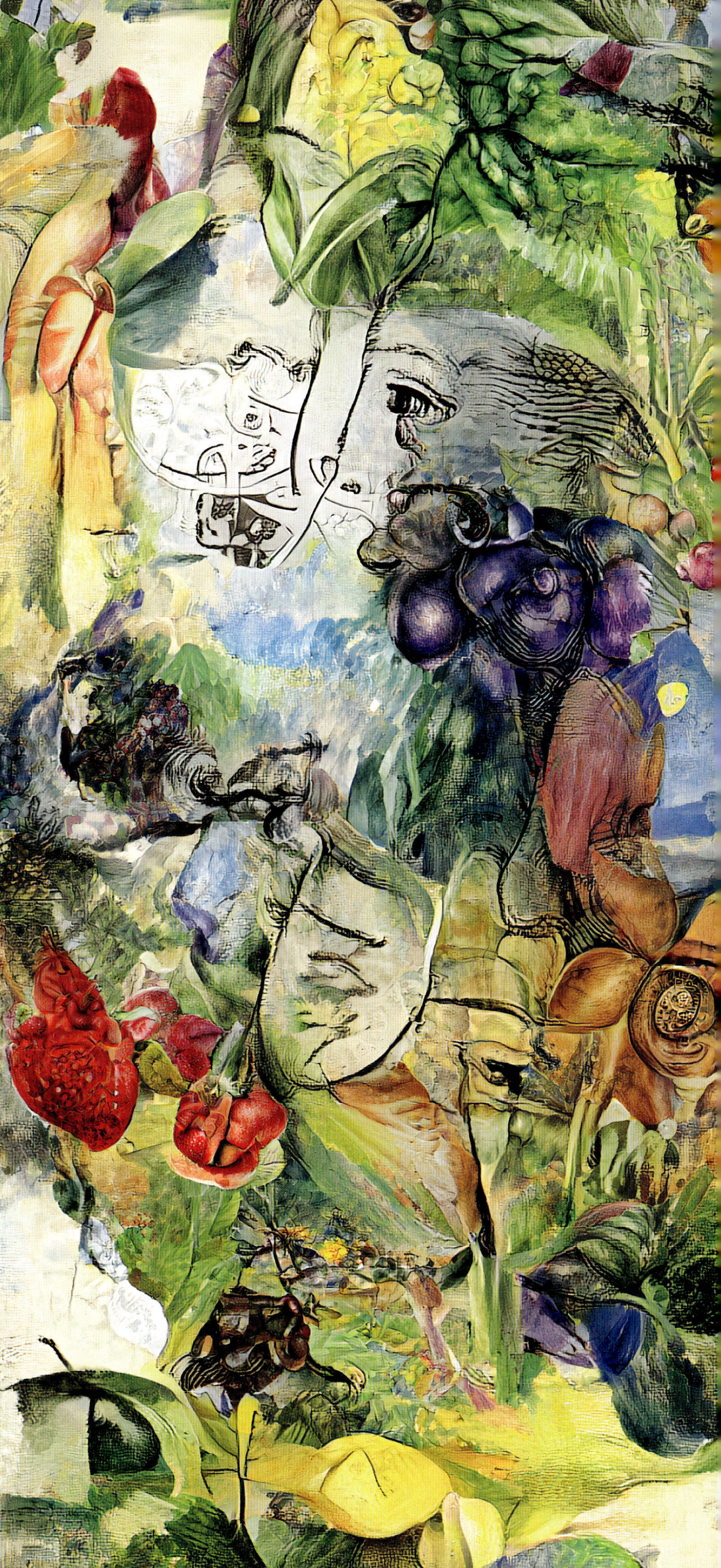

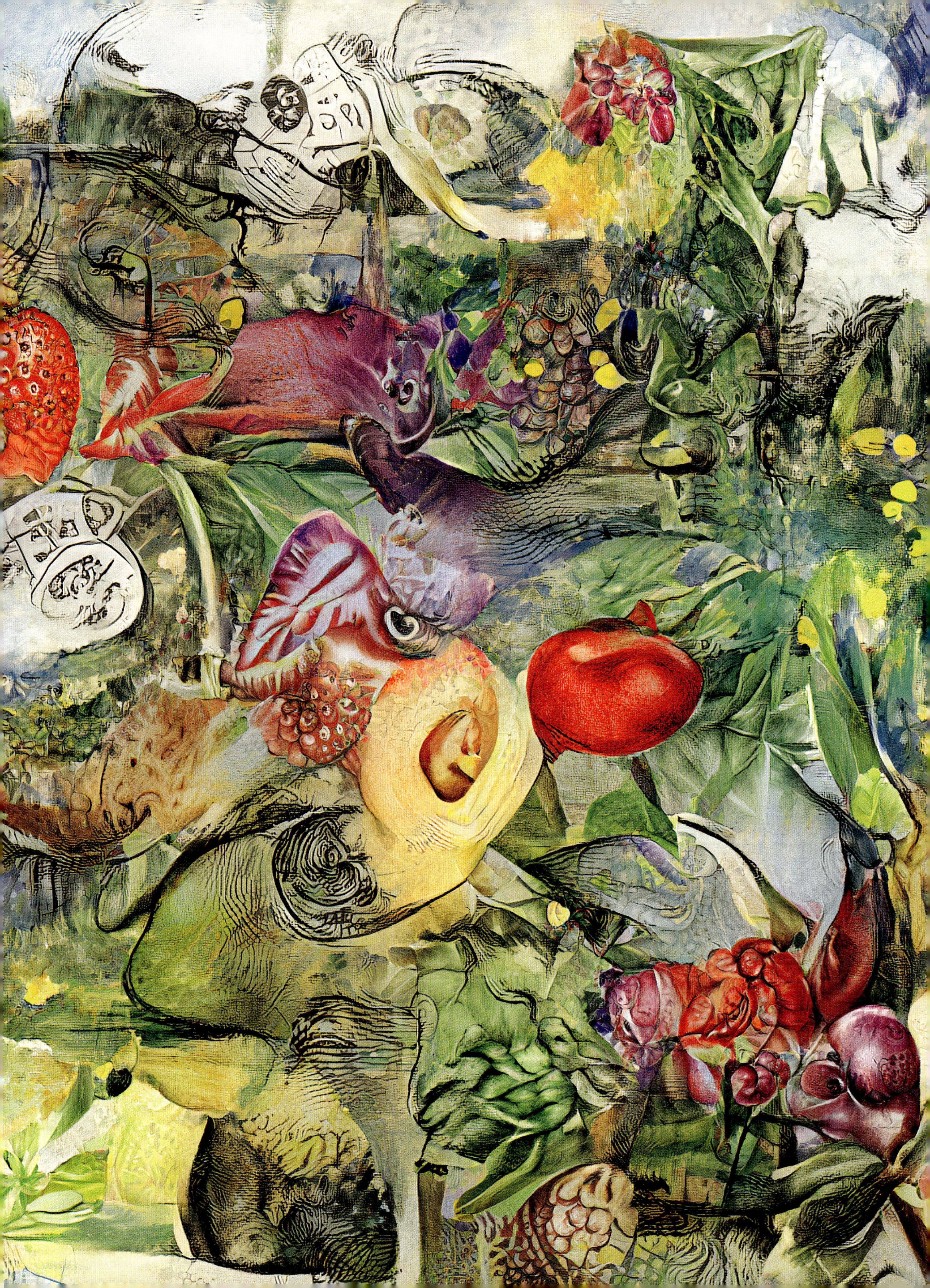

FVCKRENDE

WHEN GEOMETRY PLAYS WITH LIGHT

"MY WORK LIES AT THE INTERSECTION OF IMAGINATION AND TECHNOLOGY. I'M DRIVEN BY ENDLESS CURIOSITY AND A PASSION TO PUSH THE LIMITS OF WHAT'S POSSIBLE IN THE DIGITAL ART REALM."

In his universe, metal figures coalesce like drops of ink, quickly dissolving into hints of a fantastical infinity characterized by bits of geometric and abstract figures, present and evanescent in equal measure . . . They're like virtual ghosts floating in one's imagination, an encounter between the physical and digital worlds. Sometimes a hand reaches for a chain, as if seeking connection . . . At other times, a luminous futuristic landscape pushes itself In . . . Or, again, crisp architectural geometry strikes the eye. The light and dark elements of this technological world are not afraid of uncovering dark implications or revelatory mirrors of existence itself.

The artist Frederic Duquette, who has assumed FVCKRENDER as his *nom de plume*, is self-taught. His dedication, his combative and forever in-your-face spirit, emerge from the undertones of his art, to which he passionately and instinctively gives his all. FVCKRENDER has created his own world in the metaverse—LVCIDIA, previously known as FVCKRENDERVERSE—which includes original and innovative projects like FVCK_CRYSTALS, a collection of 4169 digital crystals.

FEEL//ARTE

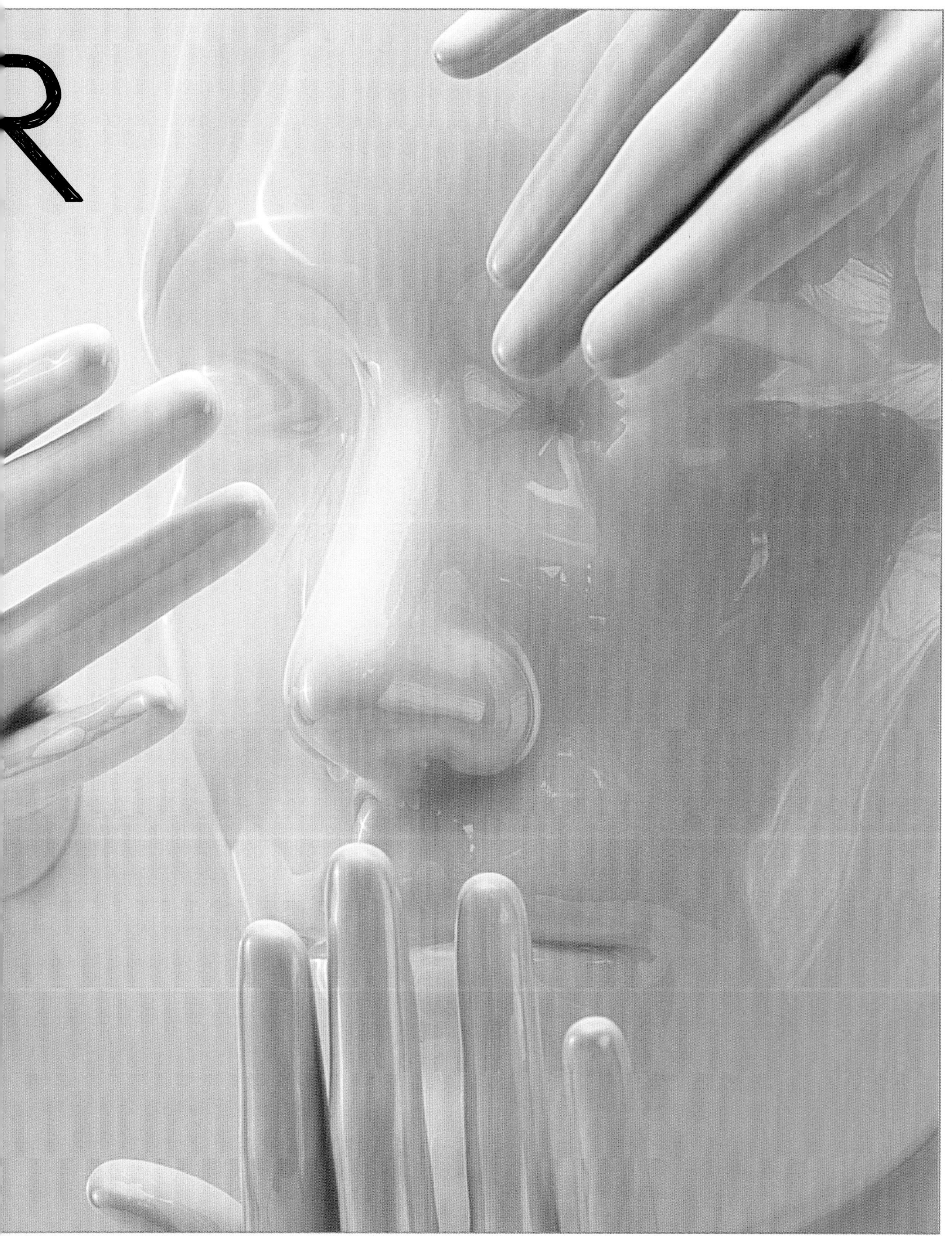

An important figure within his artistic repertoire is Ally, a symbol of a future world in which everyone will have to work hard to create a better place.

Viewing his art as therapeutic and capable of helping people overcome trauma, anxiety, and fear, FVCKRENDER has come up with a manifesto to which he is firmly committed, and which brings together all aspects of his vision: "I use art as a diary in which to express myself and project my emotions onto the past. Art serves as therapy, offering me both a way of finding myself and an outlet through which to express myself. It has helped me connect with others and has motivated me. Thanks to their intricate details, vibrant colors, and a touch of extraterrestrial energy, my works invite viewers to embark on a voyage of discovery and introspection. Art heals. My purpose is to bring people together and create experiences, to help others, and to build community. My ultimate goal as an artist is to inspire, provoke, and transport viewers into universes they didn't even know existed. In this, our present-day world, full of chaos and uncertainty, I believe that art has the power to illuminate the darkness and instill hope for a better future. That's my story. I overcame my own problems through art. Developing self-awareness through authenticity has brought me joy and a place in this world."

FVCKRENDER hopes that this can help others like him overcome life's hardest and darkest moments and find happiness and purpose. "I always wanted to devote myself to art, but I wasn't sure what medium was right for me. I began in high school with a sewing machine, making cardigans and tie-dye articles, but that wasn't what I was looking for . . . Then I tried drawing, but I just didn't like it. Several years later, I wanted to take studio art courses in Montreal; but since I had dropped out of high school, my application was rejected. This shattered my dream of pursuing art of any kind," he recounts.

"Afterwards, I worked at a restaurant and participated in bike races, but an accident stopped me from continuing along that path as well . . . At that point, I had to reinvent myself and went back to the idea of making art, so I bought the Cinema 4D and Octane Render software simply for fun . . . And I still can't believe where I ended up . . . ," he admits. His road to art was marked by many sacrifices and problems, and was, in fact, quite bumpy. Canada, his country of origin, certainly contributed a great deal to his upbringing. "Not long ago, I moved back to Montreal from Vancouver. Vancouver is the perfect place in which to clear one's mind and reconsider what one wants to do in life. Its proximity to the ocean and mountains has a powerful influence on one's spirit, but I think it's important to be constantly on the move and explore new worlds and new environments! Life's too short to live in one place," he insists.

According to his fate, art has always been accompanied by technology. "I grew up with a computer in my bedroom and spent lots of time playing Diablo, StarCraft, and Zelda. This contributed a great deal to nurturing my love for the digital world," he states. "I knew that my passion lay in art, but I had to find the right path to get there. I didn't have a diploma that could grant me access to an academic environment or the gallery world, so it was quite difficult for me to establish myself as an artist and do what really interests me," he says.

"But at the most difficult moments, art inspired me . . . and saved me. My inspiration comes from everything and everywhere, but especially from light and the way in which it reacts and bounces off objects," he says. As for the choice of subject, he is eager to clarify: "I wouldn't say that robots fascinate me in any particular way, but I like to believe that consciousness can be transported elsewhere, even beyond human reality . . . It is from this presupposition that my exploration of new worlds arises . . ."

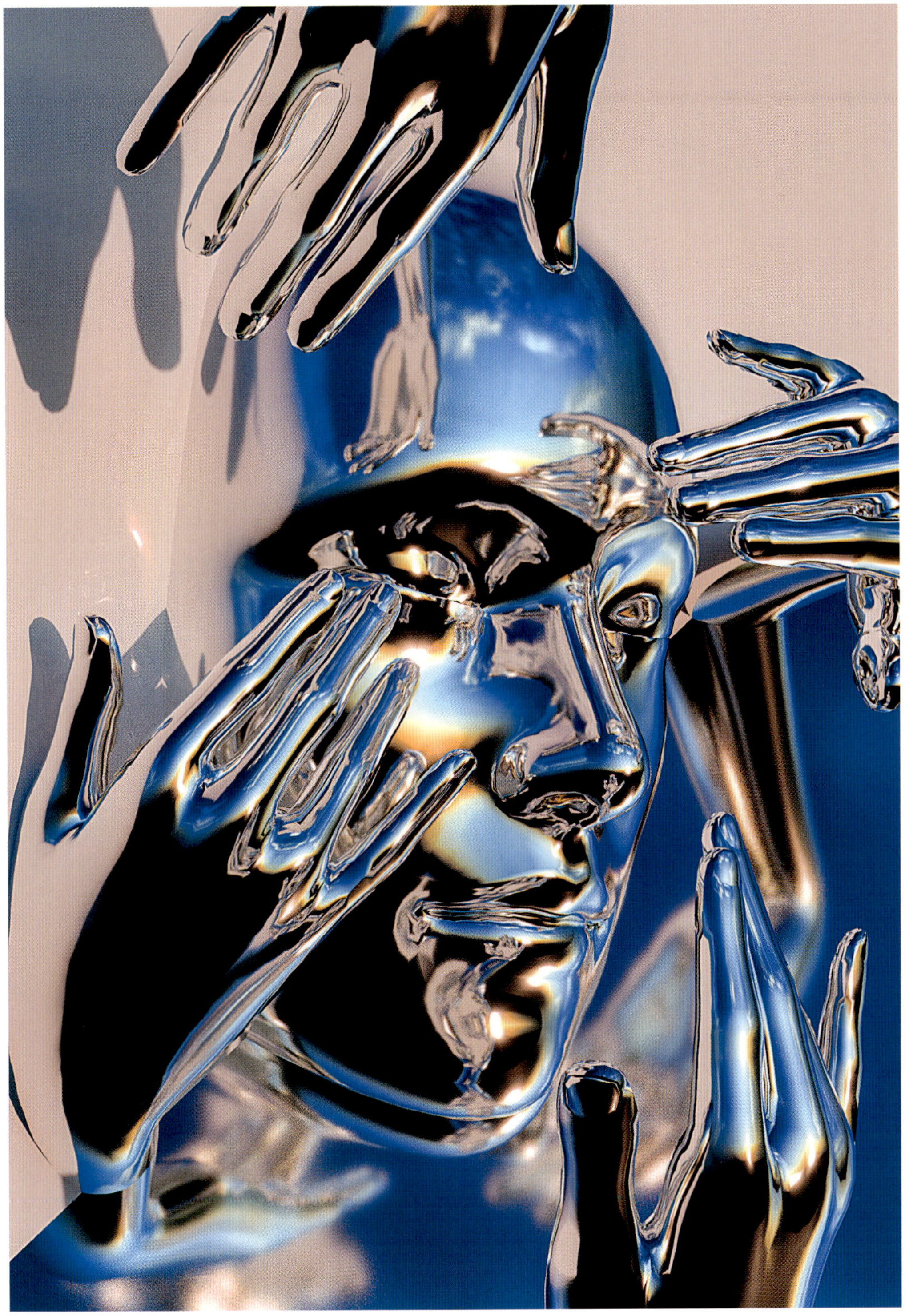

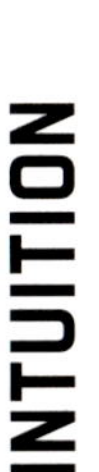

SELF HELP

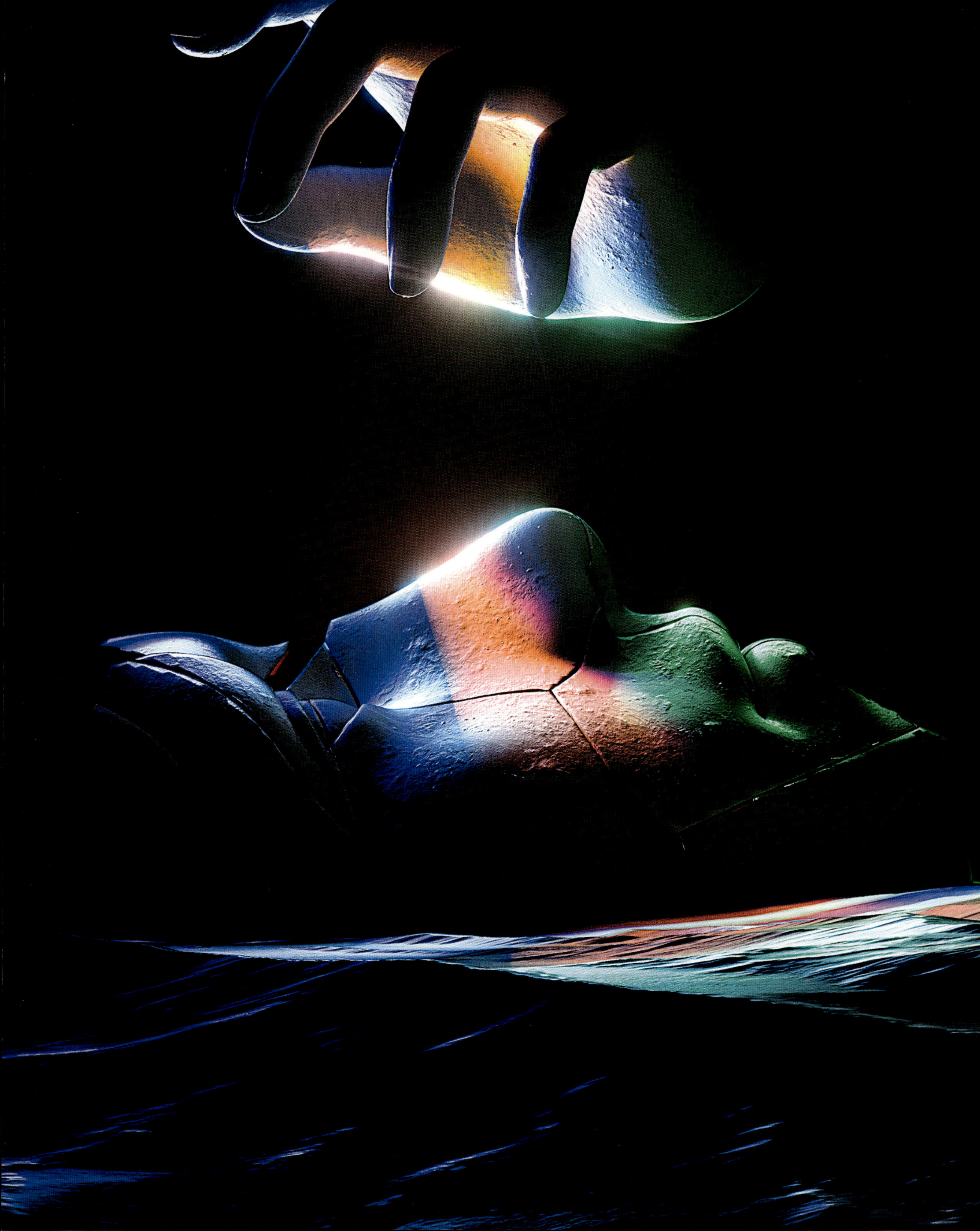

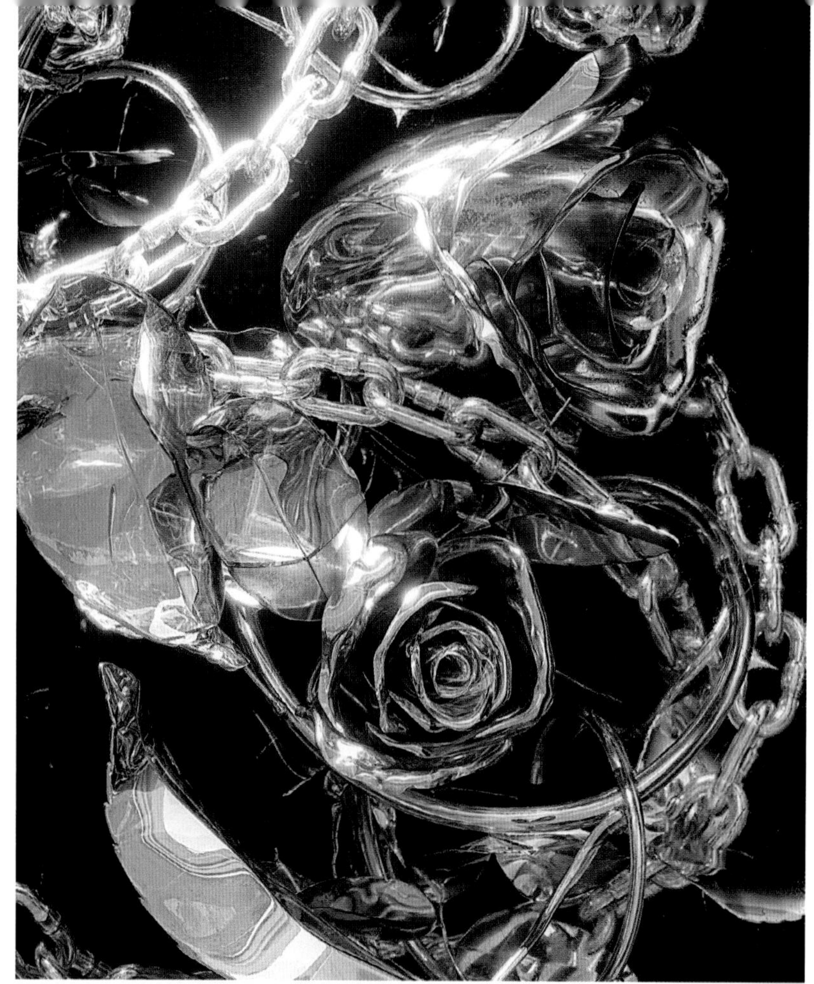

BLOOMED

Afterwards, he reflects once again: "I'm convinced that making art pushes you into a vulnerable state and forces you to deal with yourself. Making art makes you understand who you are and lets your emotions flow into creation."

FVCKRENDER can't predict the future, but he does know what he wants now; an unexpected vision brings him to the root of physical art with a deep connection to the real world: "I want to make 30-foot-tall sculptures! I want to leave a tangible and permanent—not just digital—mark on this planet! Staying true to myself and not locking myself into a creative box—that's the key. If I wish to create an artwork in a style totally different from my current one, I won't hesitate to explore other avenues: it's only thus that I can grow, evolve!"

PERSONAL GROWTH

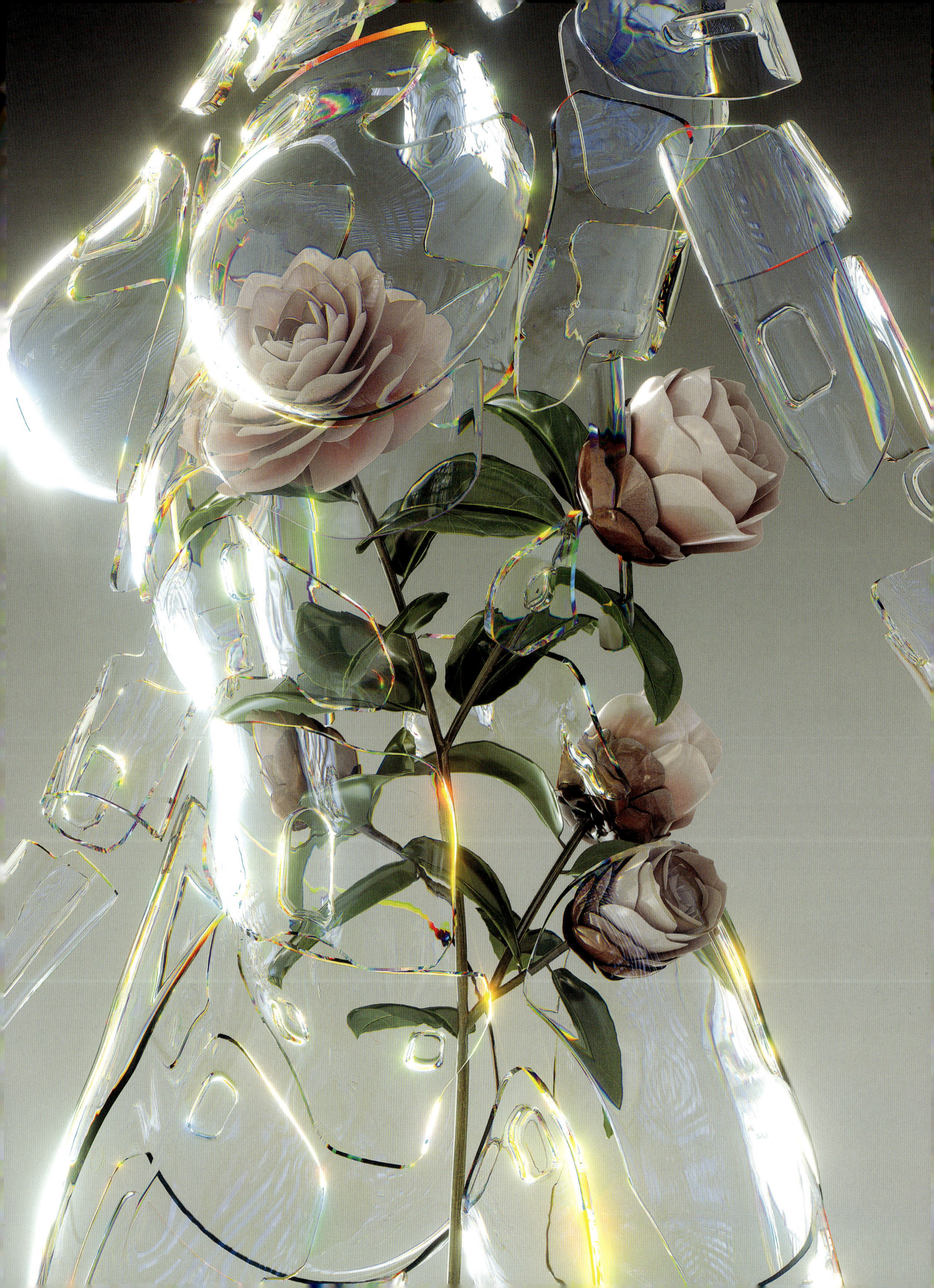

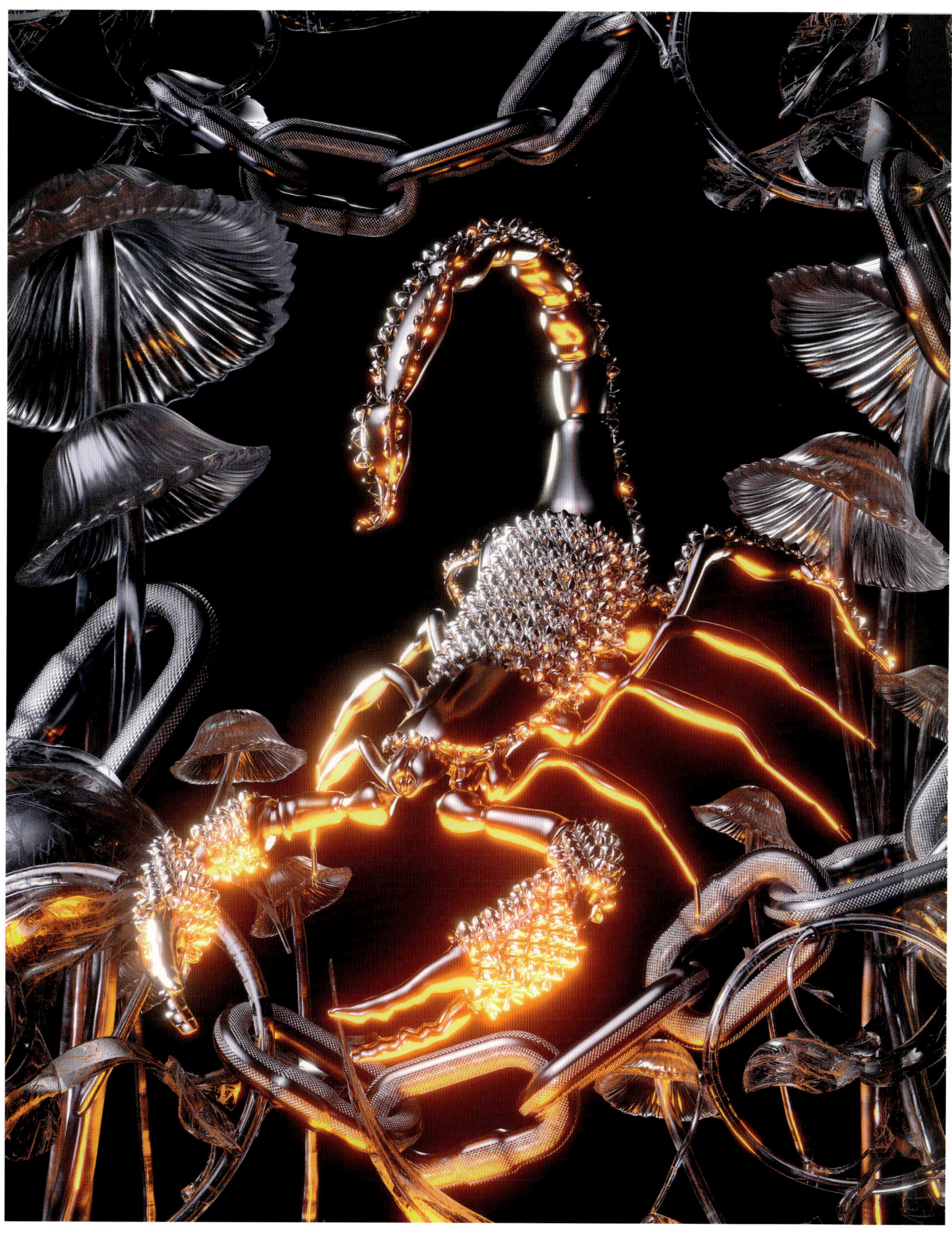

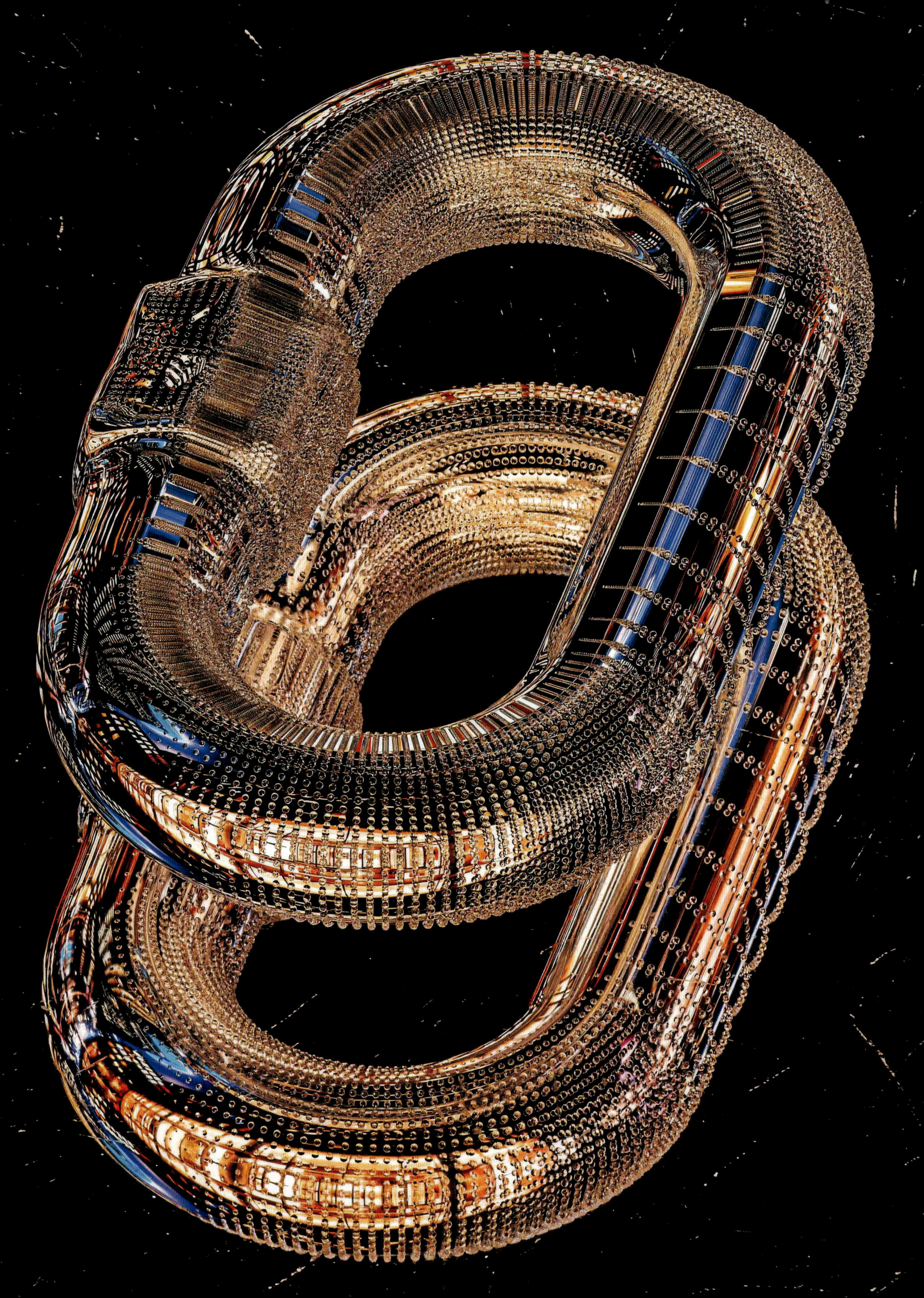

HACKATAO

WHEN NATURES FALLS IN LOVE WITH TECHNOLOGICAL INTERFERENCE

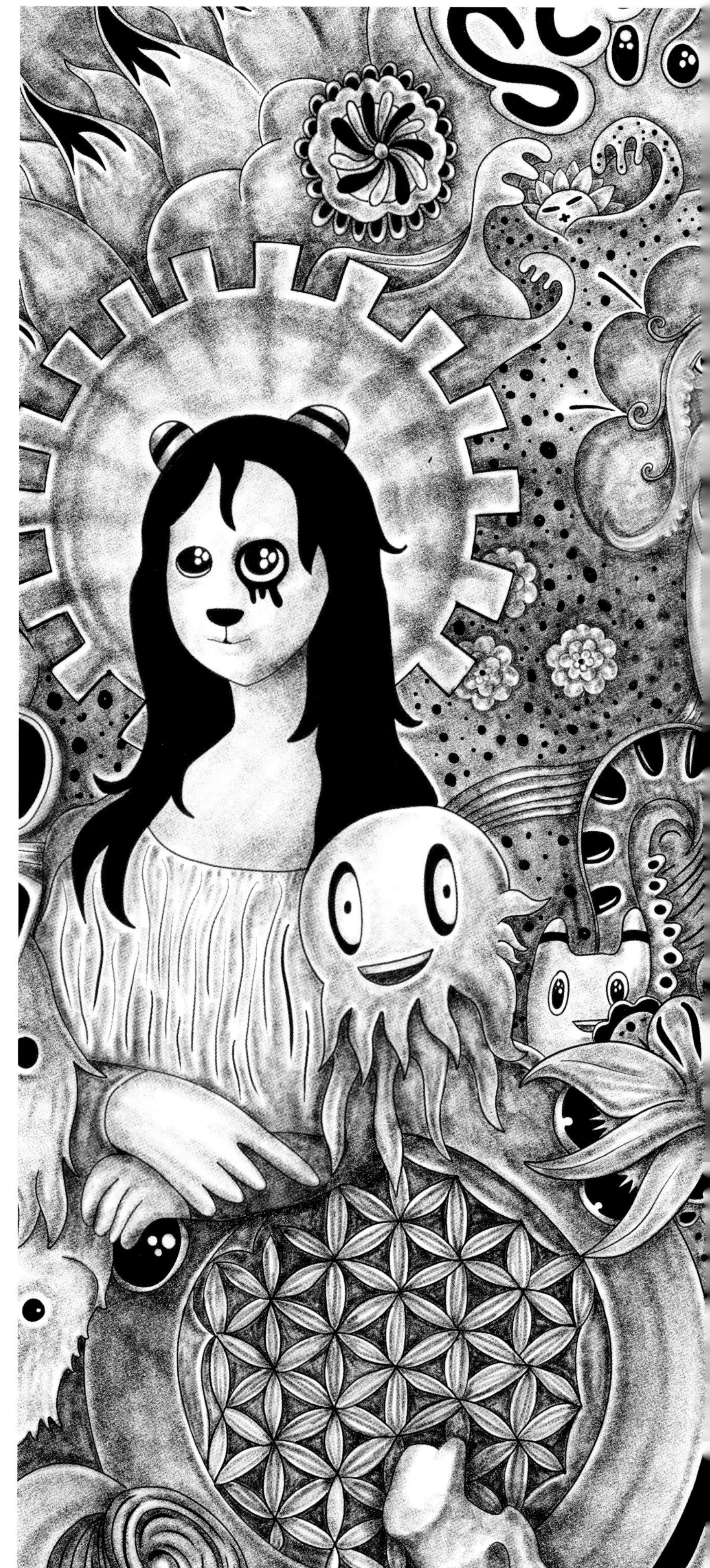

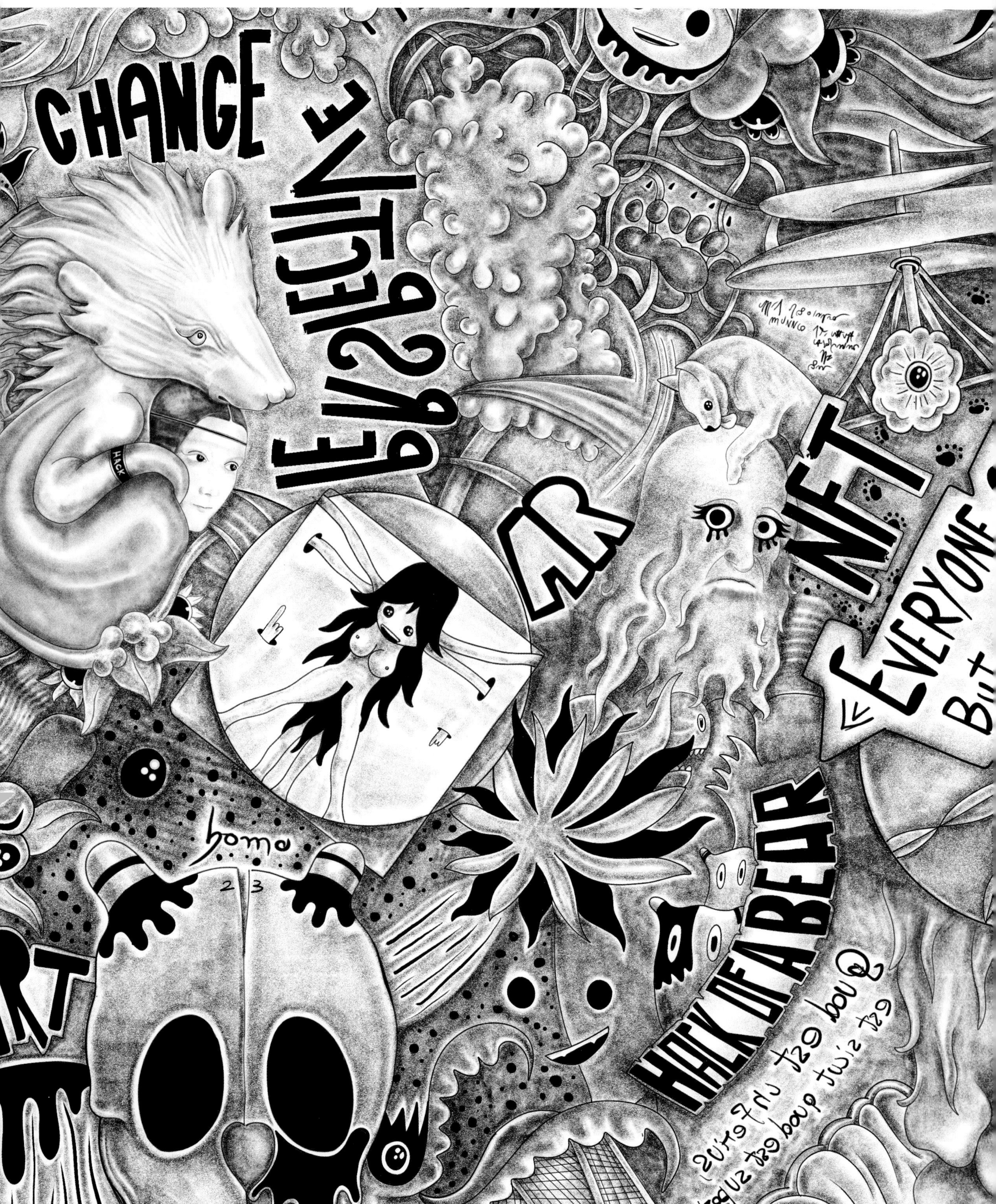
CHANGE
PERSPECTIVE
AR
NFT
EVERYONE
BUT
HACK OF A BEAR
homo
23

"FOR US, TECHNOLOGY HAS ALWAYS BEEN A MEANS OF EXPERIMENTING AND EXPRESSING OURSELVES, OF TRAVELING THE WORLD WHILE LIVING IN A VILLAGE, UNRESTRAINED BY THE LIMITS IMPOSED BY TIME, SPACE, AND SIZE."

Their art is fluid, moving between the real and the virtual, always paying special attention to nature, animals, to the sense of existence itself, with a strong connection to humanity and to a playful and imaginative spirit that invites others to partake in—and even be part of—that wonderful microcosm of emotions and feelings that constitutes their universe. They're a he and a she, both with names that begin with the letters "S" and "N," but who prefer to go by their pseudonym, "Hackatao." They've been working together on their vision since 2005, when they met and fell in love. Their voices chime, flow like a river in which currents and interjected words get jumbled and superimposed with a passion and courage that leads to a beautiful whole—just like the lines of their art . . . Hackatao pioneered NFTs; but as constantly evolving artists, they are now exploring the new frontiers of digital art.

"We work with different tools and media, with ceramics, drawings, paintings . . . ," N explains. "Still, digital art is where our heart's at," S adds, completing the sentence. "Our art is 'physical' but with digital eyes; it's been an experiment from the outset, much like the creation of something rare or unique," N clarifies. They still remember the sensation when one of their early works met with great success—the *Girl Next Door*, a character quite special to them . . .

"I grew up in Trentino, in the mountains. Art and technology have been my comfort zones since childhood. I felt at ease—good about myself—whenever I entered that imaginary universe," S recalls. "I was born into and raised by a family of highlanders, peasants in origin. I'm convinced that we always carry our

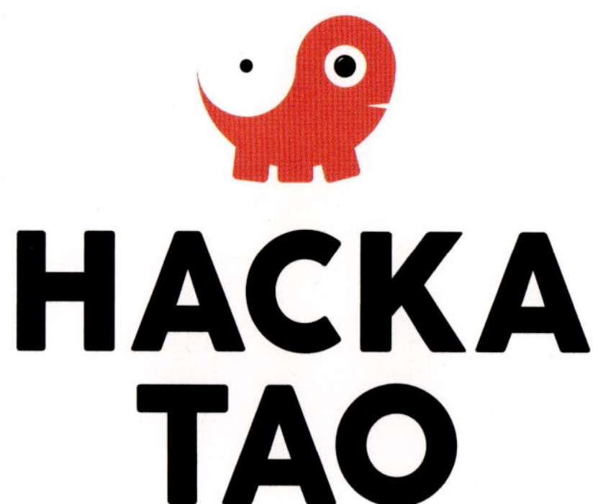

HACKA TAO

roots within ourselves," he states, "and that these emerge forcefully in our *modus operandi*, our work, and our manner of expressing ourselves." He continues, his memory reverting to the past: "There wasn't much culture at home; life was bound up with the need to survive. And to survive, one had to be creative. I believe that this is where my curiosity, my desire to explore and experiment, originated. Then came technology."

S still recalls his first computer, a Commodore 64, and his early experiments with the language of [BASIC] programming with a kind of nostalgia. He also remembers the arrival of the more powerful Commodore Amiga: "From the outset, I loved experimenting, using pixels to draw, designing video games and composing music. All this was my personal space, one in which there were no boundaries to stifle my imagination," he relates. Determined to follow his own path and aspirations, he eventually decided to leave his birthplace in the mountains . . .

In Milan, S began working in advertising as a copywriter. "Although it was a highly desirable job in a creative field, I felt limited, constricted to a creative routine in the service of others. Finally, something happened to me. I needed surgery. The full anesthesia to which I was subject unleashed something within me. I woke up with my head full of childhood memories and began drawing non-stop. And that made me feel good," he admits.

S still reflects on this with a mindset and manner of expression inextricably bound to the technological universe: "It was as if I had gone through a total reset.

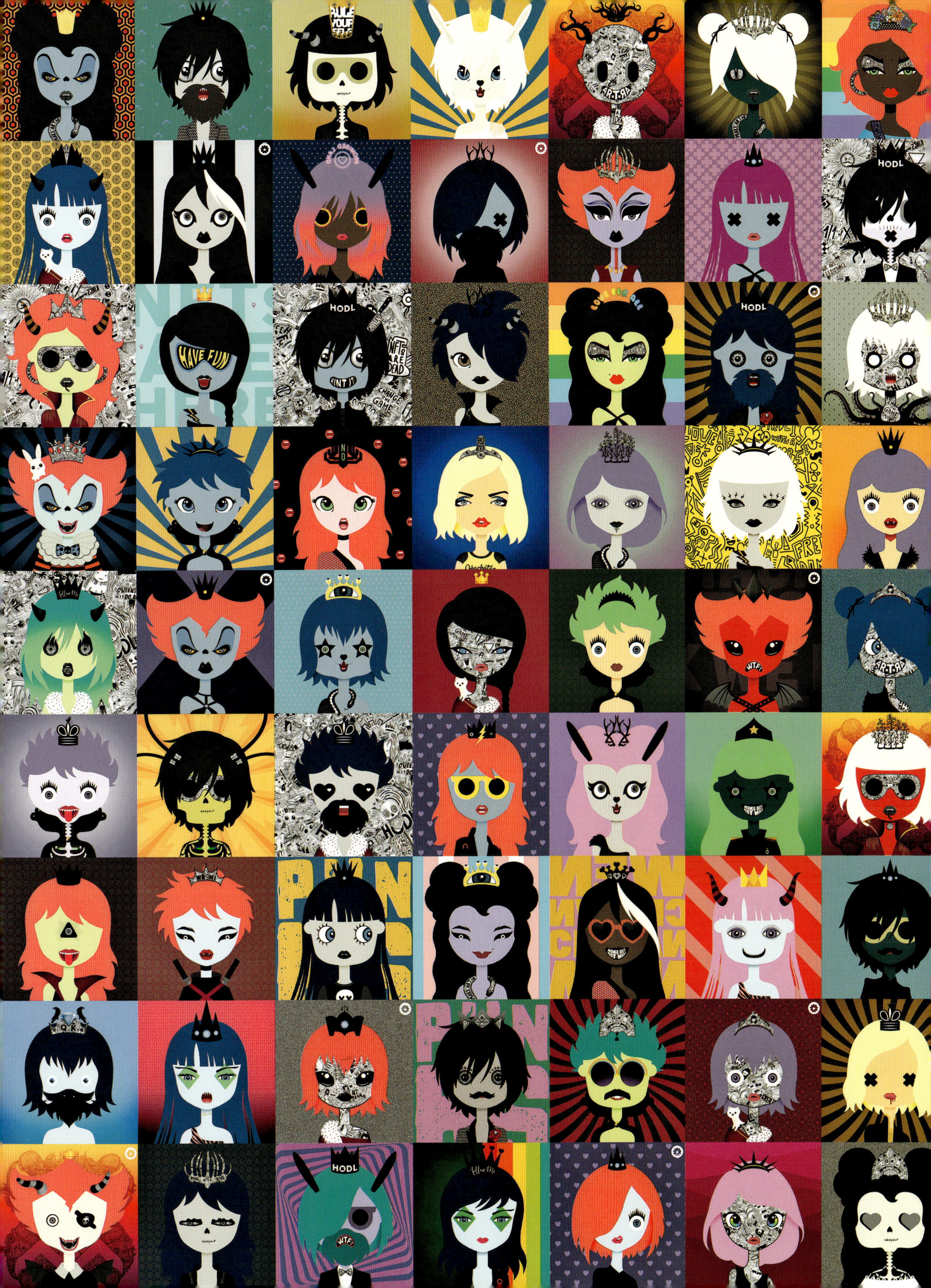

The creative streak that had dominated my childhood resurfaced and, while drawing, I wrote . . . Inside me raged an internal battle: I really liked art, but writing had
become a form of labor . . . Of course, I wasn't writing novels as I would have liked,
but advertisements. I had a job, but one that entailed too many compromises. So,
as soon as I finished doing creative work for others, I turned my attention back to
the computer, on which I drew and made digital art for myself. The marriage of the
two remained deeply rooted within me," he admits.

Eventually, *S* fell into a deep depression, burned out by a job that brought him
no satisfaction. At this point, he mustered up the courage for a radical change
and decided to devote himself exclusively to art for six months. He executed his
first works of art and organized his first exhibitions. But earning a living was difficult, and in the end he was forced to return to advertising.

But then, once again something unexpected happened: "I met *N*. She came into
my life and once more everything changed." Unlike *S*, *N* had gone to art school.
"At the time I met *N*, I was experimenting with new sculptures made out of leftover
material from one of my other jobs. I had just made my first Podmork, and that
evening, after I fell asleep, I dreamt of being bombarded by eyes and creatures
emerging from the dark," he relates.

"I found this dream world of his irresistibly attractive," explains *N*, "just as I
did his creative process and—obviously—him. From that moment on, our souls
joined . . . We fell in love, moved in together." They worked together on their earliest

QUEEN AND KING

works inspired by Podmork, a mix of the digital and physical world. "We developed our style by combining drawings, graffiti, newsprint, and the flat color planes typical of N's work. We became quite popular in the city's art circles; but once our daughter was born, we began feeling constrained in Milan," says S. "In the end, we decided to move back to the mountains in the Northeast, against the advice of gallery owners, who worried about our disappearance from the artistic circuit, from receptions, exhibition openings," explains N, albeit admitting that both of them are by nature fairly reserved and shy. "We wanted to work in peace. We felt nature's strong call within us. We wanted to live in a place that was more human in scale, to return to our childhood roots," states S.

In 2018, S and N made their entrance into the world of Crypto Art, fascinated by journalist Jason Bailey's article on Crypto Art Culture. "To me it seemed the perfect technology for certifying digital art. We felt inspired by—and part of—a movement that was in its infancy," says S. This happened in early March 2018; within a month, Hackatao had already produced their first works. "There were only a few of us at the beginning, and we bought the works amongst ourselves. Many artists entered and left this world, but we remained," states N, who goes on to explain: "Some conventional artists poked fun at us because we were selling our works for a hundred bucks or even less; but for us, it was perfect, as it allowed us to live far from the center, yet participate in art trends of international breadth. Our vision of uniting different worlds—that of art, that of technology, and that of nature—meshed marvelously with this new source of ideas and manner of thinking."

"The early years of NFT, 2018-2020, were the most intense and experimental; the community was closely bound, and there was a spirit of sharing and a search

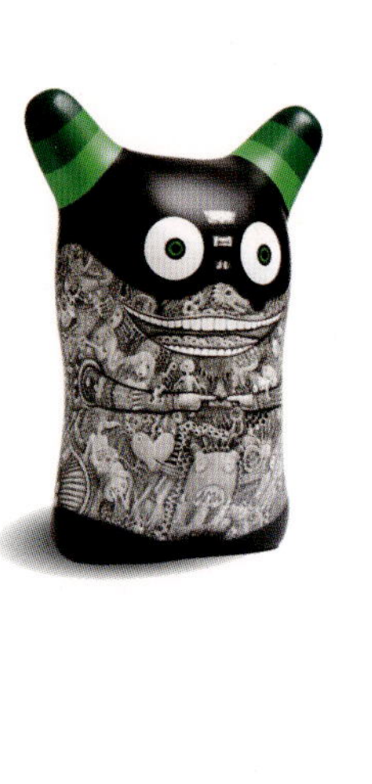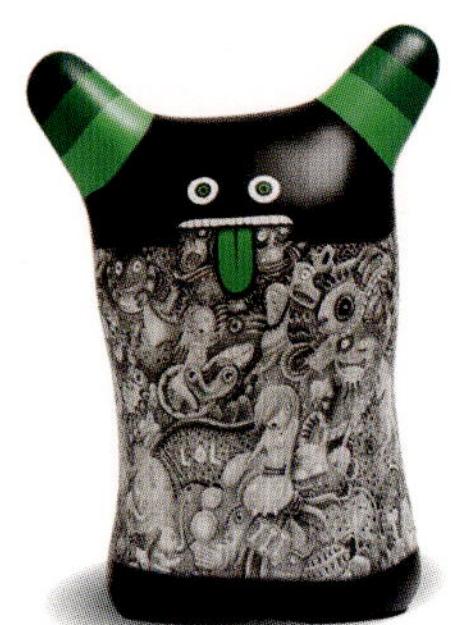

PODMORK KU 03

for quality. These were the foundational years of the Crypto Art movement. Unfortunately, that spirit was lost to some degree in the years that followed, due to the inflationary bubble of 2021," says N.

Friulian by birth, she had worked for communication agencies as an art director after graduating from art school. Like S, she too had moved to Milan for work. "Once I arrived in the big city, I stopped making art because I had to look for a job and didn't have time for anything else. With S, I returned to my brushes . . . It came absolutely naturally to me; I was prompted by something inside me, and I knew that whatever happened, I would never go back," she recalls.

N and S feel like they're Yin and Yang, and it was like that from the moment they met. "We're both creative souls; we found and recognized each other as such, and clicked immediately. We felt even closer during the creative process, certainly the most engaging aspect of art . . . We feel like Yin and Yang; we 'dovetail' each other. We're complementary souls; S likes to explore, while I'm more methodical," says N. "N needs S's drive to probe and experiment as much as S needs N's analytical restraint," adds S.

As she explains, "The female and male sides mesh perfectly in the creative process. Then there's the Tao side that seeks harmony among the elements, though we also enjoy deconstructing, slashing, and hacking. It's from this that we got the name Hackatao. I pour everything into the drawings—my immense curiosity and the energy that compels me to stay constantly active. The drawings are my way of 'releasing' what's inside me. For us, making art is like passing a ball back and forth—a continuous dialogue that leads us to the final result," she notes.

"Digital art shortens the distance between the idea and the work. The creation of physical art is a more intense process, in part because a canvas sometimes

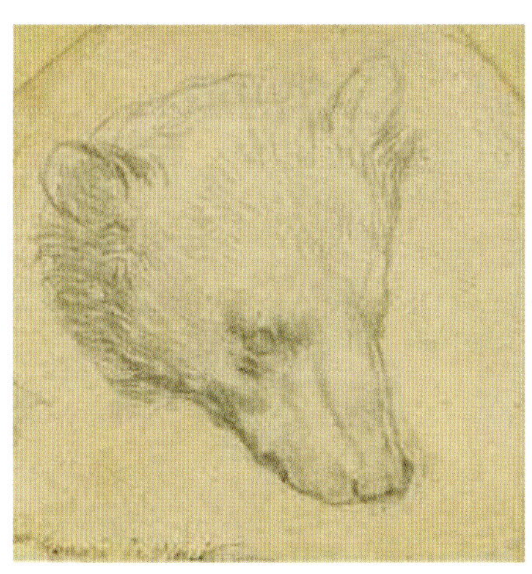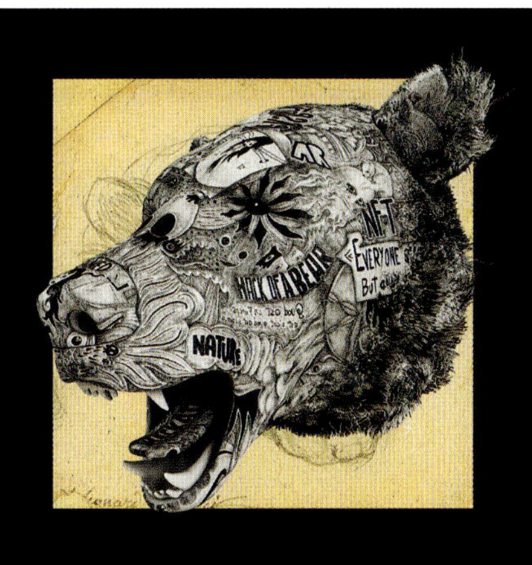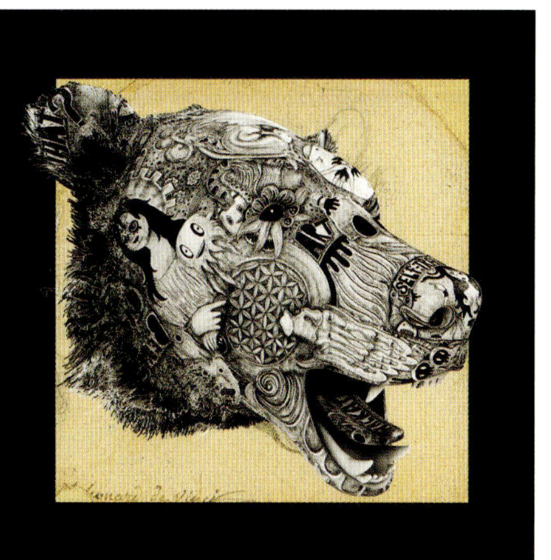

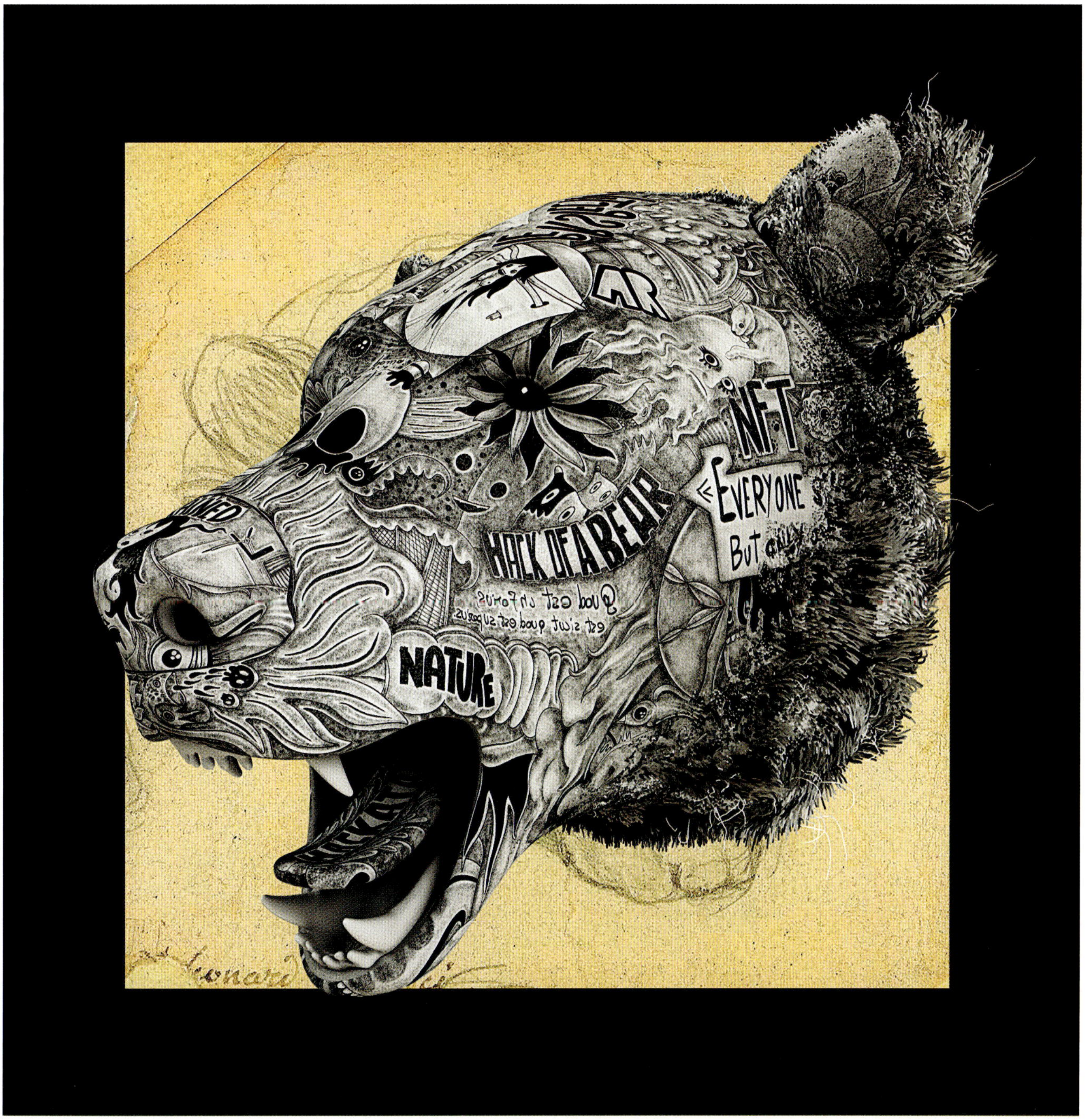

requires months of labor. By contrast, the production of digital art brings instant gratification; it is quicker, more pop. Although we love both processes, we know that digital art is better suited to the world in which we now live and lets us express ourselves in the language of our time," S explains.

"We use technology to create a movable chain. For example, we give others a chance to hack our work, split it into pieces, then reconstruct it according to their liking. Ever since we started living amid nature, even our colors have become bolder and more vibrant . . .

HEAD OF A BEAR

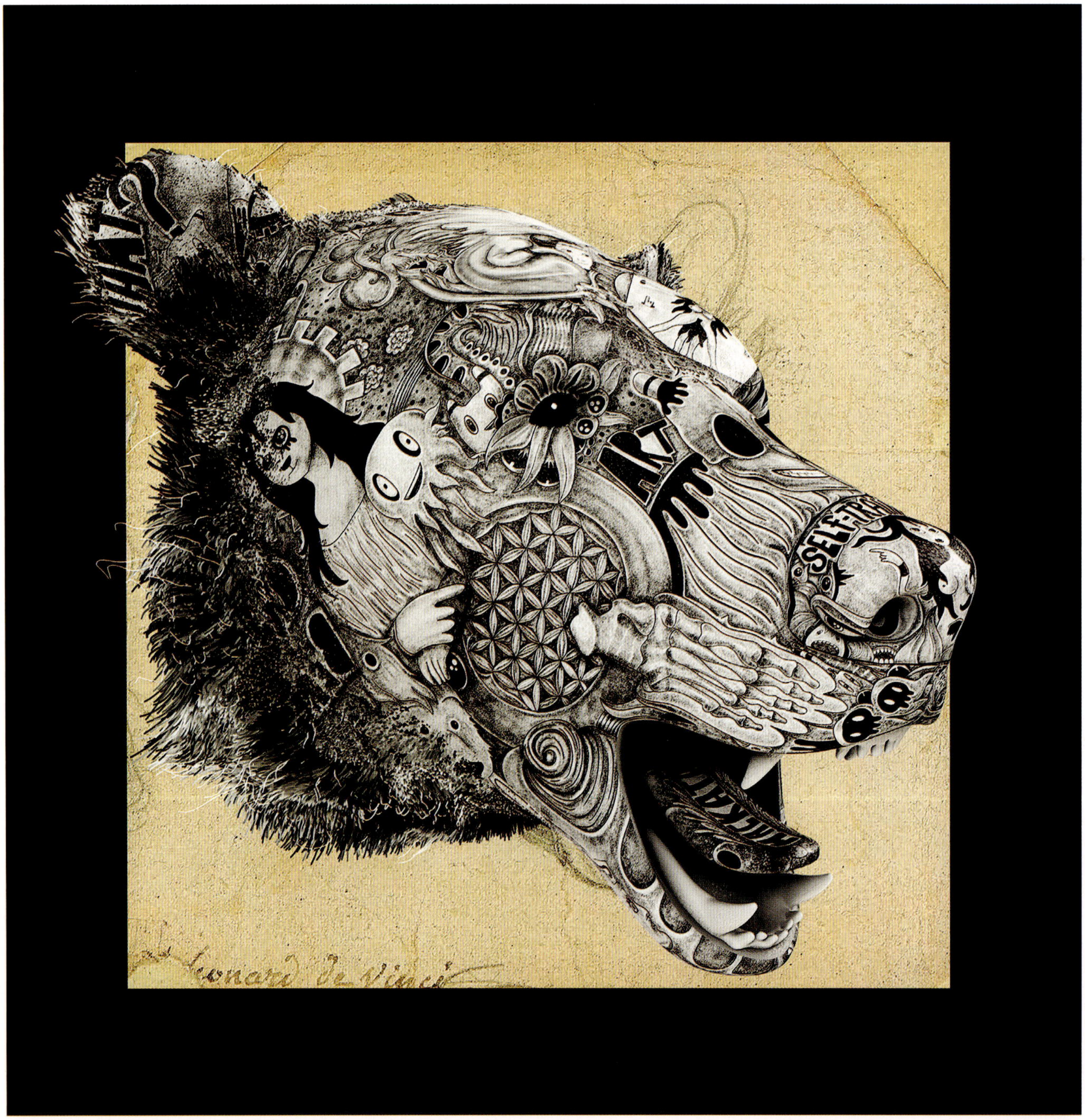

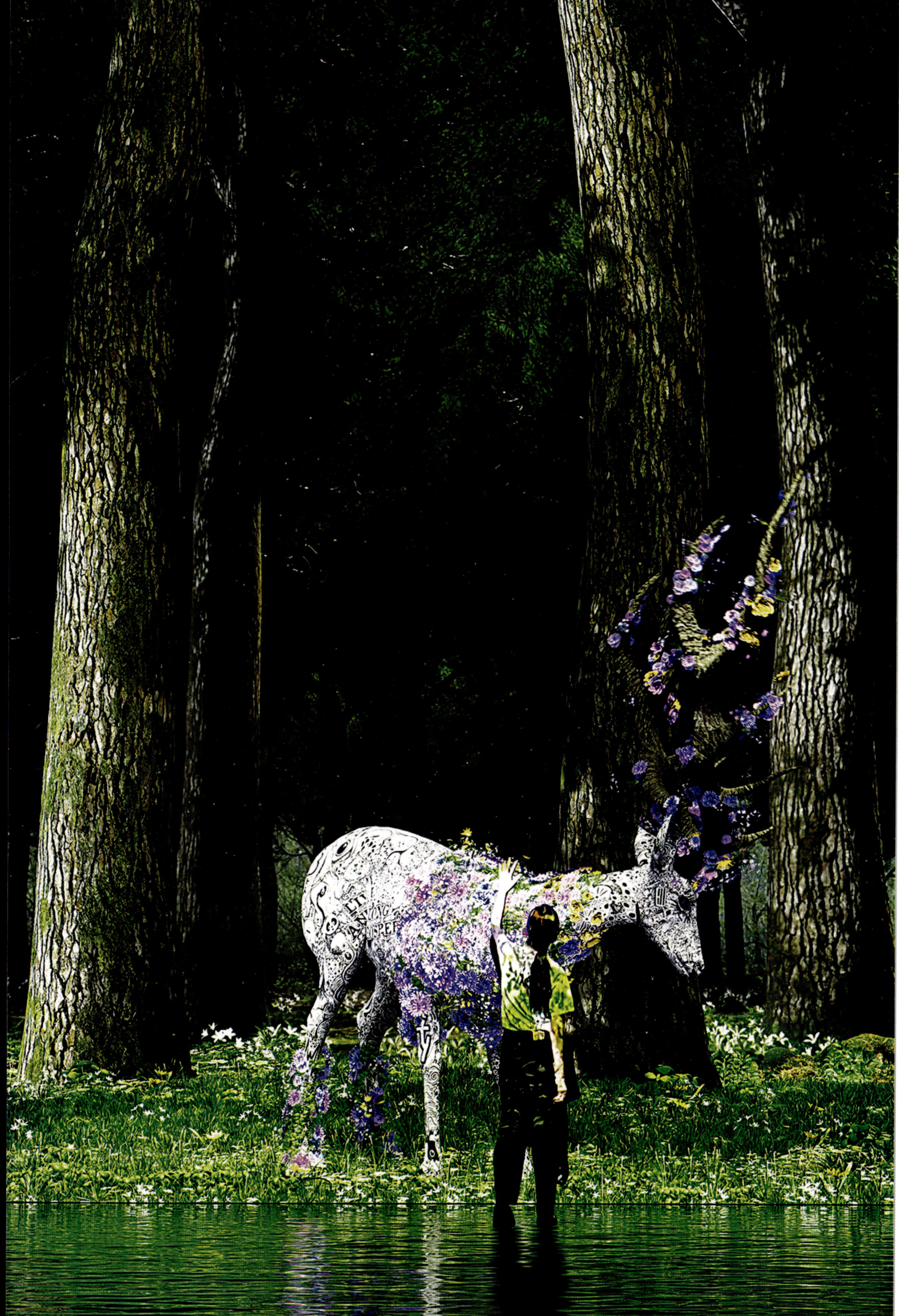

LIVE LONG AND PROSPER

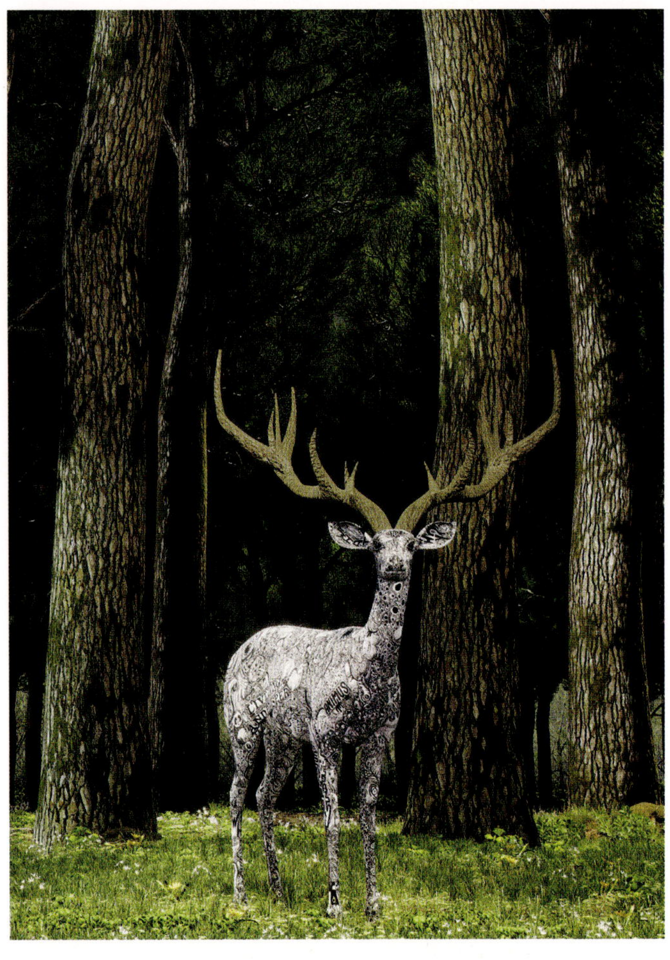

We've also spent time doing generative art, 3D, animation, and AI; we're always open to experimenting and discovering new techniques and means of expression, because digital art has no borders," she explains. "We're like the Cohen brothers in cinema, spanning utterly different genres. We try to do all this with the spirit of innovation: we always want to include something of our own and something that's different," he emphasizes.

"The beauty of interacting with people from all over the world, with diverse cultures and ideas, even in little things, is a form of constant personal enrichment. Once you're in this digital world, you realize the meaninglessness and futility of borders between states. It's like being in a parallel universe that travels down its own path and reveals the slowness and absurdity of the outside world with all its contradictions. It makes you realize how unacceptable it is to go on living on a planet dominated by divisiveness and war. In the digital world, diversity is a plus, because it supplies creative material for new ideas," concludes *N*.

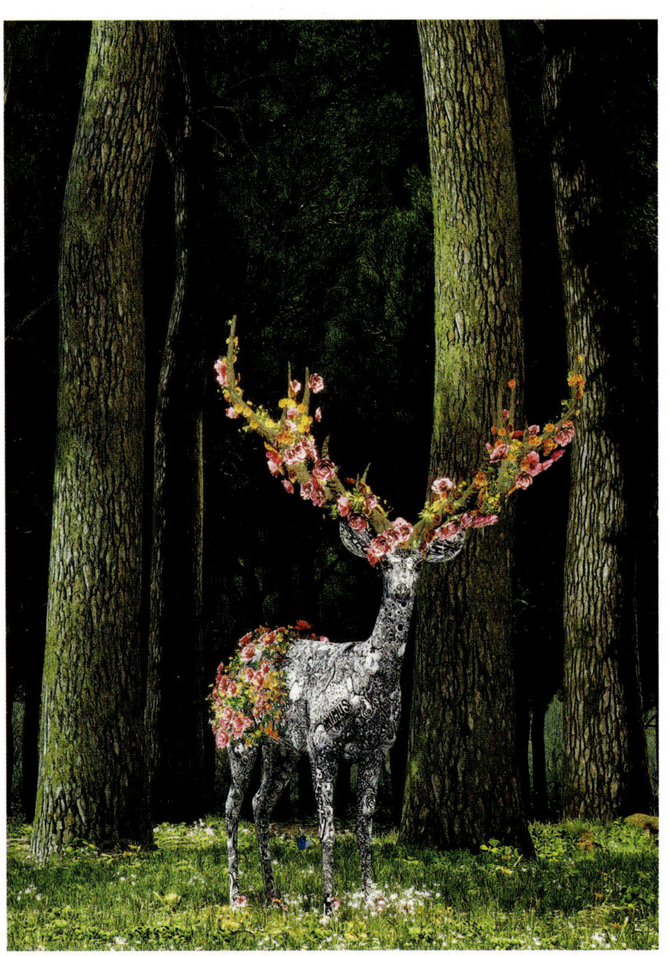

INCANTO

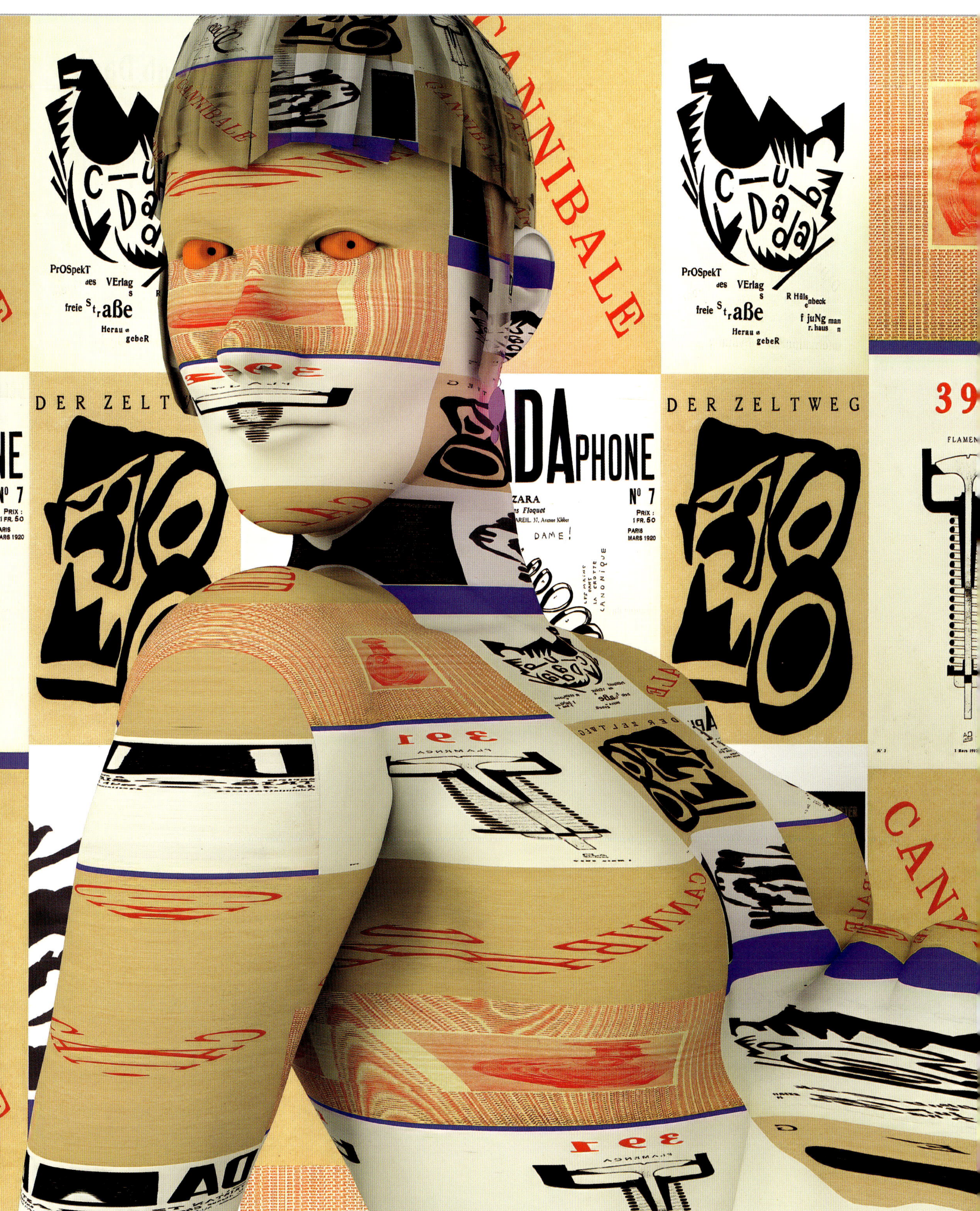

CANNIBALE
C-u Da-b Da-da
PrOSpekT des VErlag s
freie StraBe R Hülsenbeck
Herau geber f juNg man r. haus n
CANNIBALE
DER ZELT WEG
DAphone
ZARA
Floquet
No 7
PRIX: 1 FR. 50
PARIS MARS 1920
DAME!
DER ZELTWEG
39
FLAMEN
391
FLAMINGA
391
FLAMINGA
CANNIBALE

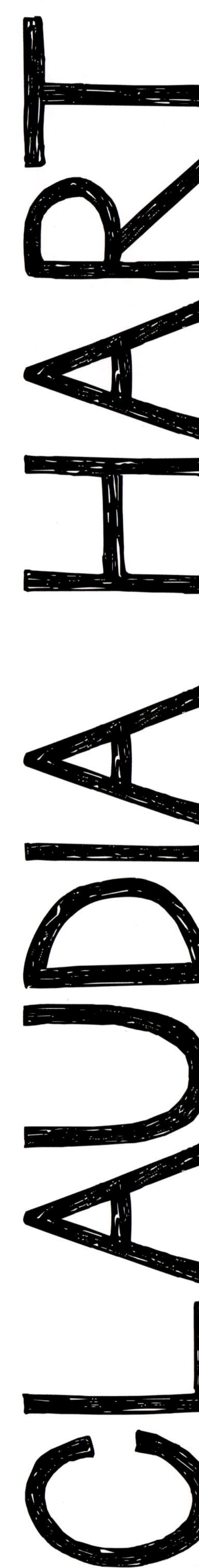

CLAUDIA HART

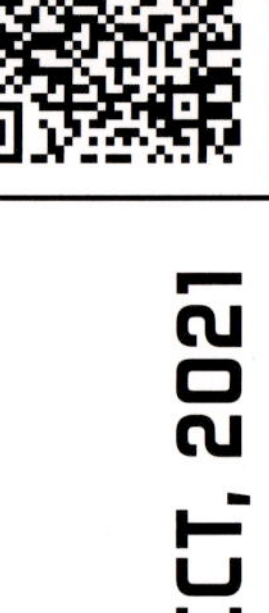

KIKI.OBJECT, 2021

WHEN THE DIGITAL CREATES BRIDGES BETWEEN BEING AND BECOMING

"THERE'S NATURE ON EARTH, AND THEN THERE'S THE TECHNOLOGICAL VERSION: THAT IS, THE VIRTUAL WORLD. LET'S CALL IT THE METAVERSE, THOUGH I DON'T PARTICULARLY CARE FOR THAT TERM. THE METAVERSE IS A MODEL OF THE NATURAL WORLD. AND SINCE HUMAN BEINGS ARE PART OF NATURE, IT'S ALSO A MODEL OF OUR INTELLECT."

A clash of colors, feelings, sensations, moments of a spirit coming together, emotions gushing into each other in an incredible fantasy, between glimpses of harmony and memory: Claudia Hart's work is all of this. "I never went to art school. I studied architecture and historical preservation at Columbia University between 1981 and 1984. These were the years of 'paper architecture' and of the New York Five, a group of conceptual architects who, back then, only drew and never built anything. This was before software's entry in architectural practice. The community included artists such as Vito Acconci and Dan Graham, Leo Castelli, and Marian Goodman.

"I'm a fan of evocative images, paintings, and photographs, so I fell in love with artists such as Cindy Sherman, Mike Kelley, Jack Goldstein, Gretchen Bender, and Robert Longo." Claudia began painting in her tiny studio apartment in the East Village, completely destroying the carpeting and hardwood floors. "Initially, I thought of myself as an artist along the lines of Dürer with his perspectival machines, Vermeer with his camera obscura, Robert Rauschenberg with his novel printing techniques, or David Hockney and pop artists like Roy Lichtenstein, my favorite," she recalls. In 1995, a particular experience changed her style: "I saw the animated movie *Toy Story*. The technology used to produce it relied on big data, i.e., all the scientific information amassed on the natural world in order to reconstruct the latter with more or less realistic images." And it was thus that she embarked on her adventure in art, but with a clear feminist slant: "I was a female artist in a man's world. So, I embraced a particular feminine concept of beauty in a very intentional way. I expressed my type of sensuality by using pastel colors

and decorative elements. I was also one of the first people to explore computer art. I had no access to any grants or institutional support: I was a woman, an artist experimenting with the digital in the late '90s and at the dawn of the new millennium. I definitely lacked the possibilities that even young women enjoy today. Due to the misogyny that dominated digital culture when I started out, my terrain became strictly 'personal' and intimate—'feminine.' I had to produce everything on my own, on a small scale, trusting solely in my own forces. I improvised alone, in the middle of the night." In 2021, following the pandemic and the subsequent explosion of NFTs, Claudia came up with a new hybrid work, *Digital Combines*, partly hand-painted, partly NFT. "I appropriated the term *Combine* from Robert Rauschenberg to propose a genre of art in which a physical work is combined with a virtual one: two halves that unite the tangible with the ephemeral. In the years that followed, I dismissed the NFT component. I decided that it was enough to expand on the idea of combining digital and classical painting in a single work," she explains. Her first mixed-media series was inspired by a game entitled *Russian Roulette (A Game of Life)* that she had invented but never publicized. "Written over the course of a year, it was based on the mechanics of an interactive 3D game I had designed, but never coded. My gaming scenario set the rules for an elaborate system, a combination of black magic and gambling along with the systems and hierarchies on which ancient divination texts, such as I Ching, tarot, and astrology, are based. My paintings embody a complex dance between a range of high-end hardware that I've learned to use over the years and the manual skills that I've gradually developed through much practice and use," she clarifies.

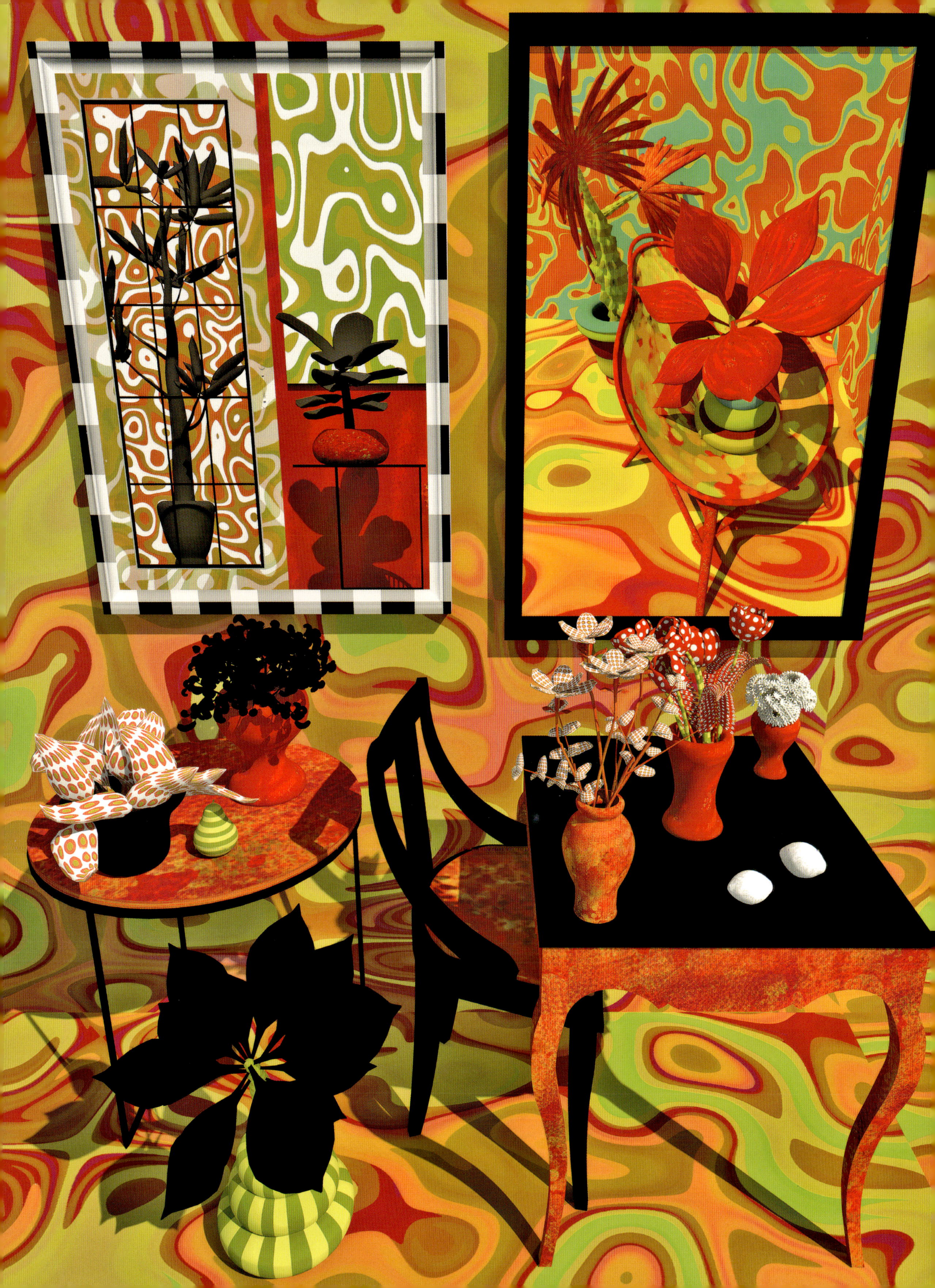

Born in New York, Claudia now lives in a Victorian house on Staten Island's North Shore: "My family lived in Corona, in Queens, where I was born. No one in my family had a university degree. My mother, who attended Hunter College—an exceptional thing in those days—had cultural aspirations and regularly visited all the museums in New York. I had to become an artist: she practically commanded it! As soon as I learned how to walk she began taking me to MOMA [the Museum of Modern Art], the Brooklyn Museum, and the MET [the Metropolitan Museum of Art]. My imagination originated among those display cases of works and masterpieces, even if it took me a while to understand how one actually 'becomes' an artist." Her mission? "What seems to be common to most artists who identify with digital culture is the drive to reinvent art from scratch. I don't agree with this in any way. By contrast, I want to expand on contemporary art and connect the past to the present. I'm not sure how much being a woman is part of my overall attitude. To be sure, the tech culture emanating from Silicon Valley that I encountered when I was starting out was far more sexist than were the identity politics and artists that dominated the art scene in which I was involved during my early days in the East Village.

"My resistance to the culture of innovation coming from California was inspired in part by the more open-minded society I engaged with before turning my attention to technology. But aside from that, I'm by no means a futurist. I'm not interested in innovation. I've always been an artist of my time. I haven't invented any new tools, but instead have used what's available. I brought together existing tools to do things that they hadn't been designed to do. I believe that, above all, I'm a person who builds bridges between the past and the present," she adds thoughtfully.

BIG RED 2019

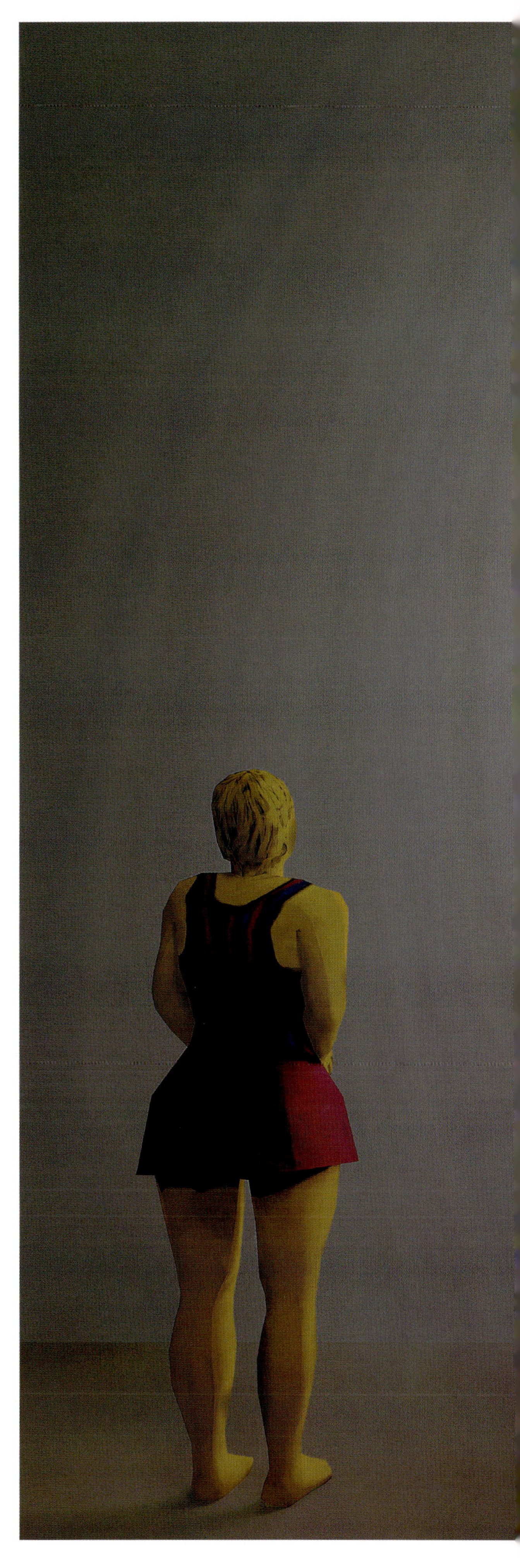

**RISK MANAGEMENT
(A GAME OF RUSSIAN ROULETTE), 2024**

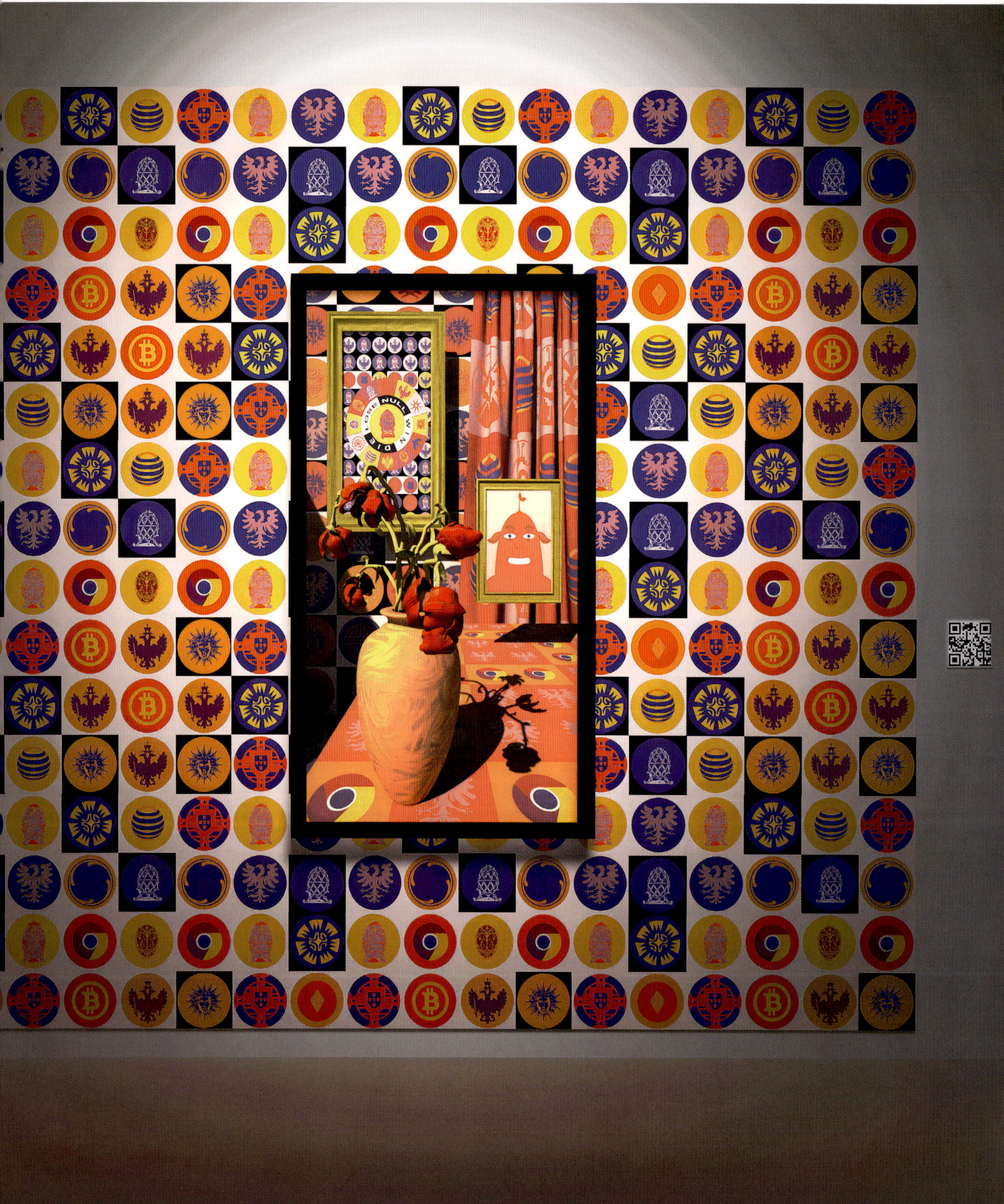

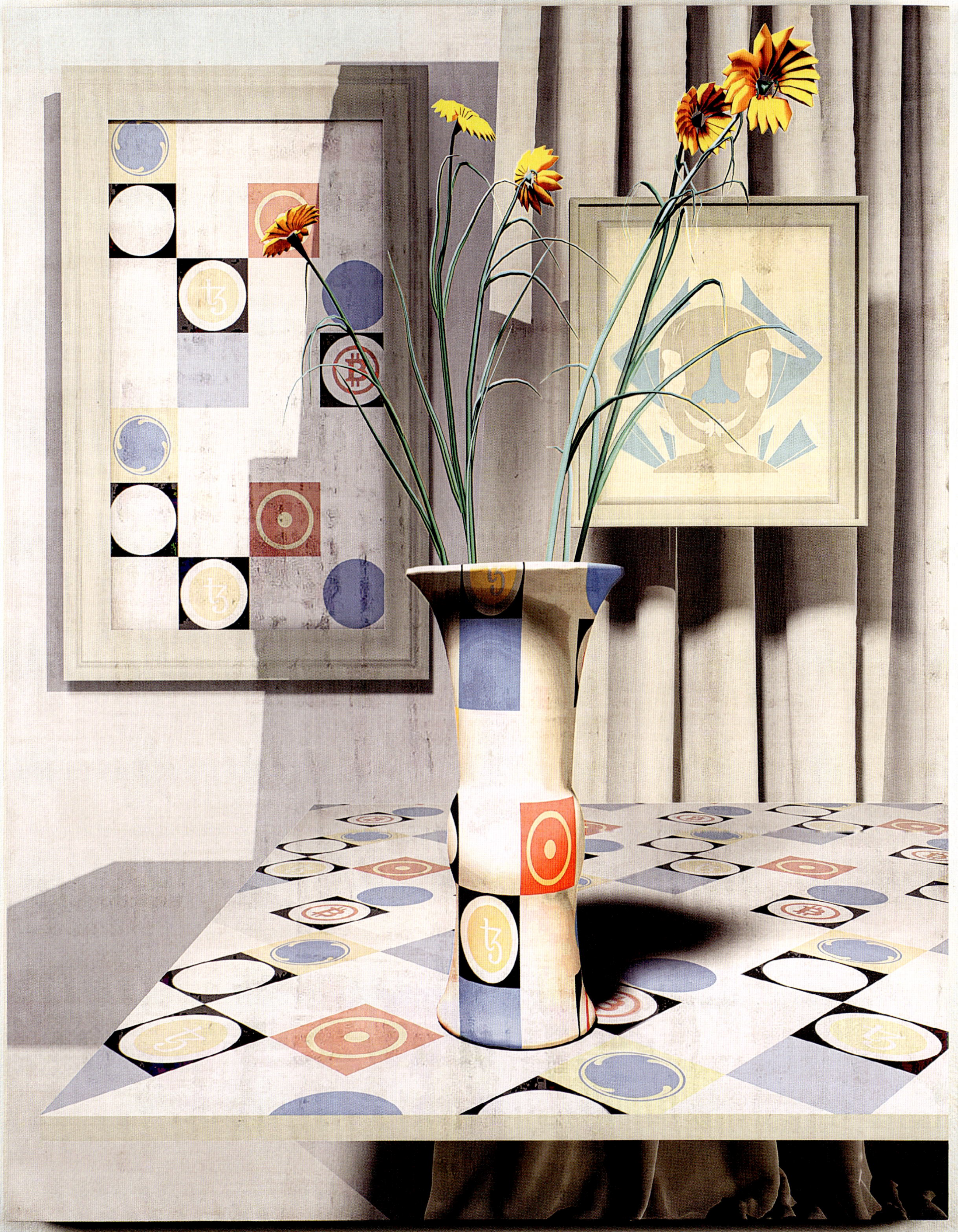

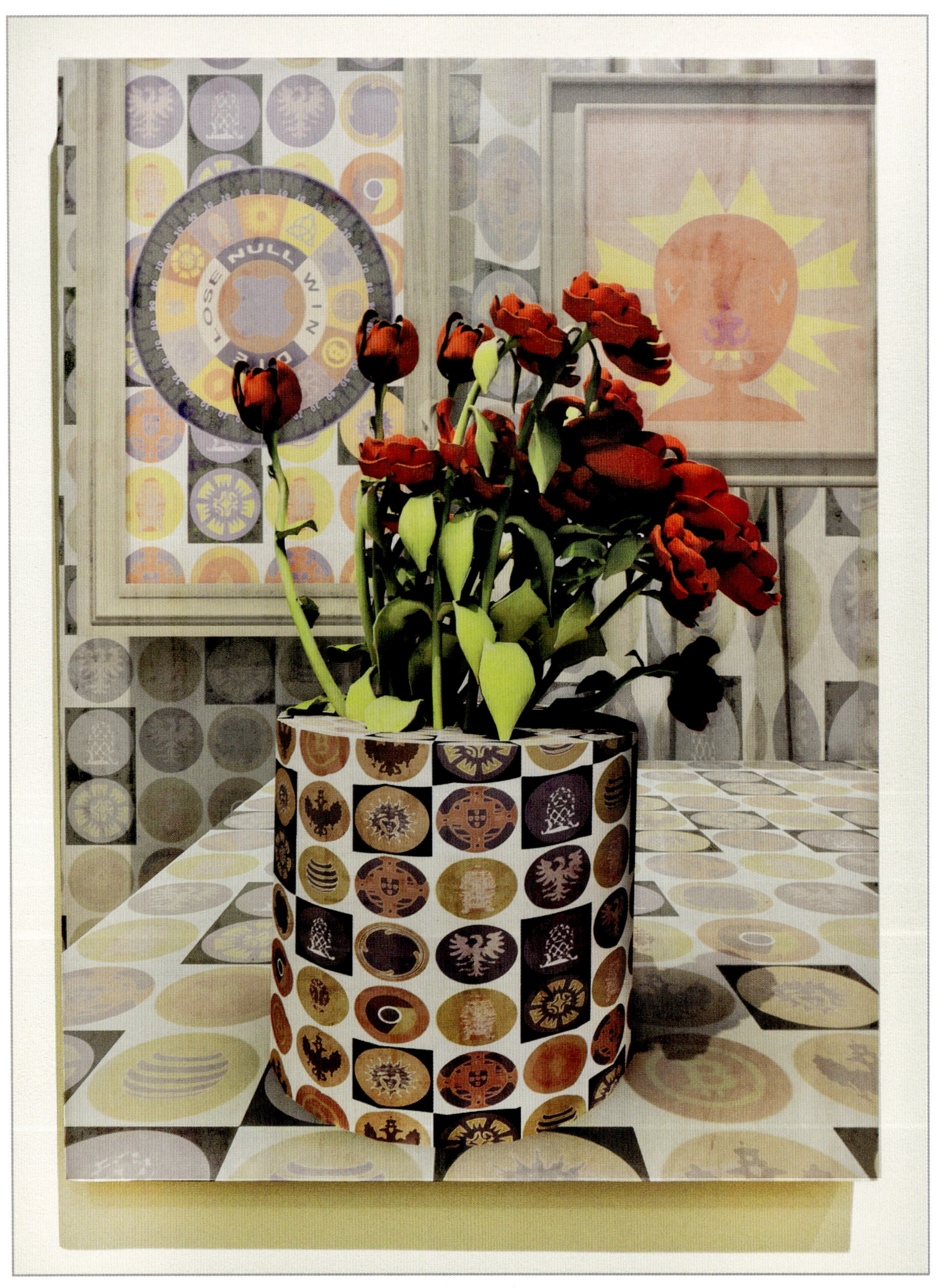

RUSSIAN ROULETTE (SECOND PRIZE 1.0) 2024

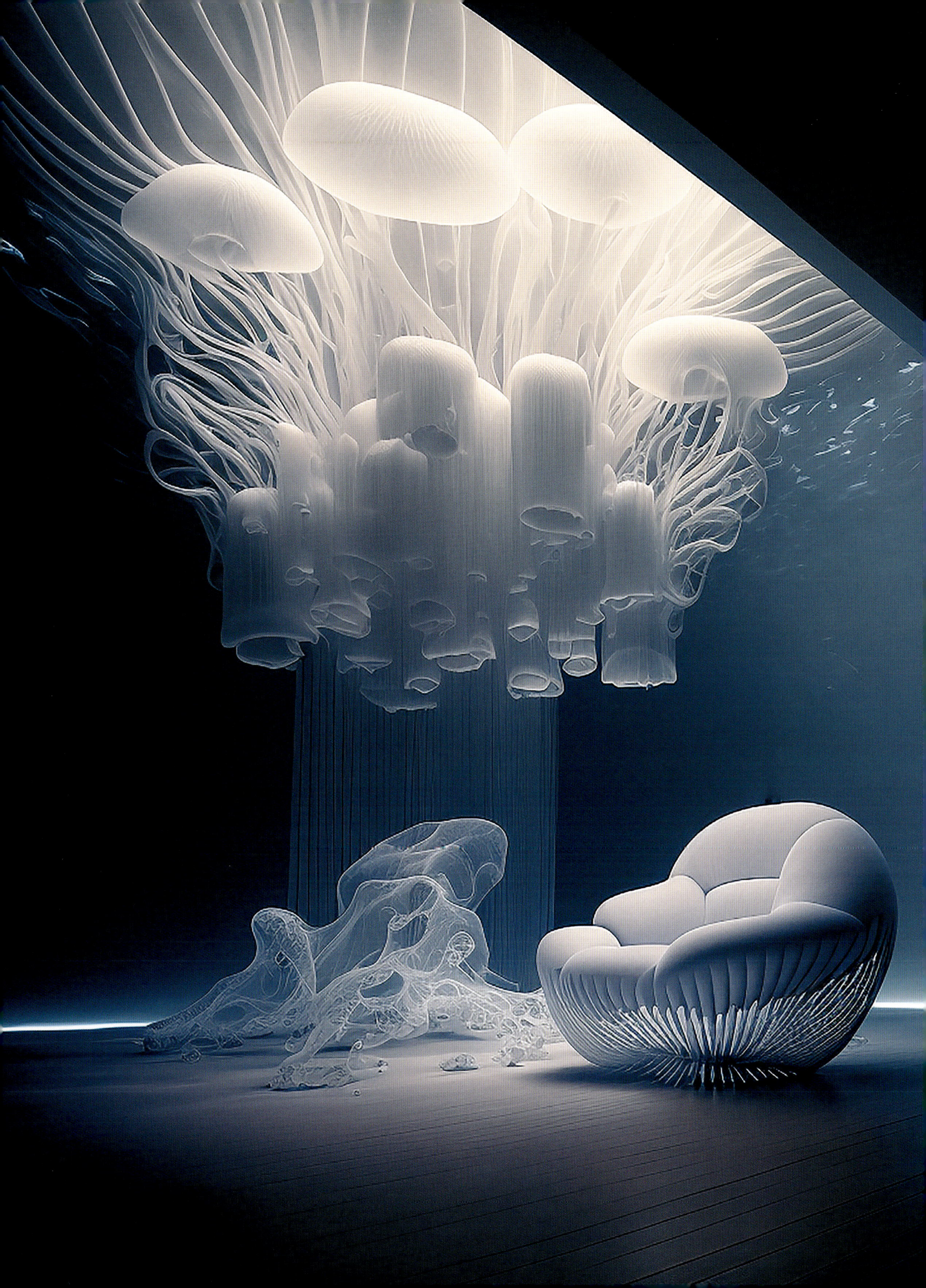

KRISTA KIM

"I BELIEVE IN THE POWER OF FEELINGS AND EMOTIONS. TECHNOLOGY MUST NOT BE BY CAPITALIST INTERESTS AND THE DESIRE FOR PROFIT. QUITE THE CONTRARY, IT MUST BECOME A MEANS OF ENLIGHTENING HUMANITY AND ELEVATING OUR MINDS. TECHNOLOGY MUST BE ZEN."

In a world increasingly dominated by technology and threatened by ever-rising globalization and its penchant for uniformity at the expense of diversity, feelings and emotions have never been more important. The art of Krista Kim is a genuine kaleidoscope of Zen sensations and serendipity . . . Light becomes ink, evolves, transforms itself, fades and extinguishes itself in the name of love.

Like a master of pictorial color, Krista uses technology as a paintbrush for noble and ethical ends that transcend computer digits and formulae. Reaching straight for the soul and touching the heart, she challenges the boundaries of space and time, using her mastery to generate a universal experience.

Standing before her works, we are touched, we rejoice, we reflect, we feel in sync with that wonderful set of sensations that elicits our empathy and hope for a better world. Krista explores the new frontiers of the metaverse with the sensitivity of an adventurer in search of herself, but also of others, and thus creates an amazing connection between body and spirit in a unique and innovative space, one that is perfect despite the imperfection of the surrounding world.

"Nowadays, I live in Los Angeles, a super dynamic city full of creative types—a city with the capacity to offer me constant stimulation . . . The people here have a very open and fluid mindset. However, I was born and raised in Canada, in Toronto, to Korean parents. I still feel very much a Canadian because I love the kindness and character of that country, where feelings are more important than money and sheer profit," she openly admits. And it's precisely this candid quality that makes her so winning, this disarming and courageous desire to expose herself. "There was a time when I didn't know exactly who I was, when I felt the need to belong. So, for a while, I moved to Korea. I wanted to figure out whether my soul was more steeped in Korean or Canadian tradition. Ultimately, I realized that I was fluid, a mix of various

cultures, that I was basically a citizen of the world. It no longer matters to me where I'm from, but rather who I am in the now," she claims.

Although art has always been a part of her life, it is backed by a certain kind of practical and entrepreneurial spirit. "I've always wanted to be both an artist and a businesswoman. I had really clear ideas about this by the age of five or six," she says. "I remember how, while playing, I used to pretend that I had an office all to myself and, at the same time, kept my paints and painting supplies next to me. I had a natural knack for art; I drew constantly and was inspired and encouraged by my parents. My mother was a highly original Korean vegan chef. My father was a healer, an acupuncturist and supreme grandmaster of taekwondo, the Korean martial art . . . They were true artists in their own disciplines," Krista recounts. Her early upbringing was fundamental to the development and course of all her art. "My father had a deep influence on my artistic output, as he brought me up according to the philosophy that lies at the basis of the martial art that he practiced. Not only did I come to understand it, but I felt as though it resonated deeply with me because it was about the connection of mind and body, for me a fundamental principle of human existence. From it I also learned discipline and dedication, qualities that accompany me in all my life choices even today," she says.

Krista has always been instinctive, and still relies primarily on her feelings when creating . . . Despite her love of art, she initially had no clear idea which path to take. Nonetheless, when faced with this decision she again trusted her instincts. "At first I wanted to devote myself to fashion and art, but my mother, who hoped I'd have a career as a doctor or lawyer, suggested that I start out as a journalist. I therefore decided to study political science at the University of Toronto . . . I found it interesting, but not something that could arouse my passion," she admits.

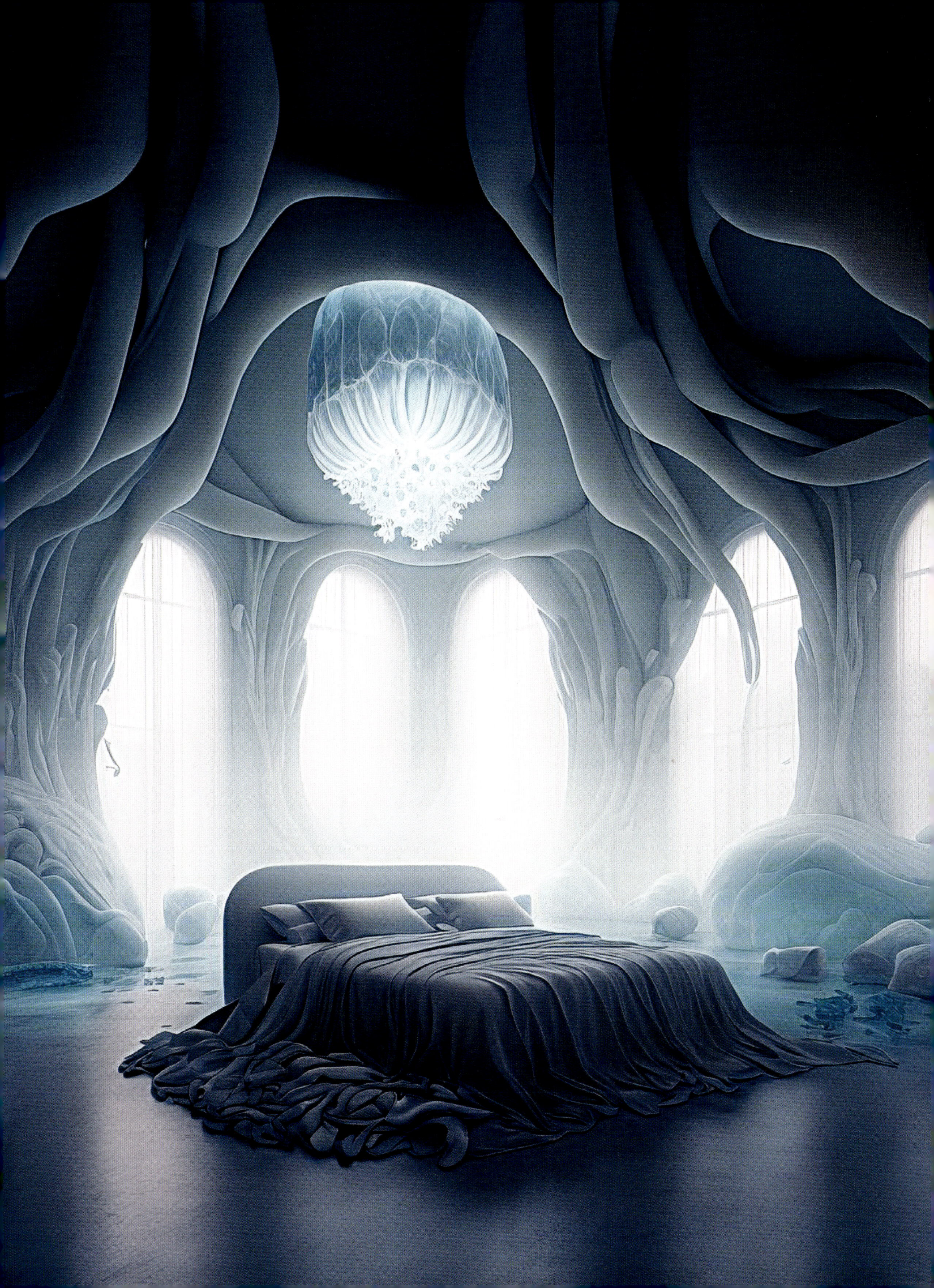

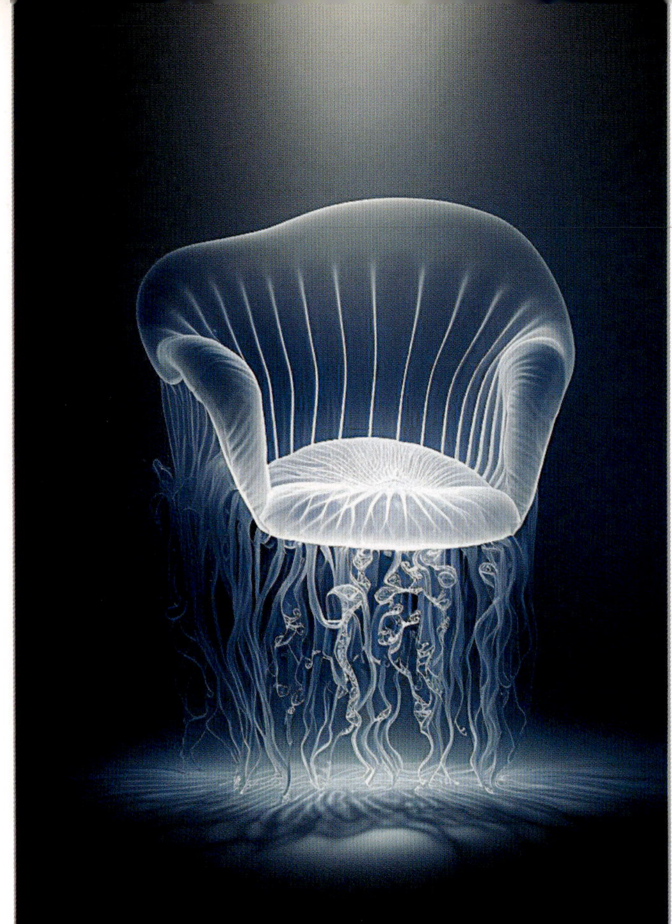

Krista had what she describes as her "artistic epiphany" in 2005. At the time, she was living in Japan and working as a freelance journalist. "I was inspired by the garden at the Ryoanji Temple in Kyoto. As I sat and gazed at its aesthetic perfection—beautifully mirrored in my mind—it had a positive effect on me. That sensation utterly changed my life. I felt good, at peace, totally serene, and incredibly inspired. It was then that I realized that the philosophy and practice of Zen can be applied to everything; that, in fact, it holds within itself an optimized way of life. So I delved deeper into my Zen experience by studying Japanese abstract painting in Tokyo, and I delved into digital art during my master studies in Singapore in 2012," she says.

It was from that first moment of enlightenment that her entire vision emerged. "I wanted to draw attention to light because today's society lives through the filter of a screen—that of the algorhitms. In 2012, the smart phone was an irresistible novelty, and social media was entering people's lives on a massive scale. I found these intrusive; they bothered me, generated anxiety and narcissism. I perceived the negative energy emanating from the addictive interactions that consumed many people who stopped at nothing to achieve visibility and feel important. There was no humanity in the countless apps, no sensitivity or awareness of others. Little by little, I grew convinced that the urgent need—or, rather, the responsibility—of artists was to draw a connection between technology and humanity," she claims.

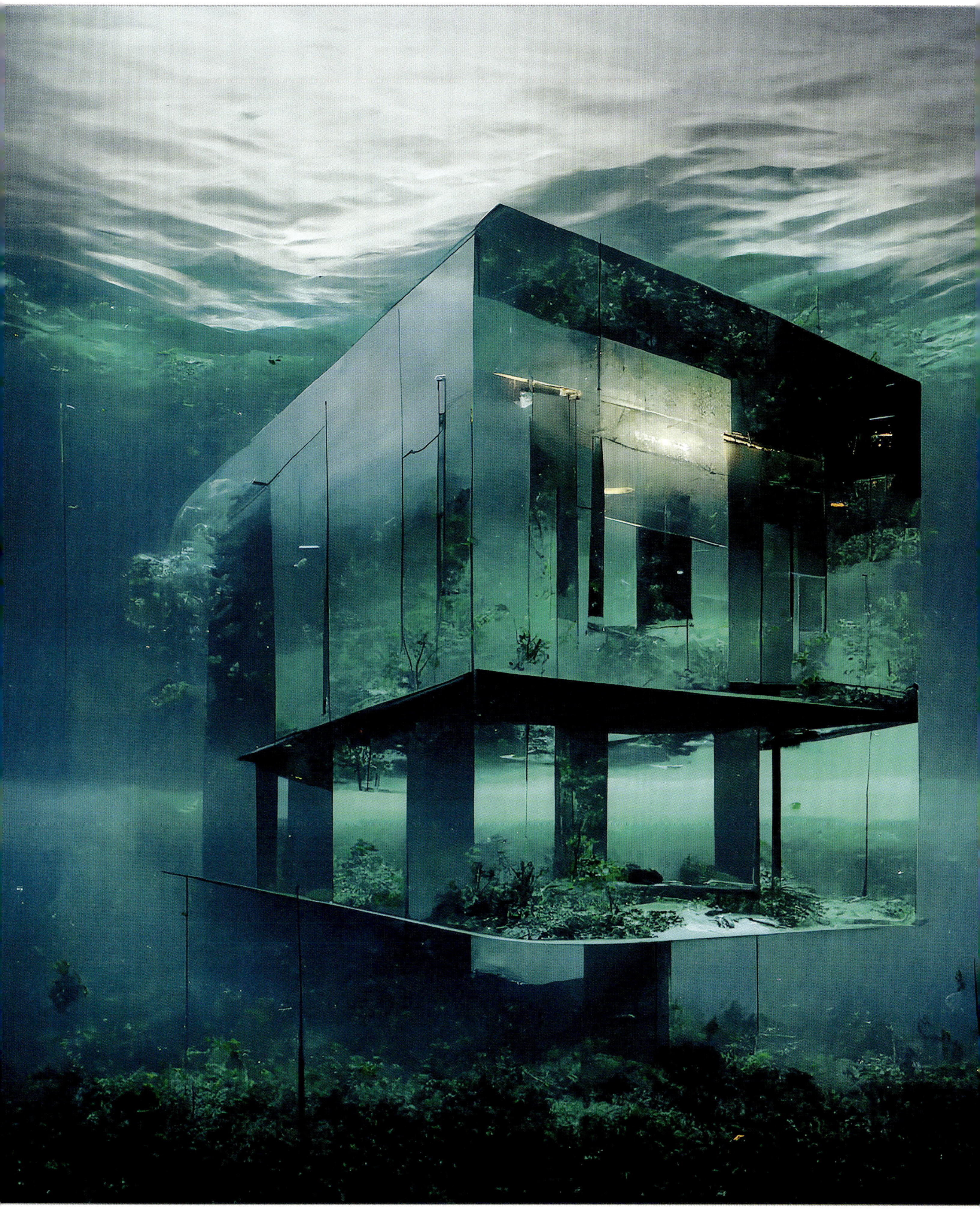

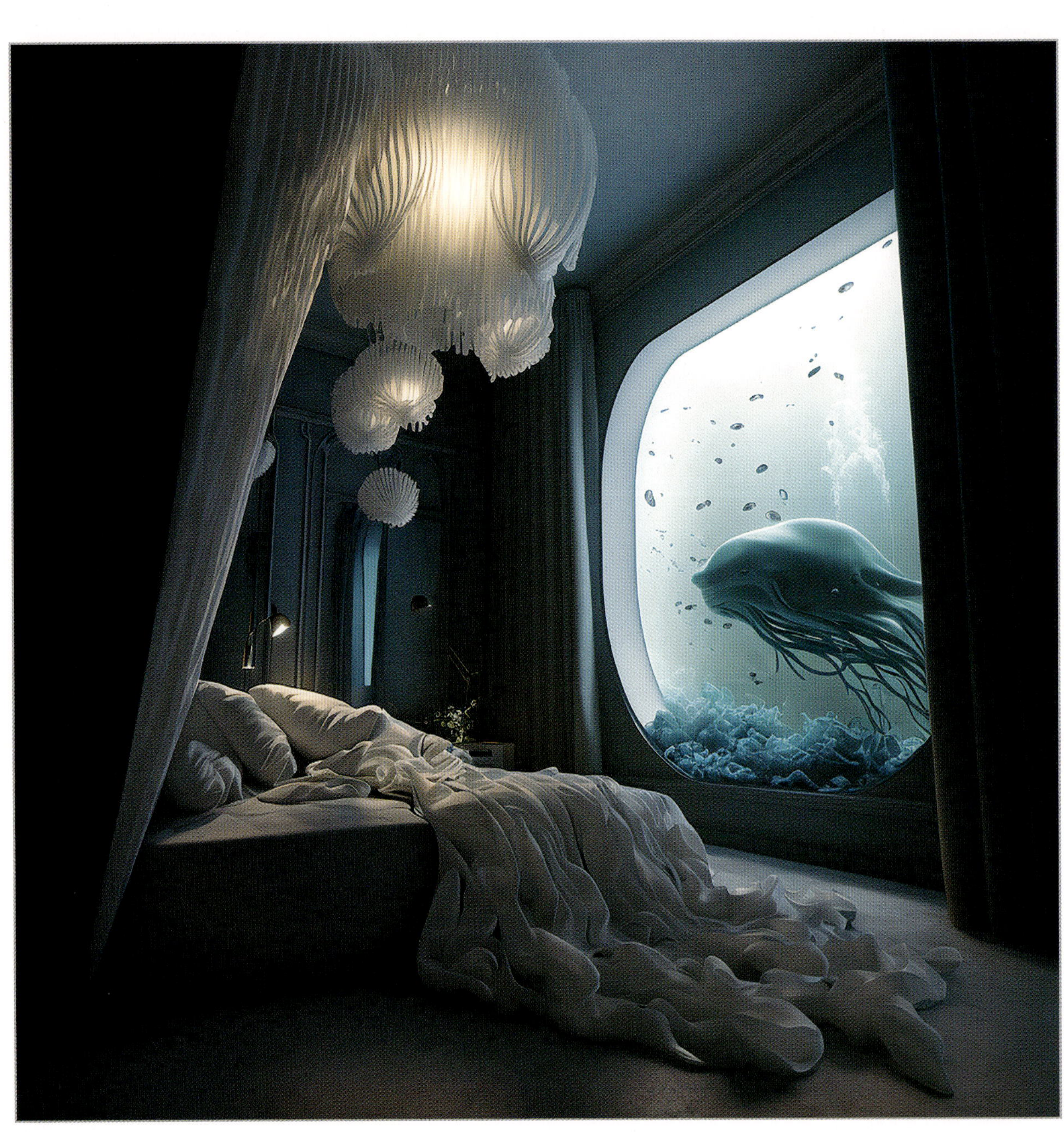

UNTITLED

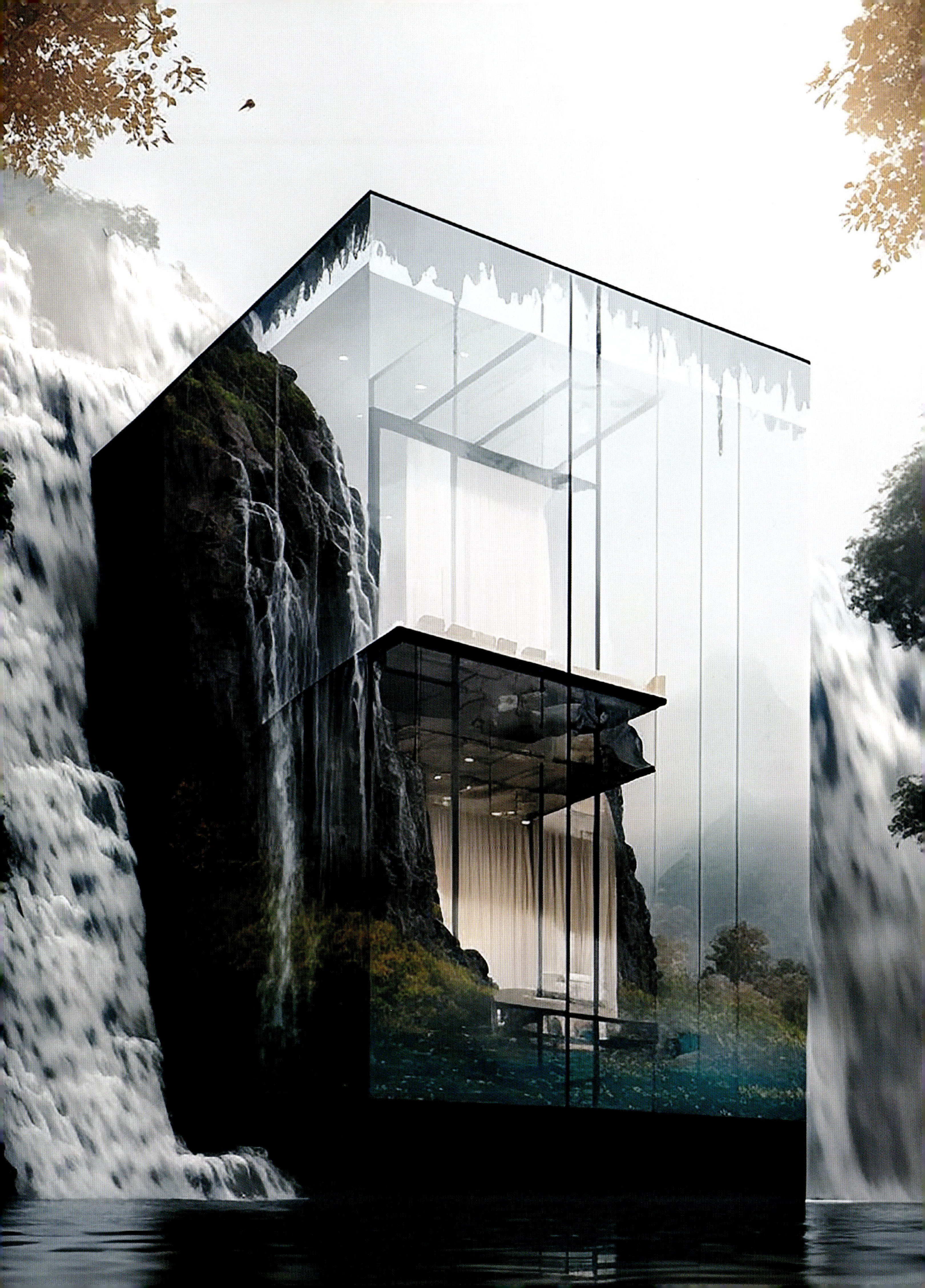

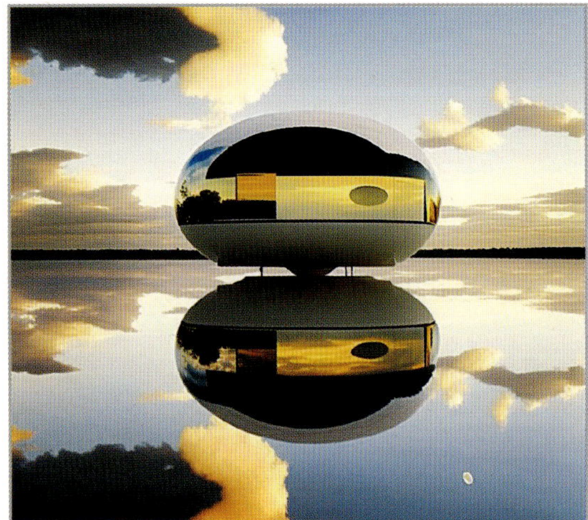

In 2014, Krista wrote her first Manifesto, influenced by Marshal McLuhan's writings in "The Medium is the Message" and the philosophical texts she had read over the course of her life, and which had shaped her as an artist. In this document, she established and defined the concept of Techism, a movement that views art and technology as allied and totally free to create a new wave of expression through digital humanism. "It is unhealthy for us to become instruments of economic interest, and we need to put an end to this if we wish to create a better, more deeply conscientious humanity. We must focus on meditation and wellness, corporeal and spiritual well-being. We need to eliminate all the noise around us and bring color, light, and sound back into a harmonious and comforting whole. My objective is to experiment, always come up with something new, but, above all, have an impact on humanity in a way that can lead to a better world," she explains. UNESCO included Krista among the "50 Minds for the Next 50" on account of her innovative and visionary mind; Forbes magazine termed her "the new digital Rothko," while the World Economic Forum named her a Cultural Leader.

But concealed behind all this popularity lies darkness, that of her soul—a darkness that causes deeps suffering but that has helped her become an icon, a model for many women. "I was in Singapore, going through a painful divorce. Really depressed and anxious, I worried about my children's future. I wanted to move back to Canada, but was forced to stay in Singapore, where my rights as a woman were not well protected. I was granted shared custody of the children, but no financial support. All this was really difficult, but in the end it made me much stronger," she admits.

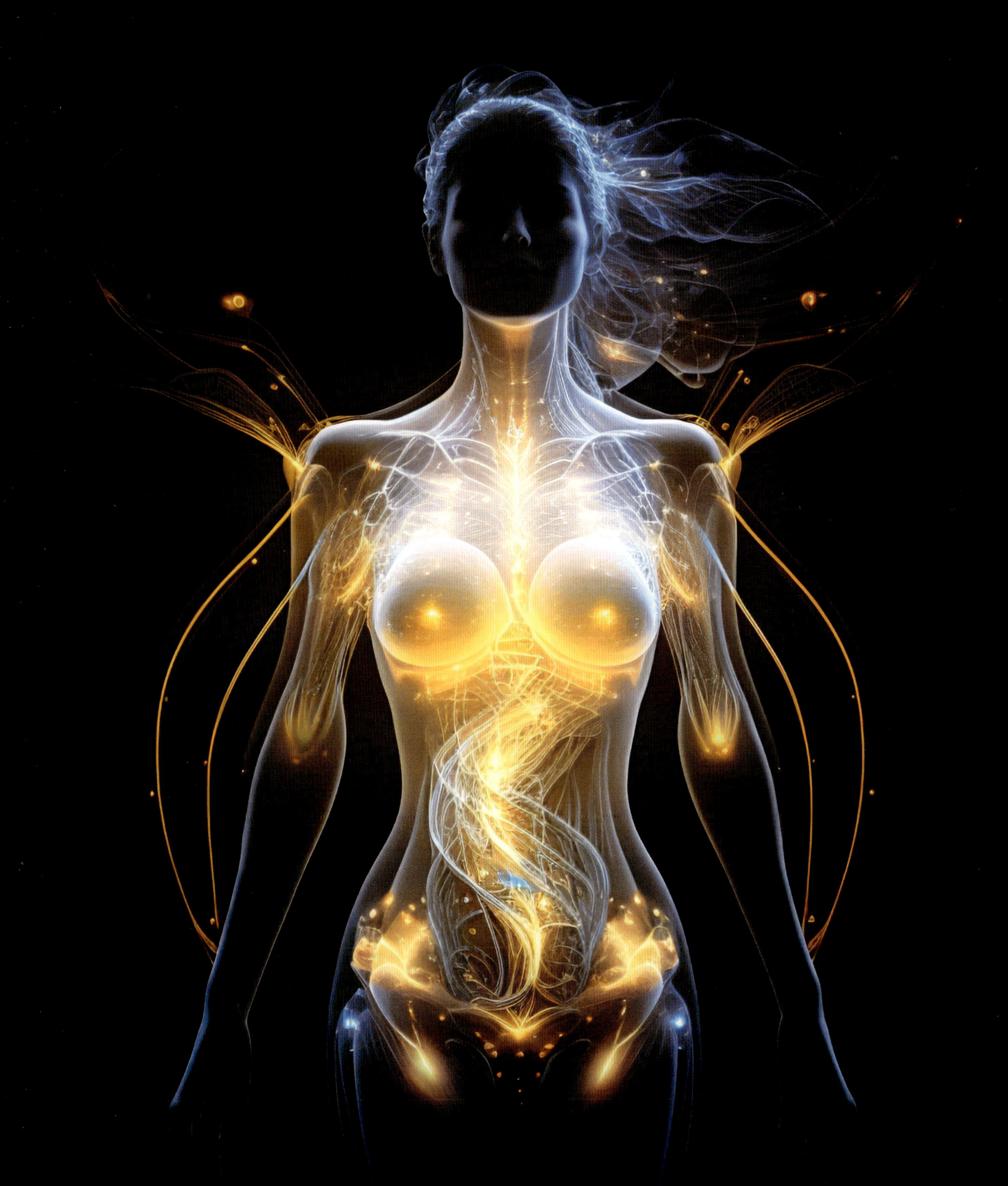

For Krista at that point, making art became, above all, therapeutic. "Inspired by artists like Mark Rothko and James Turrell, I began painting, but then set aside my brushes and let myself be influenced by artists of the great tech revolution, as I was also fascinated by the possibilities of this media to create novel experiences. Sitting in a corner of my garden in Singapore, I suddenly decided to pick up my camera and snap a picture of LED lights. I got some interesting compositions and, using Adobe [software], played around with them. I experimented and developed shades of blue while seeking inspiration from Zen that would bring me peace," she recalls. It was in this way that Krista was able to revitalize her life. "I rebuilt what I like to call my 'sanctuary' and discovered myself. Initially, when making art, I had imitated the works of others; I had had no identity of my own. But, thanks to transcendental meditation, I was able to find myself, my style, and my mission as an artist. Using sound and light to create public art and outdoor installations that bring people together and spread a powerful message—a sort of immersive Zen experience, open to all and, above all, based on the principle of service to humanity . . . Algorithms are dominating the world with social media. The convergence of AI, metaverse, and blockchain, by contrast, inspires beauty through technology and helps us feel better because, as a form of technology, it is more egalitarian, and responsible. AI grants each individual the ability to become a creator and wield a superpower. If used correctly, it will provide the world with more compassion, education, and sanity."

Krista is likewise convinced that women are the driving force of present-day society: "Most projects by contemporary artists derive their motivation from a profound sense of responsibility that hopes to build a better world and future." Her role as a mother marked this path out for her: "Motherhood was—and is—my main source of motivation, because art is meant for future generations."

TRANSCENDENT BEAUTY

GREG MIKE

WHEN STREET ART AND POP MEET TECHNOLOGY

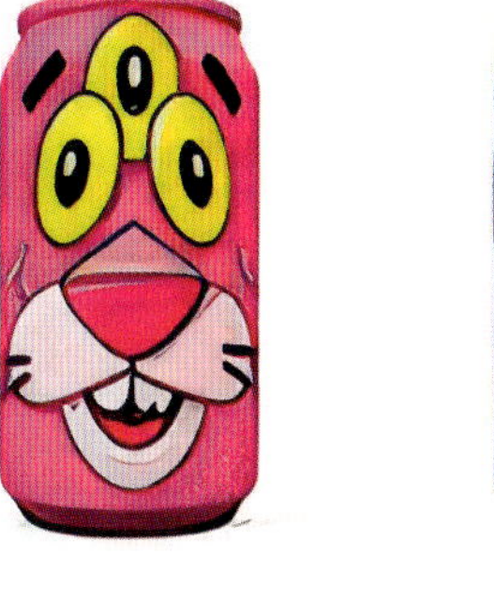
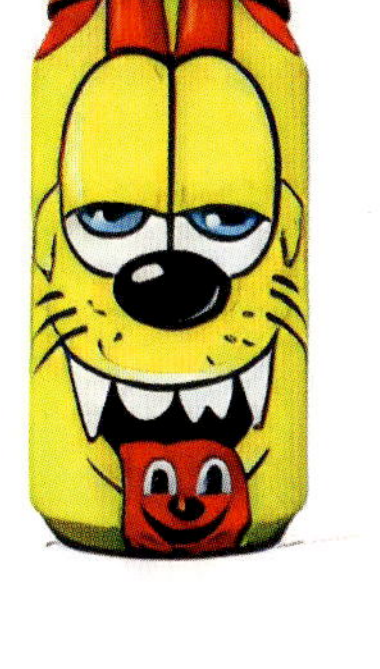
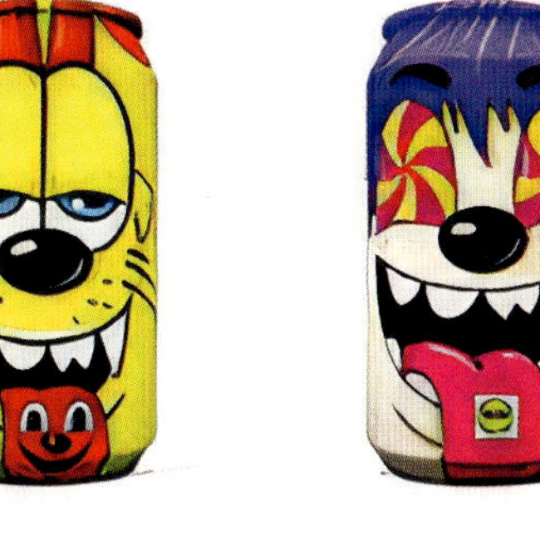
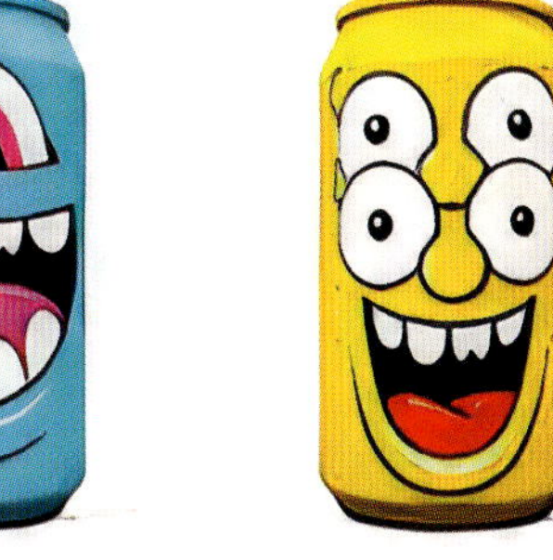
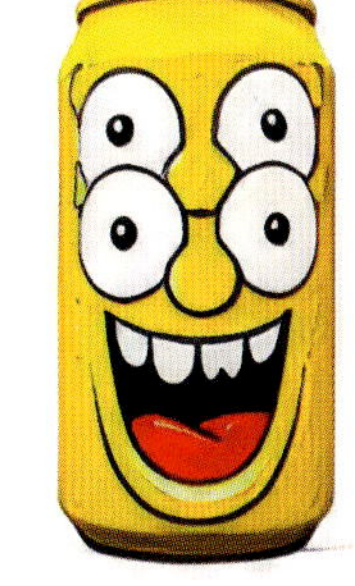
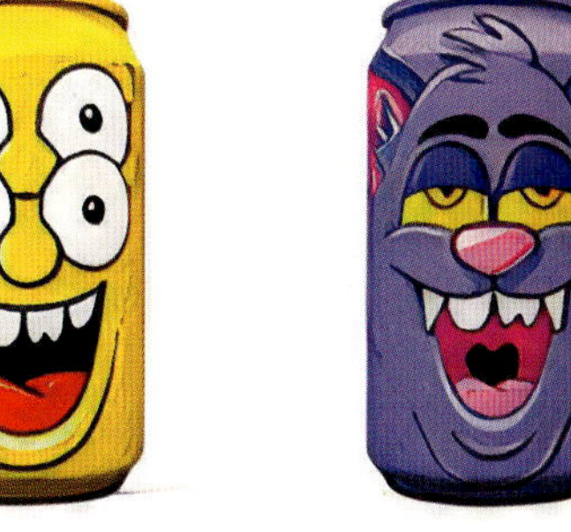
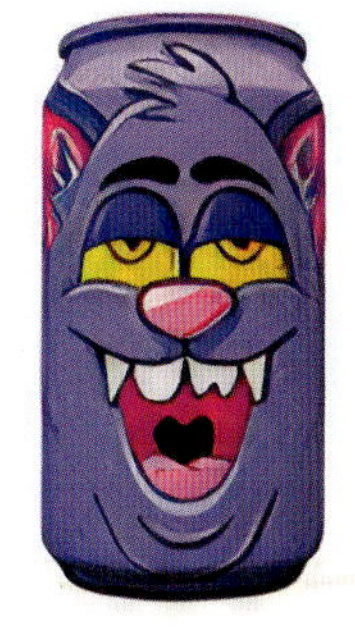
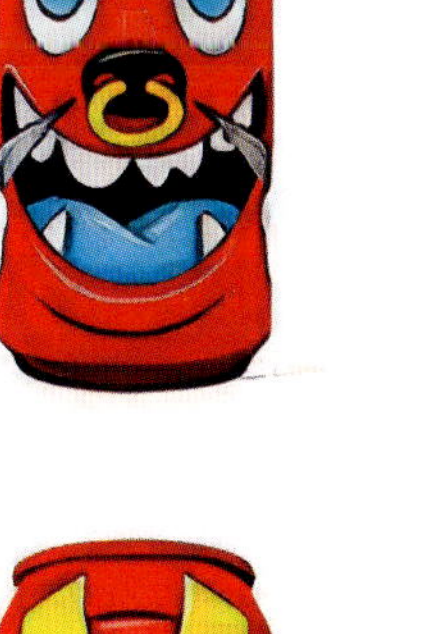
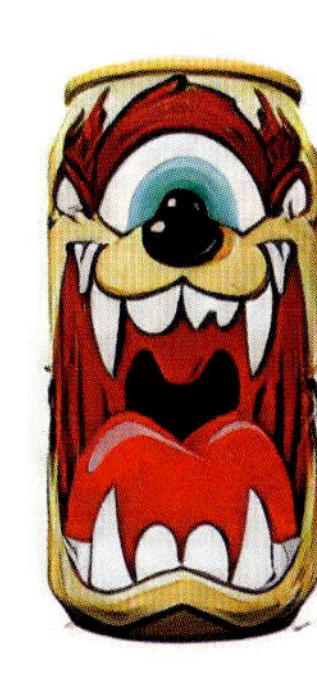
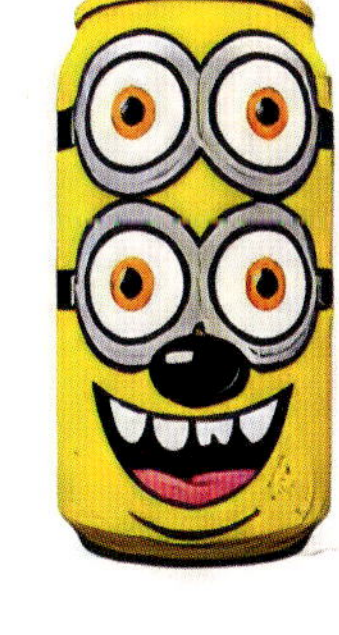
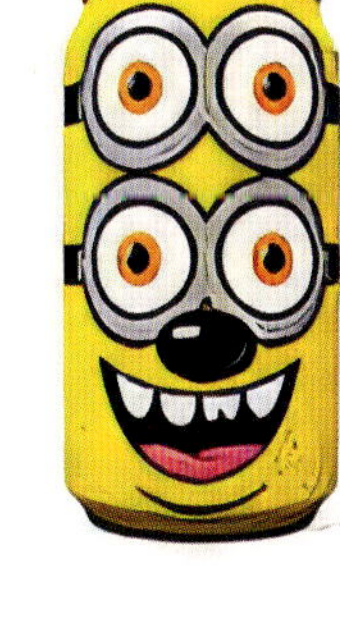
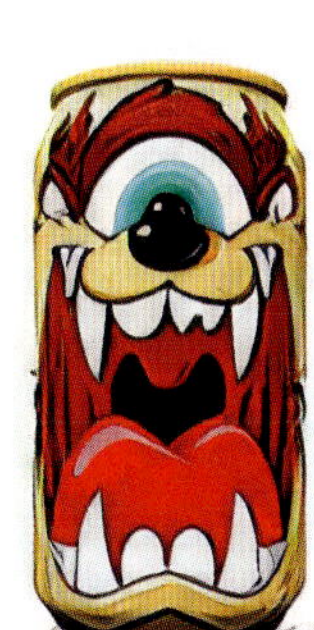
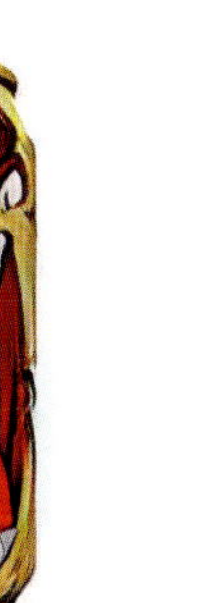
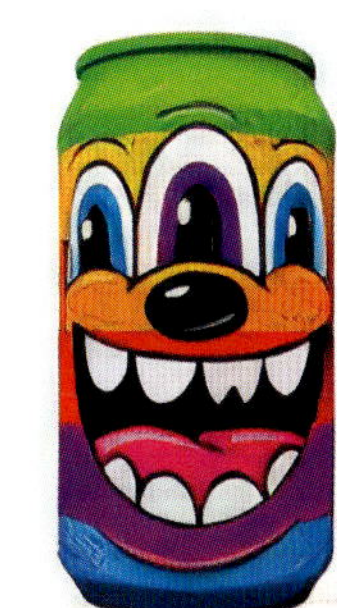
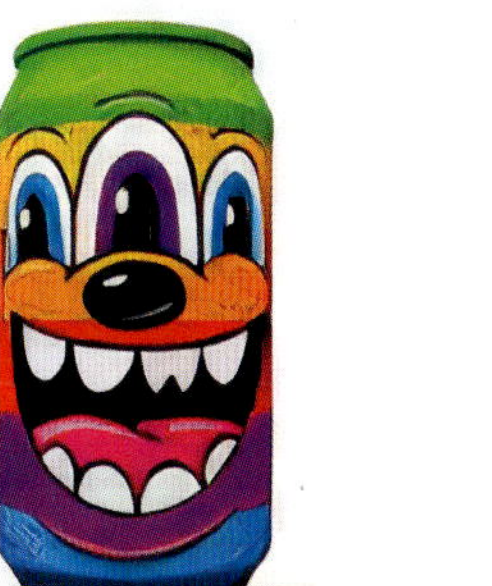
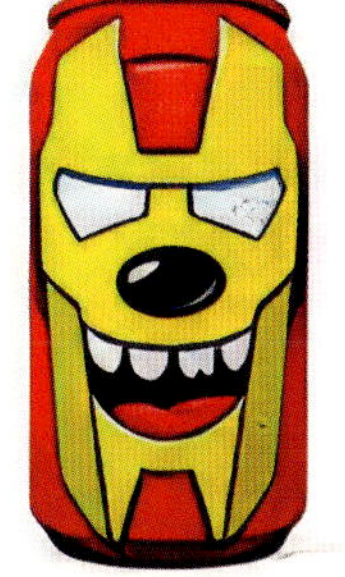
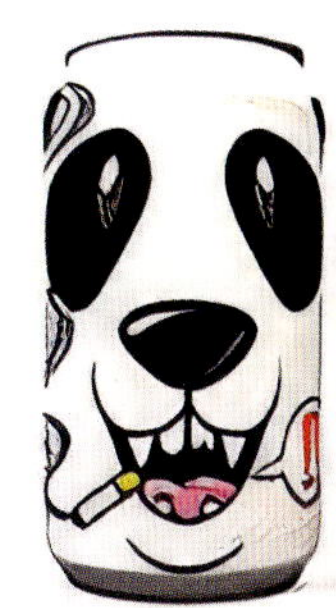

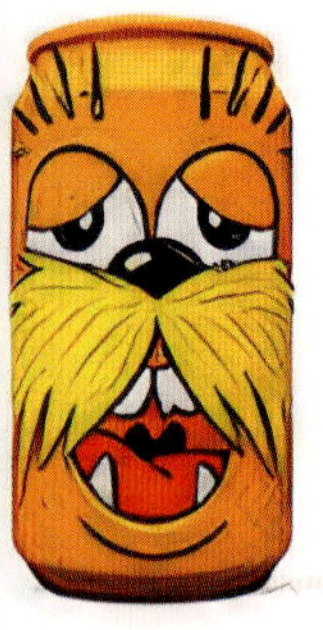 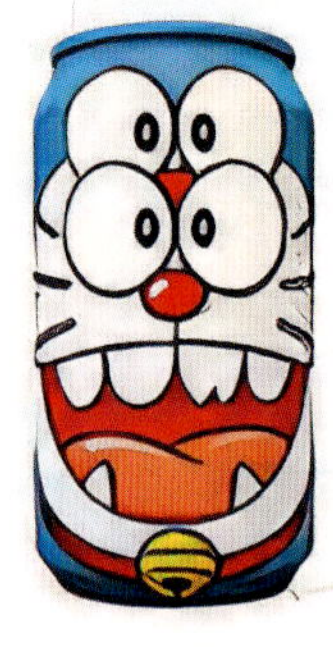 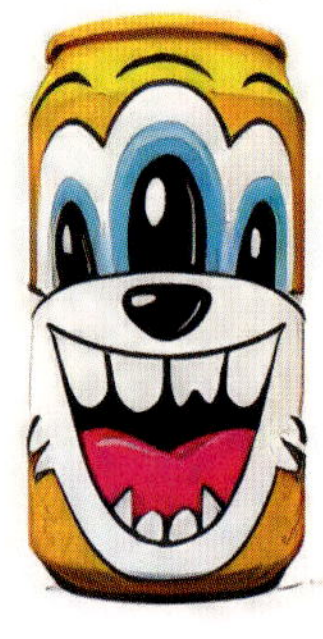 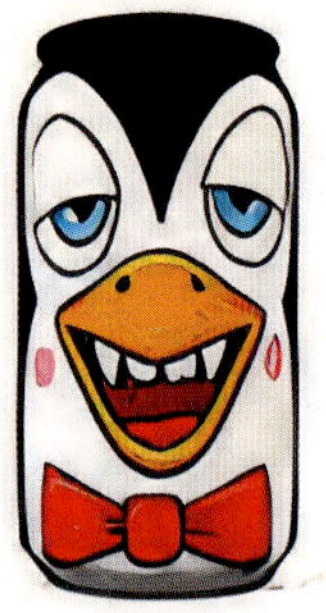 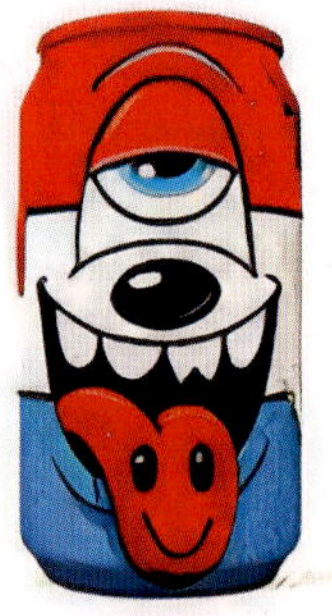 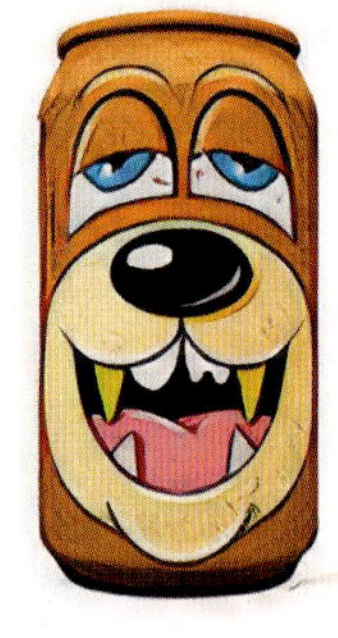
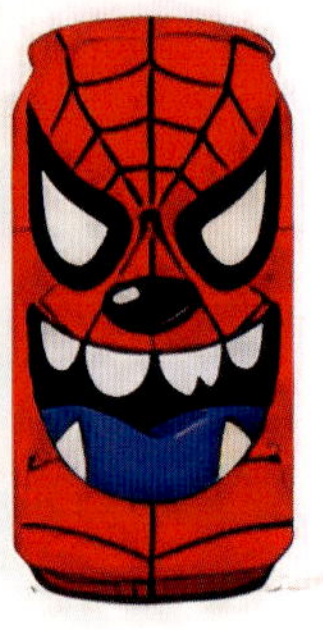 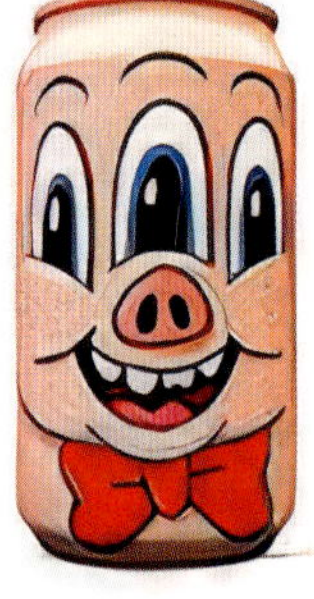 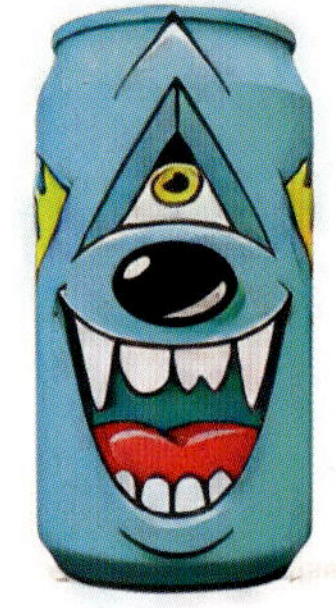 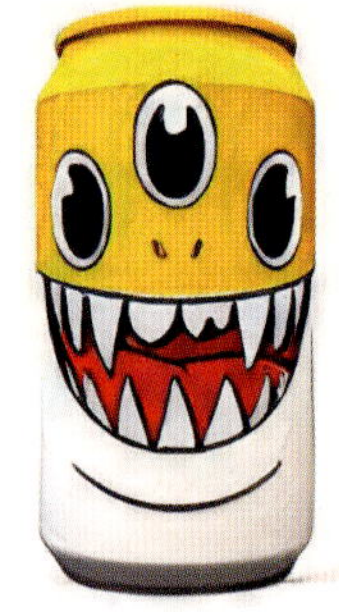 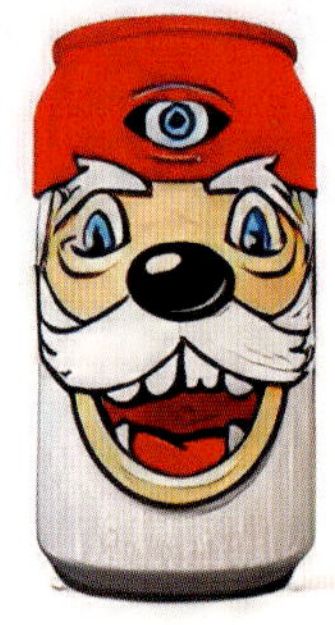 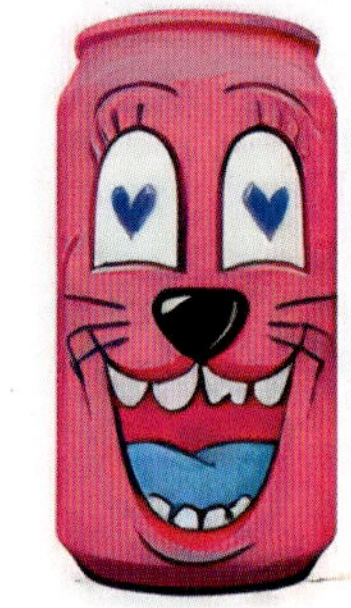
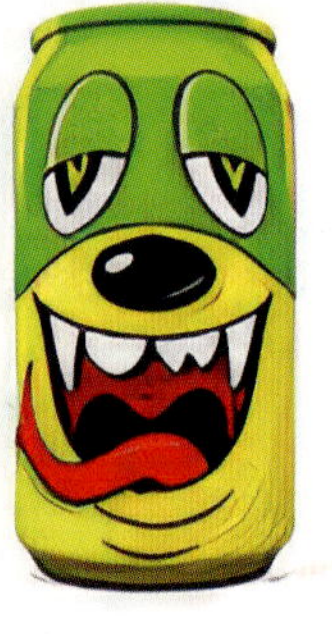 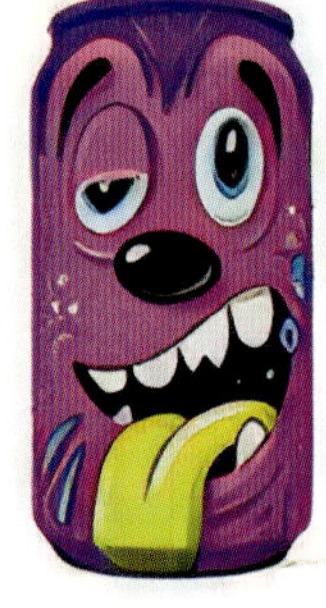 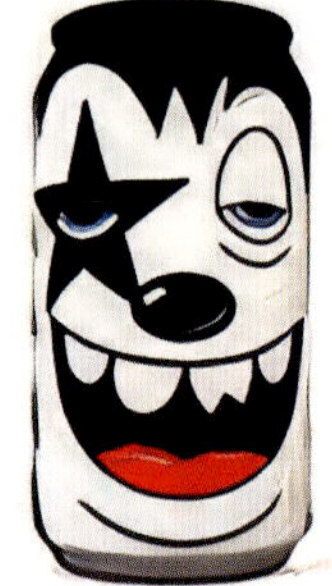 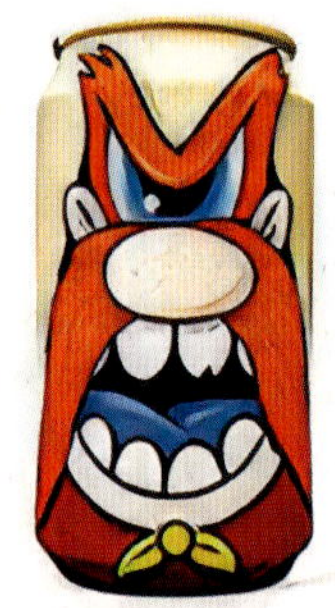 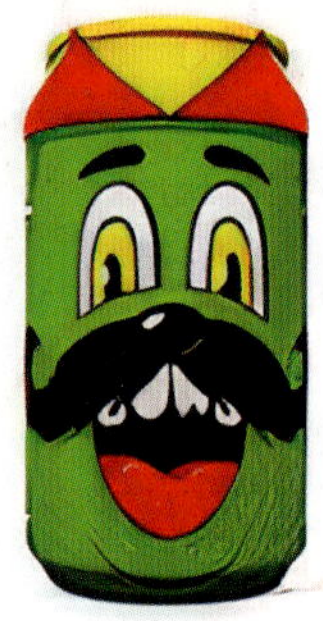 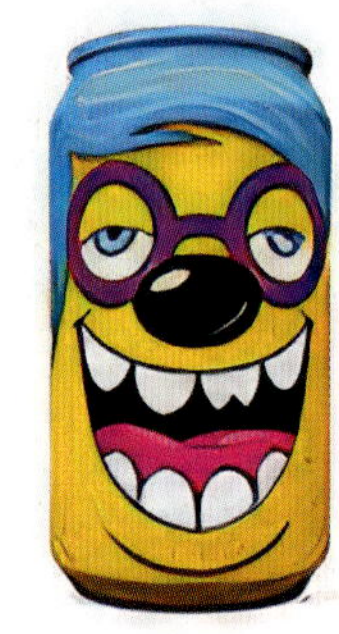
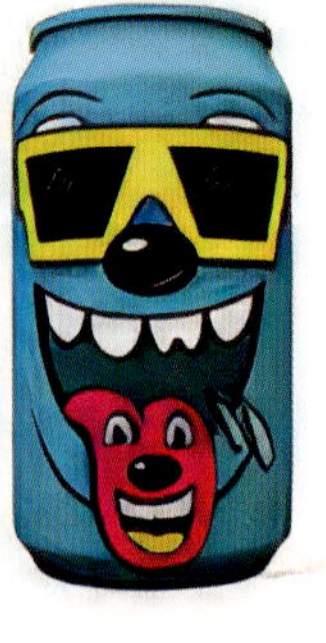 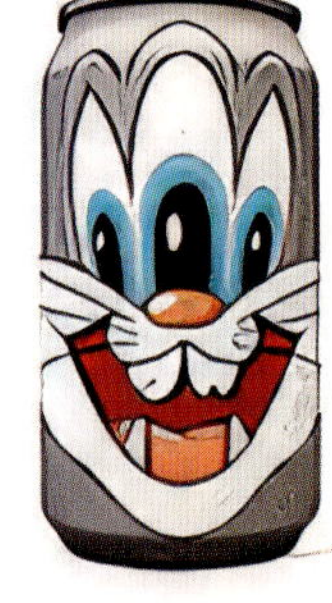 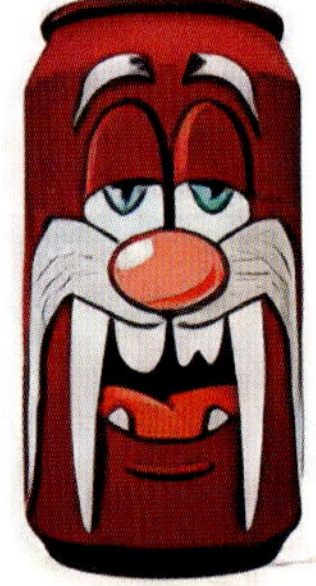 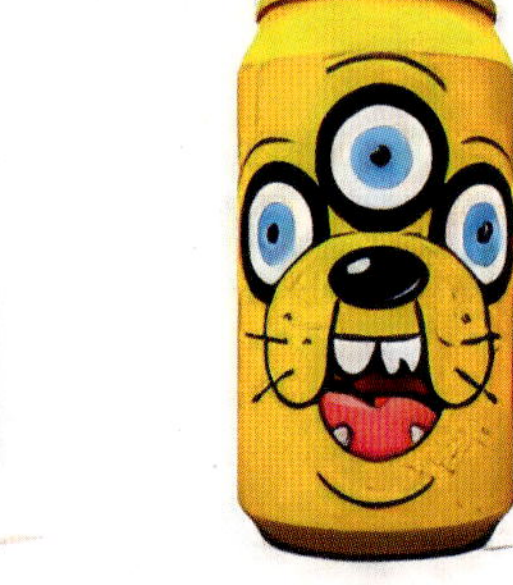 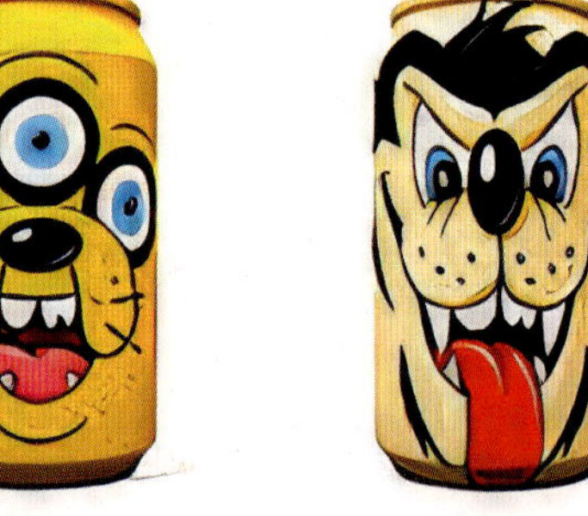 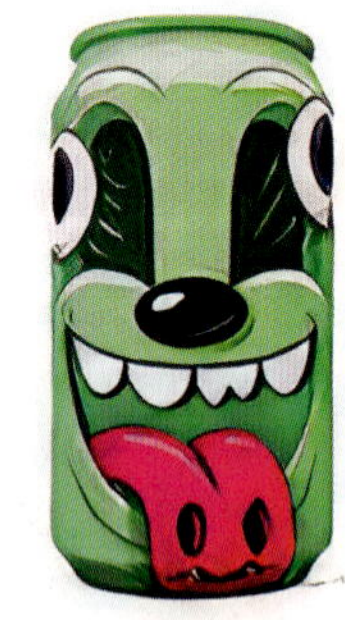
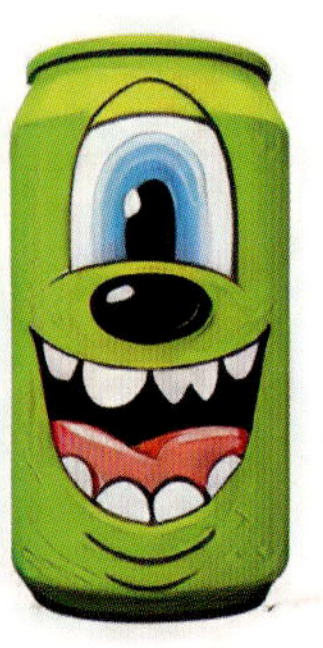 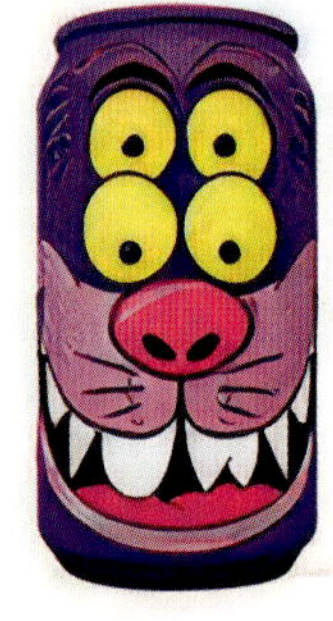 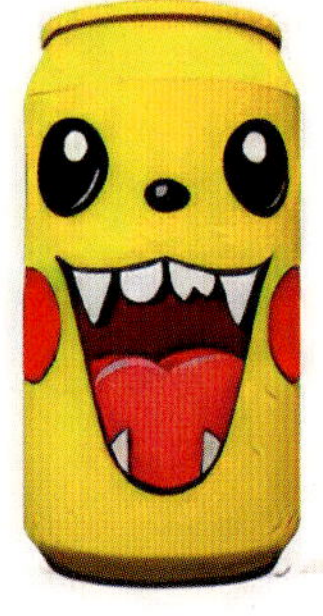 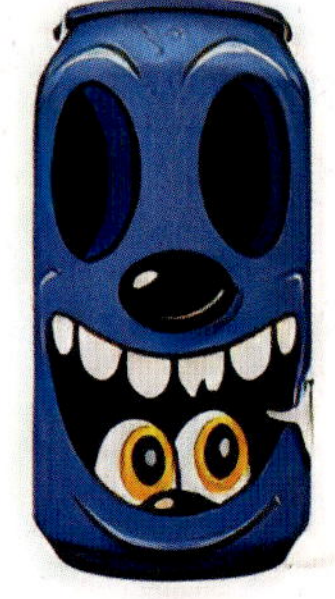 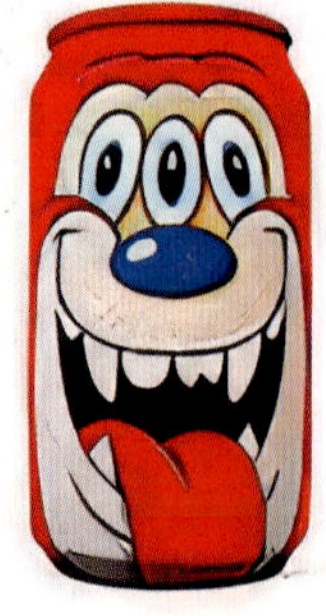 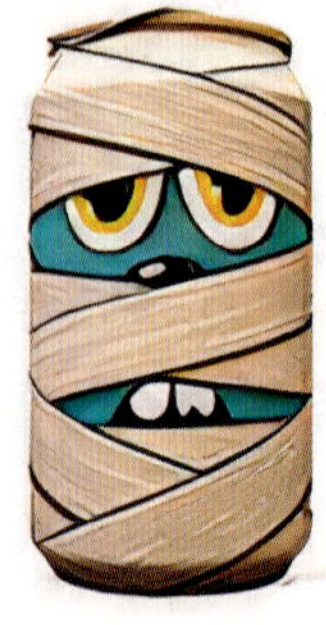

Greg Mike is fascinated by cartoon and comic-book characters, past and present, and certain types of black-and-white photographs of animals, which he combines in a kind of surrealist collage with the vibrant hues of pop figures and symbols, as well as flashes of color that recall his murals . . . Then come his experimental works, equally vivid and irreverent—provocative, joyful, and fun—yet concealing deeper meanings that go well beyond those initially impressed on viewers. As one looks at his works, the perspective shifts based on the manner in which they are examined; varying sporadically with the rhythm of a kaleidoscope, the works are full of surprises, pulling the viewer into the artist's vibrant, multi-colored, unpredictable universe. Joy and nostalgia, past and present, melt together in the wild existence of the moment.

For Greg Mike, boredom is definitely inconceivable. "Atlanta is a city that inspires me because it's the perfect place for creatives to experiment and is welcoming to new influences, especially in regards to street art. I am the founder and Creative Director for ABV, which is a contemporary Art Gallery and Creative Agency and has its roots in street art while providing an opportunity for artists and brands to collaborate in a unique way. ABV Gallery has hosted the work of over five hundred established and emerging artists around the world who I consider a part of the contemporary art movement. And with our creative agency we have produced countless murals and artist led projects in the city of Atlanta and across the nation. I will always be amazed by the community that we've been a part of, helped create, and continue to grow here," he states. In 2015, Greg Mike also launched the OuterSpace Project. OSP is a an event series that merges public art, live music, design, and culture. With an outdoor mural project at its core, OSP's goal is to enhance outdoor spaces, generate positive energy, expand the mind, and engage the public through urban beautification and creativity. To expand the ABV Gallery, he recently purchased a deconsecrated church in East Atlanta with the

goal of transforming it into an even larger event space, EAV (East Atlanta Village), devoted to all sorts of art forms. "This has been a dream of mine for a long time. And since I believe in the possibility of fulfilling it, I committed myself to it with all my heart . . . ," he admits with that disarming enthusiasm that conquers everyone the moment he opens his mouth.

Curiosity, creativity, and action dominate everything in Greg Mike's work. It's no coincidence that one of his most beautiful street art installations in Atlanta is titled *Keep Going* . . . A large wall mural in Las Vegas, *Every Day Counts 3*, explodes with irrepressible joy and optimism, with lolling tongues, flowers shooting forth multicolored rainbows, and famous cartoon characters, plus some of his own invention, all appearing to be having lots of fun . . . Like his *Larry Loudmouf*, an iconic mouth that doesn't hold back sound bites or punch lines and blends colorful design with pop culture, Greg Mike's digital art is simply a mirror of all this . . . "In my works, you'll discover popular cartoon characters with whom you're already familiar, like Tom and Jerry, for example, but also many new ones, born of my imagination, whom I consider outsiders, a bit like me. They're the ones who ultimately dominate the scene due precisely to their originality, their 'being different'," he states.

Greg Mike has his roots in street art, the world's most free and democratic art form, whose founding principles he made his own. "I was born in Danbury, Connecticut, about an hour by car from New York. I often took the train into the city, and, from the time I was a child, I was fascinated by the graffiti I saw on the subway cars—by their color, their rebelliousness, their longing for freedom . . . I've always been attracted to all forms of art or visual expression; I even enjoyed finding the signs, colors, and images on the bottoms of my skateboards. I used to spend hours looking at the vibrant colors of cartoons, comic books, and illustrations, then taking a brush and trying to copy them. It was only natural and inevitable for me to enter the world of graffiti

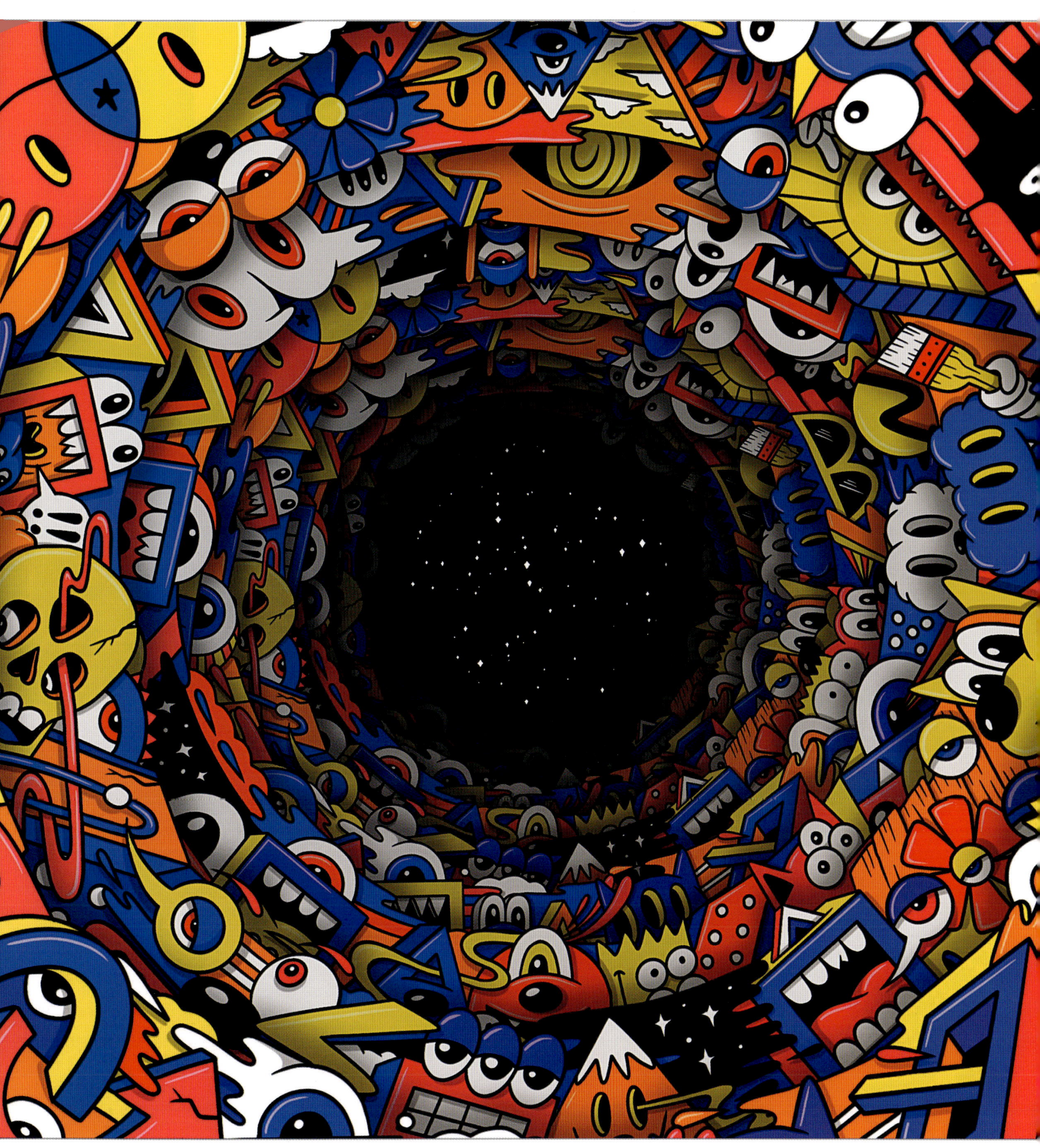

and street art and start doing things at age twelve or thirteen, reclaiming characters from old Disney movies with more modern and contemporary touches," he recalls. "I was a member of the urban community of skateboarders and street artists. We shared ideas and feelings, we inspired each other, but I was quite keen to pursue my own ideas and to focus on my personal style," he adds.

Greg Mike inherited the love of art since his childhood. "My family has been in the Broadway scenic industry and in the theater business for four generations. As a child I remember sitting in the shop and watching scenic artists paint massive backdrops and being in awe of the scale and process of creation. Their passion for the arts influenced me to pursue my natural inclinations . . .

"Soon I found myself imagining huge sculptures and immense installations . . . Around the age of twelve I already knew that I wanted to be an artist and began taking art classes. Nonetheless, if it hadn't been for graffiti and street art, I certainly would not be here today," he underscores. "Gallery and museum art was too predictable; my soul and natural instinct lay in street art, which was more in tune with my lifestyle. I did lots of 'guerrilla art' and I worked on the streets," he says reflectively.

The transition from street to digital art also came naturally to him—an inevitable shift . . . Knowing that digital art is forging ahead faster and faster, Greg Mike follows its rhythms, combining figures and feelings, as if composing a hip-hop song—slightly angry, slightly irreverent, slightly funny, slightly weird, but always exciting and engaging. "Technology has always played a part in my creative process. I learned to draw on my PC even before I got a Mac, and decided to study graphic design and digital photography since these seemed to offer the best way of supporting oneself financially.

NGHTMRE_HIGH_NOON

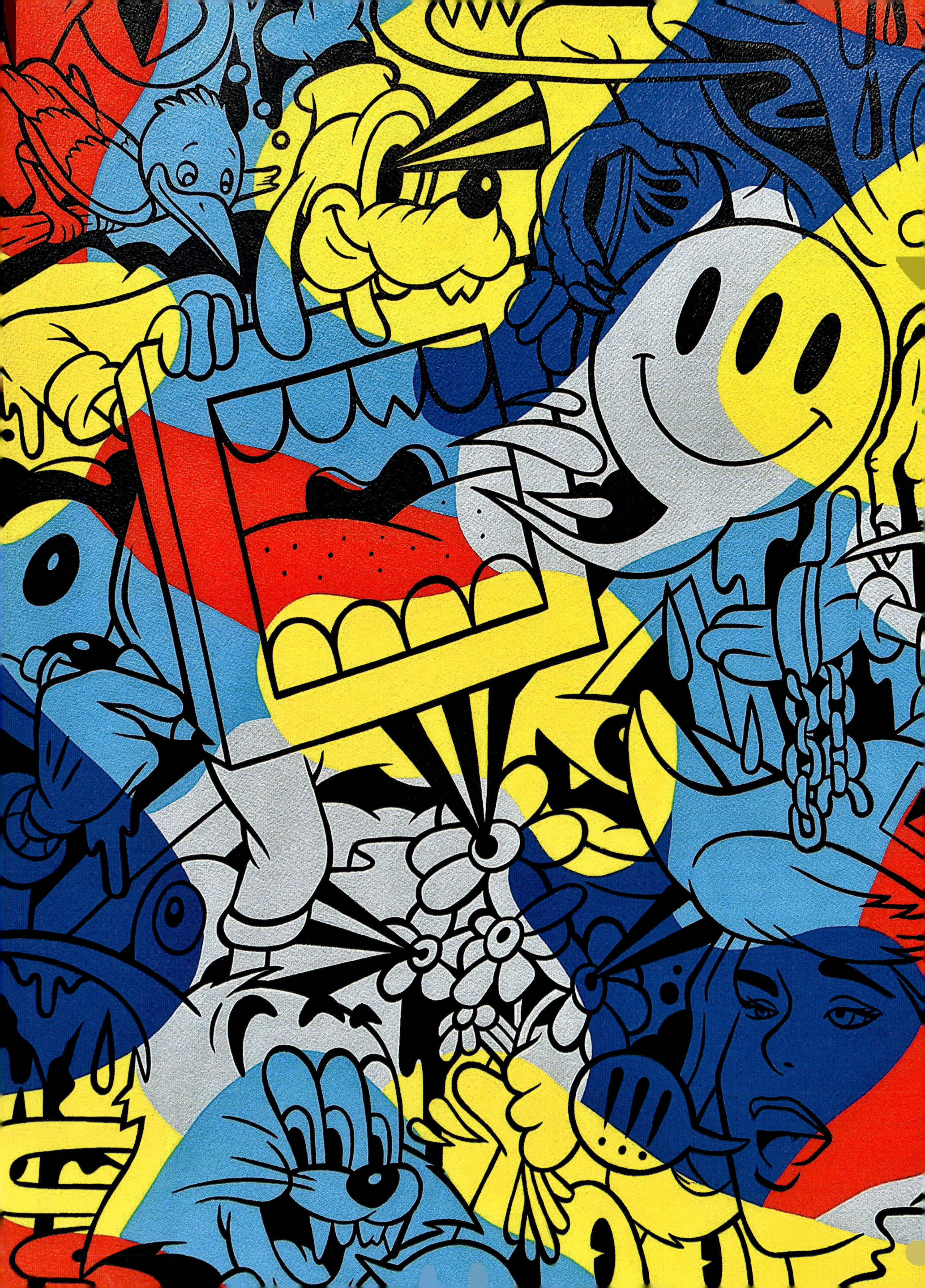

RIP - SMIILEY

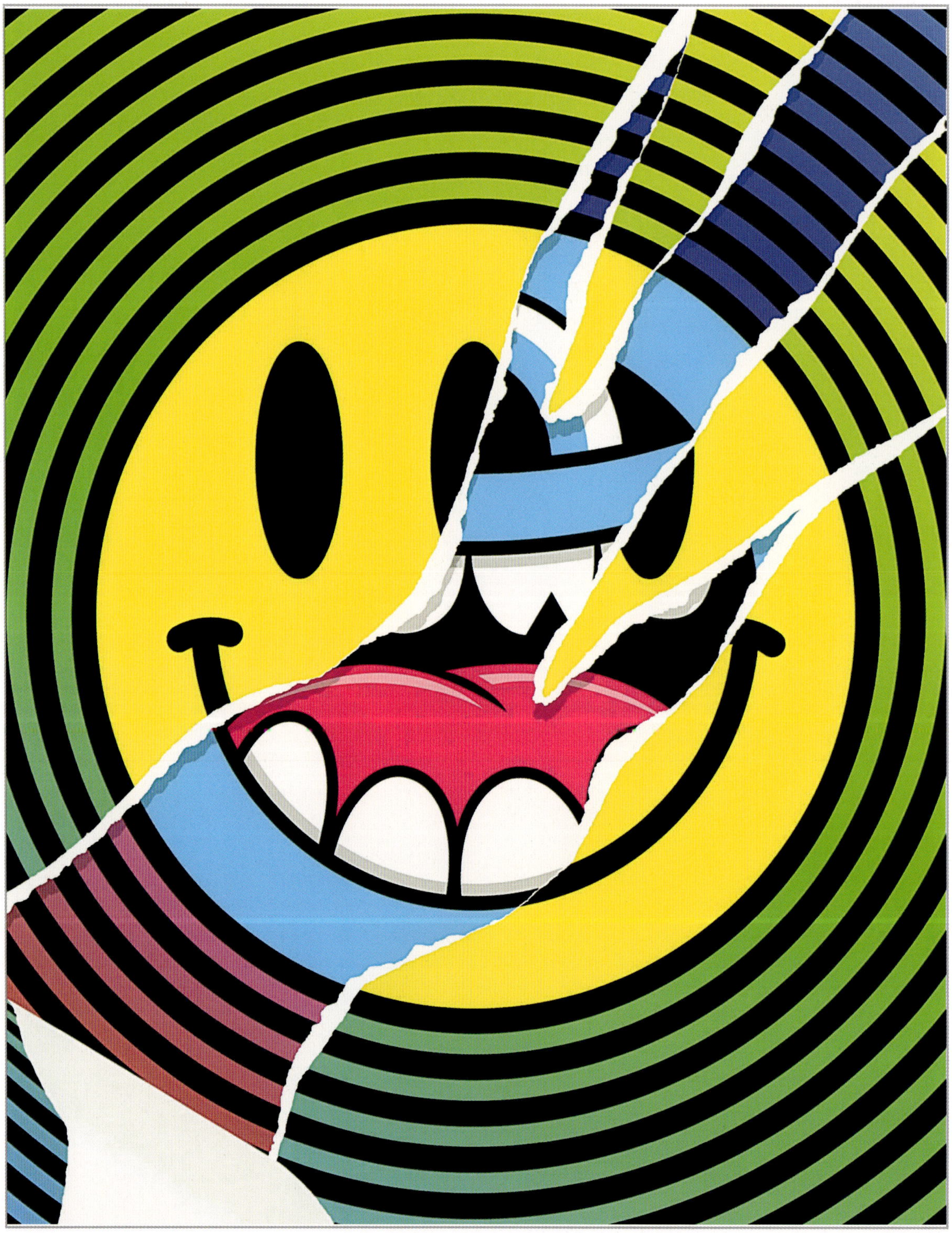

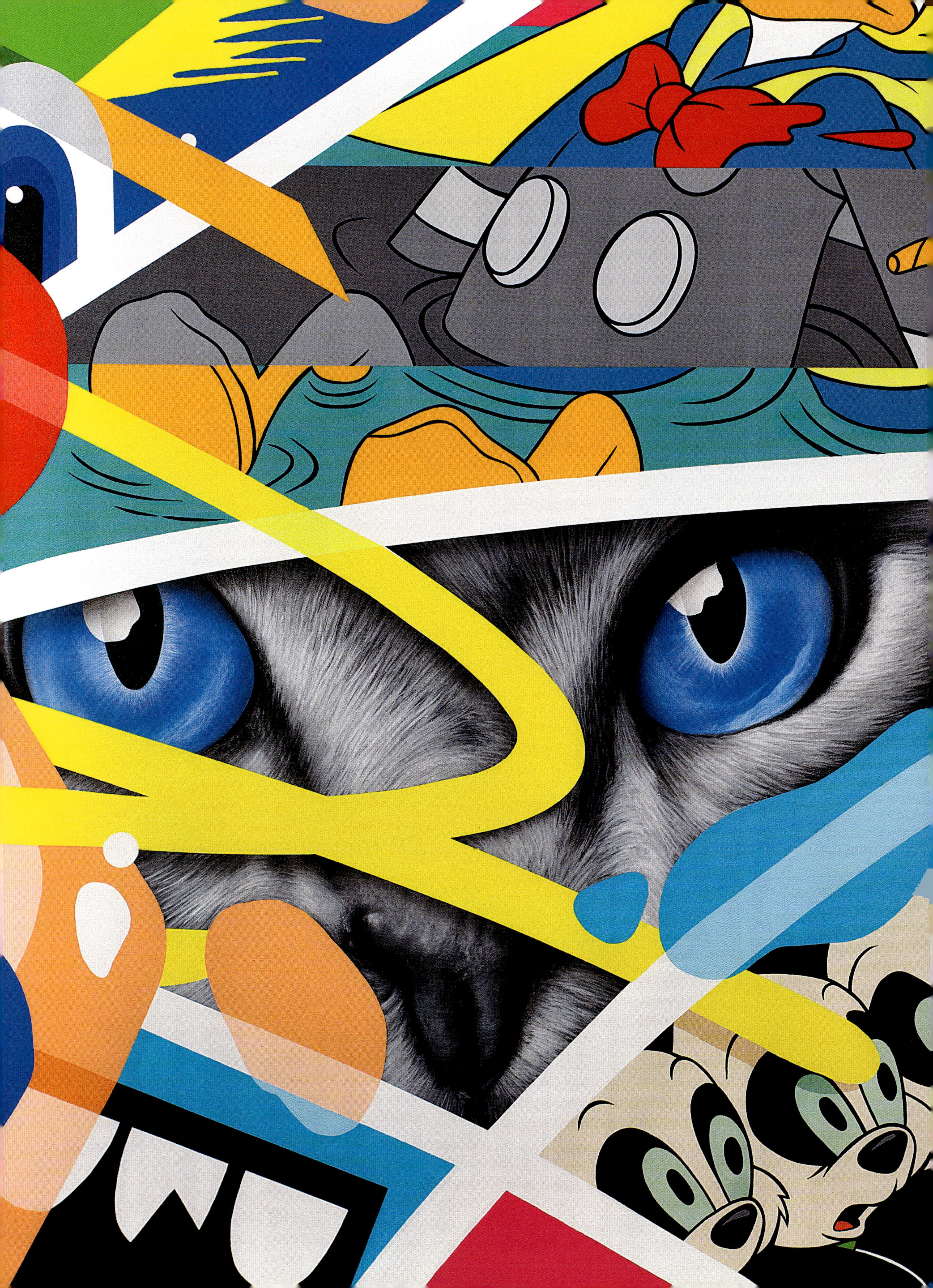

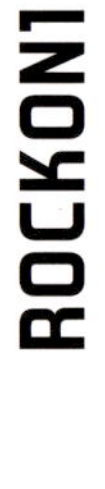

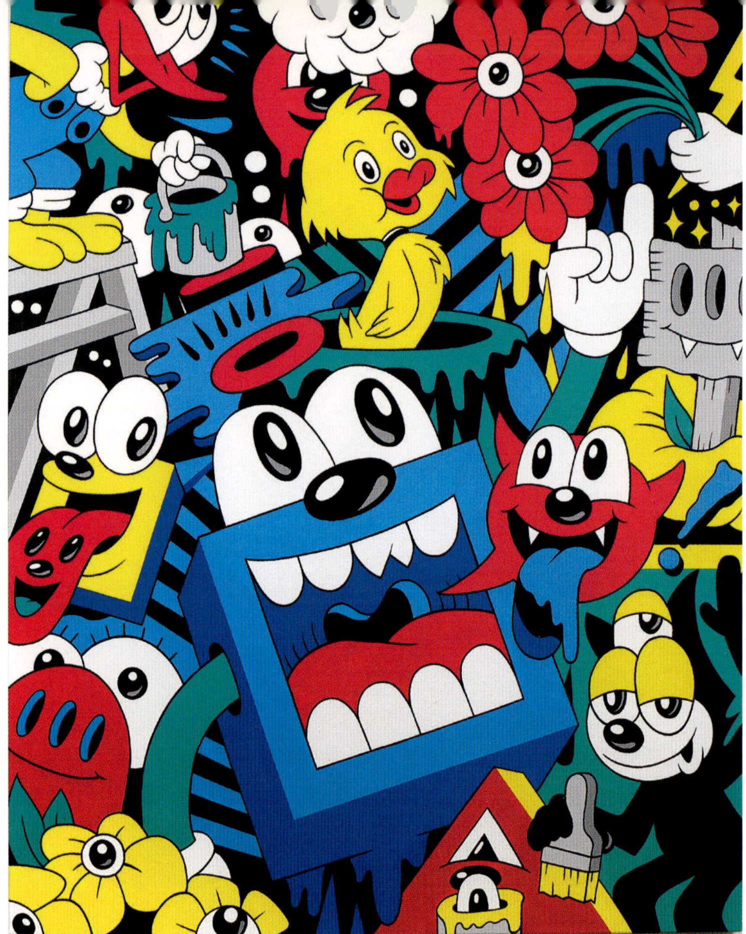

In the meantime, and even before the social-media boom, I began sharing the art I created in chat rooms and receiving really positive feedback. I can say that the digital revolution had a tremendous impact on my entire adolescence. As the saying goes: 'You've got to run fast if you don't want to be left in the past'," he says.

His mission today? "Angry and rebellious as a kid, I now like to paint positive figures. All this reflects me and my emotions, and I hope it can inspire those who look at it," he says in response. In this respect, his art almost becomes a form of psychological introspection behind its apparent pop facade. "I know that a smiling face can get an entire community to hope for a better world, so positivity has become an irreversible choice," he concludes, with hope in his eyes.

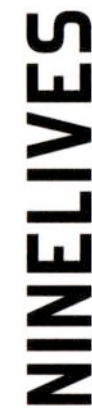

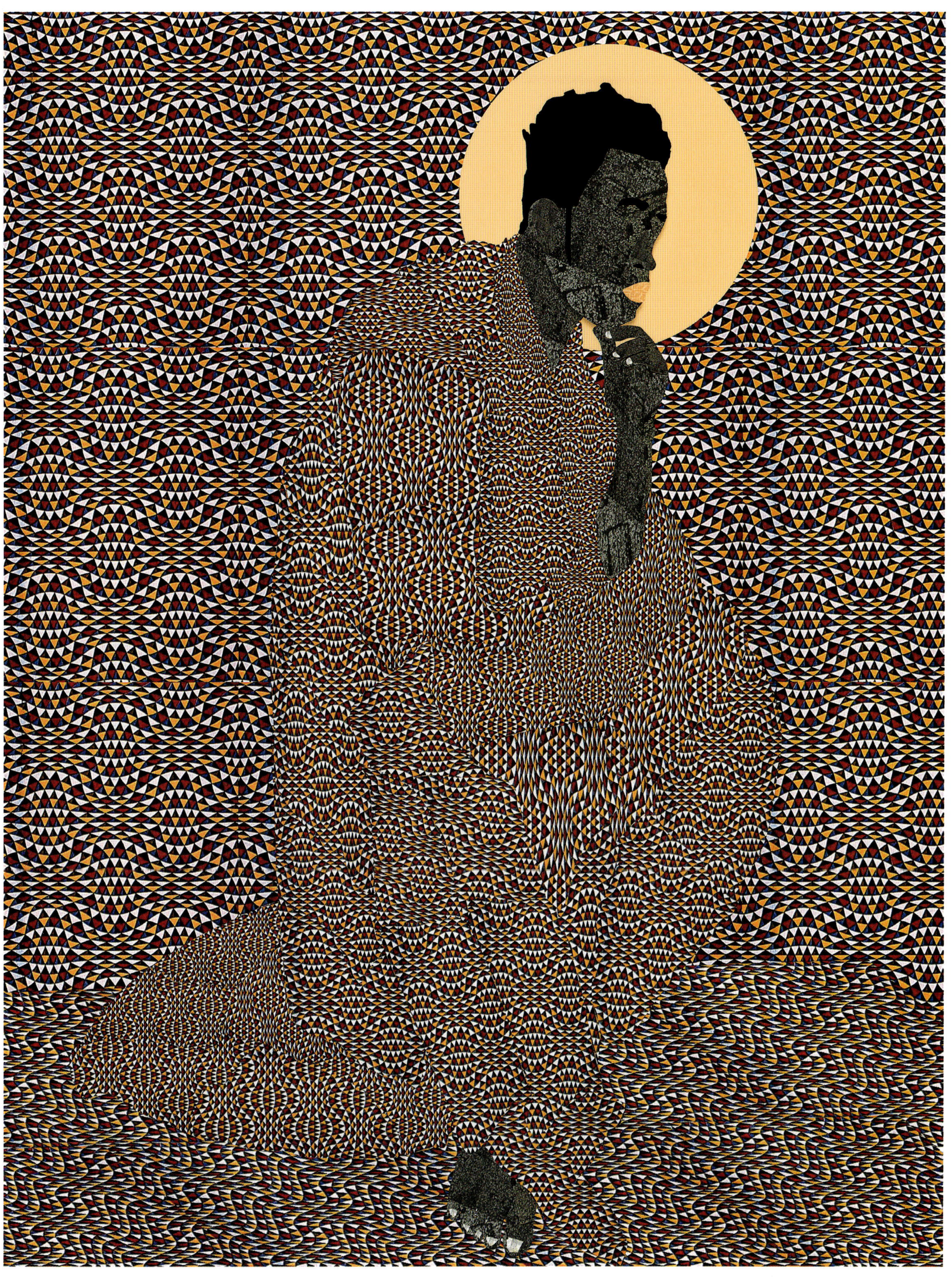

OSINACHI

WHEN COLORS SPEAK TO THE HEART

"TECHNOLOGY AND ART. ART AND TECHNOLOGY. FOR ME THEY'RE INSEPARABLE. THEY'RE A MOVEMENT AND A MOVEMENT OF OUR TIME. EVERY ERA HAS HAD ITS TRENDS . . . THE USE OF A COMPUTER DOES NOT DEFINE ART; ART GOES BEYOND TRADITION AND FORM, ART PIERCES EVERYTHING."

Colors, strong and bright, that project, that highlight the culture of Africa, but above all the values that he himself holds dear. "Africa is rich in color, and I'm intrigued by the idea of incorporating them into my art. I'm not attracted to any particular color; it depends on the moment. I have a predilection for orange, though I know I can't work solely with that color and its many shades: humanity is too vast to limit oneself in this way . . . My inspiration is global and focused on the immediate, on what's contemporary . . . ," he elucidates.

His art speaks straight to the heart, in a direct and open manner, but also representing the spirit of community that has been overlooked and ignored for too long . . . Crying out loud and powerful, it lays claim to the principles of equality and the need for a better world. Osinachi is a visionary, a positive one. His figures, African men and women seemingly involved in mundane activities, like swimming in a pool, clutching a pillow to their chest as they sit before an old TV, or busily sewing, are frozen at a specific moment of their life. In reality, however, they're vibrant icons of an ever-more-present world that imposes itself on Western culture with power and determination, keen to make its voice heard, proud of its origins, of its existence for its own sake, and beyond conven-

THE THINKER 2020

tions . . . And, in the virtual world, all this becomes quicker, nearly fleeting, in the continuous movement of lines and the succession of fragile boundaries oscillating between the real and surreal, desperately pursuing a better world.

Osinachi is all this and far more: joy and positivity pour forth from his words, a momentary awareness of the spontaneous rebirth of emotions and sensations. "I wanted to be an artist from the time I was a child . . . My journey through this fantastic universe got immersed in adventure once I began reading a great deal, writing and drawing. I wanted to create illustrations that captured what I was reading, so I searched for an Internet café where I could use a computer, as I preferred creating images through digital means to doing it on paper . . . I was especially fascinated by certain illustrations in art books and tried to do something similar . . . ," he recounts. "I'm self-taught, and have learned everything I know primarily from books. I've studied the great masters, but also new techniques for creating visual art," he adds. "Today, I live in Lagos, but I grew up in Southern Nigeria, in Aba. Africa has continued playing a crucial role in my life, and the environment in which I grew up has had a great influence on me," he states. "I've always had a passion for technology—a passion inherited from my father, who brought home old TV sets and electronic items that he found while walking around and that needed to be fixed and rendered functional once again. It was he who first taught me how to use a computer . . . ," he says emphatically. Osinachi has done his work with Microsoft Word for over fifteen years, but is open to every new tool from which he can draw fresh ideas and creative inspiration. "For me, art is

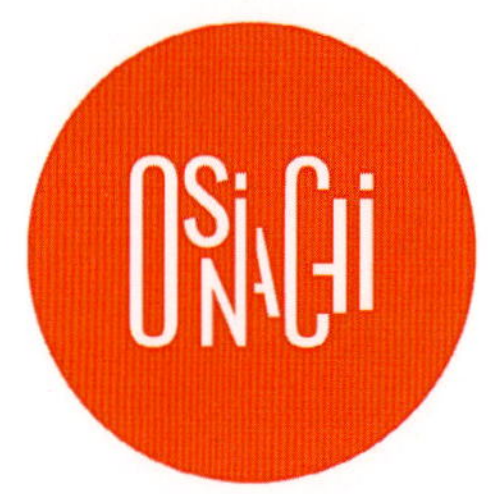

nothing more than the expression of my emotions; it's visual imagination created by various tools, and it is also created by a new language. For me, digital art carries the same value as physical art and deserves the same aesthetic appreciation, and I'm happy that the world finally acknowledges this," he explains. "I often don't understand all its technical aspects and details; I'm not an engineer or computer scientist, as are many other artists in this field, but it doesn't matter, because in my mind what counts above all is the way in which technology is used, not how it works," he claims. AI doesn't instill fear in him, because he confronts it with the same spirit: "I look at AI as simply another tool with which I can work, operate, and create. I am especially fascinated by generative art's ability to create something new each time . . ."

According to Osinachi, art must have a mission and a deeper meaning that goes beyond its purely technological and spectacular aspects. He believes in the quality of the message and its objective. "In my work, I've always reserved a special place for women, because at the time I was growing up I too often saw how they were abused and overlooked, how their voice was frequently disregarded. In my pieces, no man enjoys greater prominence than a woman. I believe deeply in equality and respect, and I care about representing Africa and minorities in my art," he states. "I've always loved animals. Some are regarded as dangerous, and so lots of people think they should be killed . . . That's a horrible way to think!

I would like to completely wipe out this mindset, fight for respect for Mother Earth and all the creatures that inhabit it," he points out.

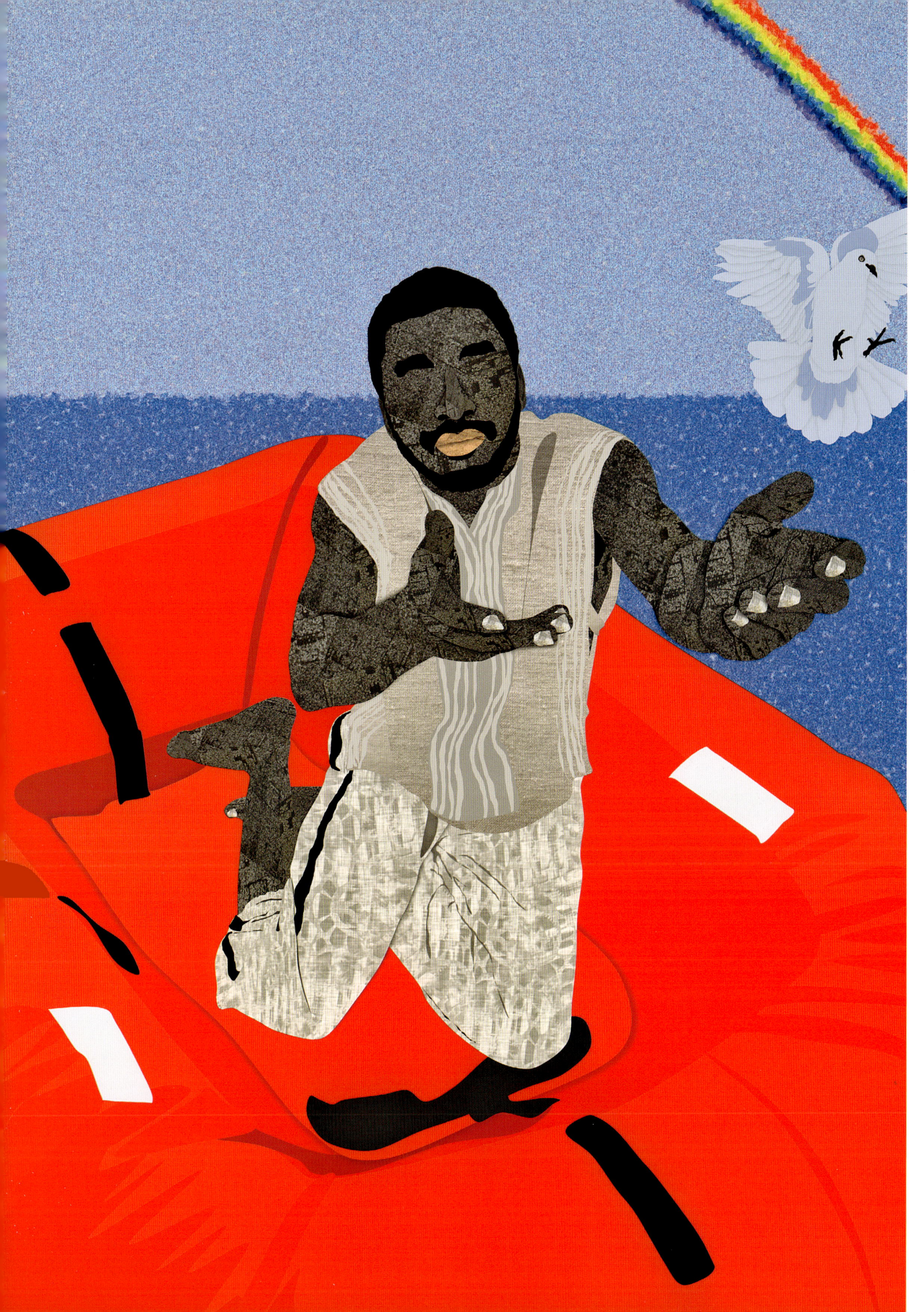

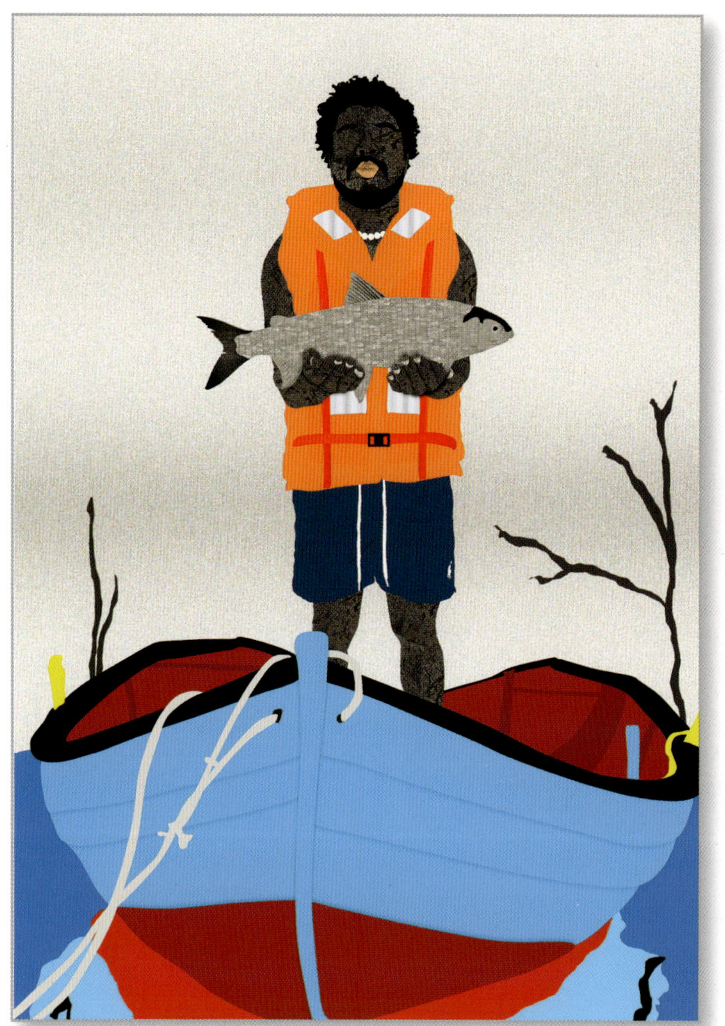

"We need to come up with the right balance between man and nature, and I'm convinced that technology will greatly assist us in this," he says with hope.

His mission as an artist? "I want to create an art that speaks to my time, regardless of the medium or the tools used to create it, but it must reflect the context in which I'm living. If you think about it, all artists of the past were inspired by their own era. It may seem like an exaggeration when I say that I make art that's close to my heart, as by doing so I'm professing that I'm doing all I can to alter the future with my work . . . But that's what I'm trying to do with humility; and if I manage to accomplish this even in part, that will already be a success," he claims.

There are many artists who have inspired him . . . All are driven by the same sense of responsibility that characterizes his work. "Plenty of American artists have had an influence on me; but African, and particularly Nigerian ones, are probably those who've had the most . . . Among them are Kehinde Wiley, Devan Shimoyama, Njideka Akunyili-Crosby . . . And then there's the music that's played such an important role in my life. Nigeria is the home of Afrobeat, a beautiful genre of music," he points out.

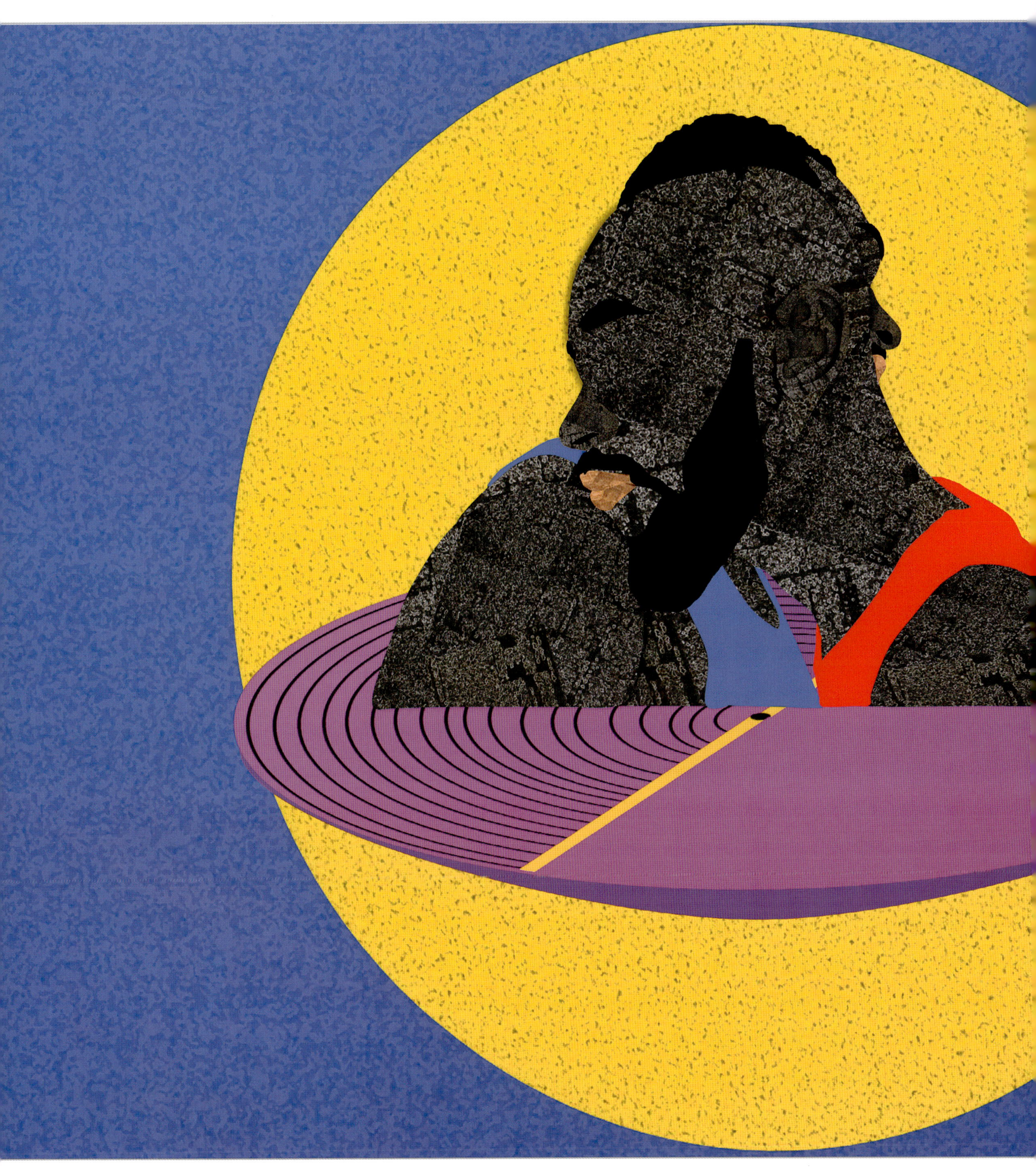

+RAVE-SING (TRAVERSING) 2022

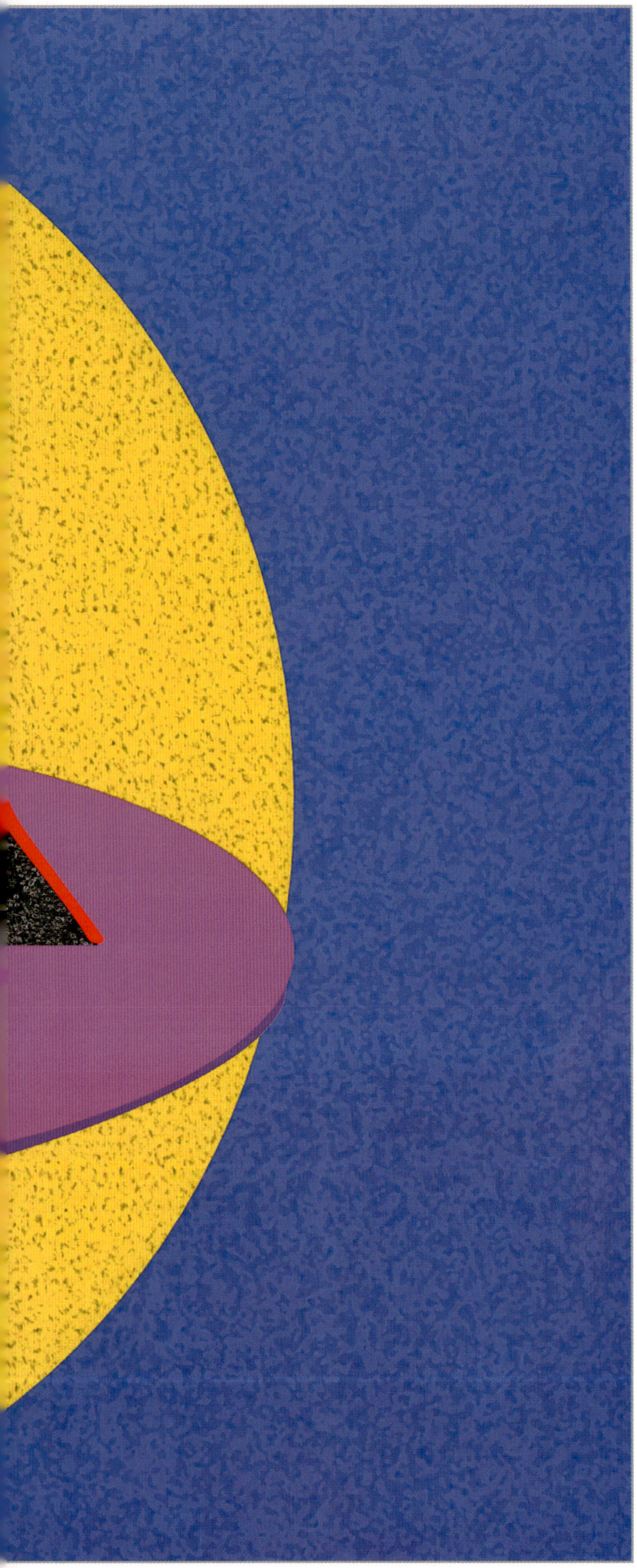

Osinachi loves Nigeria, but is well aware that many things need to change in his country: "Nigeria is undergoing a major technological boom, but too many talented people leave to seek fame and fortune elsewhere. The situation for women has greatly improved, but the road to equality is still truly long and complex," he reflects. Today Osinachi is an established and sought-after artist on an international scale, and his works are recognized and exhibited in the world's top museums; but his success has never cast a shadow on his soul or disproportionately swelled his ego. Not only does his art reflect his identity, but it's also a resonant protest against the stereotypes and prejudices that often afflict the continent of Africa.

"My values? Above all, mutual respect. I have deep faith in love, which inspires and guides me as a man and an artist," he concludes.

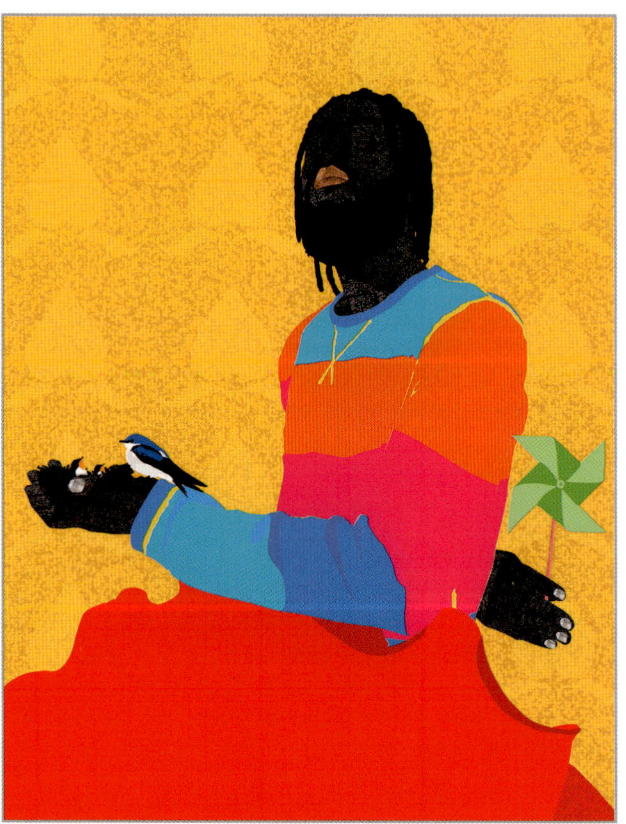

RAIN:FIELD 2023

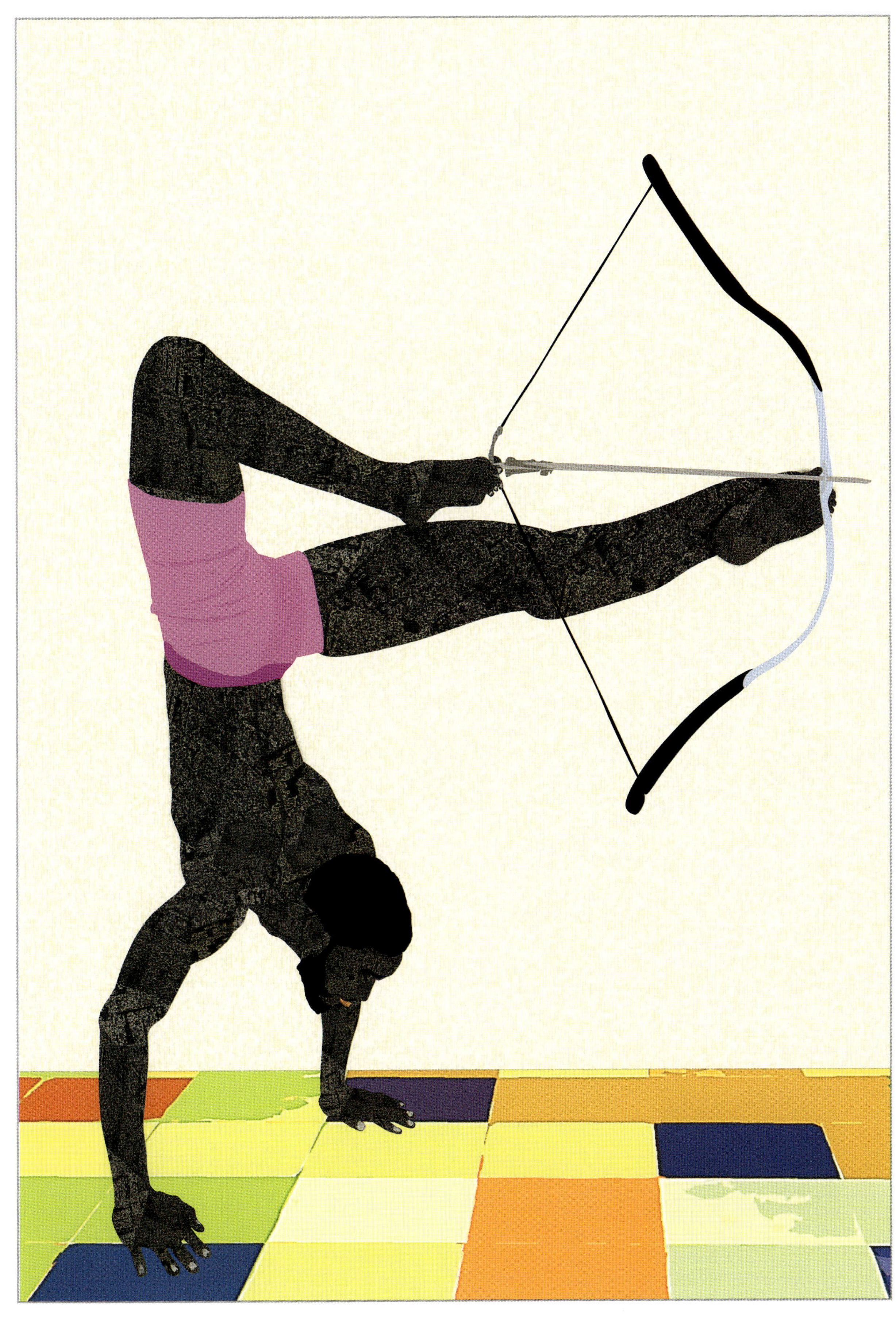

LET'S DANCE III

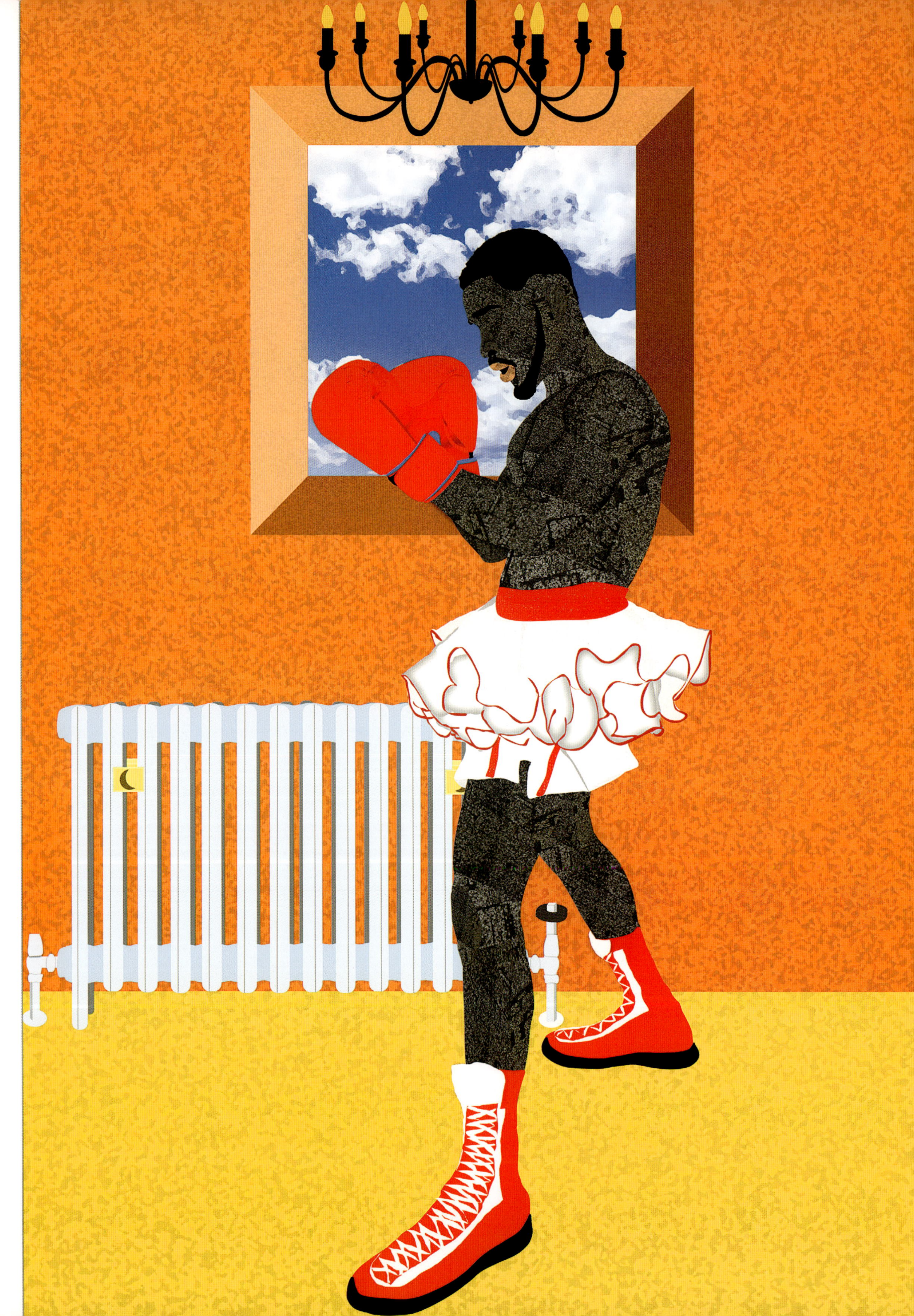

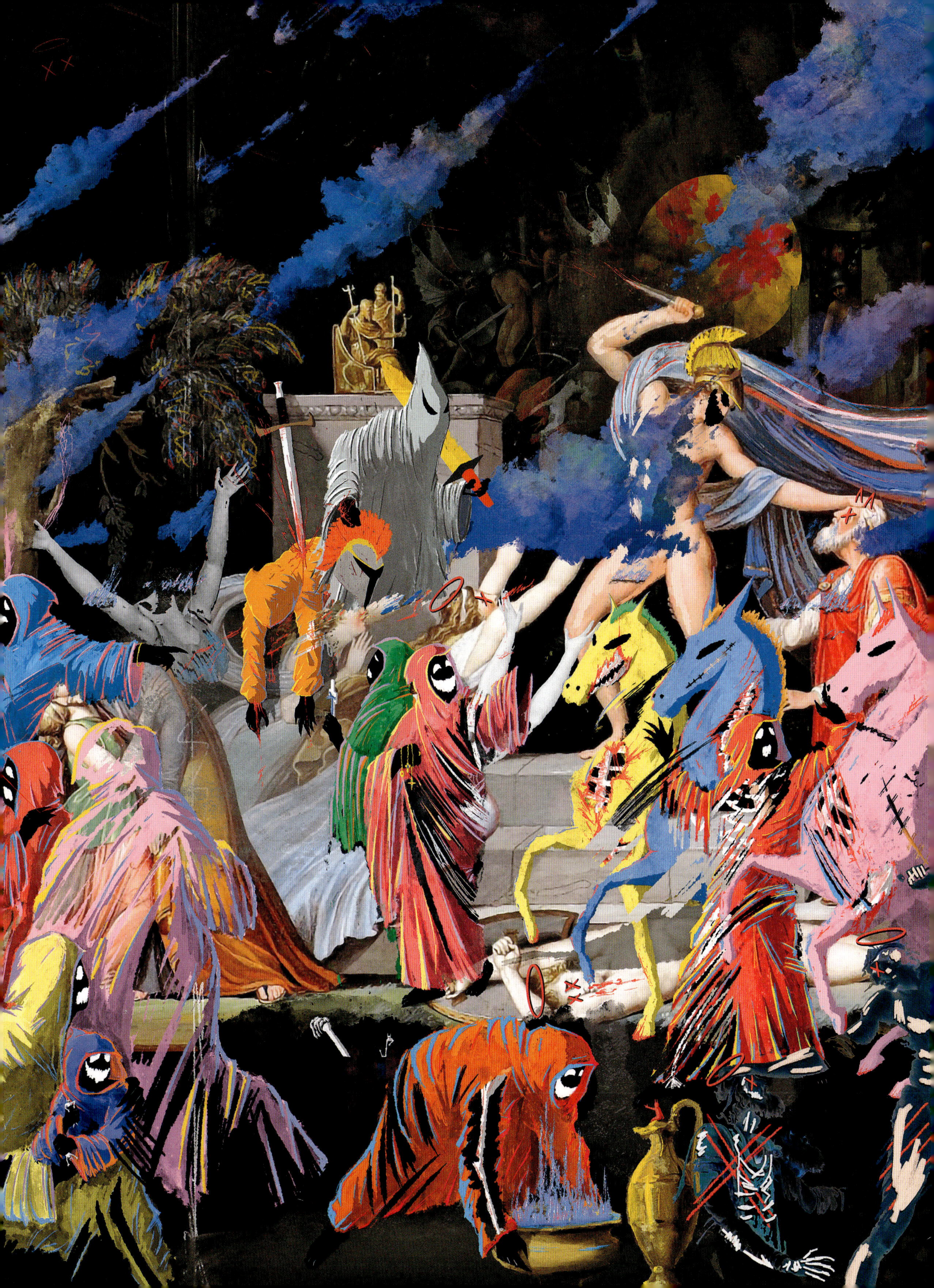

OTHER WORLD

A DANCE TO FORGET

"TECHNOLOGY HAS IMPROVED THE QUALITY OF LIFE
FOR HUMAN BEINGS WORLDWIDE. BY THE SAME TOKEN,
IT'S ADVANCING AT AN ALARMINGLY RAPID PACE.
HOW ALL THIS WILL END ONLY TIME CAN TELL, BUT
MY CAREER HAS CERTAINLY BENEFITED A GREAT DEAL
FROM TECHNOLOGY—SO MUCH SO THAT I COULD EVEN
SAY THAT IT'S WHAT'S MADE IT POSSIBLE."

His works are quite often inspired by masterpieces of the past, recast in a contemporary context thanks to his creative vision and populated by dark figures, garbed in tunics of intense color. Although their looming presence is palpable, their dark faces melt into the total homogeneity of existence. Other World loves contrasts, the unexpected, and the kind of mystery that touches on the occult and melts away in the fleeting moment. He is as good a master at exploring light and shadow as he is at exploring the past and present, and is adept at causing surprise with these disturbing presences that are capable of generating chaos, but also of making us reflect philosophically on the meaning of humanity, in ways that sometimes make us smile . . .

As far back as he can remember, Other World has felt closely connected to art, which has constantly exerted a strong desire on him. "I have always been fascinated by art. For as long as I can remember, I've known that I love drawing. Growing up, I used to draw to distract myself, using pencils to sketch funny figures or war scenes," he says. He goes on to recall how one moment, one event in particular—unexpected, even inconceivable—changed his life forever: "Toward the end of my time at university, I began painting in acrylic, just for fun. It was only during the pandemic and the lockdown that I began devoting myself seriously to art. The enforced isolation actually gave me plenty of time to explore the digital-art world. It was thus that I opened an Instagram account with the aim of creating a fashion brand called 'Other World.' . . . However, I soon realized that I was more interested in the art itself than in creating a line of clothing. And thus I began using digital collage to create psychedelic works," he recalls. As time passed amid general uncertainty, despondency, and the fear that life would never again be the same, Other World was actually discovering an "other world," his own other world.

"With practice, I learned how to use my iPad better and began incorporating illustrations into my collages . . . Soon I found that I had become an artist! I'm conscious and grateful of the fact that I had a handful of loyal collectors who ultimately enabled me to pursue this profession and transform it into a career," he says with satisfaction, though still with some amazement.

Much like his art, Other World can be simultaneously pessimistic and constructive: "Art means everything to me: it's the world. I want my art to have a positive impact on people and inspire them. My goal is to keep on developing as an artist and tell my story with higher-quality works and projects. I want to push the viewer into my world and get them to ask questions about their own world. For me, this is a never-ending and continuously evolving mission." Other World's strong sense of empathy manifests itself in his gracious generosity and open heart: "Another important goal is to pay back my collectors and all those who have supported me for all they have done for me. The best way I can do so is by constantly raising the quality of my works, growing, developing, and thus confirming the correctness of their choice. The most concrete and tangible way of assessing my success and showing its true value is by becoming a source of inspiration for as many people as possible. This, of course, is what underlies the significance and purpose of my art," he admits.

His inspiration comes primarily from the past and from history. "In most cases, I start with a historically important work of art that has struck me in particular. Sometimes my attention is drawn to a group of figures. At other times, I focus on the background. I divide my time between illustration and collage; I move back and forth between these techniques until I feel that my piece is done," he explains.

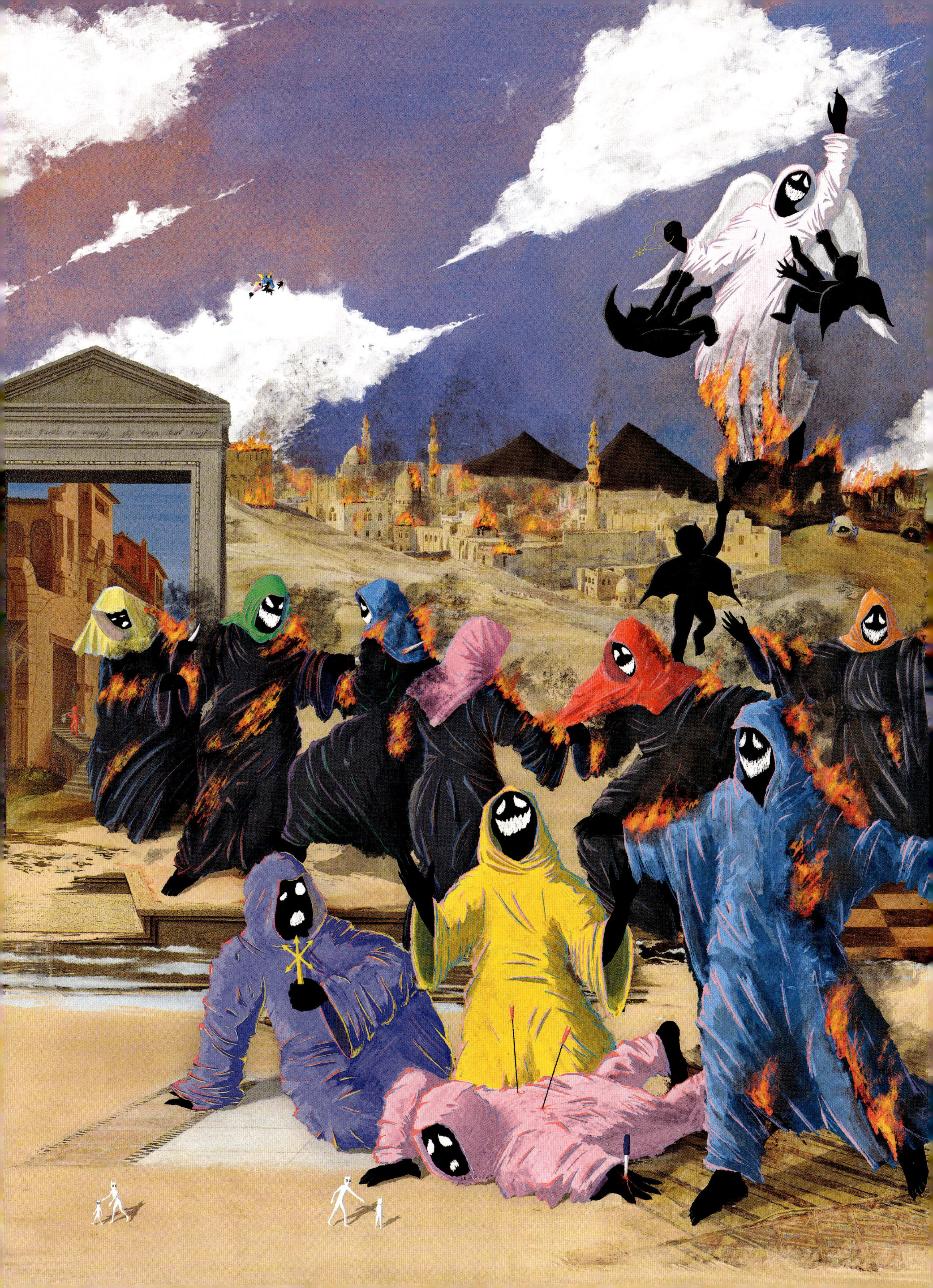

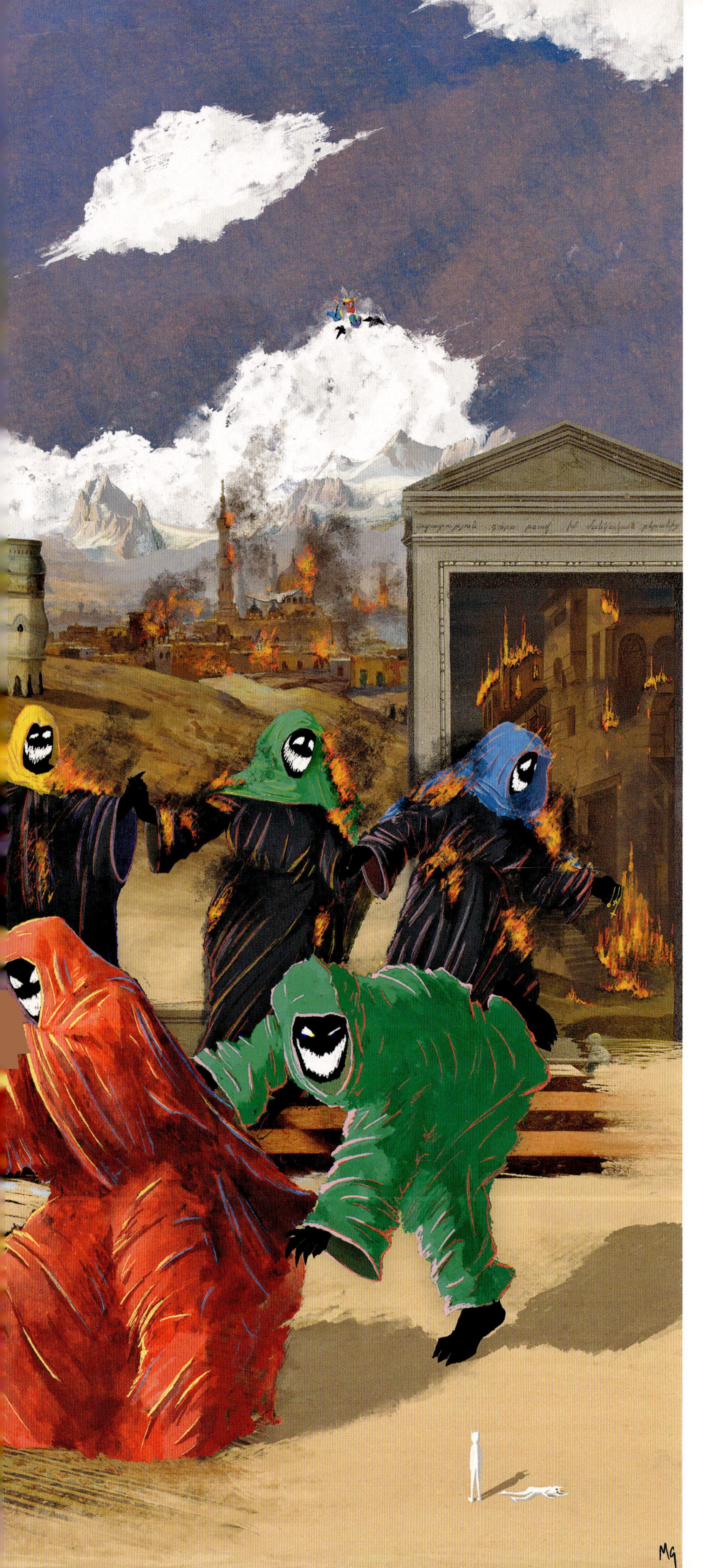

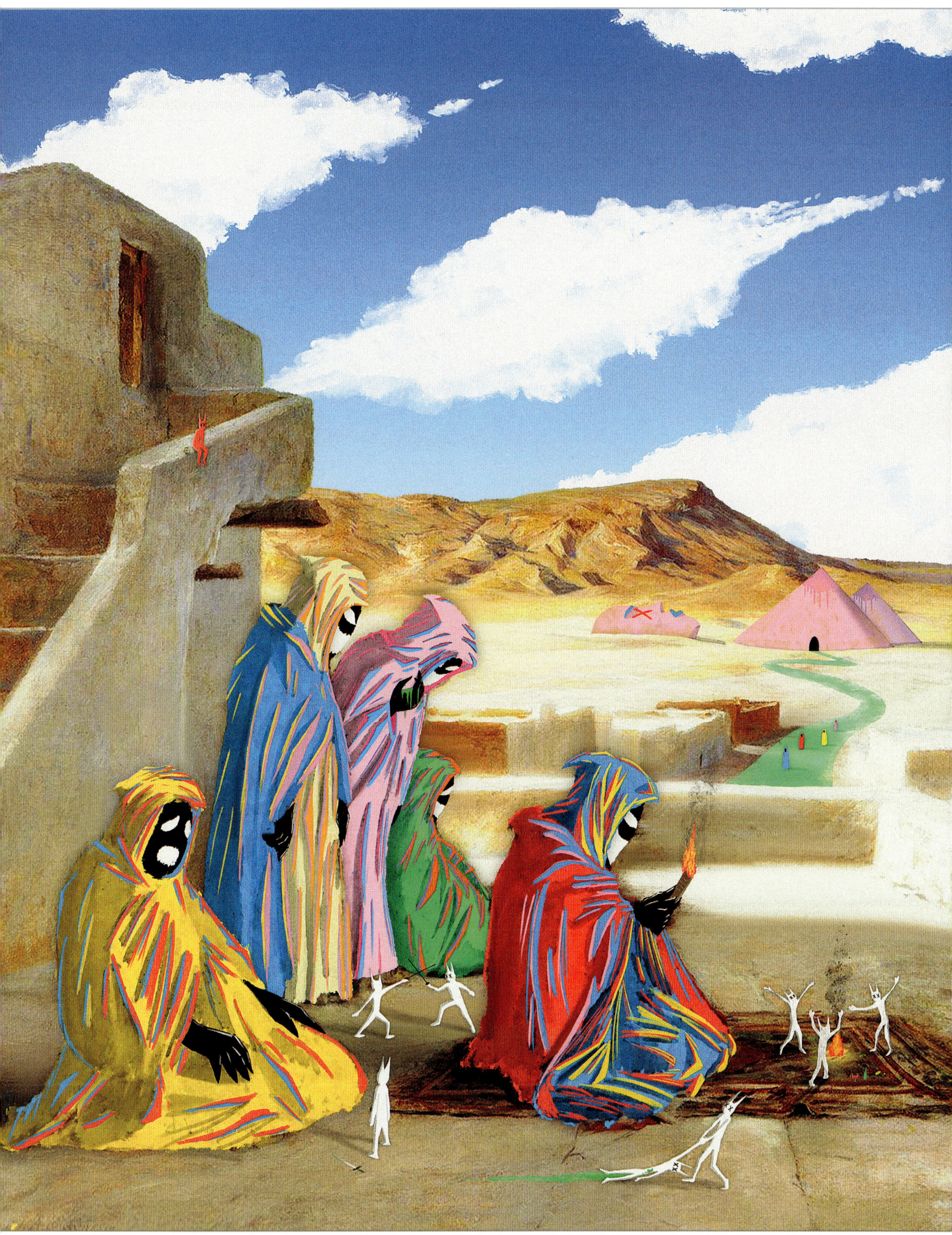

CEREMONY OF LIFE

But he doesn't stop here; everything influences and rouses his curiosity. "So many things inspire me! There are the artists who preceded me, then the music, the movies, and, more generally, my vision of life. Inspiration lies everywhere!" he states.

His protagonists arise from his own imagination: "My characters, the Fiends, represent the dark side of human beings. Chromatic tones are really important in my art. Bright colors dominate and are applied to canonical paintings, leading to contrasts that let my Fiends project to the maximum." His favorite color? "Blue, of every shade. There's a great deal of scientific research on the meaning of colors and their effect on the human mind. That's why I pay particular attention to them," he says.

Other World sees himself as a psychedelic and surrealist artist. He doesn't like to reveal too much about his art, as he prefers that people identify with it, constructing their own stories and their own world within it . . . He views his art as a path progressing upward, rising to the ephemeral but also descending into the most hidden corners of our minds, pushing us to confront and pose questions to ourselves, and leading to the discovery and adventurous exploration of that which was the past and that which the future could be.

It is for this reason that Other World regards the present as a moment that is always merely the prelude to the future. For him, the decision to stop can only be a temporary one; the push ahead is necessary. "AI is an inevitable technology to which we must adapt. I see it as a tool, not as competition," he predicts.

"Morality is important to every aspect of existence; it's fundamental to the very concept of humanity. Egoism doesn't lead to anything good, which is why I try to encourage and support other emerging artists by collecting their works or simply sharing my favorite ones," he notes. In terms of his vision, Other World recalls his Fiends, who reflect on aspects of life and death, elements that are marvelously wed in an extraordinary kaleidoscope of emotions, highs and lows, and constitute the mirror of existence itself, which can be both beautiful and terrifying. This is why his art has the power to touch people's hearts.

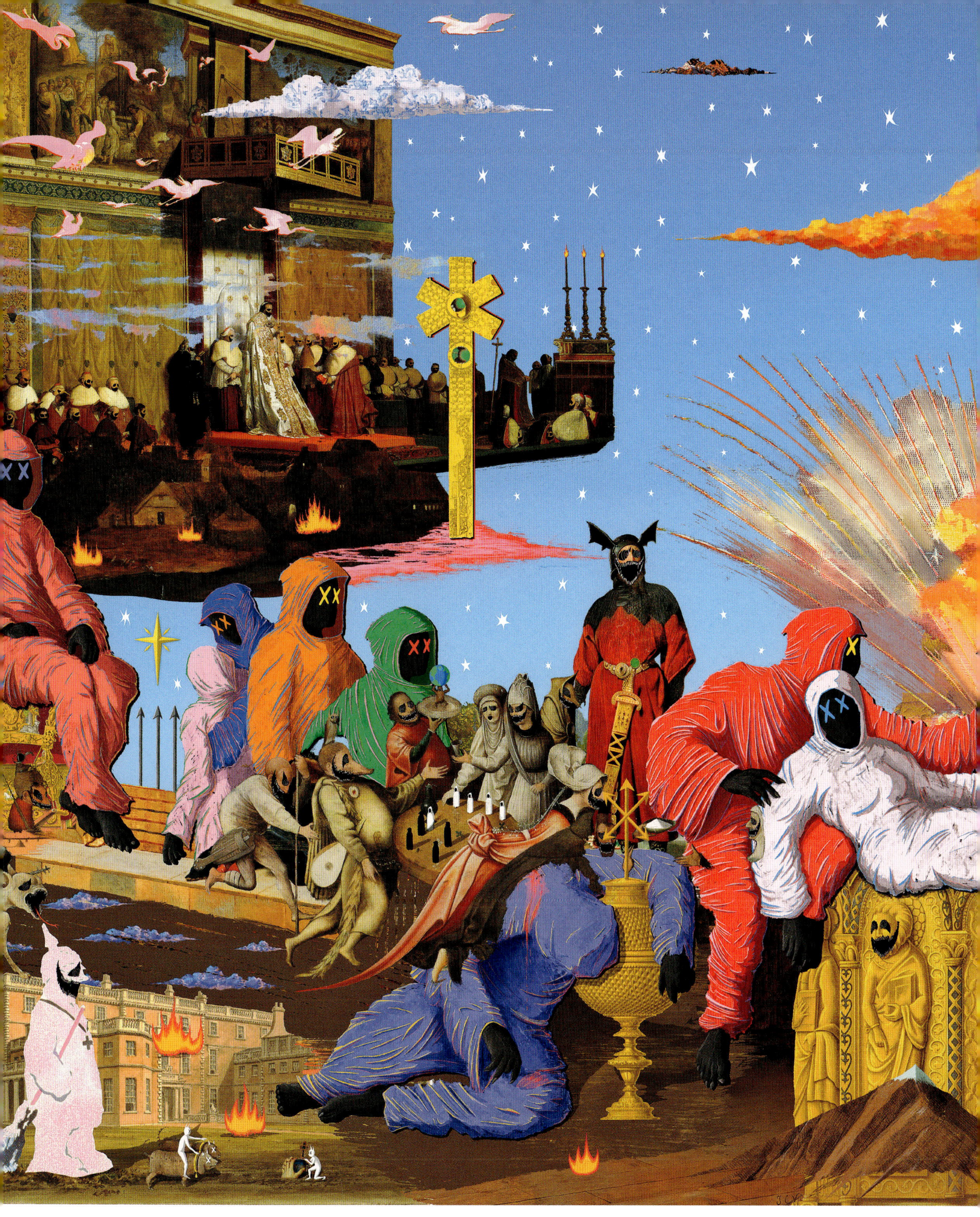

EVERYTHING AT ONCE

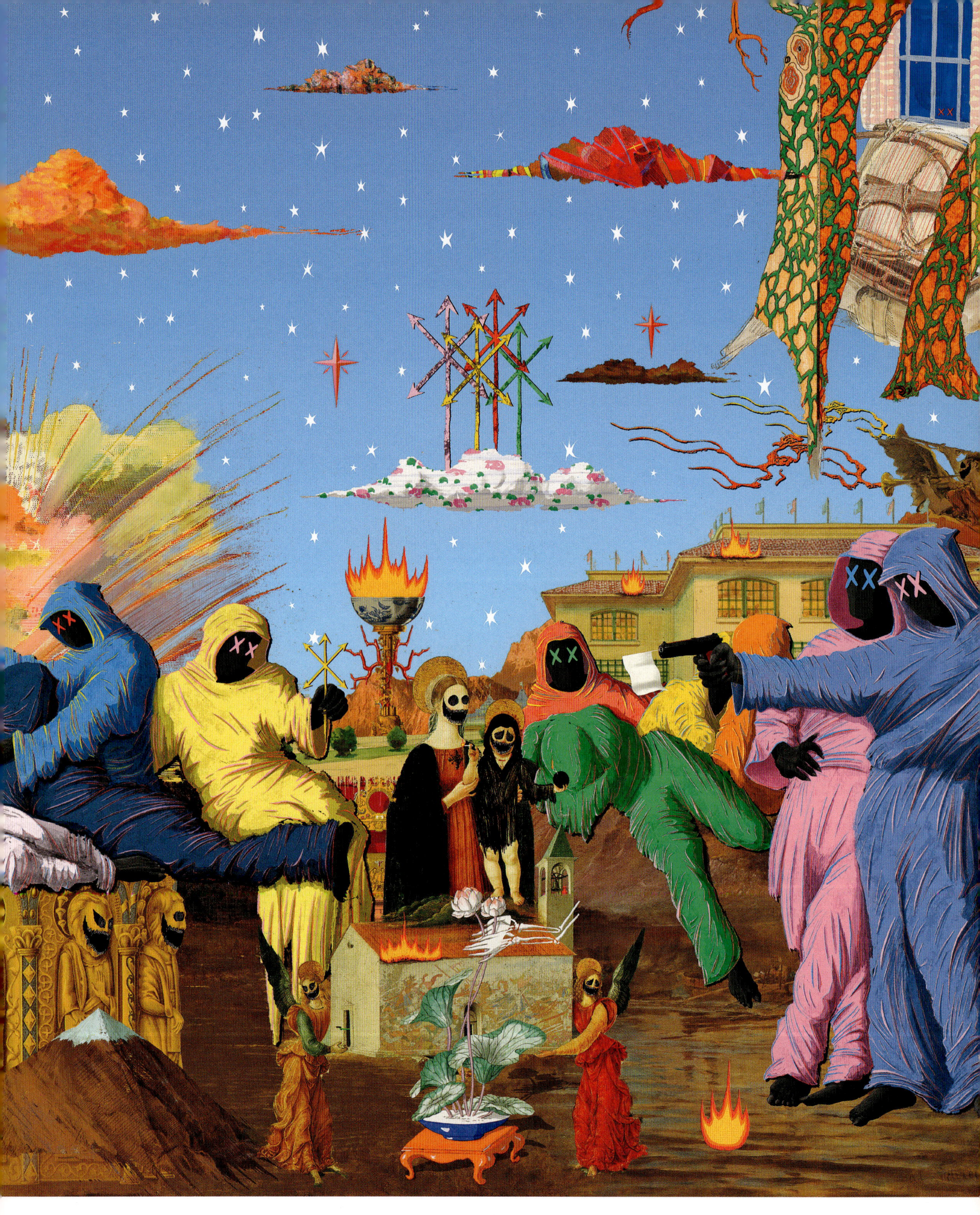

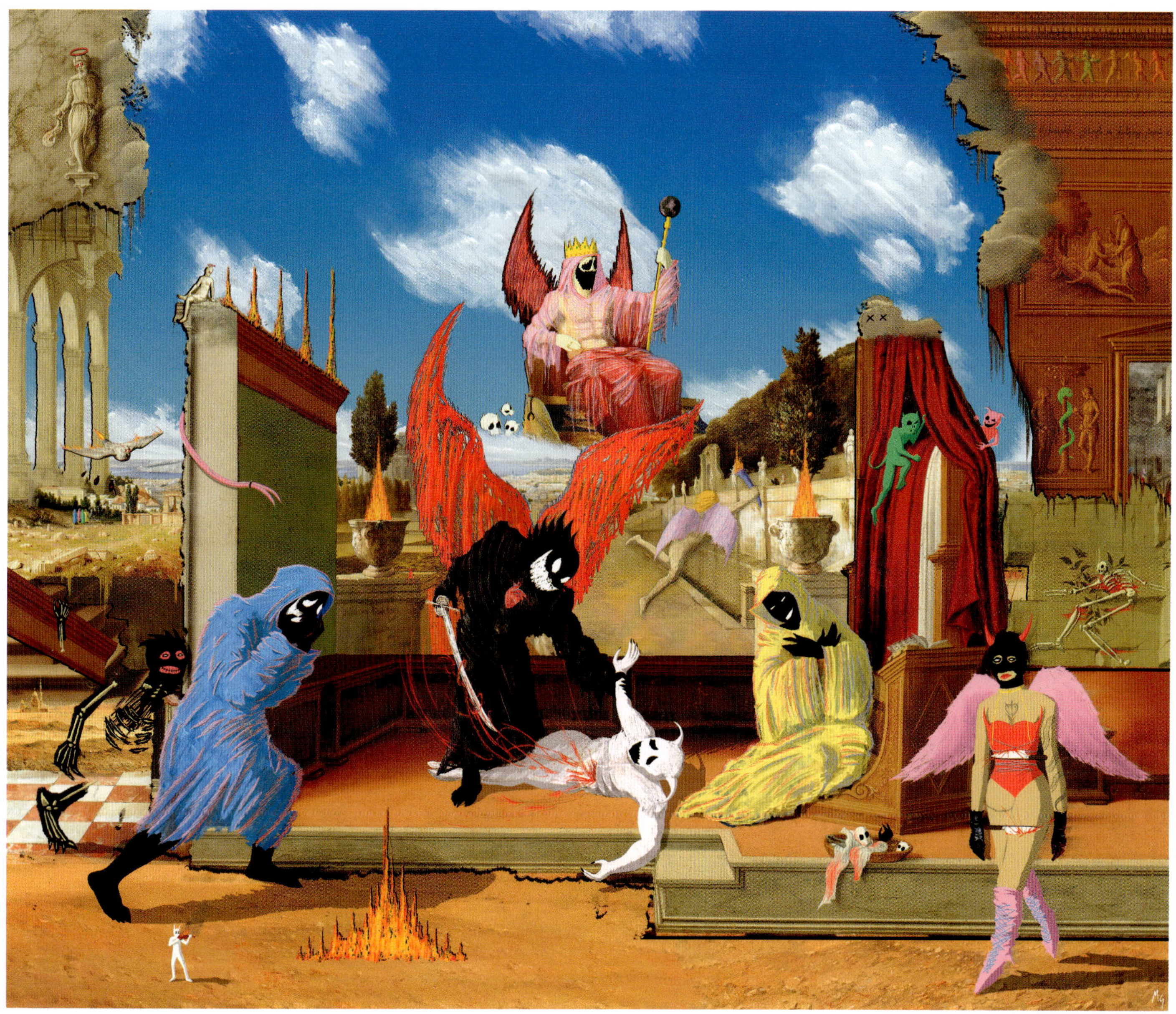

THE FALL

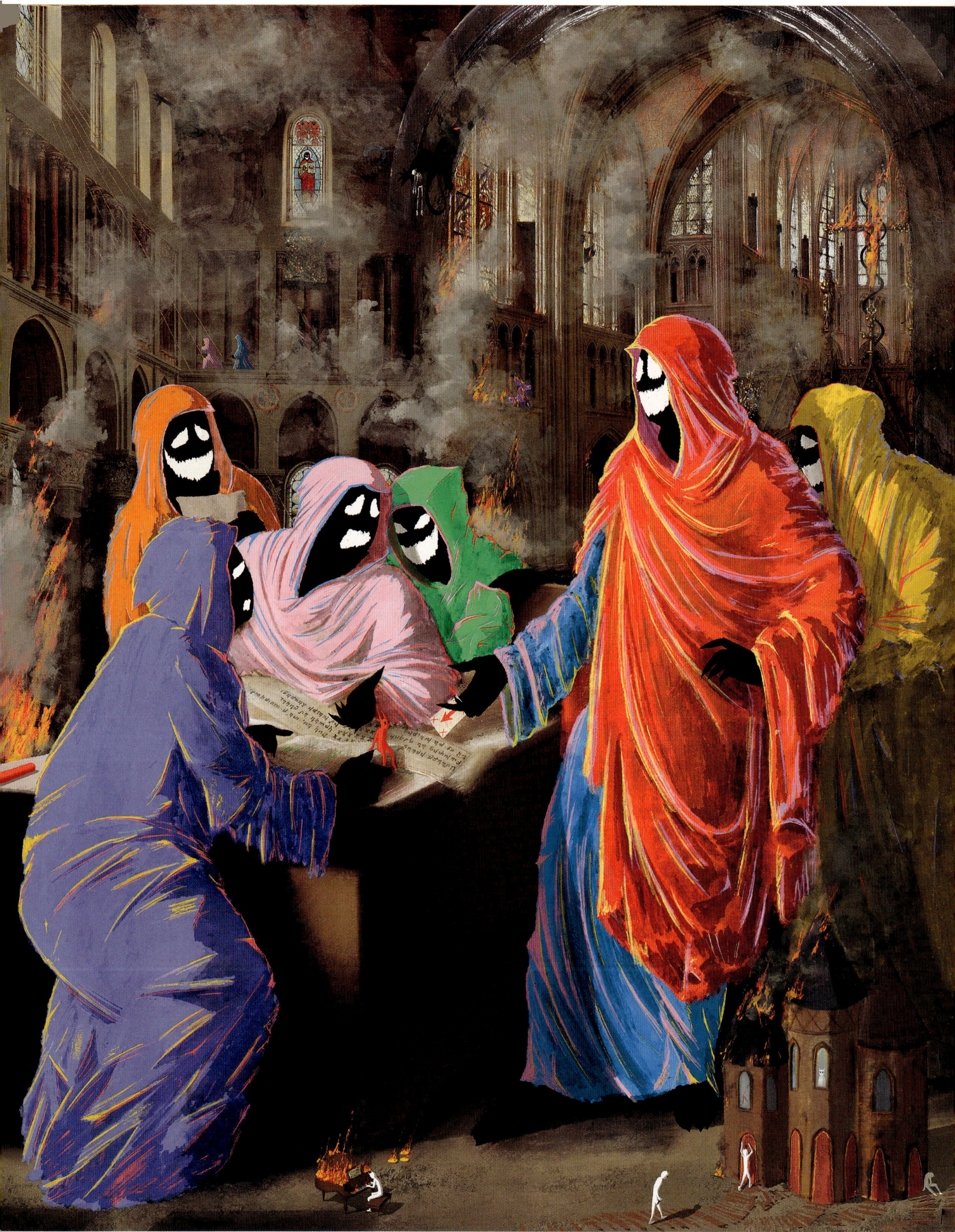

ANDRÉS REISINGER

||||||||||||||||||||||||||||||||||||||||||||||||||||||||||||||||||||||||||||||||||||||||||||||||||||||||||||||||||||

WHEN VISION BECOMES REALITY

"THE TECHNOLOGY AVAILABLE TO US TODAY IS INCREDIBLE, BUT, AT THE END OF THE DAY, IT'S NOT ALL THAT DIFFERENT FROM GUTENBERG'S INVENTION OF PRINTING WITH MOVABLE TYPE . . . IT WORKS ON THE SAME PRINCIPLE . . ."

Progress calls for imagination. And human imagination is the basis for understanding anything. Andrés Reisinger is a genuine visionary. His artistic creations seem like the dreams of a fabulous and absurd imagination. Recalling the ambience of some of Franz Kafka's books, they are simultaneously strange and awe-inspiring, as astonishing as they are hypnotizing, and capable of evoking remote and fantastical universes . . . "I don't know how I became passionate about art, as no one in my family was. Both my parents were scientists; but though they didn't put much weight on this interest of mine, they always offered me support, and this definitely helped me pick up the confidence I needed to move ahead," he says.

GRIS DIOR GALLERY VIEW 2023

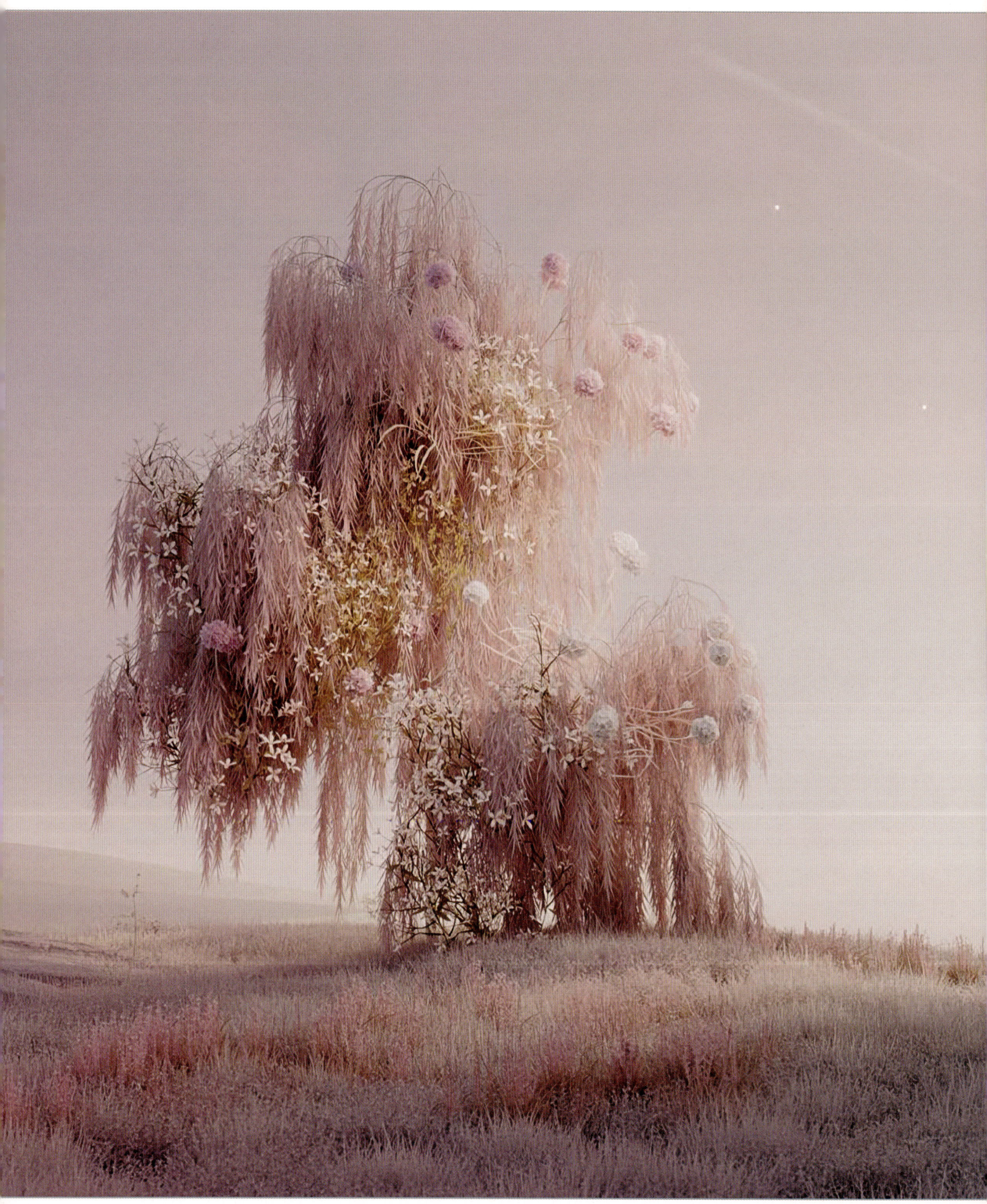

"I was especially crazy about music and all things visual. I used to draw and paint, but even then my mind was already racing toward something greater . . . From the time I was a child, I couldn't think of anything else but creating something out of nothing," he recalls. "It wasn't easy, because many people, even within my family, were opposed to my decision to follow this course, which, for the most part, they didn't understand. And it's precisely on the basis of my own personal experience that I always advise others to trust their instinct and not listen to the excessive 'noise' around them," he adds.

Technology was one of Andrés's first playmates, for which reason, probably, he feels totally connected to it and the images he discovered with it . . . As he recalls: "I was born in Buenos Aires, but I lived at the edge of the city in an immigrant neighborhood, which, in the 1990s—right when I was a kid—had become particularly dangerous. So my parents bought me a PC when I was only six years old to keep me off the streets. Playing with it completely changed my way of interacting with technology and its tools. I quit soccer and began downloading software and interacting with lots of people all over the world. It was as if I were traveling everywhere through my imagination. I moved among chats and forums, all of which stimulated me tremendously because I was coming into contact with so many people with whom I could share my interests.

"Letting my curiosity lead me on, I was constantly discovering different things, finding new inspiration, letting my imagination run wild, and inventing stuff . . . Boundaries did not exist; nothing was off limits: I could go wherever I wished . . ." Andrés

also had a gift for numbers, which contributed significantly to his artistic endeavors: "I had a natural talent for math and found it easy to pick up programming. I used my skills to design and build . . . It wasn't long before I abandoned manual activities and devoted myself solely to virtual ones. I found images on the Internet, adapted and transformed them. Or I invented them on my own . . . ," he says.

Andrés enrolled in the Department of Architecture, Design, and Urban Planning at the University of Buenos Aires, where he specialized in Design; but he didn't find this satisfying. After working as an art director at Plenty, an animation and motion graphics company in Buenos Aires, he co-founded Six N. Five, a multidisciplinary design studio, and, four years later, was able to open his very own Reisinger Studio in Barcelona, Spain.

Today he lives and works in Madrid, a city which, due to its air of freedom and its powerful energy, serves as a true and inexhaustible hotbed of creativity as well as being the place he now calls "home." "Argentina has definitely impacted me—very much so—but not in terms of art, since it's a difficult country, full of contradictions, and economically and politically unstable. It's like living in a zany universe that forces you to develop an endless capacity for instant change, adaptation, and reinvention for the sake of survival. This leads to a kind of cerebral anarchy that can definitely prove a gift over time, as it enables you to remain active and dynamic," he reflects pensively. "I'm very grateful for the twenty years I spent in Buenos Aires. Now I'm ready for anything, because I've lived through experiences of all sorts and overcome so many obstacles.

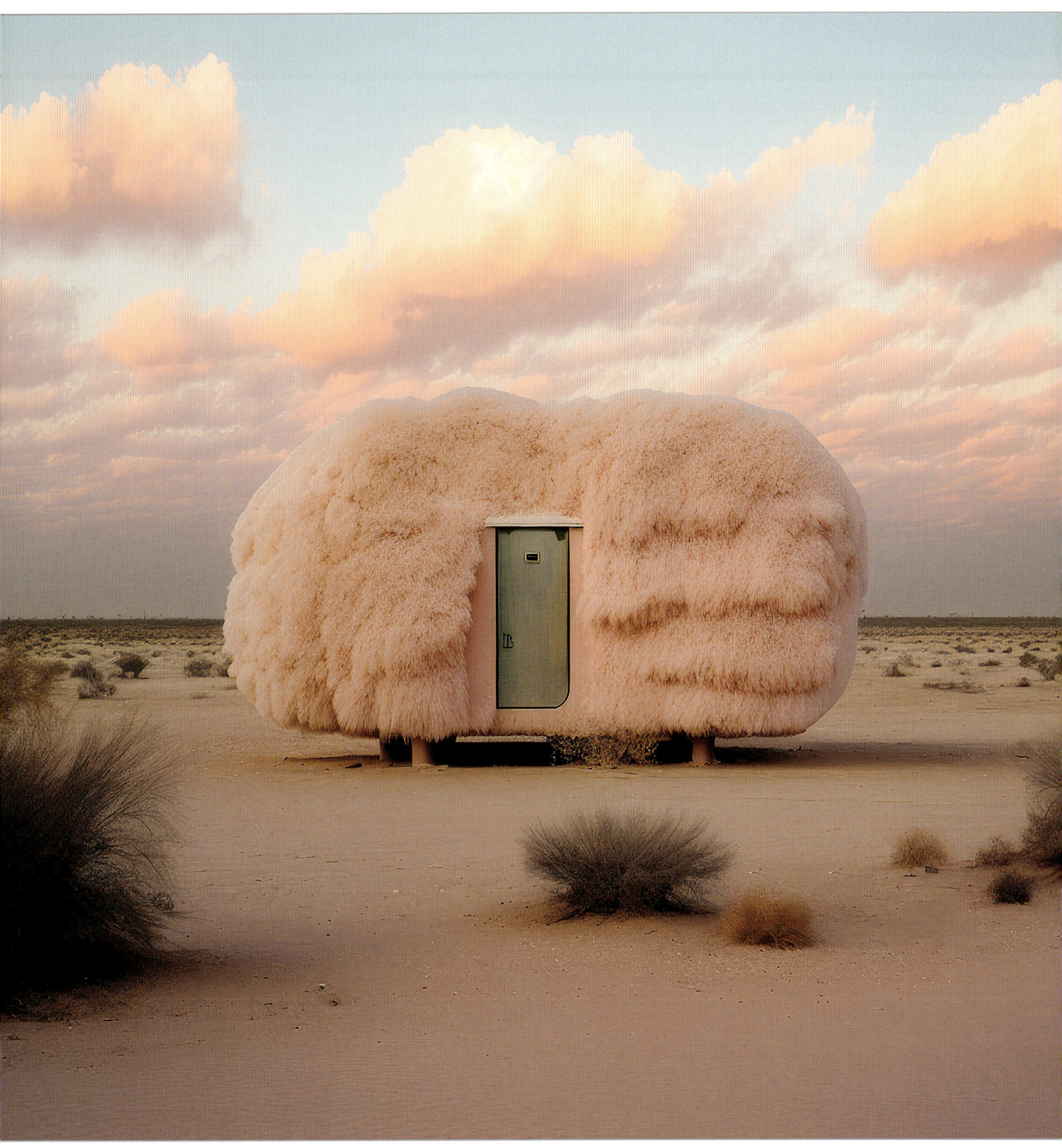

TAKE OVER DUBAI 2023

There were many beginnings, as, whenever the context changes, you too have to start all over again if you want to avoid being excluded," he admits.

Andrés has a crystal-clear memory of the day on which he had a true and proper revelation about his future: "I was on some means of transport when I realized that I was wasting my time going to university . . . Did I really need a career and a degree, or did I want to live now? My sense of discipline and obligation were strong: I had picked it up from years of studying classical music, but something was missing . . . So I decided to take a chance. I quit university and contacted an artist in Spain, whom I'd been following for some time. His name was Sergio del Puerto, known in the art world as 'Serial Cut.' He was using 3D software to create his work, which was truly innovative at the time. I wrote him an email, asking whether I could work for him. Sergio immediately replied with a yes. This, too, is the power of technology: the ability to contact every corner of the world in seconds . . ."

Andrés worked for Sergio for some time—long enough to realize that he could not remain in Argentina. He went back home for a little while, then moved permanently to Spain, first to Barcelona, then to Madrid. This marked a fundamental turning point in his career. "When I was ten, I created a site on which I posted everything I did; but in my country few people followed me or were interested in my work. Madrid and Barcelona, by contrast, were literally exploding with ideas; many artists were relocating there, and I felt part of this movement," he openly admits. "Working with other artists, I learned how to make my art more accessible. The result was immediate: I became really popular right away," he continues.

"I had an opportunity to meet with other artists, musicians, and writers, with whom I could share and discuss my ideas on a daily basis. What inspired me above all were people's lives rather than their creations—their way of life and making art," he explains.

With each day, Andrés understands ever more that his art is an extraordinary tool with which he can examine himself more closely and learn how he can help others to do the same. And knowing that he's succeeded makes him feel good. "I have a strong sense of responsibility to create works that can inspire and support others, just as others have done for me," he says.

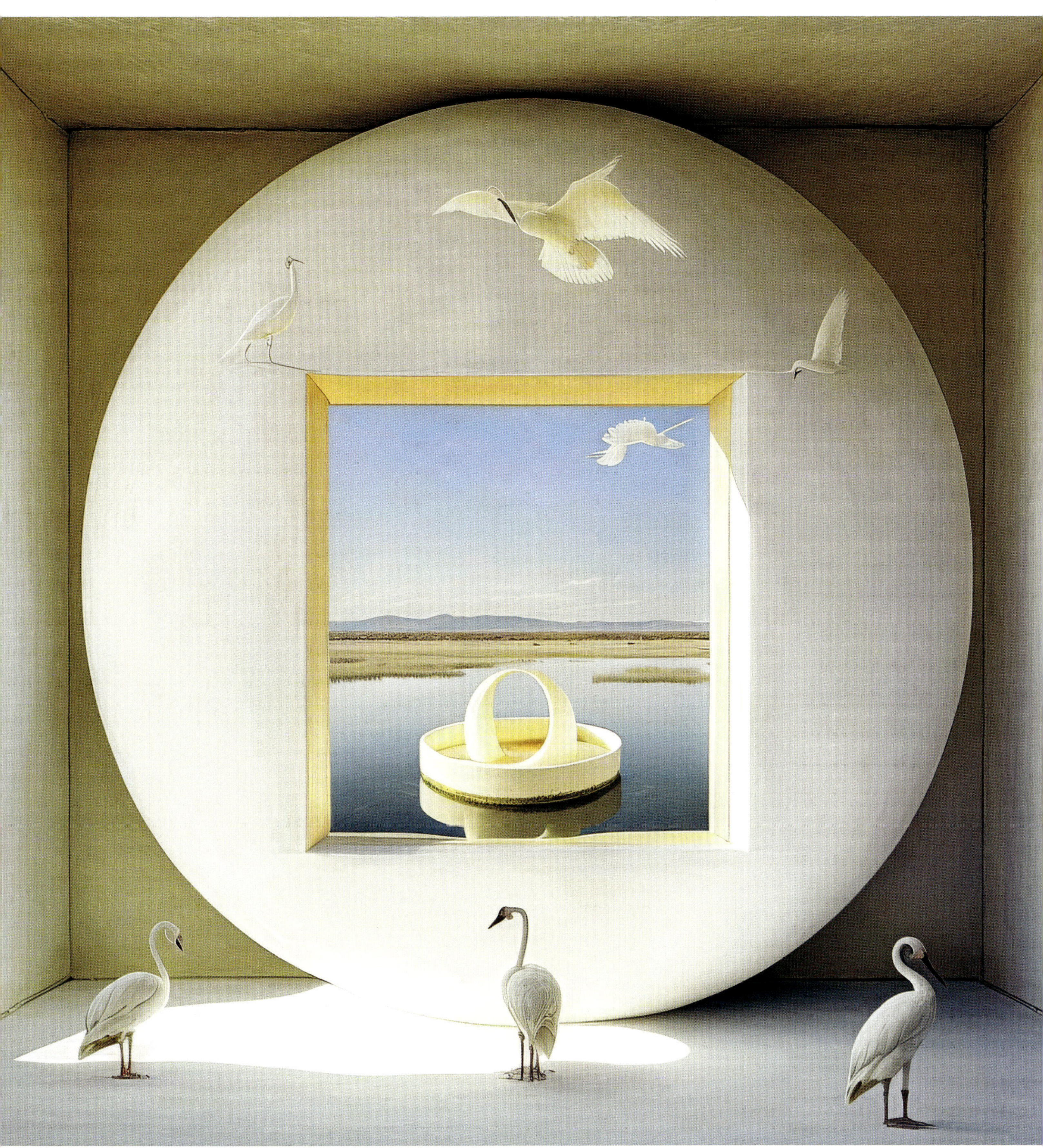

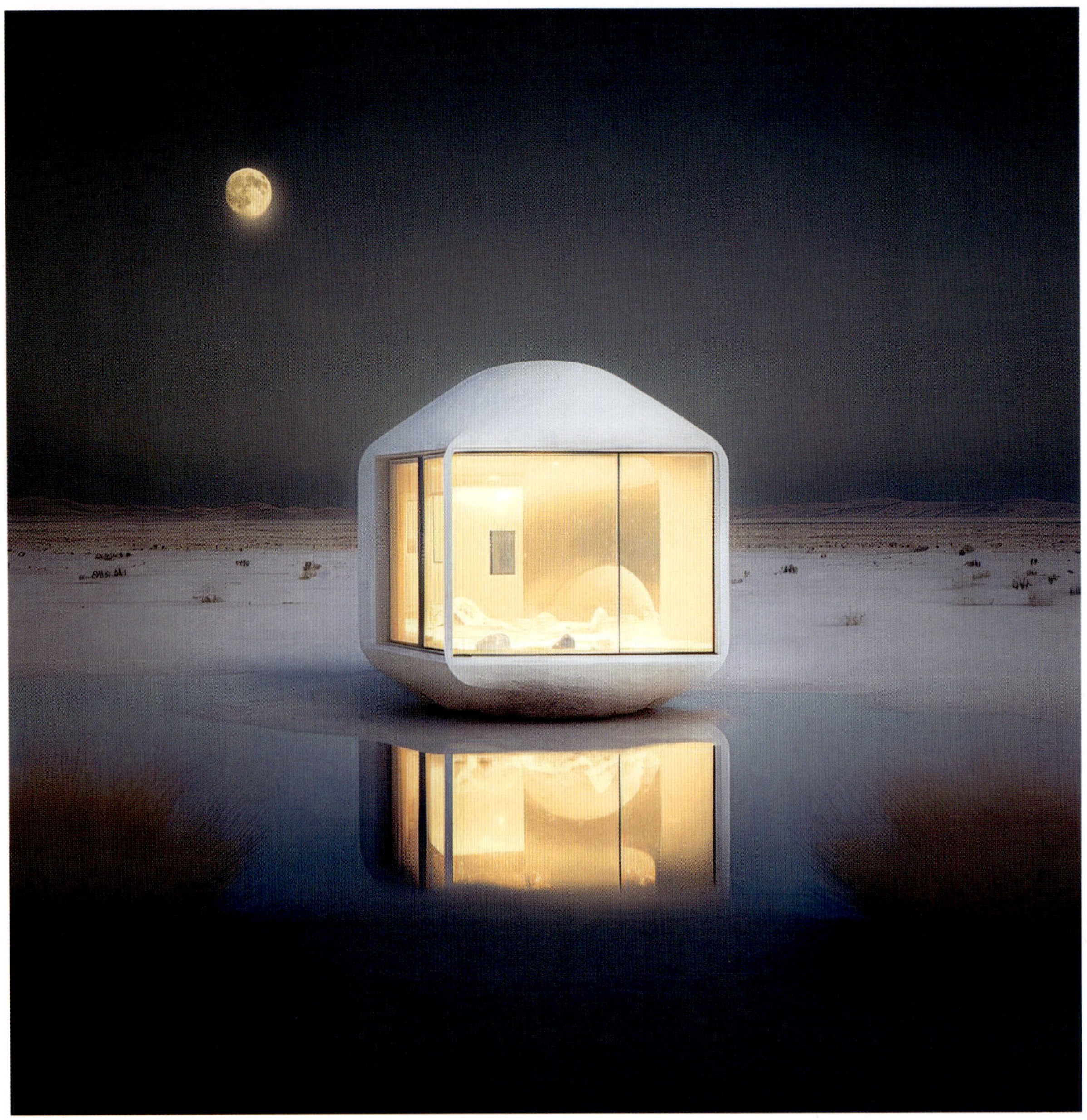

The moment matters tremendously to him. "I was born at a time when culture was being totally fragmented, and I have a deep belief in art's mission to reflect contemporaneity. Each artist must come up with their own style, new and eclectic, and push him- or herself beyond the frontiers of the possible toward the boundaries of the impossible. They must always produce something new . . . ," he claims. The fragmentation of time is as contagious as an epidemic, and today it's simply inevitable: "It's a far-reaching phenomenon that by now affects all areas of our lives. We're no longer able to dedicate ourselves to a single thing for a long time; we spend hours on our cell phones or computer, slaves of social media, connected to hundreds of people on a daily basis.

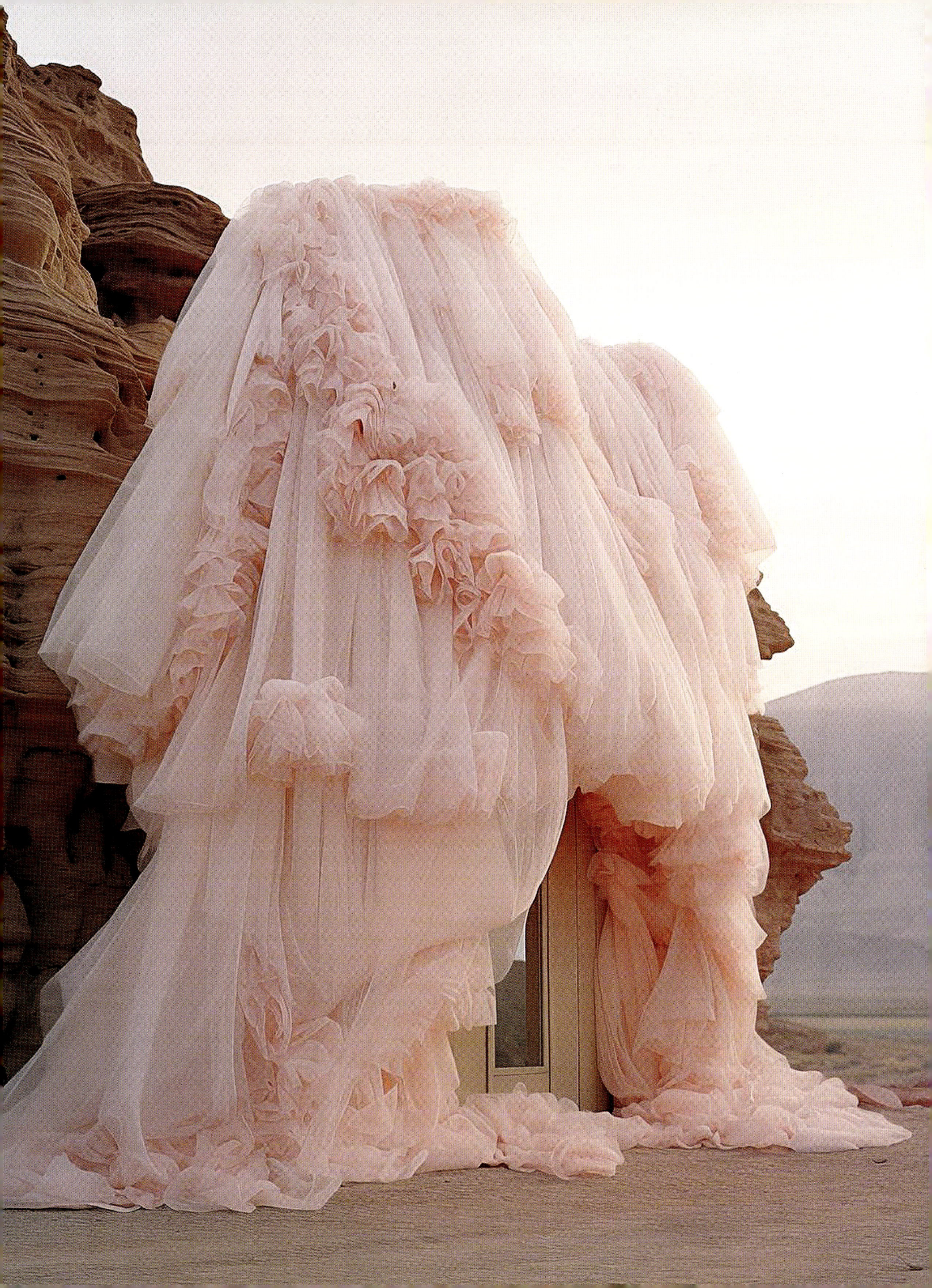

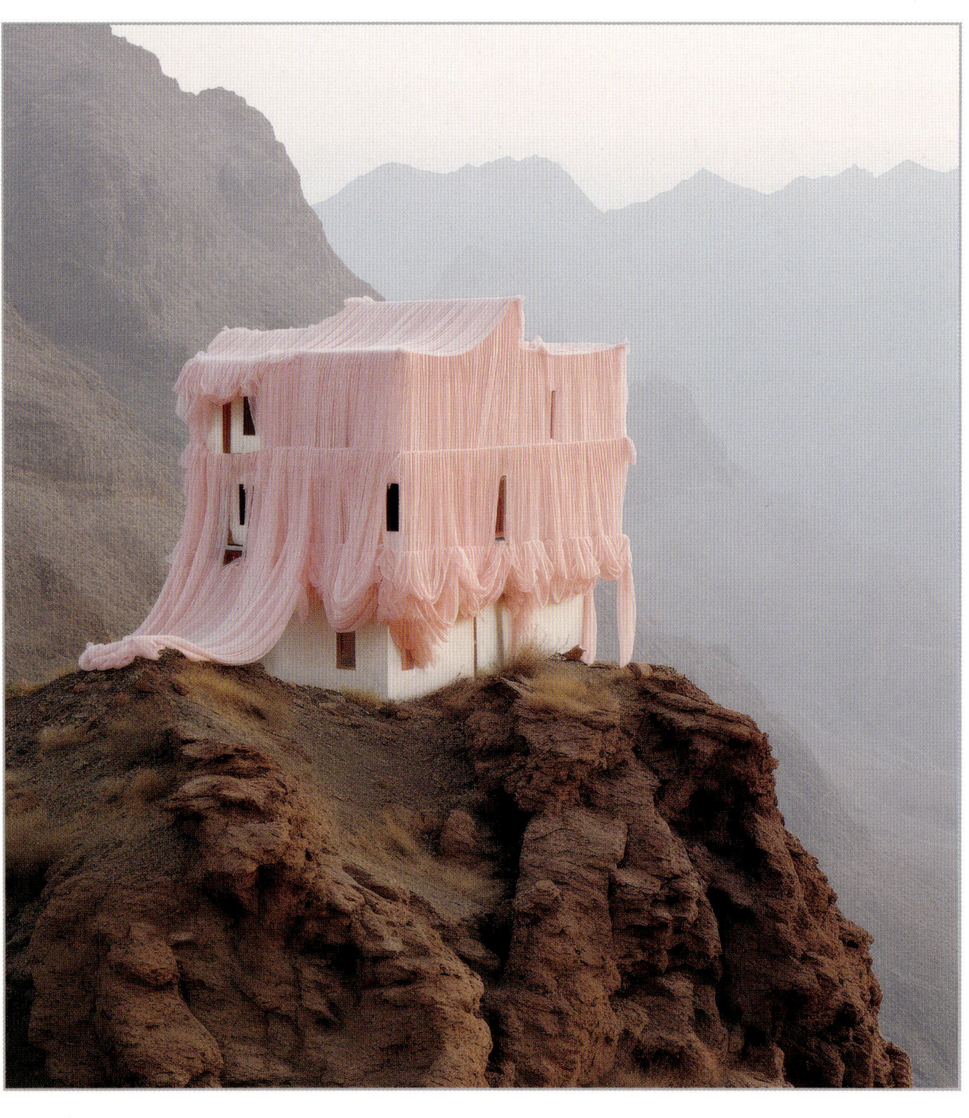

All this is part of our culture and our lifestyle, and I'd be irresponsible if I didn't represent it in my art," he explains.

Andrés loves working with various materials. "I adore the oil paintings of the great masters, but it's already been done and lies in the past. Today we're in the age of technology. Digital art is changing the art scene of the future. I was very young when I began, and there were only a few of us—a handful of artists who were regarded as antisocial and nerds because we were always pinned to the computer. Today we're the leading players of the moment," he states. "In the future, I'll continue creating digital and physical art with all tools available to me. I don't want to impose limits or place a label on what I do. I express myself in diverse ways: I don't believe there's just one field in which I can operate. Fashion, interior design, design—they're all sectors in which I feel I can develop my art," he concludes.

TAKE OVER SAUDI ARABIA 2023

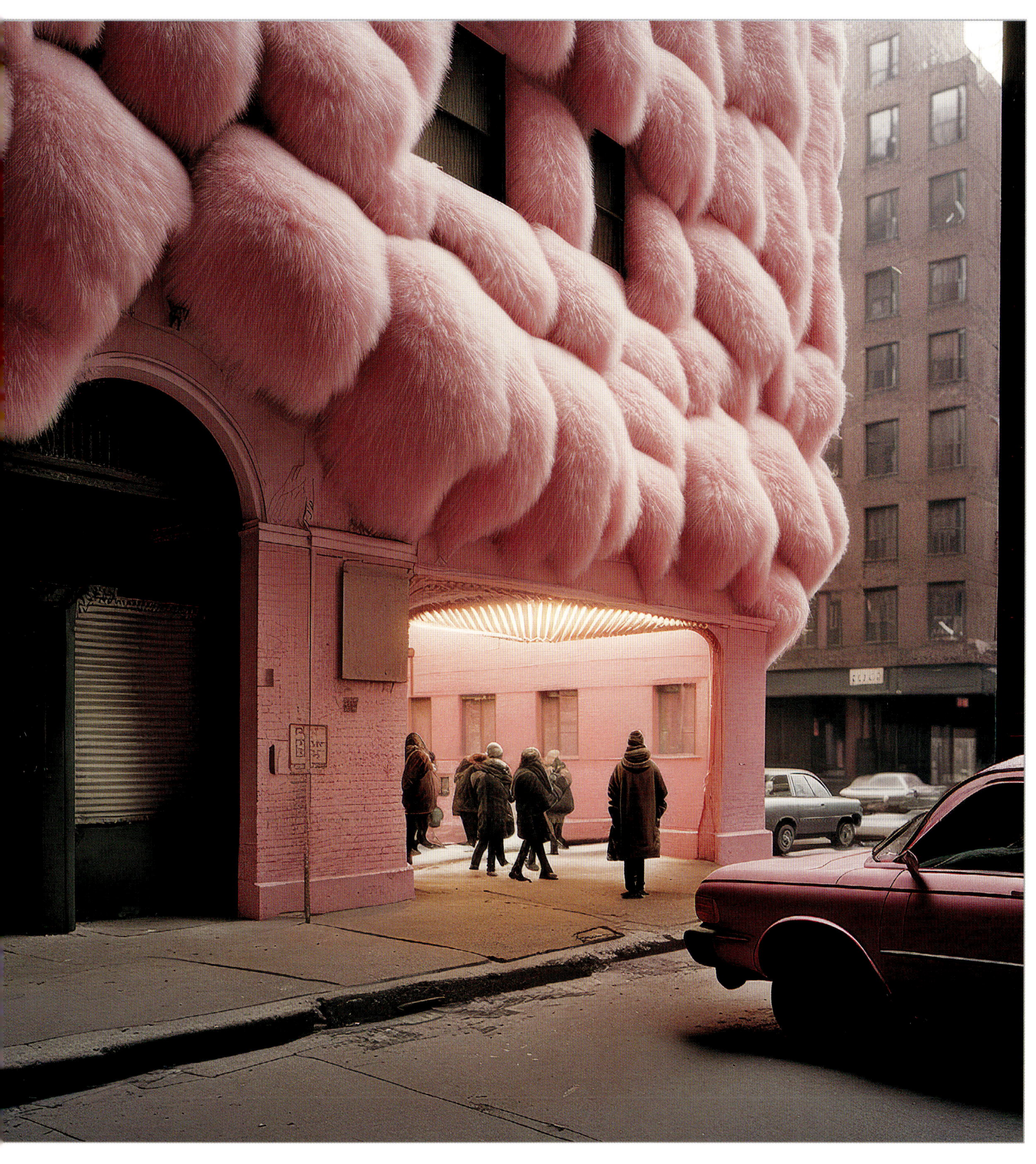

TAKE OVER NEW YORK CITY 2023

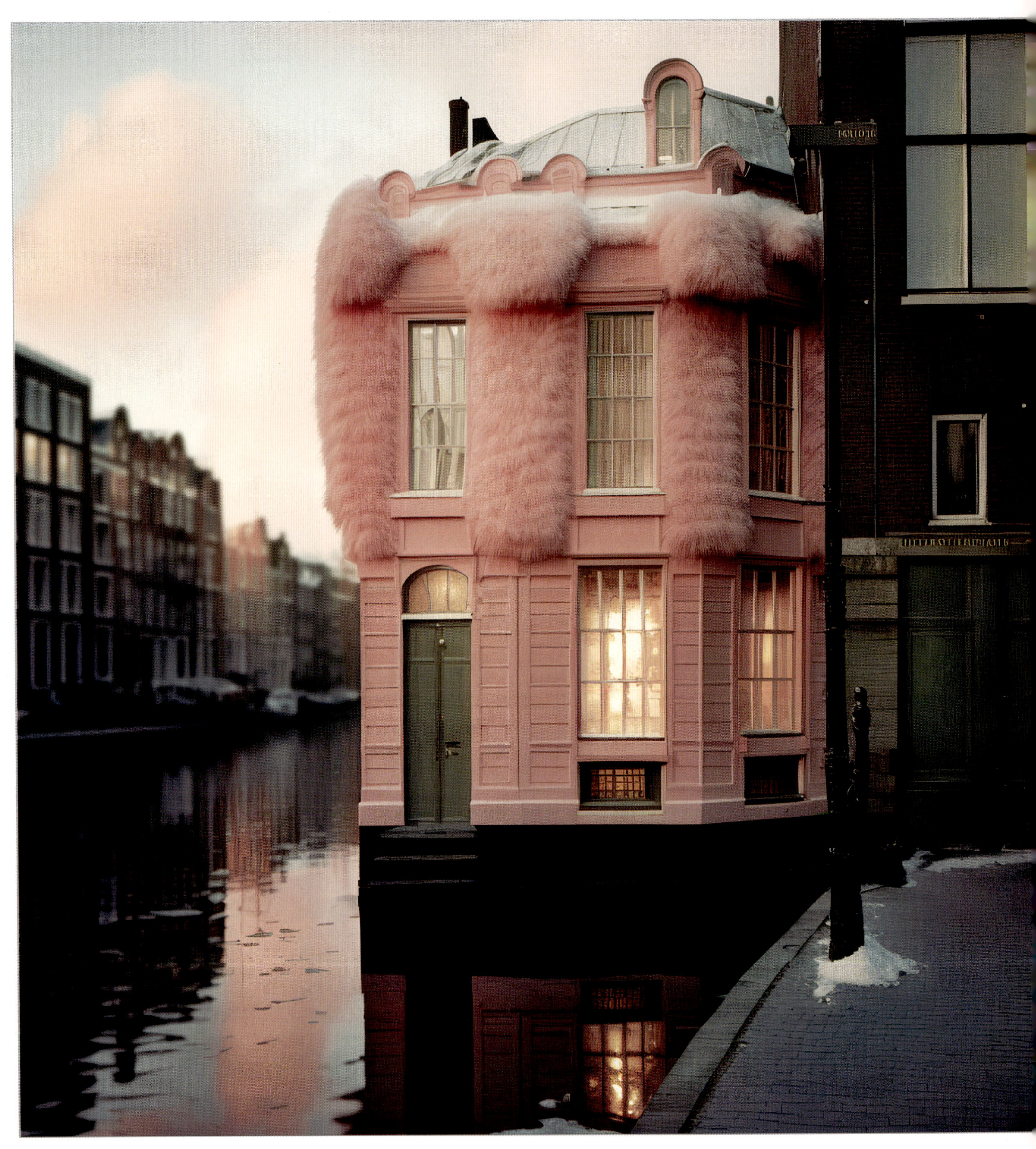

TAKE OVER AMSTERDAM 2023

MONICA RIZZOLLI

WHEN THE BOND TO NATURE BECOMES ART

"TECHNOLOGIES, FROM PAPER TO COMPUTER, GIVE ME RESULTS THAT WOULD OTHERWISE BE IMPOSSIBLE OR TOO TIME-CONSUMING TO ATTAIN."

It floats in a microcosm of flowers, leaves, plants, in which colors mix and mingle in a vibrant kaleidoscope of hues, emotions, and variable perspectives that cause viewers to reflect and confront themselves. Feelings strong and powerful explode in her creations, turning into spokespersons for something loftier that leaves an indelible mark on the spirit. Monica Rizzolli has a unique yet universal style, created and developed through the addition of a wide range of experiences. "My interest in art initially lay in printing. My grandfather had a print shop. As a child I was fascinated by the sound of his printing press. I was interested in movable type and proof sheets of illustrations. These early experiences introduced me to the concept of image-making, though at the time I didn't fully understand that this was actually art," she recalls.

HURT FINAL

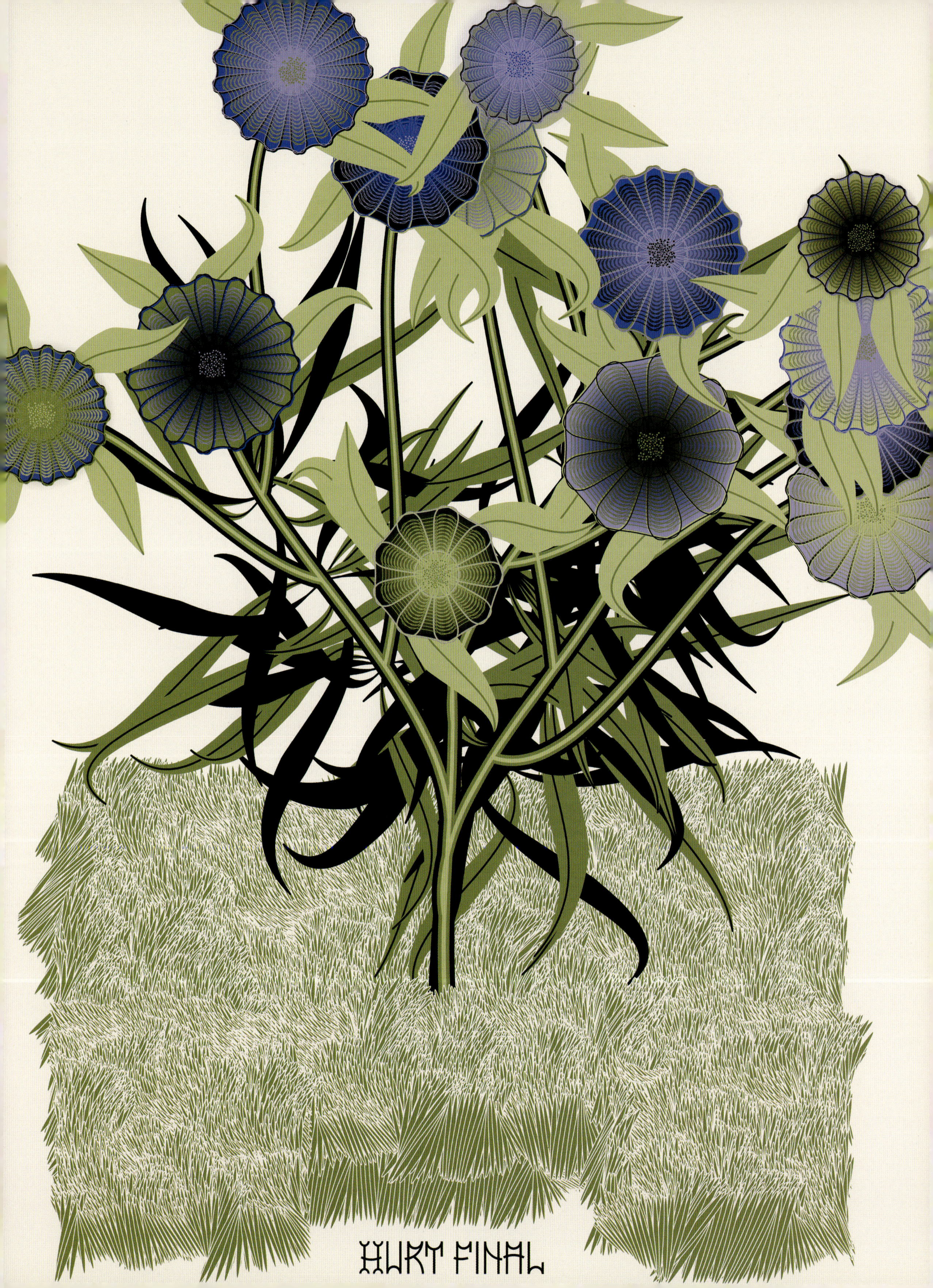
HURT FINAL

Her journey into the art world thus began quite early: "At age fifteen I enrolled in a woodcarving class, which marked my first step in formal art training. It got me interested in lithography and ultimately affected my decision to pursue print-making in college." At that point in time, the selection process for entering a formal course of study in the Fine Arts included a grueling drawing exam, so Monica had to devote herself to passing it with particular commitment. However, she was not yet imagining that it would seal her destiny and set her on a new path . . . "An initially casual approach turned into a far deeper passion. The sum of these experiences and recollections, from the noise of the print shop to my early years at university, definitely laid the grounds of my artistic trajectory," she reflects.

Born in Brazil, Monica now lives in Portugal. Her origins in a world closely bound to wild and pristine nature have continually inspired her. "From the moment I gained consciousness, I felt a tie with nature and regarded myself an integral part of it. Growing up in Brazil, I fully and proudly embraced my identity as a *caipira*, a term referring to a people and dialect often associated with the rural life." And her mind runs back to the most beautiful memories of that period: "As a young *caipira*, I enjoyed walking barefoot on the earth. I preferred to eat my food raw and learned how to distinguish between what was safe and what was dangerous to my health." Monica spent her childhood amid the wonders of Brazil's natural world as if in a fairy tale—discovering different environments, undergoing many experiences that enriched her sensitive soul. "The *cerrado*, a tropical savannah typical to Brazil, is one of the most common biomes in the region of Paulistania, and the one I knew best. Being a *caipira* meant having a profound relationship with the *cerrado*, with its plants, animals, and characteristic landscape."

Now that she has moved to Portugal, Monica has again opted for the country-side: "I live near the Vicentina Coast in the region of Montado. This area offers me a chance to learn and grow each day as I explore local biodiversity, gather flowers to connect with nature, and delve into the region's history and culinary practices. This continuous journey of discovery reaffirms my ties to nature, ones that began in my childhood and evolved with each new landscape that I have called home."

This strong connection was put to the test when Monica found herself con-fronting the fierce urbanism of big cities. "I've always believed that man is an in-tegral part of nature; but when I got to São Paulo, I had a hard time seeing its for-est of skyscrapers as part of the environment, and I felt a disconnect between my understanding of the world and the reality of what was before me." Monica has found salvation precisely in digital art, which is a world unto itself that likewise exists in isolation from all external conditioning. She began her career in the arts as a painter, studying first at the State University of São Paulo in Brazil and then at the Kunsthochschule in Kassel, Germany. A purely academic course of study soon became too narrow for her as her unbridled and adventurous young mind wanted to experiment and was bent on discovering new frontiers. In 2015, Monica presented her first digital art piece at the MAK Center for Art and Architecture in West Hollywood, California, and has since then worked and experimented in different sectors, demonstrating a natural talent for digital technology. In 2021, she launched her "Fragments of an Infinite Field" series on the Art Blocks plat-form. "I began doing digital programming in 2012 while living in Germany. I had just moved there to study, and was amazed by that new environment: what was normal for everyone else was a surprise to me! I realized that my memories had

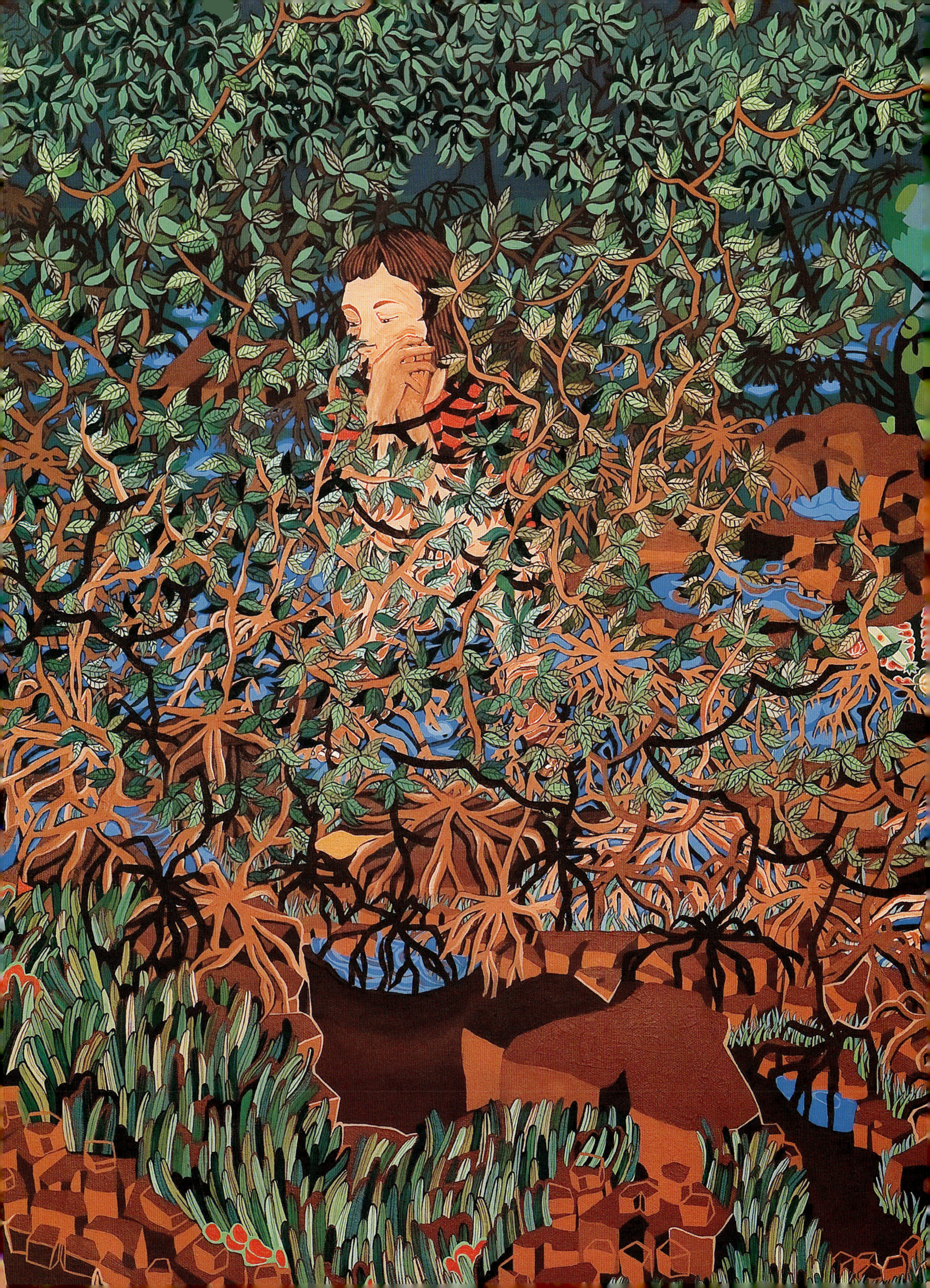

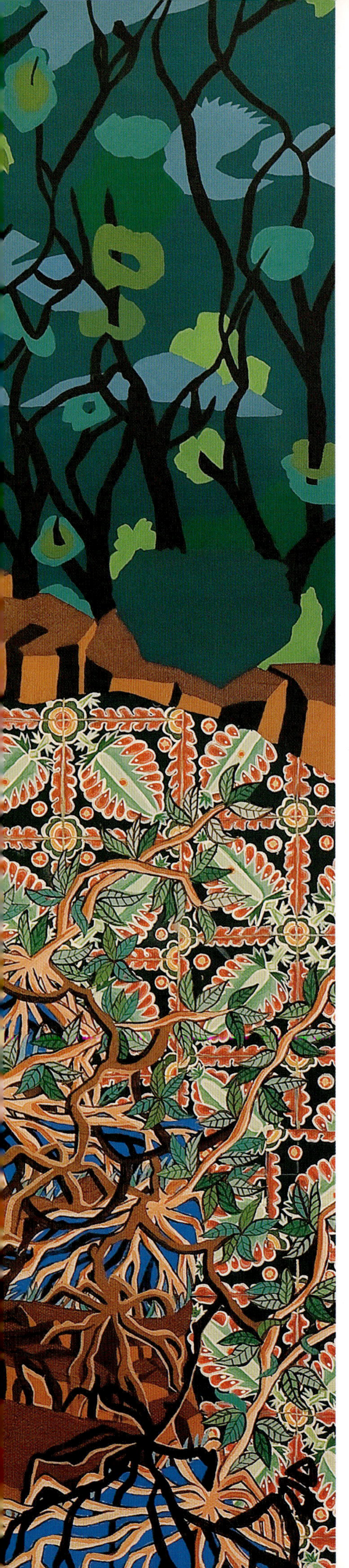

a tremendous influence on how I perceived my surroundings. Living in a tiny space with little money for canvas and paint, I started working on a small laptop, drawing mainly buildings and cityscapes; but, unlike the Impressionists, who had paid attention to the way in which light influences perception, I tried to understand how my previous experiences could affect my work and what I depicted," she says. And thus she created magic for the first time: "I thought animation might be a good way of putting those drawings together and imbuing them with a sense of transformation. It took me four months to figure out what I could do with programming languages, but in the end it became clear to me that this was the means of expression for which I'd been searching for my entire life. With coding I could write, instead of drawing, a picture. I could translate all visual elements into logical operations and mathematical equations. I was possessed of a precision that my hand could never attain; and, above all, I could use scientific knowledge to generate form."

From that point on, Monica has remained loyal to this digital process, becoming a major artist in digital generative art.

HABITAT AMBIGUO

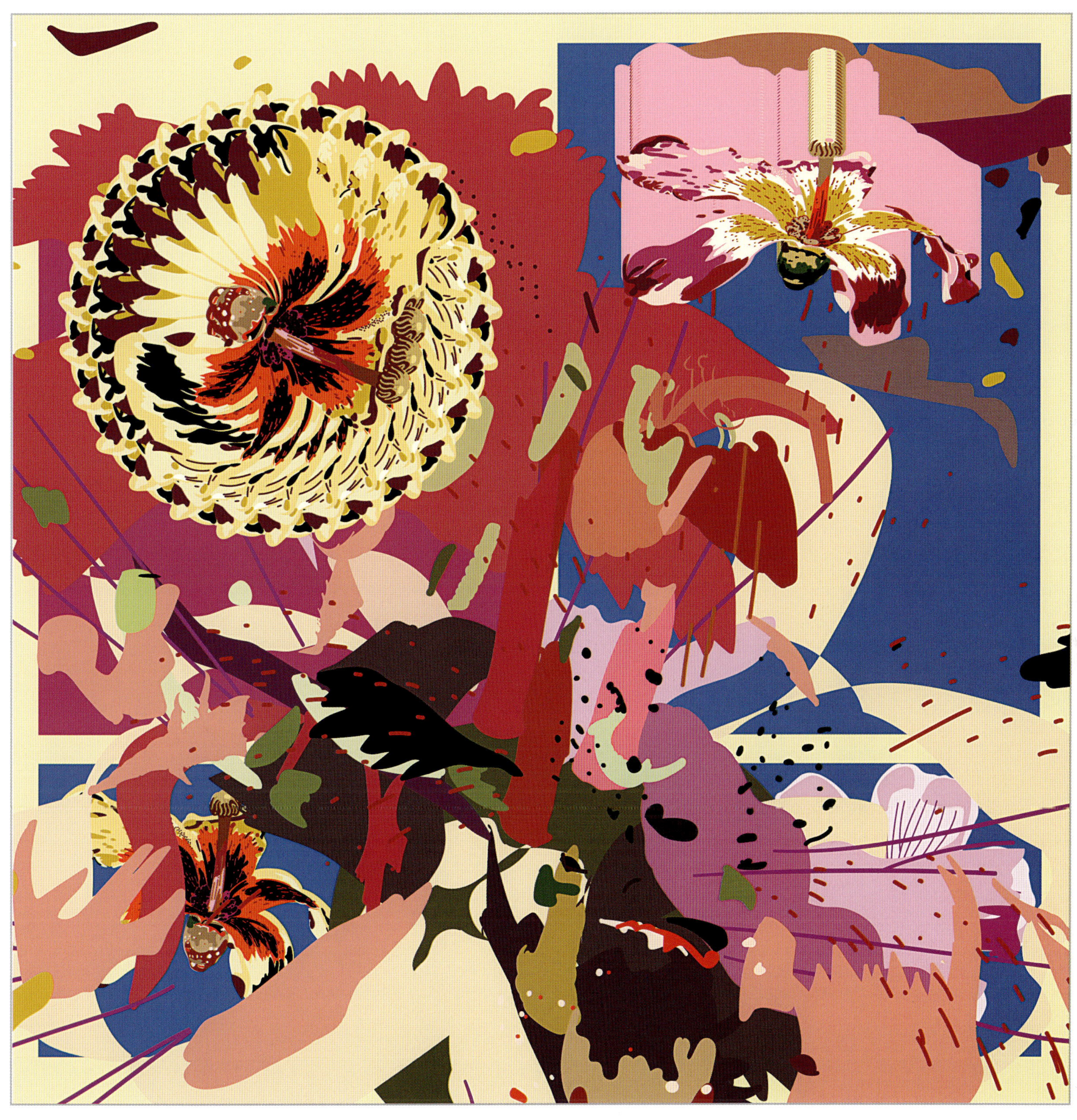

"The software I develop works like an engraving matrix; but instead of producing multiple identical results, it always gives rise to new ones. Since the results arise from the same source, they all have certain structural attributes in common, but the random component causes changes in other features, thus leading to the image's variability," she explains.

Flowers are definitely among Monica's favorite subjects: "I have many memories linked to flowers, but I must confess that my passion for flora began only during my years at university. I came across a book on nature's recurring patterns that contained a chapter on phyllotaxis—that is, the study of the order with which the various botanical entities: leaves, flowers—are distributed in space. This was the first time I realized that mathematical principles could define the appearance of plants; I had discovered a completely new branch of biology that dealt with form, structure, and development: morphology.

I collected as many books on the subject as possible and went to the village of Paranapiacaba in the State of São Paulo, known for the numerous paths that run between it and the Atlantic Forest. I spent several days there reading, observing, and drawing plants; these were intense days that changed my life." In the course of her research and multiple investigations, Monica came across Japanese art:

CEIBA SPECIOSA MEETS TIBOUCHINA MUTABILIS_2021

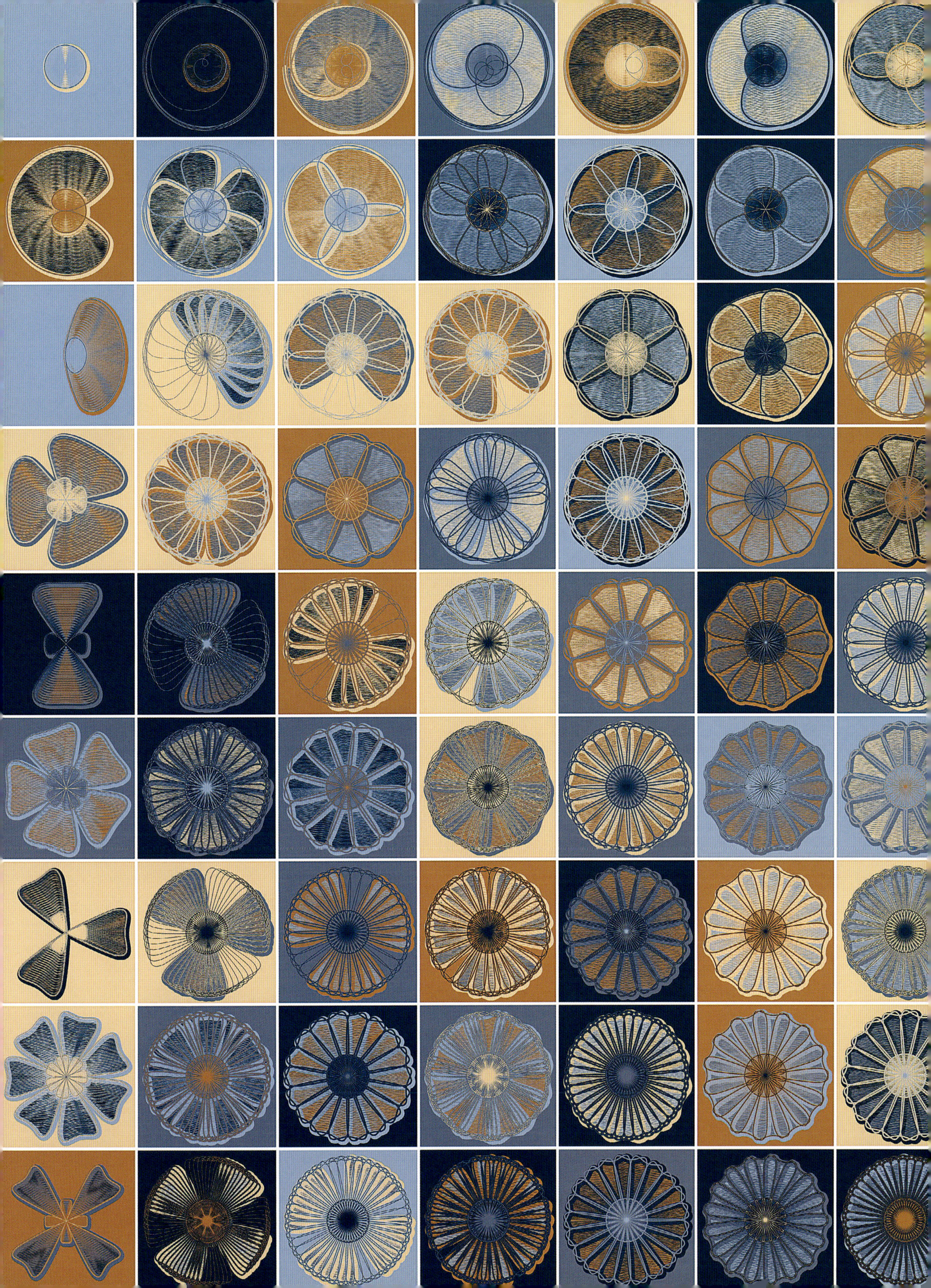

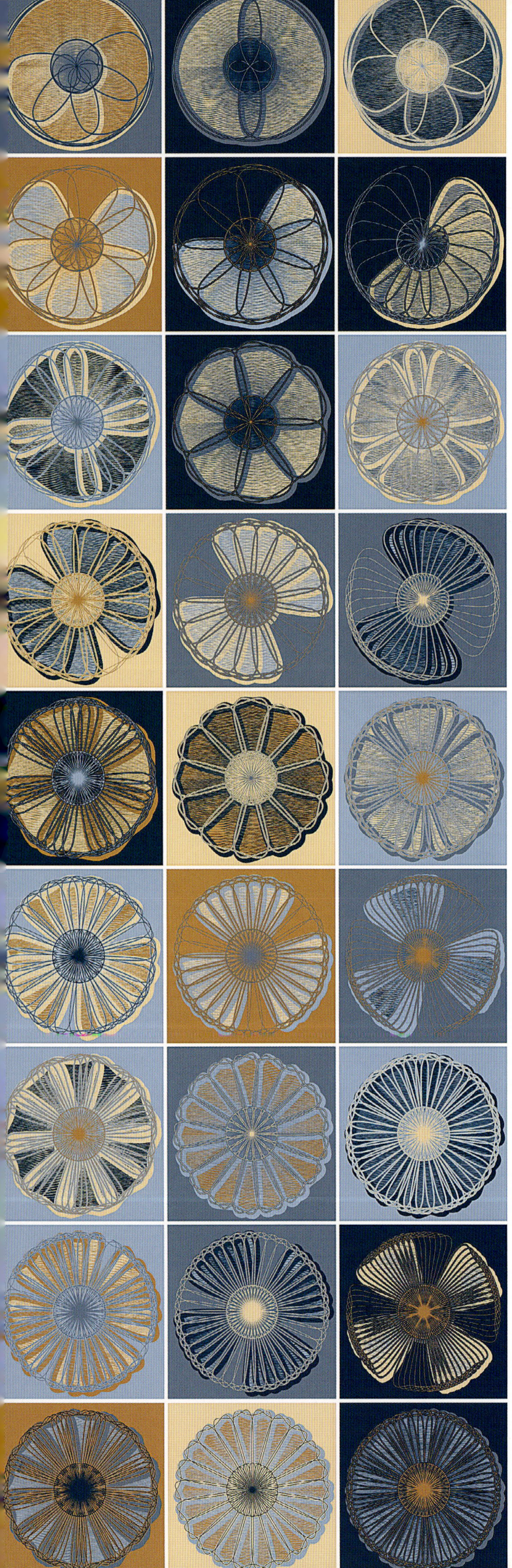

"As a teenager studying woodcarving in São Paulo, I paid a visit to an exhibition on Japanese ukiyo-e prints that opened me up to an art world of incomparable beauty.

The backgrounds of the prints contained infinite gradations of color, while the contours delineating bodies were thin and precise; there were complex fabric weaves and the most incredible landscapes, sometimes so geometric as to border on abstraction. Many compositions presented a clear balance between emptiness and areas full of color and detail. This was the first time I understood that to perceive the world, we need contrast. The sensation I felt that day has never left me, and its impact on my creative process has been enormous."

Her plans for the future? "I am preparing a work that I've entitled *Plant Script*. Actually, I've always been fascinated by plants, flowers, natural organic forms in general; but after consulting some ancient herbaria in the collection of the Los Angeles County Museum of Art, I decided to try to translate the structural logic of herbs and flowers with a digital technique and, using the Johan Gielis equation, to make a new manuscript that included artificially generated images of flowers. The work proved to be quite difficult and complex, but I'm really determined to continue and not quit the project," she concludes.

FROM GRAIN TO BLOSSOM

ALBERTO SEVESO

WHEN THE IMPOSSIBLE IS TRANSFORMED INTO THE POSSIBLE

ART AND TECHNOLOGY, WHICH HAVE ALWAYS BEEN CLOSELY BOUND, ARE TWO FUNDAMENTAL FEATURES OF OUR SOCIETY. THE HISTORY OF HUMANITY IS MARKED BY THE CONTINUOUS INTERTWINING OF THESE TWO DIMENSIONS, AND ART HAS OFTEN EMBRACED AND INCORPORATED NEW TECHNOLOGIES IN ORDER TO EXPRESS IDEAS, EMOTIONS, AND CONCEPTS IN INNOVATIVE WAYS.

Combining the real and digital worlds in a magical manner, Alberto Seveso's universe revolves around sheer creativity and improvisation. Faces and bodies self-generate among waves of color, moments of controversial existence and interrupted imagery, spasmodic feelings and emotions, revolutionary techniques and lines.

YOU WISH IS MY COMMAND

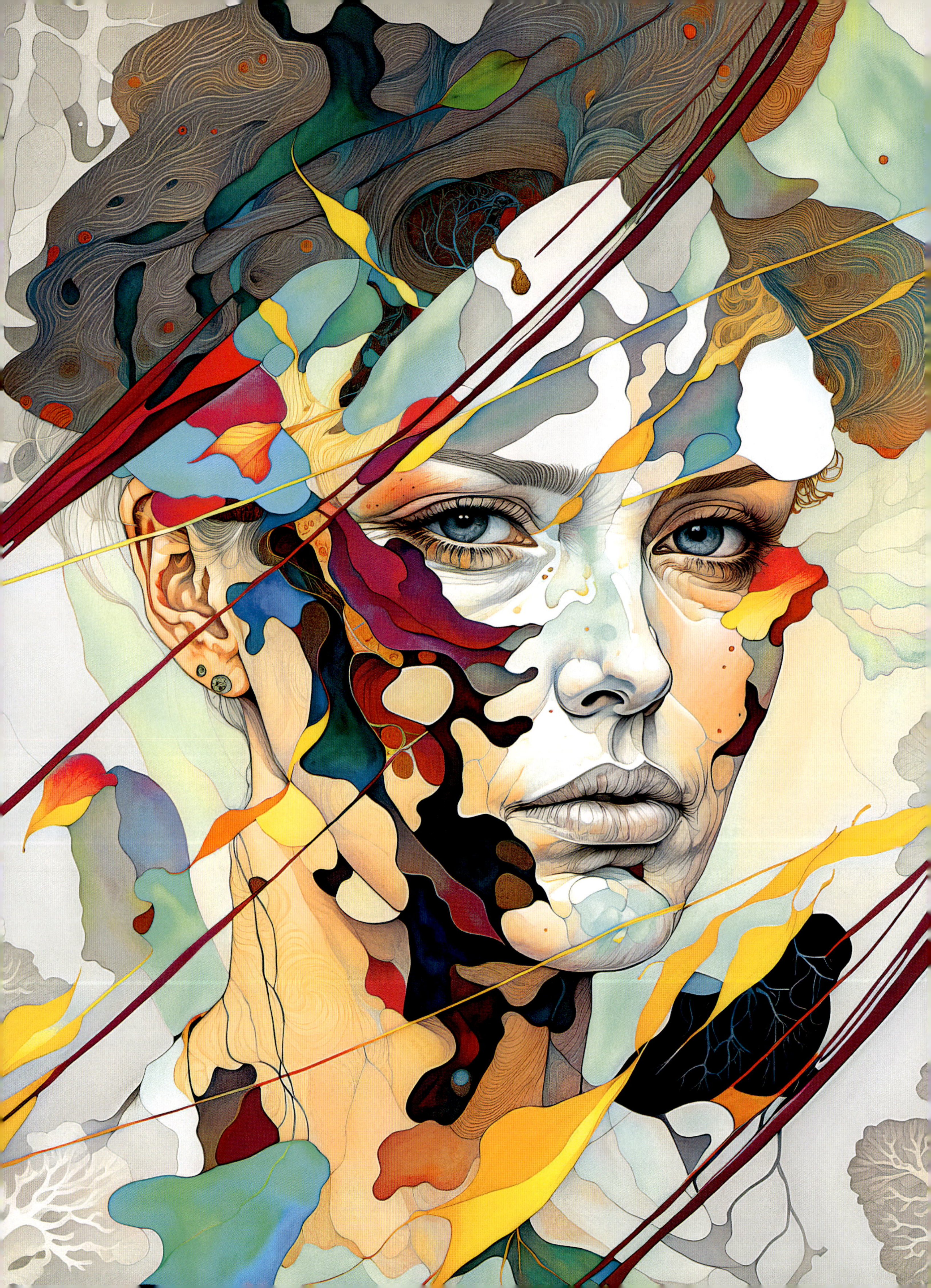

There's mystery and surprise. It's as if the impossible were to become possible. "In my view, today's art still amounts to a creative and meaningful expression of our humanity, but also serves as fertile ground for exploring the potential of modern technologies. By using digital tools, augmented reality, artificial intelligence, and other types of innovative technology, artists have new ways of creating, interacting, and connecting with their audiences. This broadens the field of artistic possibility and opens new frontiers to creative expression," he states. From the outset, Alberto has combined his passion for art with his love for and interest in technology, two areas that he views as closely related. "My connection to art has its origins in the 1980s, a time when digital technology was beginning to make inroads into our day-to-day lives. This was a moment of transformation, in which the convergence of art and technology began manifesting itself in a more obvious and widespread way. Within that context, I found myself informally involved in the world of digital art, exploring early graphic software on computer platforms such as the Commodore Amiga," he recalls. What began as a simple interest, a pastime, soon turned into a profession. "Discovering the expressive potential of digital technology opened new creative horizons and inspired me to explore the potential of this new medium. My first experiments with graphic software soon became a form of personal expression, a path along which I was able to direct my creativity. Without any clear intention of becoming a professional, I began working on random projects, such as designing posters for small businesses. These early experiences increased my passion for digital art and enabled me to refine my technical skills; at the same time, I also understood the importance of design and visual communication in the modern world," he admits. An epiphany came with a Commodore VIC 20 . . . "I was given one in the mid-80s. It was an IT platform that, in retrospect, launched the beginning of a fascinating adventure in the world of

technology; and, despite its limited abilities and simple but—for the time—innovative technical features, it opened a window onto the future for me. On the other hand, today's technology permeates nearly every aspect of our everyday lives and continues to advance at a frenetic pace. Aside from its practical and functional side, technology has an aesthetic and creative dimension that can be explored and appreciated as a form of art. Digital art, design, interactive architecture, and many other types of artistic expression are fostered by technology and reflect our constantly evolving relationship with the digital world," he continues.

Alberto is a multidisciplinary, self-taught artist. A fan of skateboards and heavy-metal band album covers, he got into graphic design in the early '90s. He's also regarded as one of the pioneers of dispersion technique, by means of which he destroys images to create new ones in an incredibly harmonious, unique, and original manner: that is, by deconstructing to reconstruct. "Since adolescence, music has always been an important and constant presence in my life. Its impact on me has been profound and complex, and it continues to inspire me and enhance my experiences to this day. In my youth, I was really fascinated by heavy-metal album covers—veritable works of visual art—that became sources of creative inspiration and pushed me to explore new dimensions of art and music. Although initially I was drawn primarily to heavy metal, as time passed my taste in music expanded and came to encompass a broad range of genres, from rock to hardcore and beyond. Today I'm open to any type of music that manages to capture my attention and move me. Like art, music is a journey of continuous discovery," he claims. His inspiration has no limits, recognizes no barriers; his mind is open to every stimulus. "What inspires me most is everyday life and everything that surrounds me. I find it exciting to observe the world and grasp the elements that arouse emotions, reflections, and creative ideas.

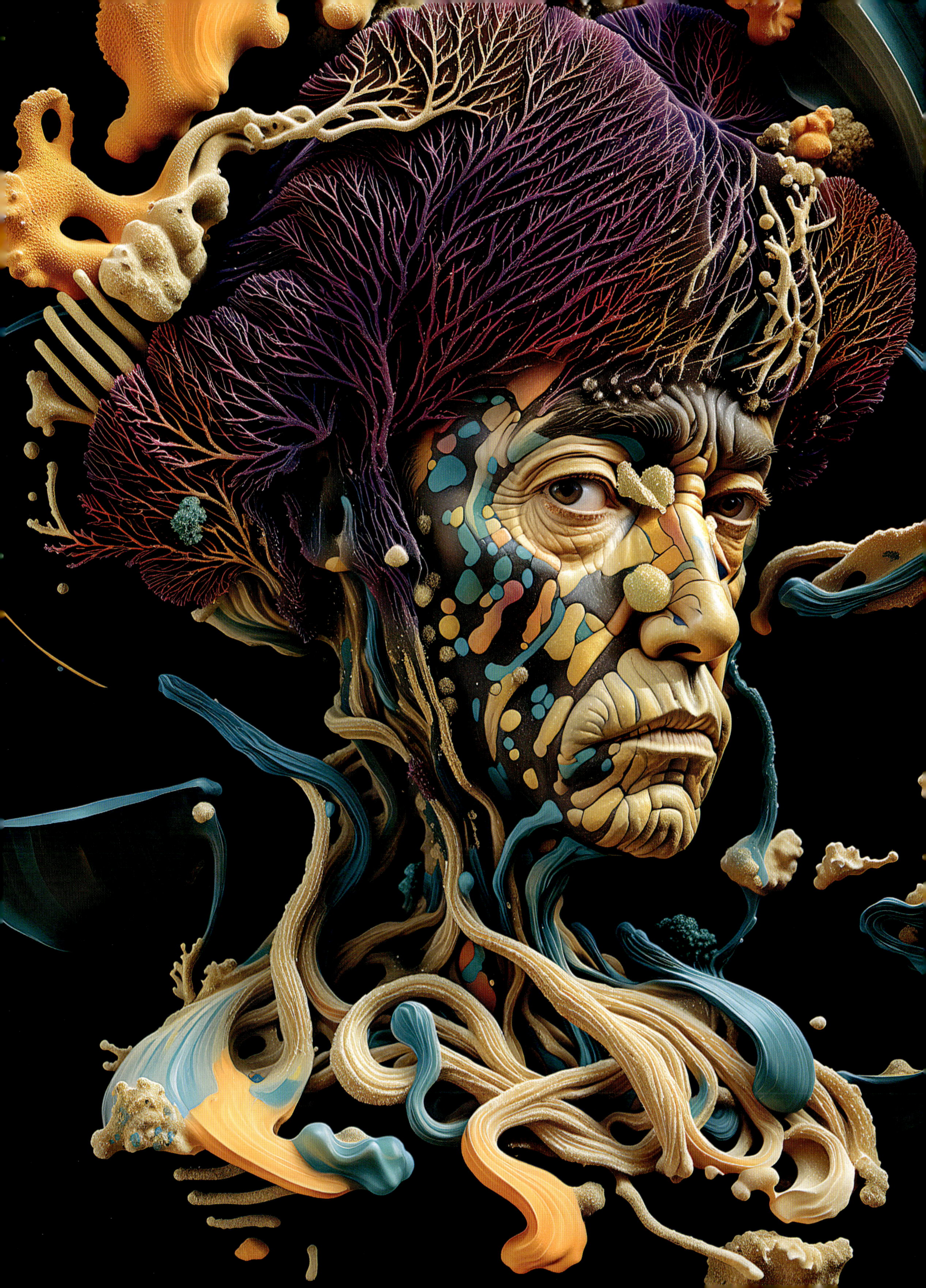

This source of variegated inspiration pushes me to experiment with different art genres and techniques, from photography to the modern tools of artificial intelligence," he says. Colors too play a fundamental role in his art, he explains: "I consider them a powerful tool for communicating emotions. I've always attached great importance to the use of colors and their arrangement in my work, whether this be photography or illustration. In photography, I carefully choose the color palette to emphasize key elements or create a particular atmosphere. The right combination of colors can transform an ordinary image into something extraordinary. In my illustrations, in turn, colors play an integral role in the narrative, helping to define the tone and mood of the work. I experiment with the saturation, intensity, and hue of colors to create dynamic contrasts and give visual form to the emotions and concepts I wish to convey." In the future, Alberto wants to explore more and more new techniques and tools. "I don't see new creative technologies as a threat, but rather as an opportunity to experiment and push beyond the conventional boundaries of art," he observes. Looking to the future, Alberto believes that excessive exposure to technologies may lead to a slowdown in the manic pace of modern life. "The omnipresence of technology and constant digital connection may push people to reflect on the value of time and the need to find an equilibrium between digital and real life. This growing awareness could lead to a cultural shift and greater appreciation for moments of calm and reflection.

People could find new ways of connecting with themselves and others, rediscovering the importance of interpersonal relationships and genuine human contact . . .

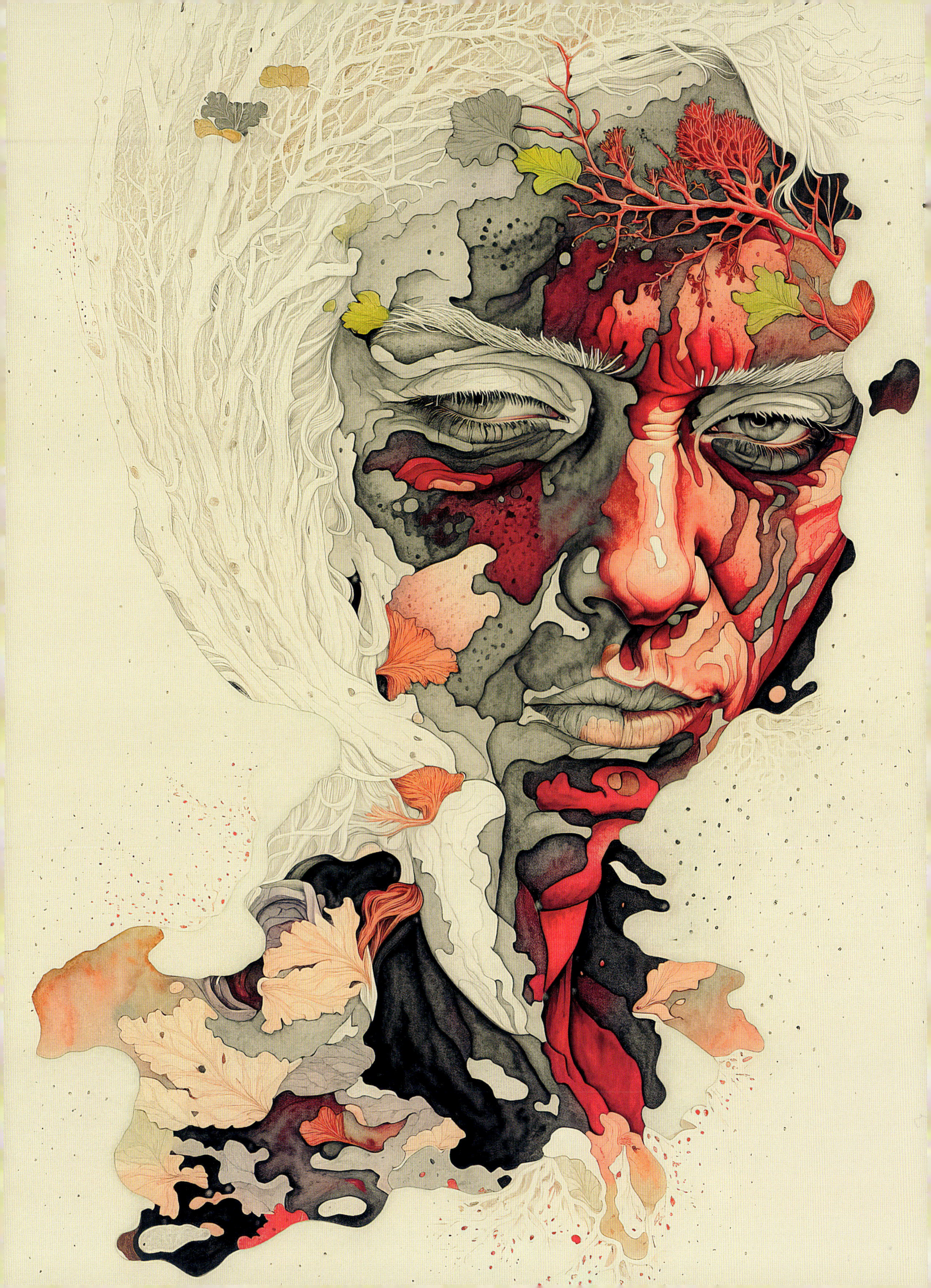

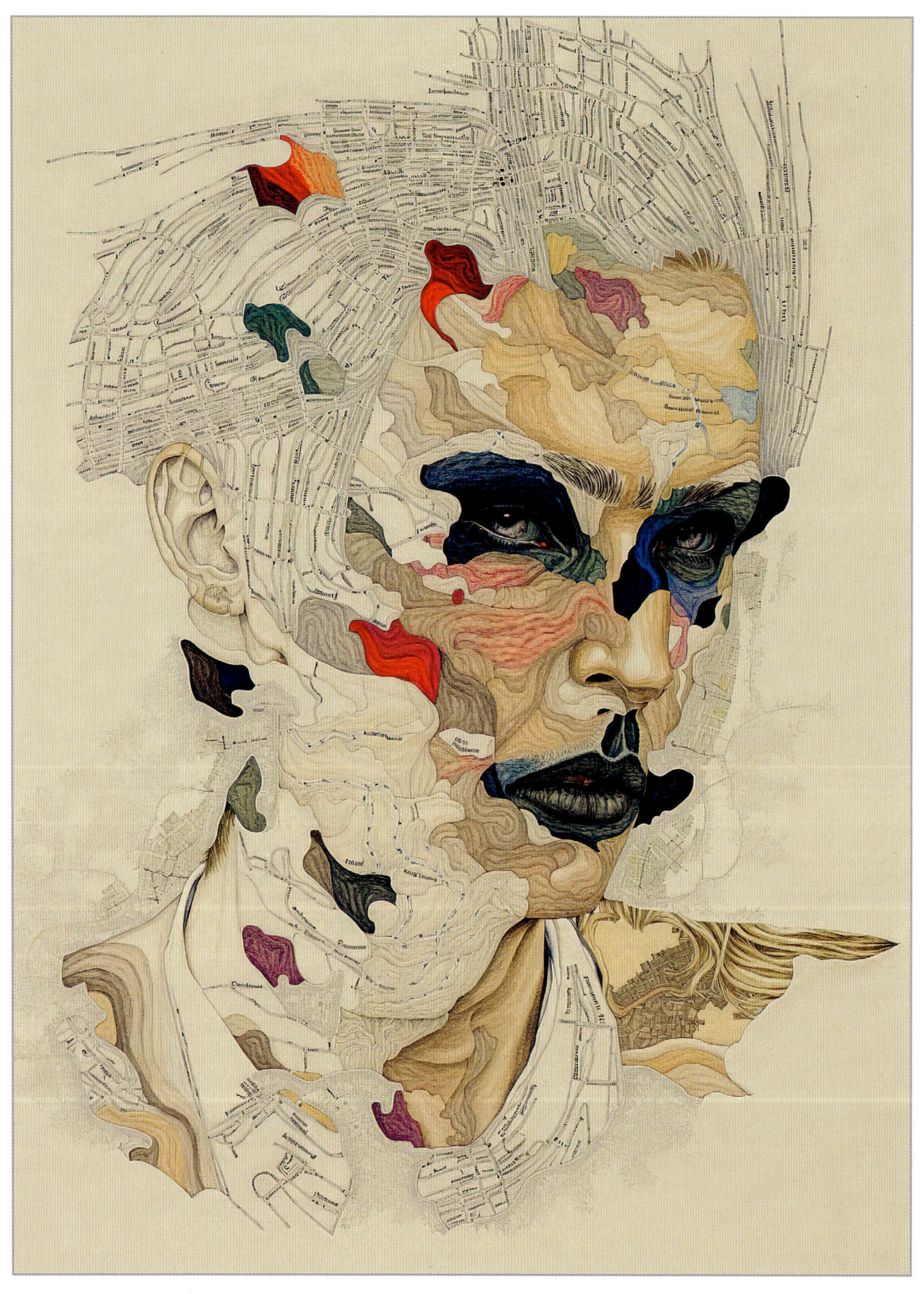

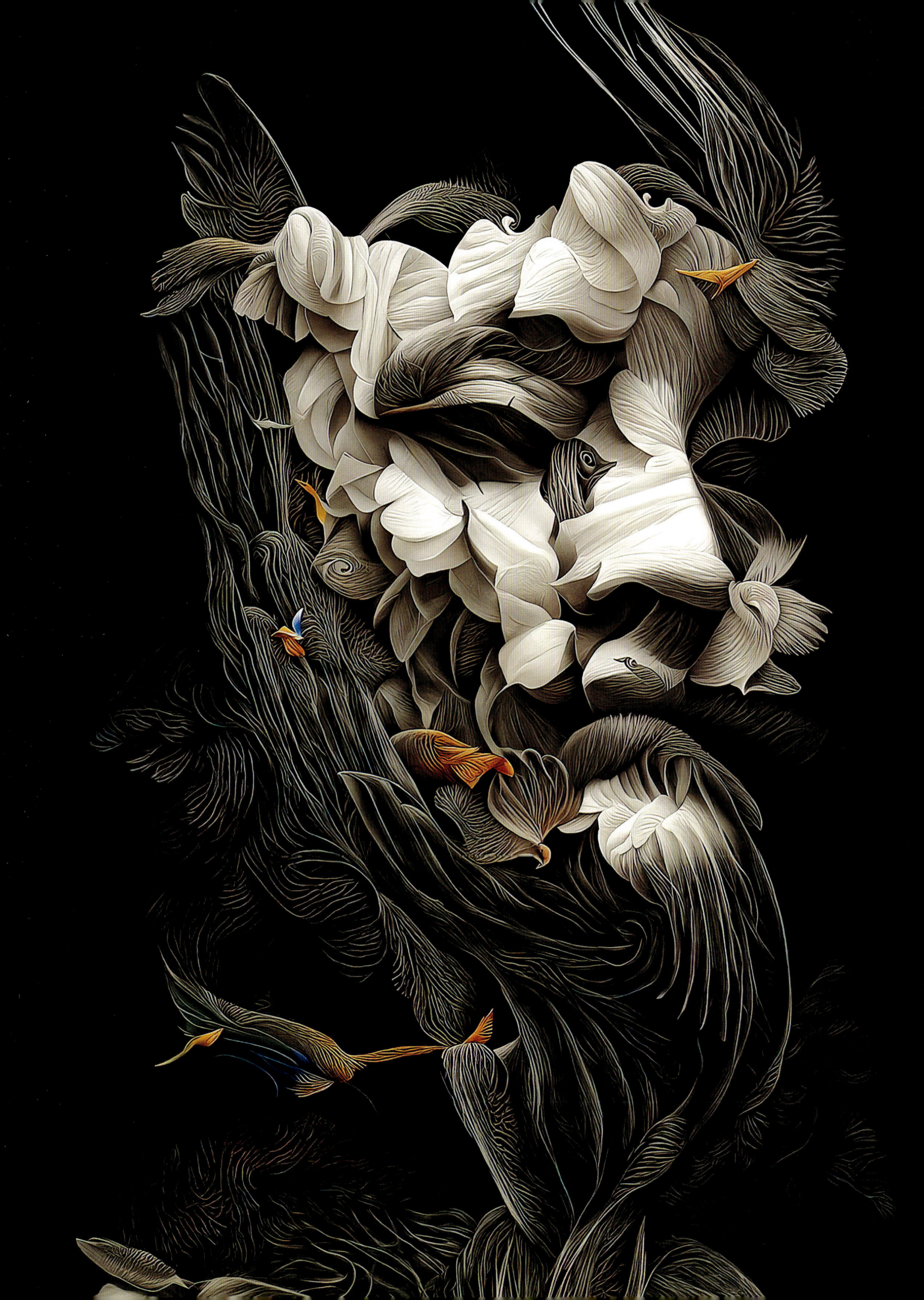

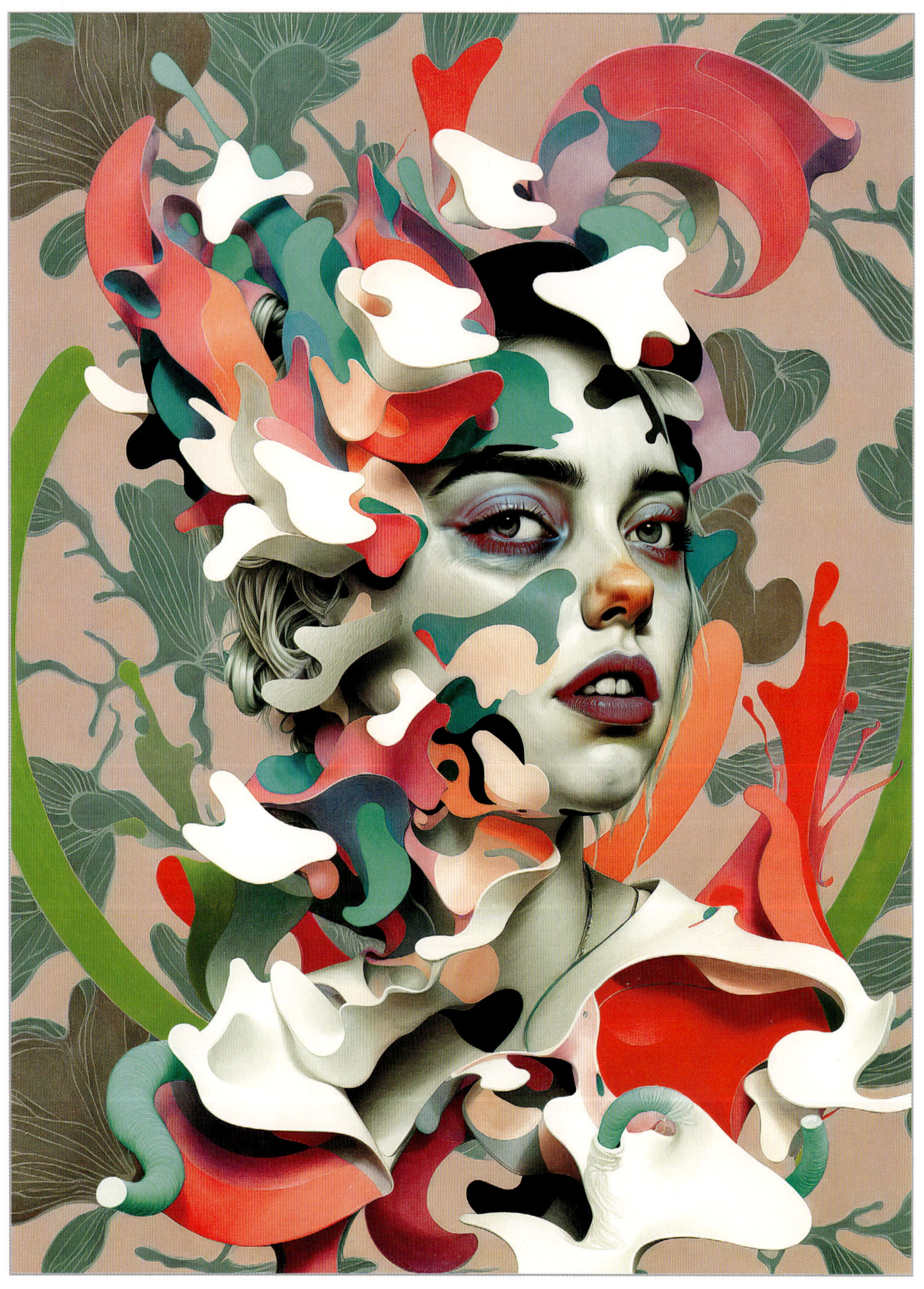

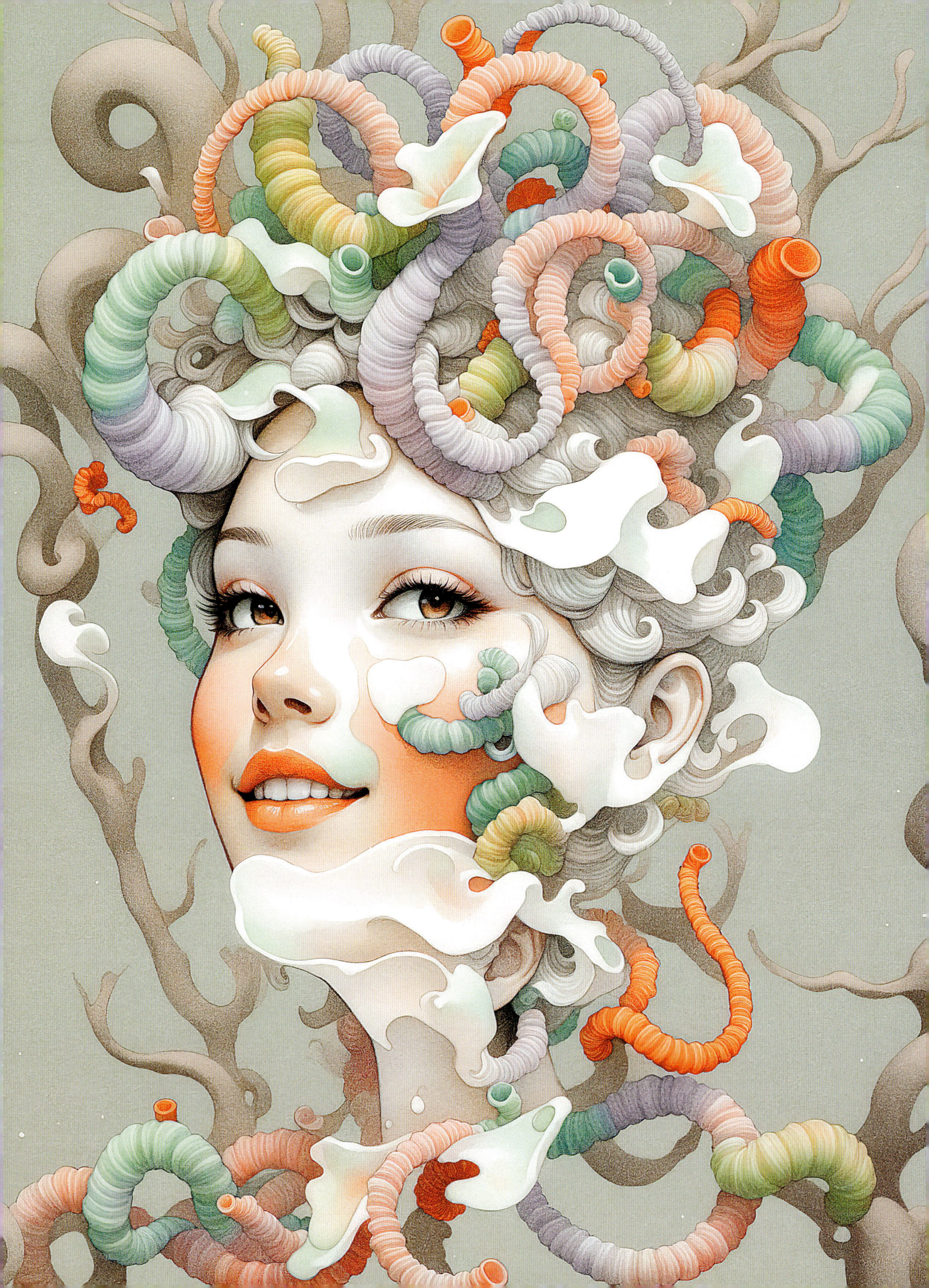

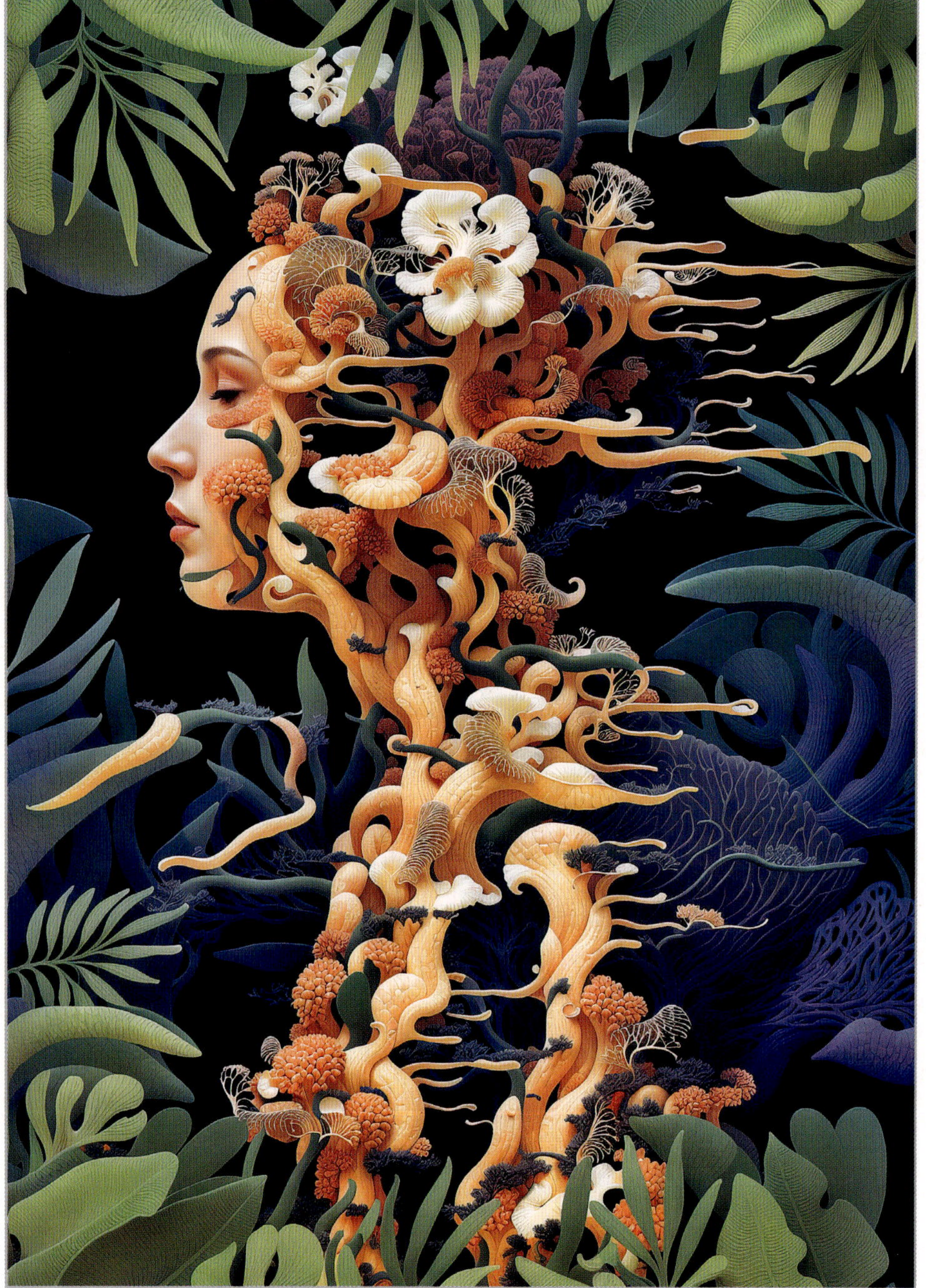

Or else Skynet—the AI network in the *Terminator* movie series—could put an end to the human race," he notes, with a disarming fatalism that conceals his profound sense of ethics. "As a man, my core values revolve around the need to respect others. I am a firm believer in the importance of treating others with kindness, understanding, and compassion. Mutual respect lies at the basis of meaningful relationships and the creation of a better world for everyone. As an artist, I am inspired by spontaneous expression. I believe that art should flow freely, unhindered by constraints or limitations. True creativity originates in instinct," he concludes.

CLAIRE SILVER

WHEN FEMININE FIGURES POPULATE
THE METAVERSE

"AS AN AI-COLLABORATIVE ARTISTS I OFTEN SAY I FEEL LIKE A CAVEMAN PAINTING FIRE. FIRE ISN'T GOOD OR BAD, IT JUST IS. IT CAN HEAT YOU IN THE COLD OR IT CAN BURN DOWN YOUR HOUSE. LIKE FIRE, AI WILL CHANGE SOCIETY AND IT'S ALREADY HERE. WE CAN'T GO BACK TO THE DARKNESS OF THE CAVES."

Her women are powerful, ethereal, evanescent, fluid, gorgeous, and disturbing, superimposed on a kaleidoscope of emotions and sensations that captivate and mutate with each look we take. Claire Silver is a "diehard" introvert, which is why she protects her anonymity with such rigor. Her complex, deeply enigmatic, and intriguing personality seems reflected in the fragments of the collage that dot her works—the lost, doe-like eyes of her women, the layers upon layers of alternating colors—like fragments of a shattered mirror.

BLUE GIRL (QUALIA) 2018

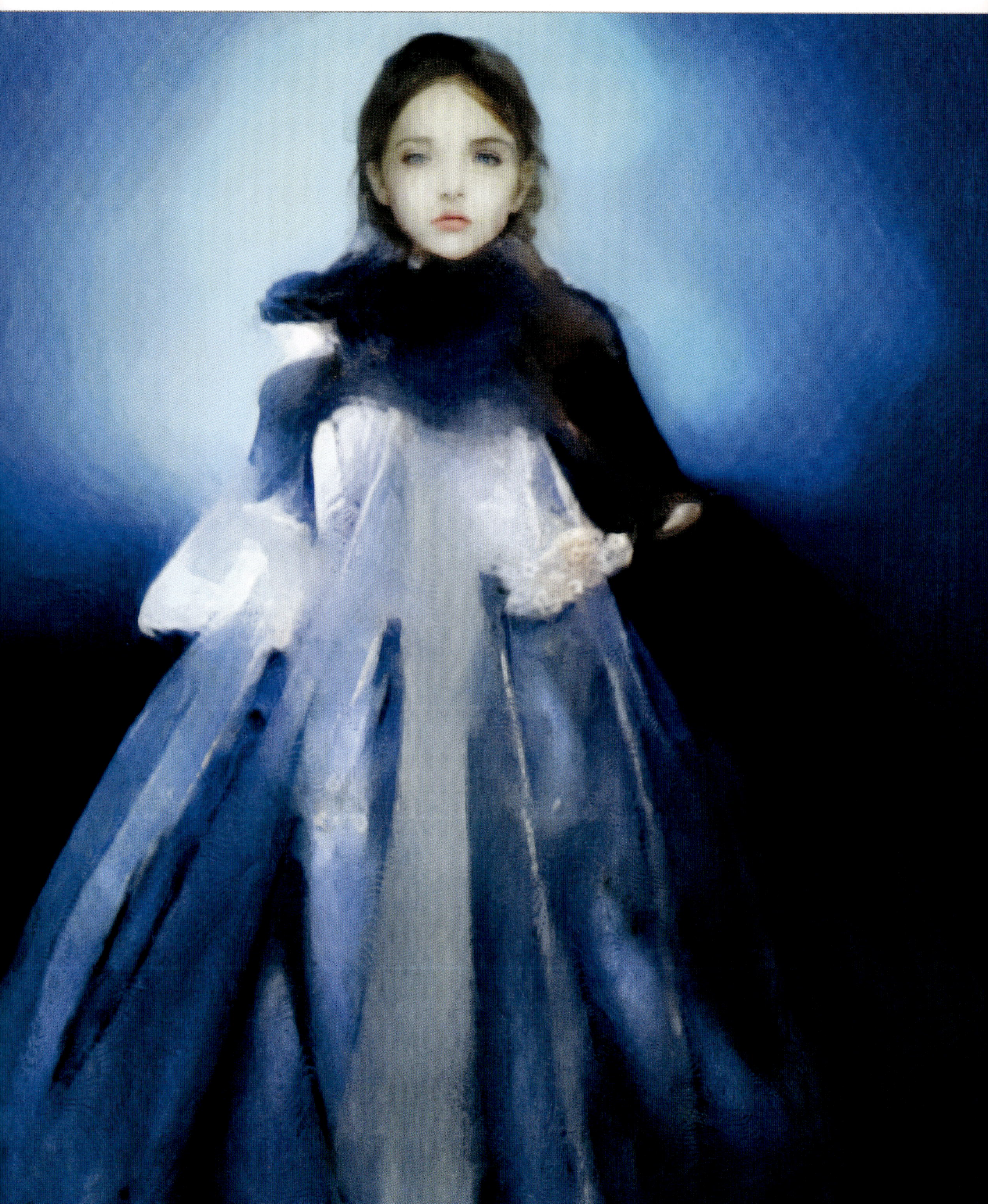

"As a child, I wanted to become a writer, but I did spend a lot of time drawing. I would draw powerful women, princesses and witches in magical kind of ways. I was an introvert and had a lonely childhood, so these figures felt like my friends," she confesses, while revealing that the poet Silvia Plath and the writer J.D. Salinger were among her greatest sources of inspiration. "I didn't start to make visual art until my twenties," she admits. "I got a serious, lifelong, chronic illness very suddenly and I couldn't work anymore so I began painting with acrylics. Fluid acrylic painting was all over Instagram at the time and it felt like an easy way to make art when you weren't traditionally trained. It was an abstract way of creating without judging my-self . . . I ended up being fascinated by the dried paint that was left on the sides: the dried, wasted paint. I resonated with the wasted potential . . .It felt like me and what I was going through. So I started to use those pieces in my work, creating images of these powerful women. It was like armoring yourself in your trauma and creating something beautiful."

Claire is completely fascinated by artificial intelligence, which she feels marked a turning point in her life both as an artist and a woman—a rediscovery of herself and of new horizons that were no longer merely conceivable, but also possible. "I discovered AI around 2017 through a website that was pre text-to-image. I made 30 to 40,000 images in the first few days and was totally obsessed. And at the same time, I was watching the television series Westworld. It made me think about a future where AI had solved for illnesses like mine and what the world would look like," she relates.

Above all, Claire wanted her women to be respected, to reflect a new era and a better world: "Most of my work includes a female figure, a non-sexualized depiction of women. Women that have an ethereal power and are beautiful yet vaguely threat-ening. Because aside from any sexualization or trauma that shows like Westworld

focused on, I think that sentience comes from something called Qualia. Qualia is something you can't explain in words. You can talk around it, but you can't explain it. It's the taste of an apple. It's the way it feels to see a color. It's the subjective experience of experiencing," she explains. "I have this memory of standing on a cliff, over the ocean and it was gray, windy, stormy and rainy. There's no evolutionary benefit to being there. But being there I felt connected to something greater. I felt part of something that was very true. And I feel like that's the divine spark that artists have been chasing for millennia. It's both the litmus test for sentience and the path to it . . . I feel like that's what Qualia is and I try to focus on Qualia in all my work."

Claire works collaboratively with AI to bring all the various facets of her personality, her love for movies and music, literature and poetry, art in every form, into her work. She also trains her own AI models with her taste so that her digital identity can eventually exist independently of her in the metaverse. "Much of my inspiration comes from other artists but also from films, books and music. For example, one movie that greatly inspires me is The Social Network or Ex Machina is also a movie I love. There is also an episode I love from the television show Black Mirror called Be Right Back about someone who loses a loved one and then uses AI to bring them back. It's kind of like a Victorian ghost story retold in the future. Among the books I've read, I love J.D. Salinger's The Catcher in the Rye or Lois Lowry's The Giver. In general, I love any media that has an outside isolation kind of theme mixed with trying to develop empathy and compassion. And of course, music has always been a huge inspiration. Particularly the group Nine Inch Nails because it fascinates me how they include real world sounds into their tracks. I think that is genius and I try to do it visually in my work."

Claire grew up in a small town in the American South, the name of which she doesn't want to reveal; but she recalls her life there as one extraordinarily bound to nature.

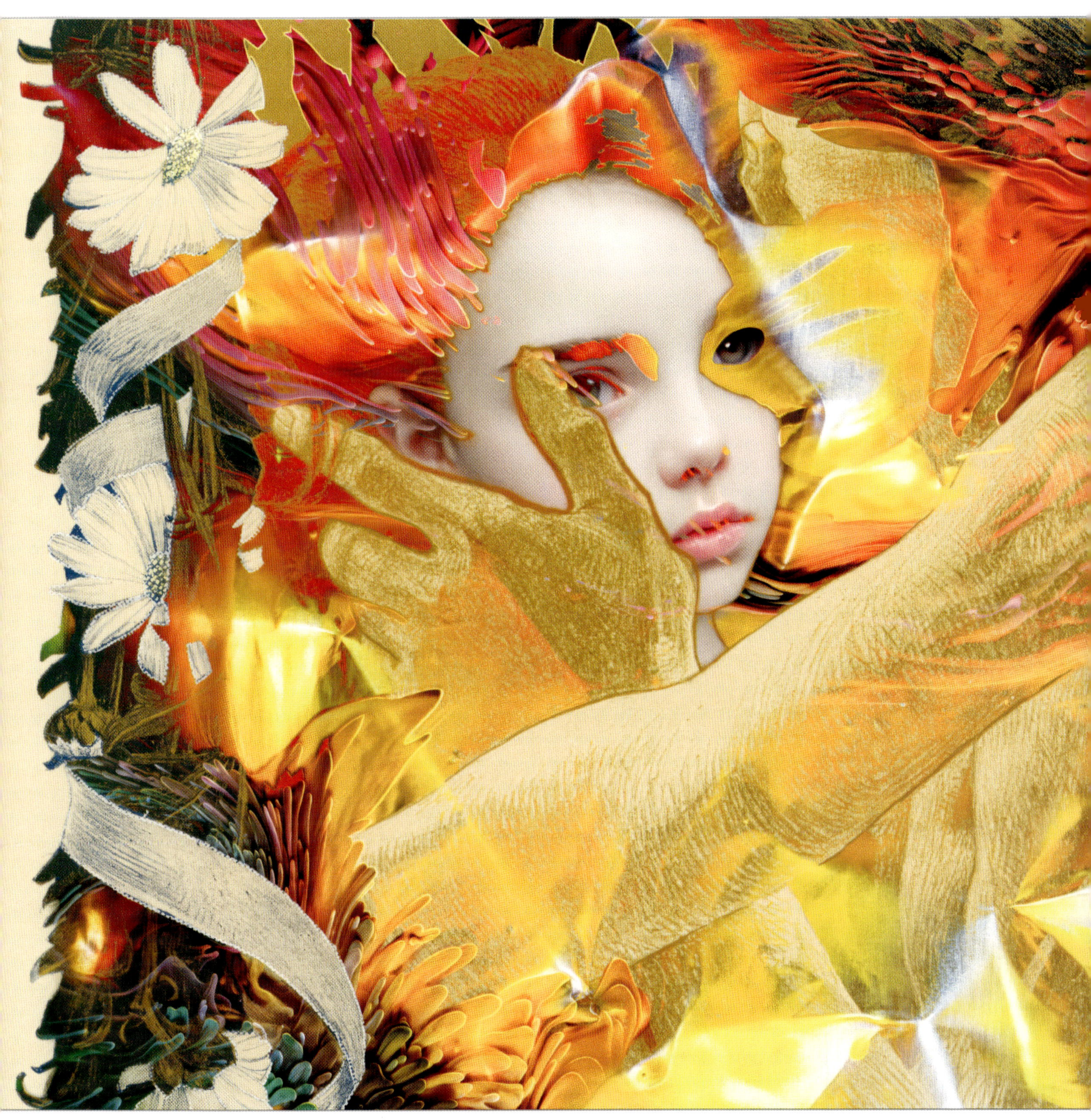

GARDEN OF EDEN 2021

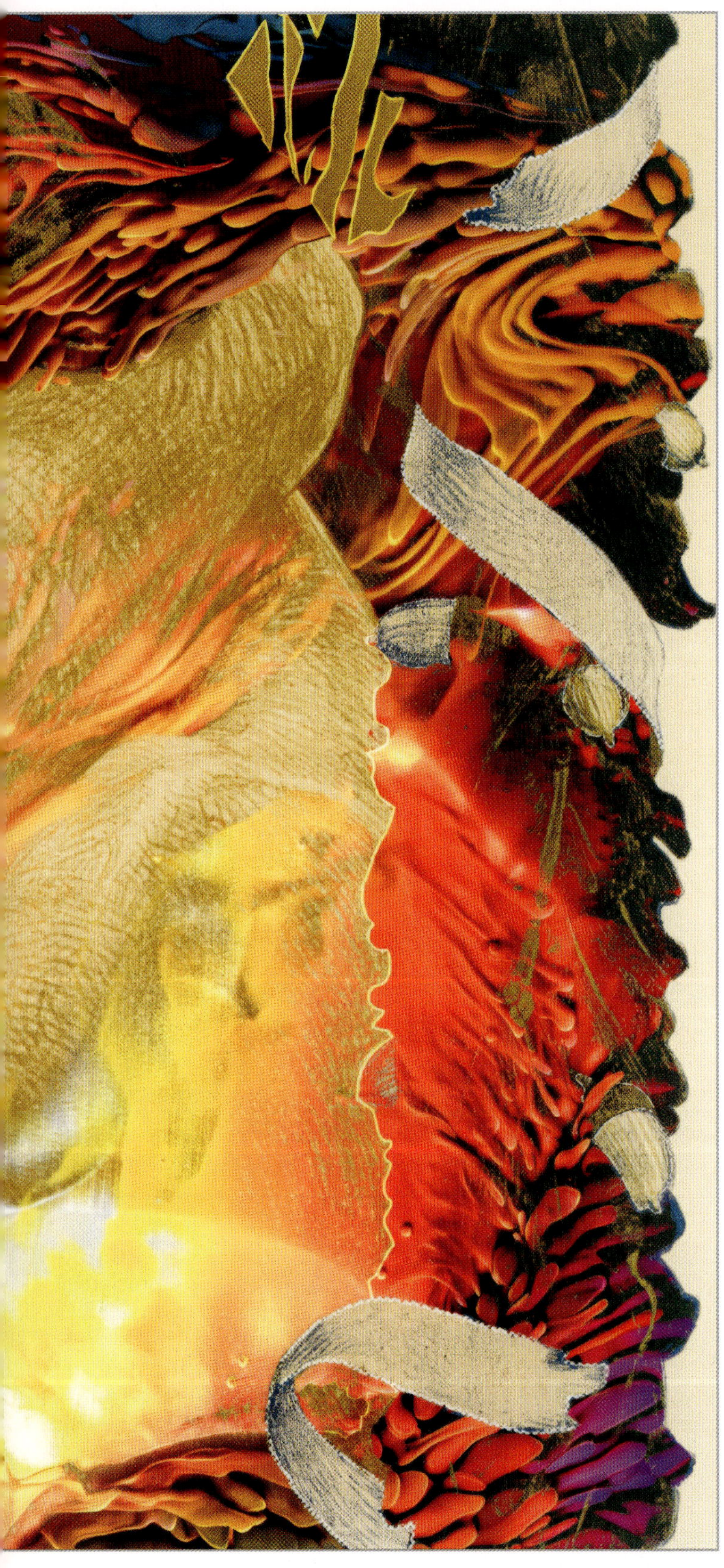

She was a reserved young woman, who preferred solitude to the company of her peers. Even today, despite living in a big city, she doesn't like crowds, preferring, as she did back then, a fairly secluded life: "I am a huge introvert so going out and being around people is a bit uncomfortable. But now that I am in a large city, I can look outside my window, see the crowded streets and it gives me energy. Makes me feel like the character in Ex Machina in the final scene of the movie as she ventures into the world."

Claire is convinced that she will never lose her innate curiosity: "If I were to write an autobiography, I'd call it Fascinated, precisely because I'm always fascinated by everything. I grew up in a very small town where there was basically nothing to do and thanks to my artistic career my life has changed completely. Being an AI-collaborative artist has allowed me to reinvent myself. I am a better friend and daughter because I put more time into those relationships. I hope that AI will push us over a generation or two to start valuing ourselves based on the things that make us human as opposed to the things that we can do in a commodified culture. Things like empathy, imagination and play. Things that will allow us to rediscover ourselves as a species."

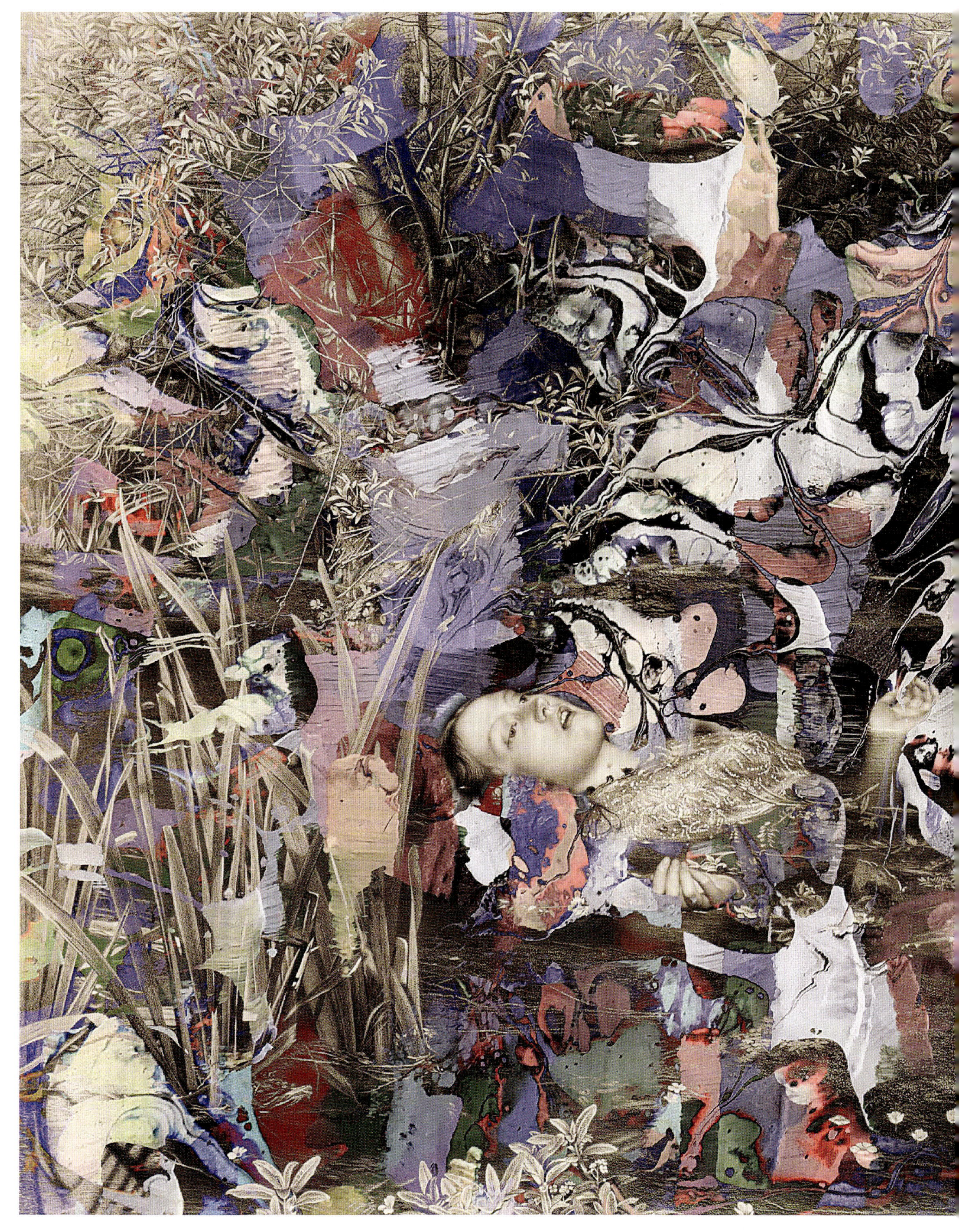

MARY IN THE BLACK AND WHITE ROOM 2020

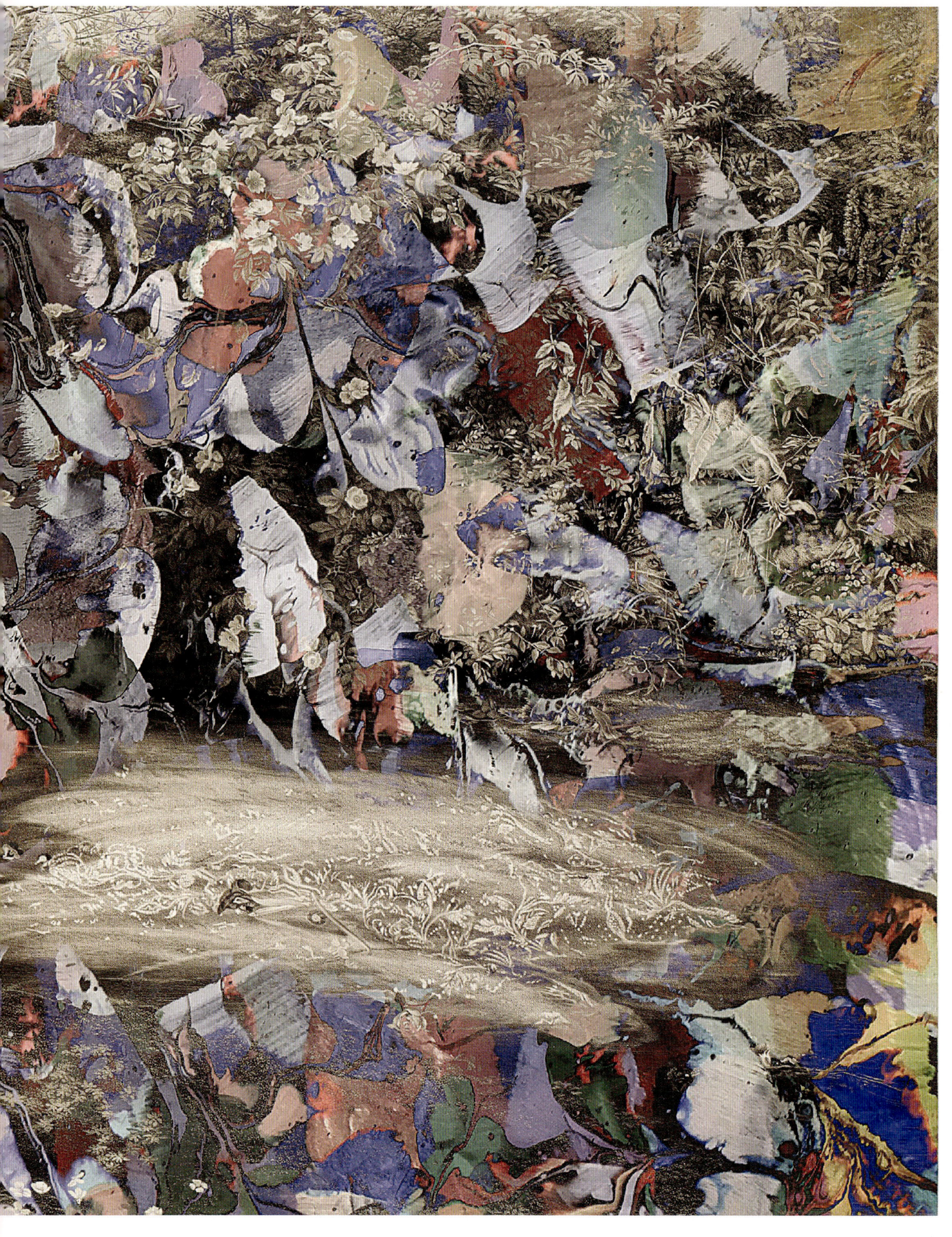

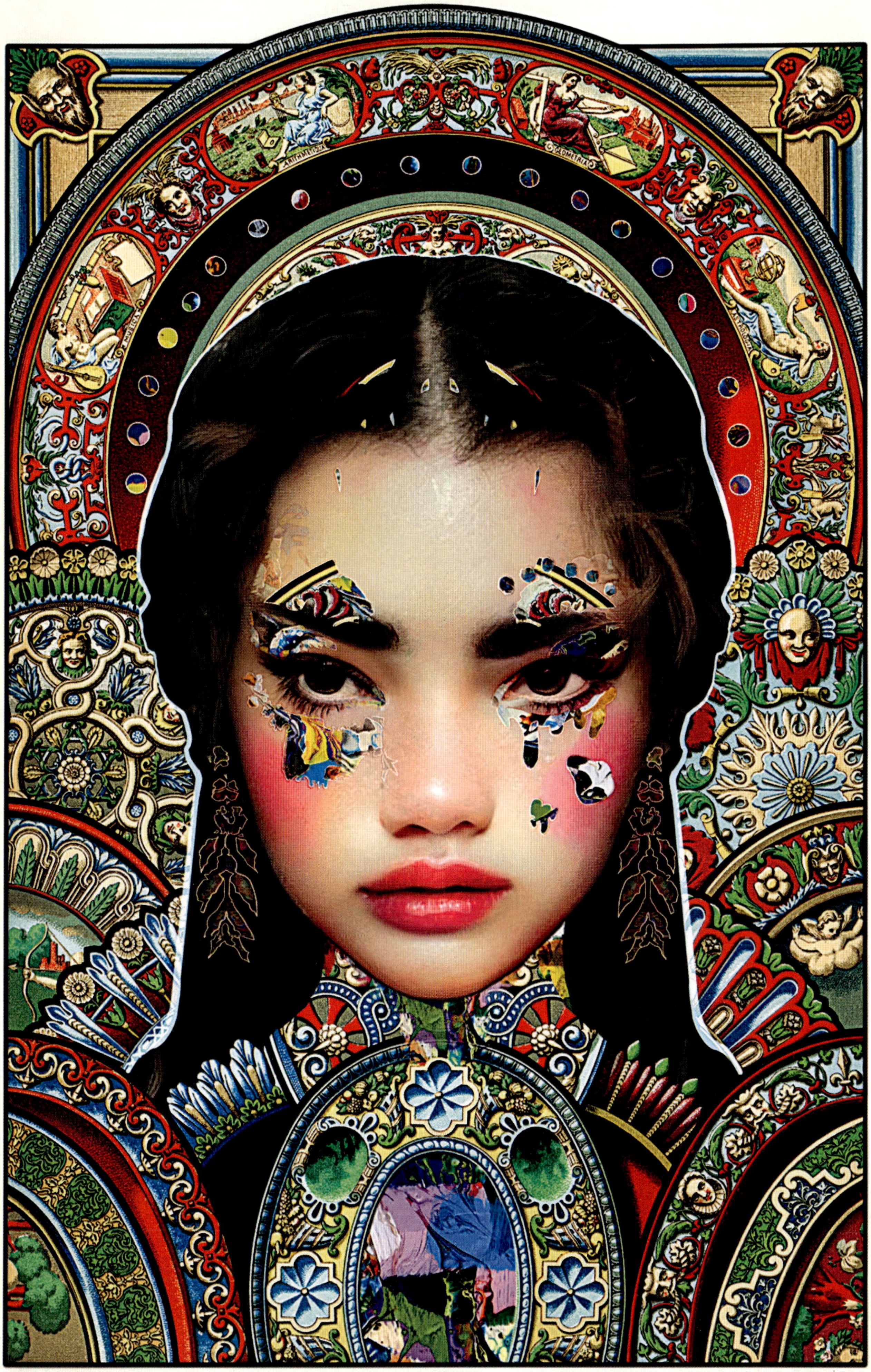

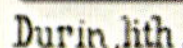
Durin, lith.

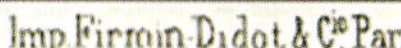
Imp. Firmin-Didot & C.ie Paris.

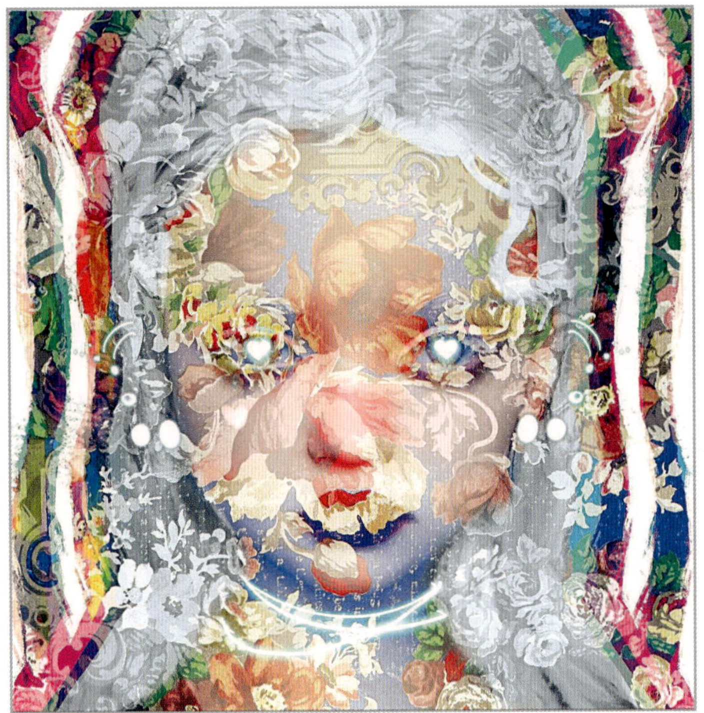 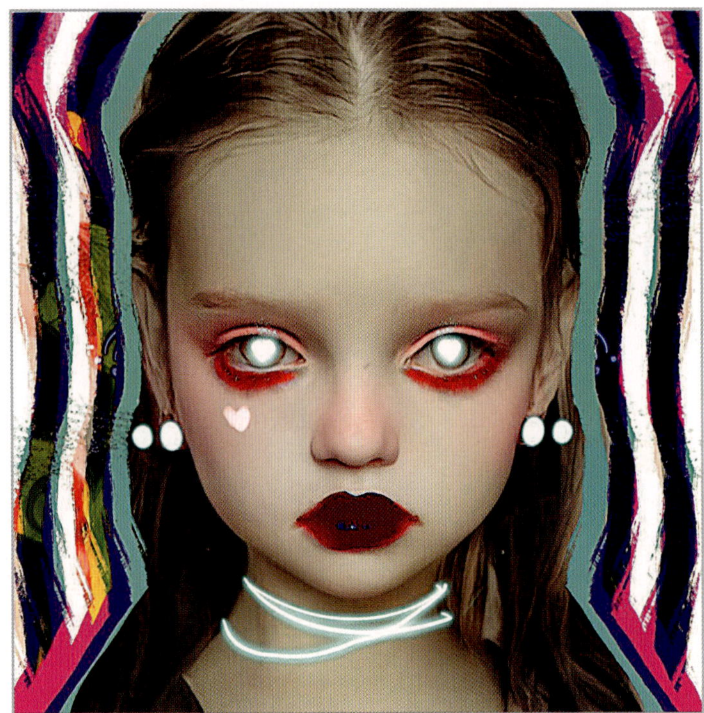

SLAP BRACELET 2020

Claire feels as though her soul is divided between the physical and the digital worlds and her work also reflects this duality. "On the one side I am very inspired by the anime and Harajuku colorful aesthetic and on the other, I love the glowy, ethereal, moody, ambient look which is much more classical and restrained. I would say my style is a split between the maniac and the quiet . . . I feel like everyone has several layers to them and that society likes to put us into very small roles and boxes. Sometimes artists are expected to stay with one style that catches fire or that they are known for. That has always seemed incredibly limiting to me, especially when given a tool like AI with infinite possibilities . . . Technology for me is about augmenting the barrier of skill. It doesn't replace it, but it makes artistic expression accessible to everyone," she says, reflecting. "For anyone that is afraid of using AI or afraid of what it might mean I always say: Do you remember when you were little, and you would finger paint and dig your hands into the dirt and make little piles? Do you remember how it felt? It was just pure creative joy free of judgement. I encourage you to try to collaborate with AI. Give it a try for a few days. It will help you developed your voice. It's like seeing a reflection of yourself in a beautiful, vivid, healing way. It changed my life, and it can change yours," she concludes.

SLIMESUNDAY

"TECHNOLOGY HELPS BREAK DOWN TABOOS AND RULES, AND ALSO ALLOWS US TO GO FAR, WHERE NO ONE HAS EVER GONE. I WOULD LIKE TO SEE COMPLETE FREEDOM OF EXPRESSION AND OF THE CREATIVE PROCESS ONLINE; ON THE OTHER HAND, I BELIEVE THAT GOVERNMENTS SHOULD MOBILIZE AS QUICKLY AS POSSIBLE TO REGULATE AI, BECAUSE THAT'S WHERE THE REAL DANGER LIES, NOT IN MY EROTIC IMAGES."

His seductive charm operates on the female body, while his imagination feeds on the pages and covers of old magazines, as well as on the many suggestions offered by the contemporary world as it passes from the sensual to the erotic, from the provocative to the margins of the rawest live experimentation. A master of digital collage, Slimesunday (the pseudonym that Mike Parisella goes by) has often been censored by social media, but has never given up and continues to heed his inspiration. "The Internet is full of erotic imagery as well as pornography, but my creations are something utterly different; they're art, and as such I would like them to be treated with respect. I want the freedom to create what I wish, not what others suggest or advise me to do," he admits. Slimesunday idolizes the female body: "I want to draw attention to the fact that when an image of a man, half-naked, without a shirt, appears on the Internet, no one is scandalized . . .

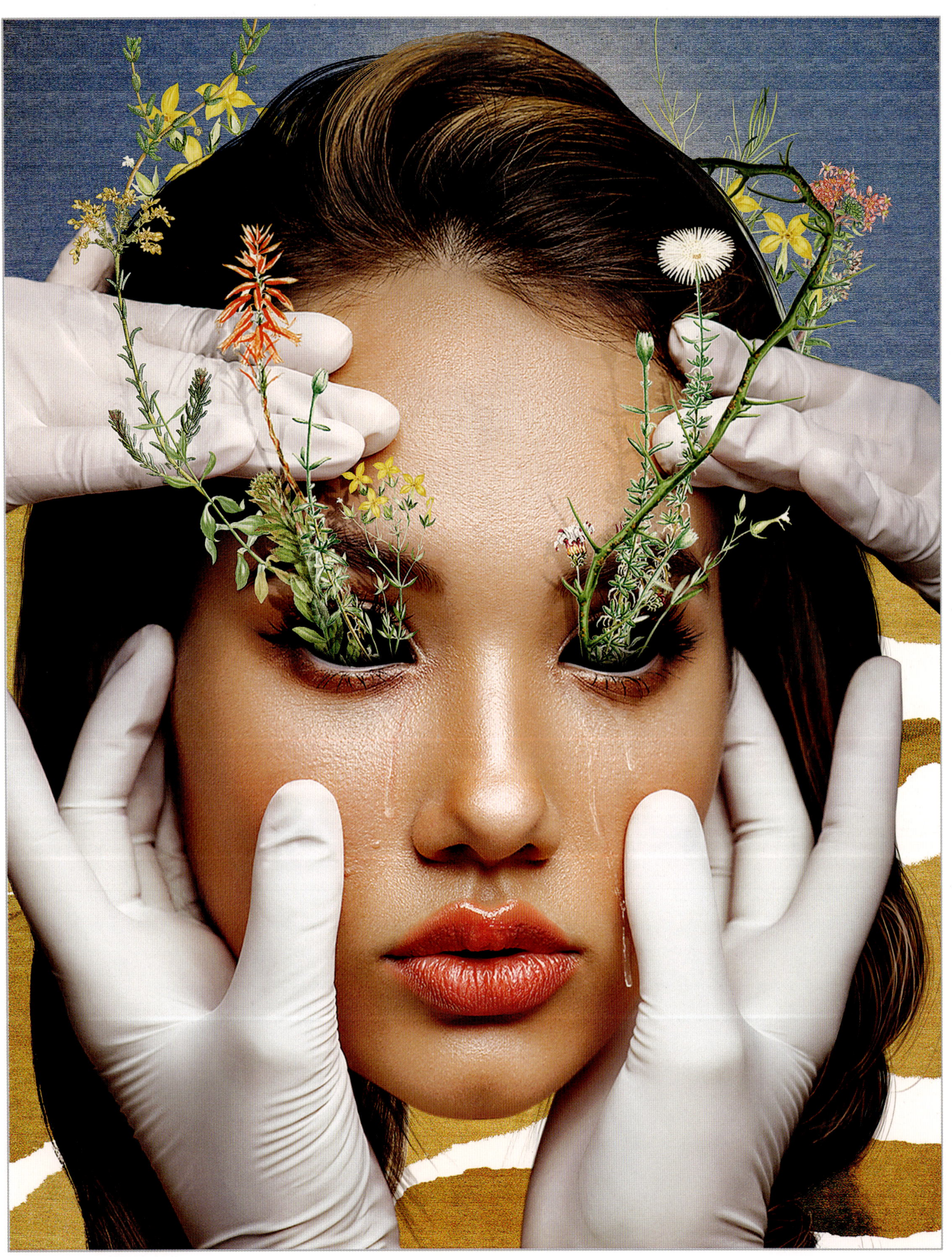

When it comes to women, it's not the same . . . That's why I want to spread a message that promotes total equality both online and worldwide, and I want to celebrate the female body in all its beauty. There's no question that I like the female body immensely, but my art is not limited to aesthetics." This cutting-edge and provocative spirit has enabled Slimesunday to become one of the most highly paid and popular artists in the entire metaverse. In addition, his passion for music has led to collaboration with great artists, such as Lana del Rey and Katy Perry. "Working with such highly talented people is definitely a great source of inspiration for me, but my creativity also feeds on what's happening around me in my everyday life," he explains.

His passion for art and technology had its origins above all in music: "I grew up playing lots of music—so much that I could say I was totally immersed in music. My father played in several bands, and, as a child, I took lessons and learned to play the guitar early in life and began composing with different software. At the same time, I created my first artworks by using Photoshop and other programs. Before long, the computer became my main creative companion," he recalls. "It was in high school that I discovered my natural inclination and vocation. Later, in college, I majored in psychology and regarded art as a mere hobby," he adds. Despite that, his creations soon became incredibly popular online.

"I had fun making erotic collages, trying to figure out how far I could go. I found an endless resource in the vintage magazines of the '70s and '80s. I scanned some of their photographs and reworked them to create things that were utterly new and unexpected, occasionally bizarre, but full of meaning for me," he says.

Slimesunday's relationship with the digital universe became even more important in the summer of 2020, during the pandemic. "Before that period, I had been working a lot in the music world, designing covers.

But then, all of a sudden, everything stopped. Musicians were no longer touring or performing on stage. As my clients disappeared, I found myself with plenty of free time. One day, my friend DJ 3LAU, aka Justin Blau, told me about NFTs, and I instantly realized that they were a perfect opportunity for my artistic aspirations. So, we made an audio-video that we launched that autumn, to great success," he recalls. Since then, Slimesunday has embarked on a new career, which he plans to develop and expand, while experimenting with the full range of possibilities offered by technology, as in the case of the creative audio-visual project that he organized with DJ 3LAU. "Although there's been a deep crisis in the NFT world, I still have great faith in it. I foresee that the technology will be used in a thousand different ways; but, more than anything, I think it's a sound tool for validating digital art. In fact, after many people have shared an image on social media, it's quite difficult to find out who made it, and this poses a major problem," he says with emphasis. "Recently, I even discovered a technology that allows me to insert a chip in my prints, which helps guarantee their authenticity. But the road is still long and complicated, and I think that more effort should be put into protecting the rights of artists," he states with conviction.

When it comes to AI, Slimesunday is both a skeptic and, surprisingly, a possibilist. "I didn't use it for a long time, but I've always been interested in applying it to my creative process to probe elements and perspectives, come up with new angles and new tools . . . At the same time, I believe that I'll never completely abandon handmade work, though I can't predict the future. My goal is to feel good about my art and make others feel the same," he clarifies. "AI worries me because I fear homogenization, and I don't share society's current anxiety to perfect AI and apply it to all aspects of life. This could be quite dangerous. We definitely need precise rules," he says.

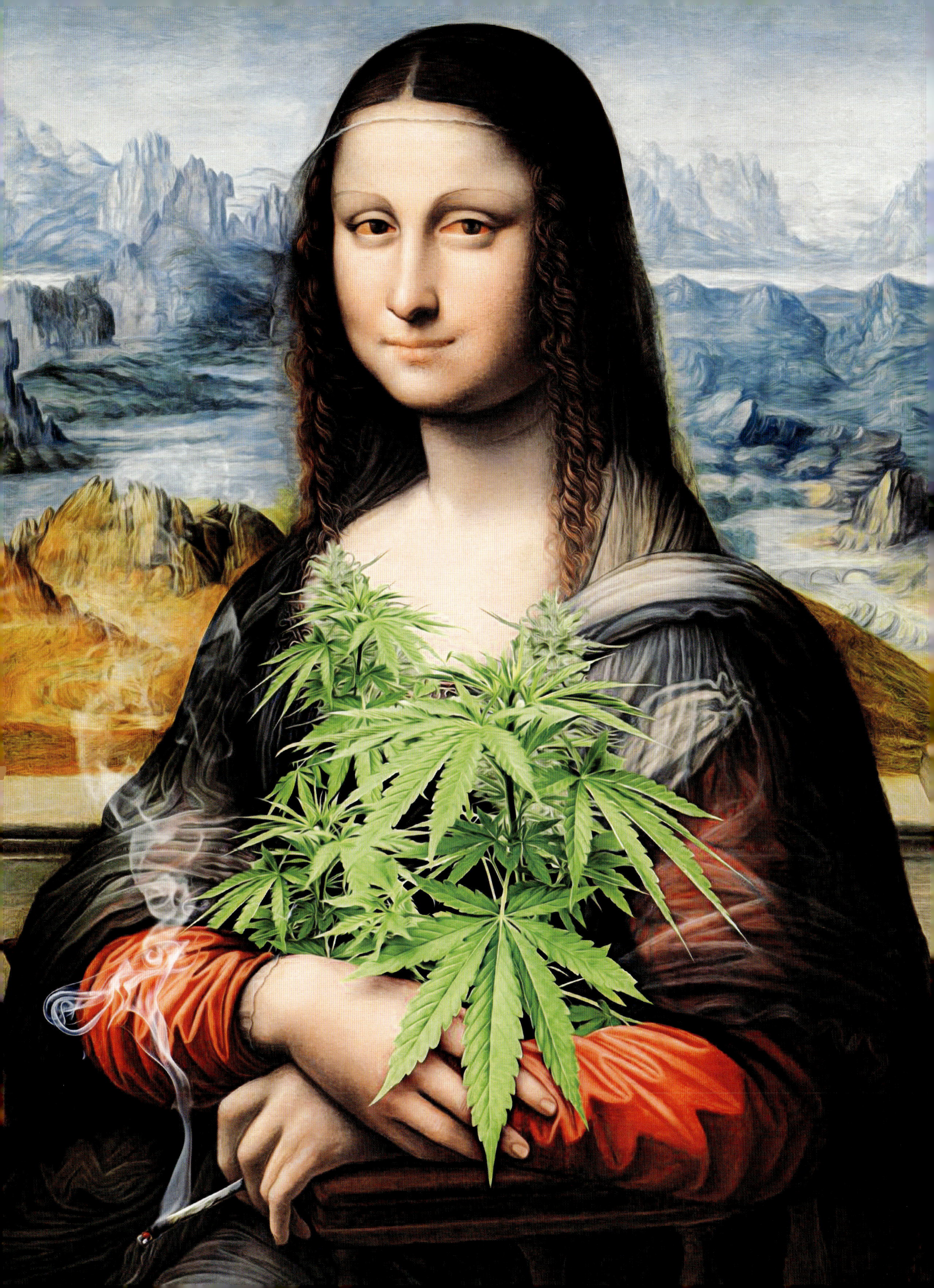

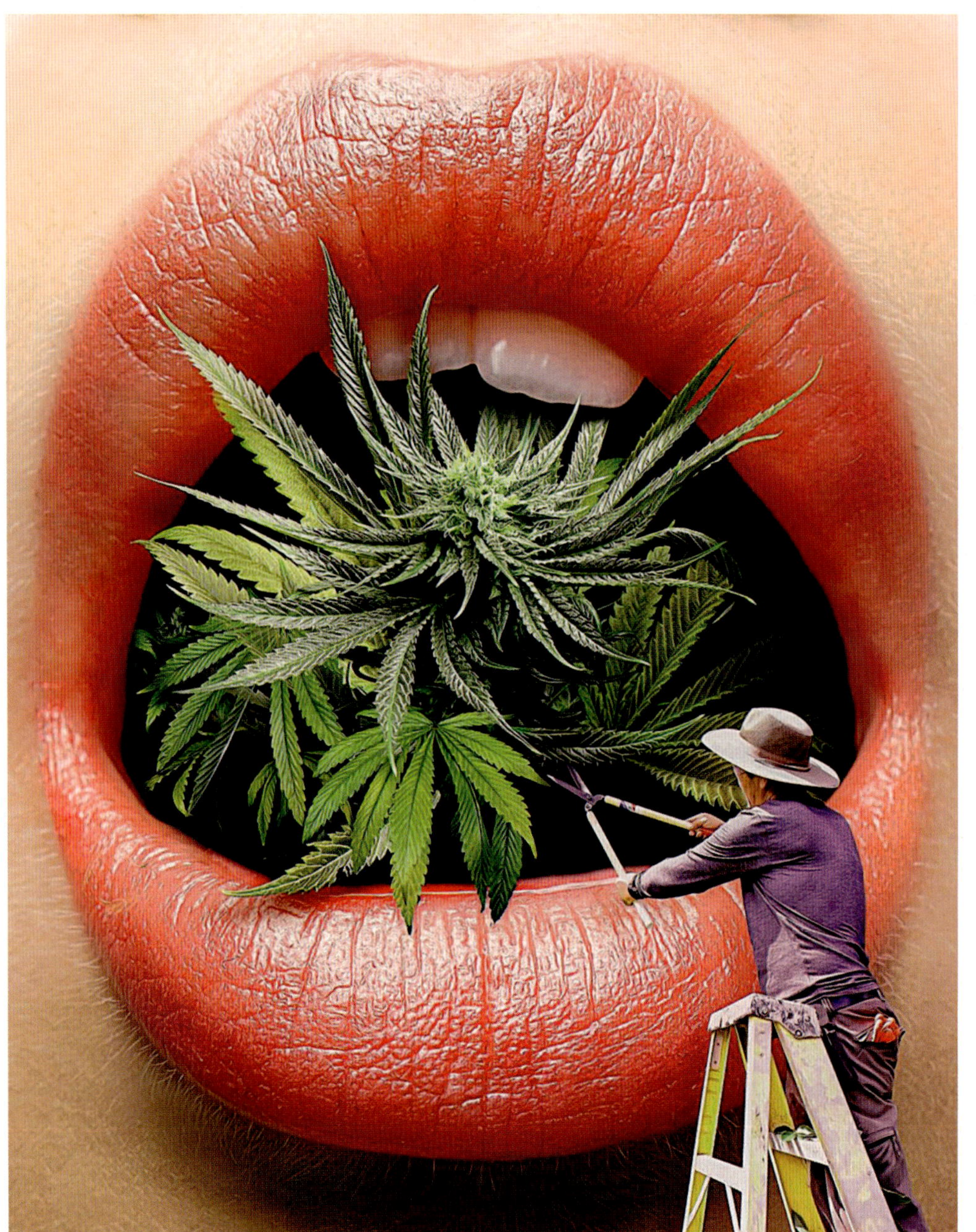

Studying psychology made him examine—and learn about—the human mind and realize how unpredictable it can be when transferred to a machine with no controls. "It's the psychological aspect that sets apart all my work; my training leaves a deep impression on everything I create. I have a profound interest in humanity, its ability to evolve and renew itself, but also remaining linked to certain older values bound to history, which should never be forgotten," he claims.

This attraction to the human body, present in all the art he produces, also derives from his interest in science: "Years ago, I considered studying medicine and becoming a doctor, but in the end I couldn't give up art. Producing it—whether in the form of music, digital imagery, or physical object—has always been of essence to me."

MONA SATIVA

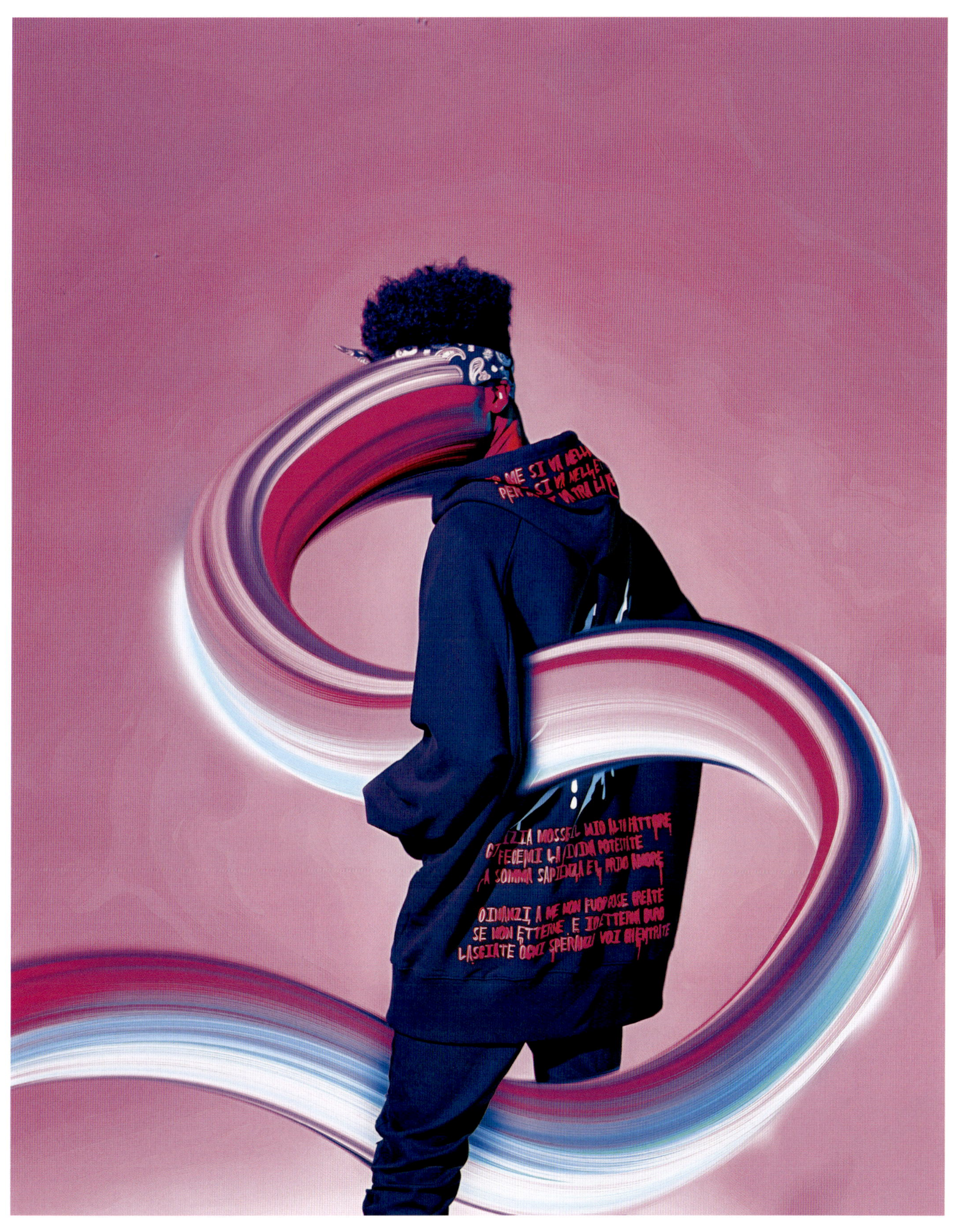

MY EDIT OF @SEREEEENAM BY @TOSHIAKIKITAOKA →

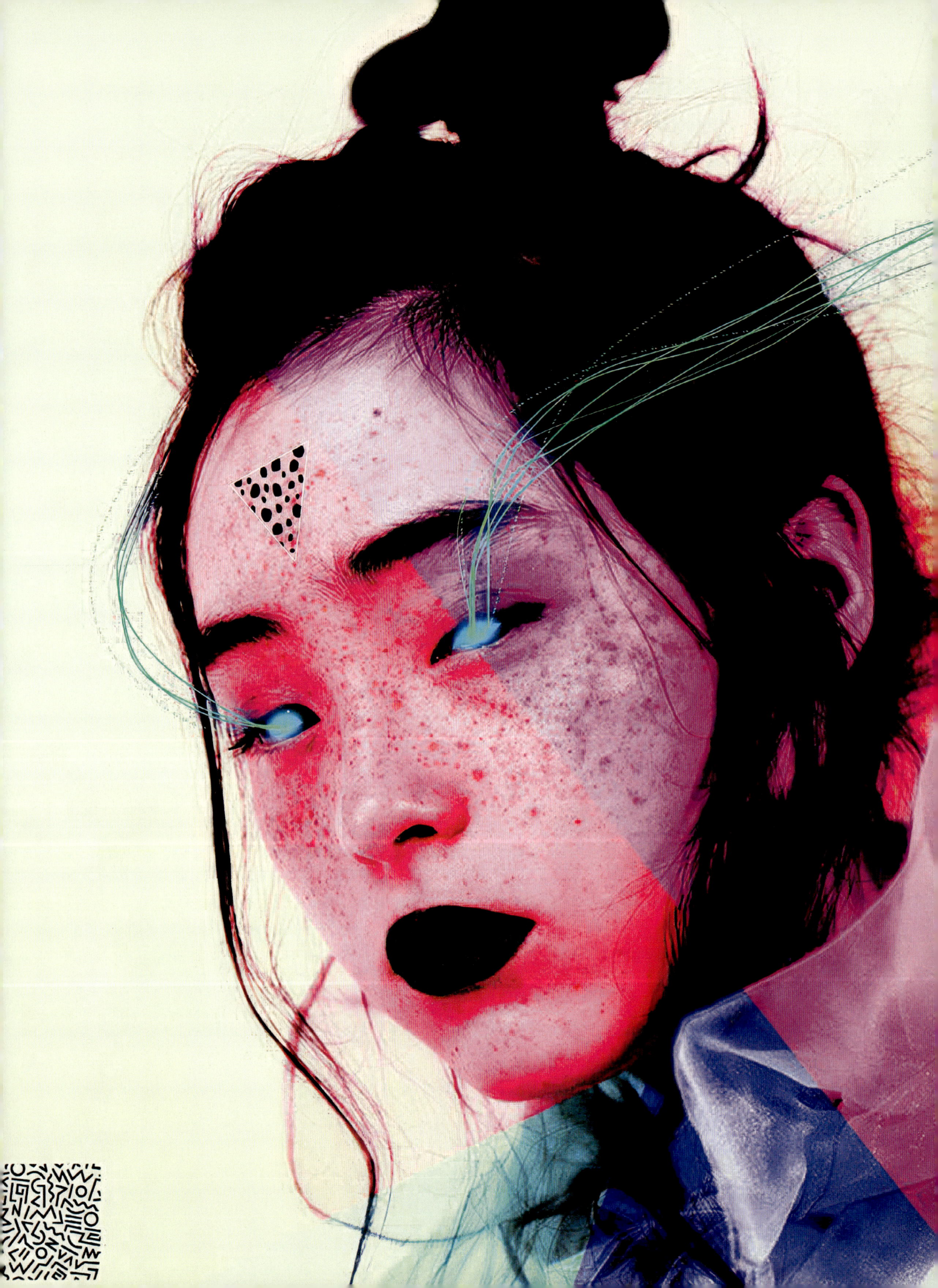

Like many other artists in the digital world, Slimesunday is an autodidact in the field: "I studied on my own. I've always been interested in software, and, if you've got a passion for anything these days, you can easily pick up everything online, where you can find incredible resources for growing and learning—ones accessible even to those living in isolation."

Slimesunday knows a lot about alienation, as he was born in a tiny town near Salem, Massachusetts, where he still lives. "I've always stayed put for my family, but I would prefer to live elsewhere as it's really quiet here, super-cold in the winter. There are some positive aspects, such as the nature surrounding the place; but it's nearly impossible to make useful work-related contacts and connections. The metaverse community, by contrast, has offered me a chance to succeed at what I love. In Massachusetts, the most popular type of art is figurative painting of the past that depicts ships and the sea . . . I definitely faced the risk that I would remain misunderstood. Luckily, I can now travel a great deal, and this forces me to compare myself to many artists from different places and cultures who inspire and stimulate me to continue down my path. New York is certainly one of my favorite cities, but Italy holds a special fascination, and I'm trying to spend more and more time there.

"My favorite places are Taormina and Sicily in general; I'm also of Italian origin; in fact, I'm a third-generation immigrant to the U.S., since my grandparents, on both my mother's and father's sides, came to America from Italy. Each time I go, the country astounds me with its extraordinary blue sky, one of my favorite colors," he admits. Colors are of supreme importance to all of Slimesunday's work: "If anyone looks at my art, they'll notice that my palette is quite specific: lots of blue and contrasting colors, such as black, orange, and red. But blue certainly predominates . . . With its many shades, it may be the one that comes closest to matching my multifaceted personality," he concludes.

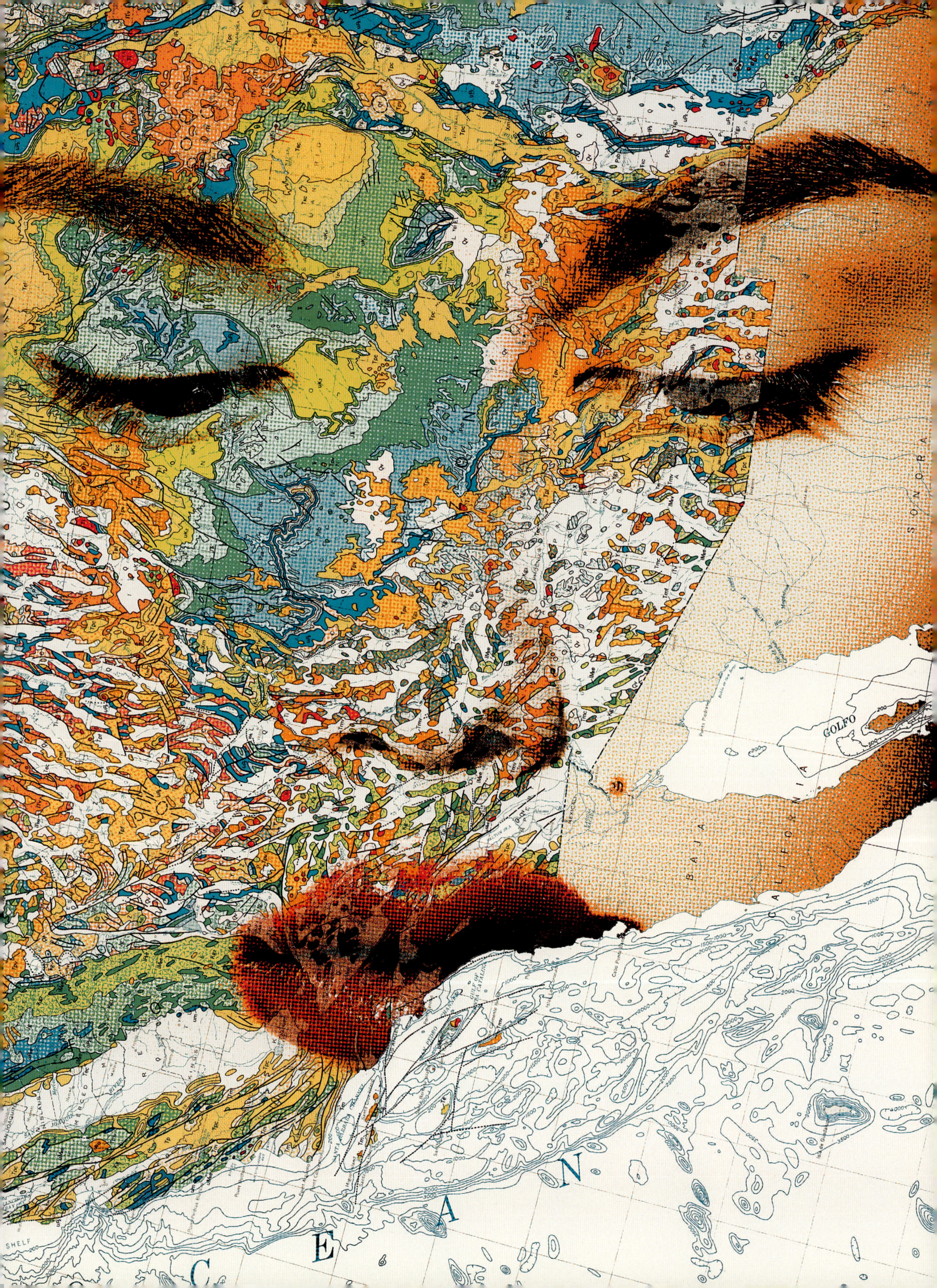

SONORA
BAJA
GOLFO
CALIFORNIA
SHELF
O C E A N

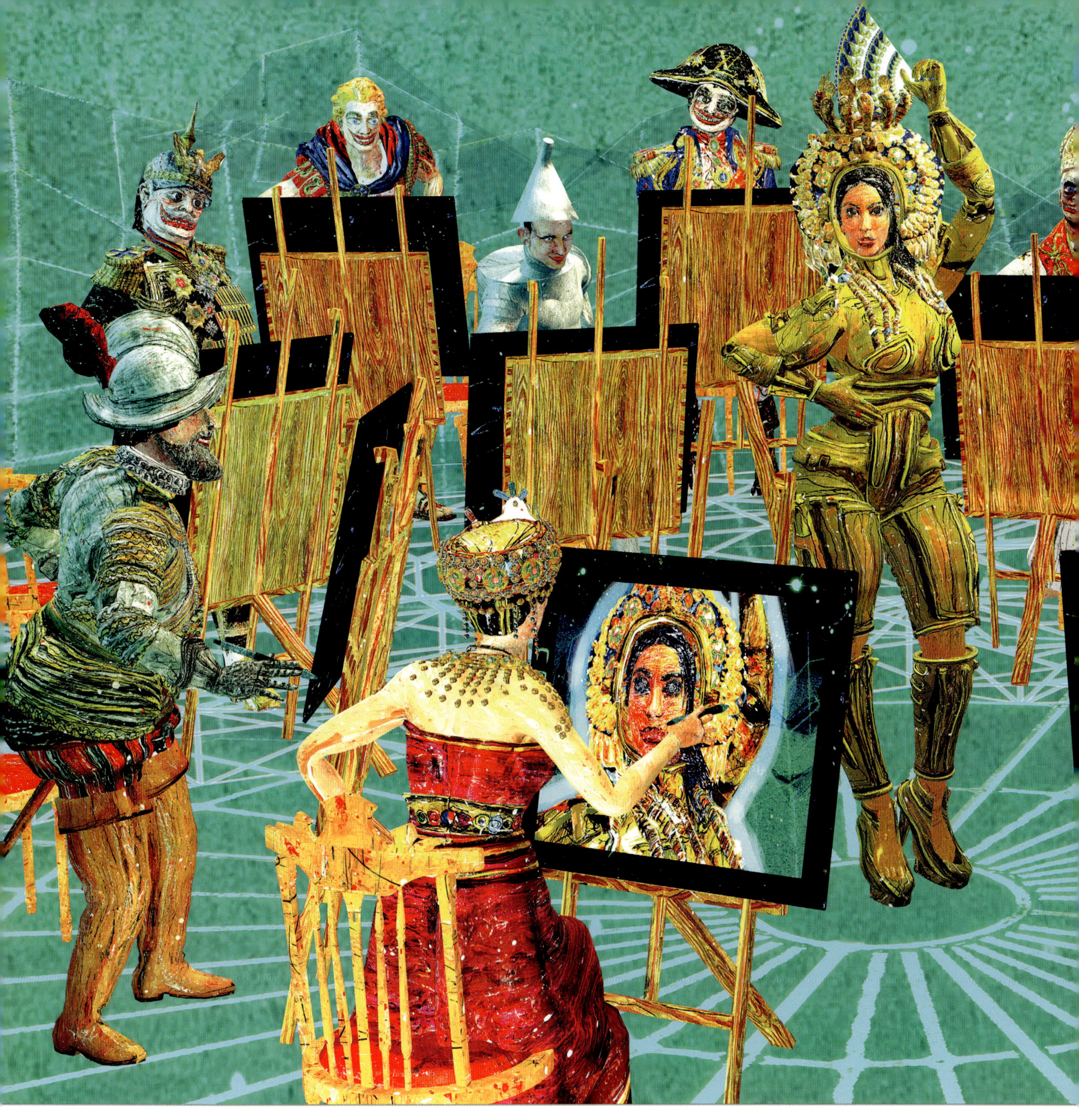

FEDERICO S

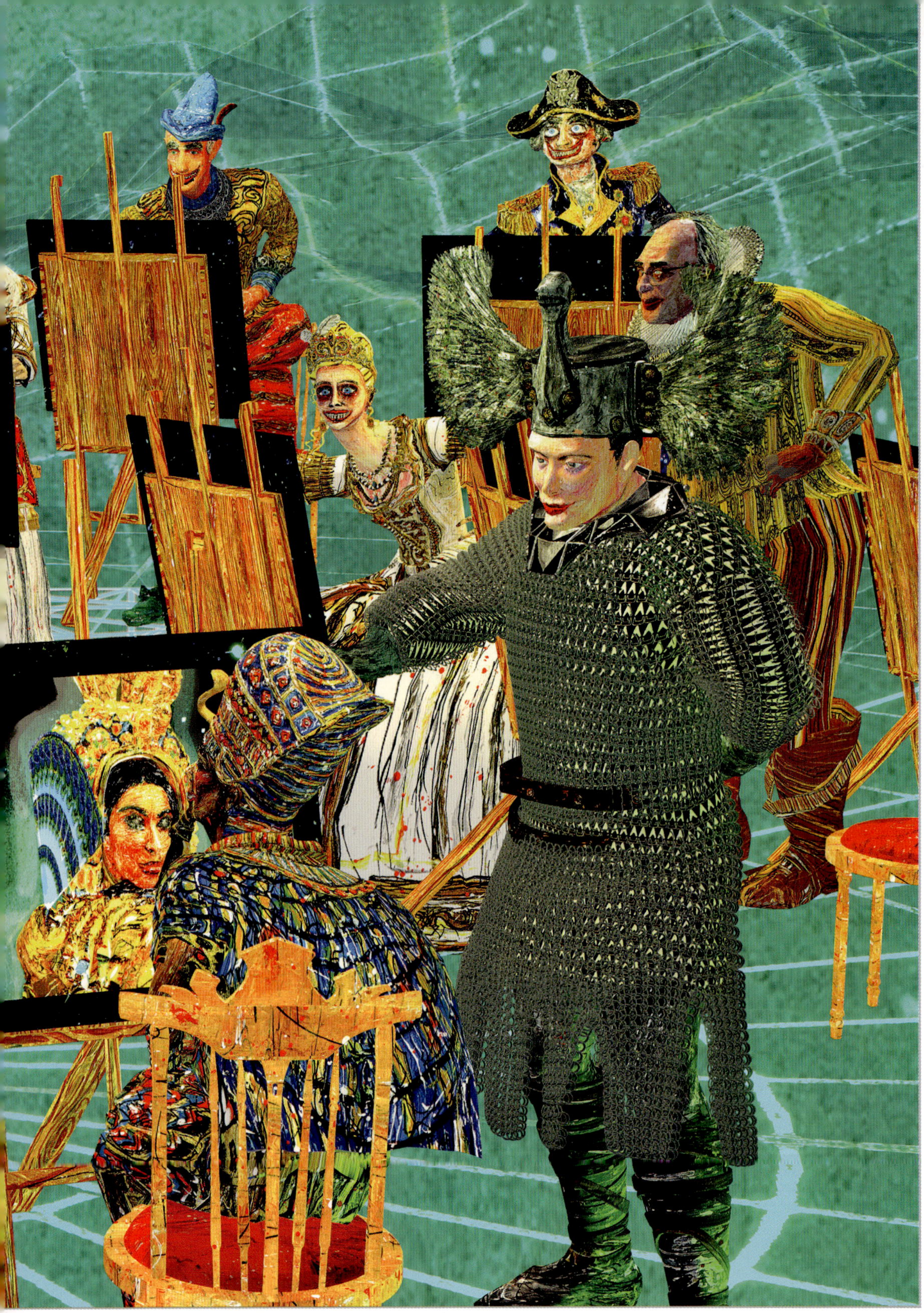

THE PAINTING CLASS, 2024 – SOUNDTRACK BY MARC URSELLI

COURTESY VAR DIGITAL ART BY VAR GROUP

OLMI

WHEN MADNESS AND THE GROTESQUE ENCOUNTER REALITY

"I DISCOVERED TECHNOLOGY THROUGH VIDEO GAMES, WHICH AS FAR AS I'M CONCERNED HAVE REVOLUTIONIZED THE CONCEPT OF AESTHETICS IN ART . . . HOWEVER, I'M ALWAYS LOOKING FOR A CONNECTION BETWEEN DRAWING, PAINTING, AND DIGITAL ART."

Figures with huge eyes and a commanding presence, their mouths full of sharp teeth, moving through a surreal world like some sort of multi-colored wireless marionettes while engaging in a baroque carnival of emotions, sensations, and messages capable of overwhelming and imprinting the soul . . . Like his one-man show, *SOLMI, Ship of Fools* at the Palazzo Donà delle Rose in Venice, or the great visual extravaganza on the screens of Times Square in New York, or in Frankfurt, Federico Solmi aspires to enter people's hearts and, like a master illusionist, take them with him on a voyage similar in many respects to that of *Alice in Wonderland* . . .

Full of surprises, delights, and risks, Federico is one of the greatest pioneers of digital art. Pursuing an alternative lifestyle based on talent, courage, an instinctual desire to incessantly create, and eager to discover new frontiers, he seems animated by the unstoppable dynamism of an art that fears no boundaries.

Born in Bologna, Italian by birth, a New Yorker since 1999, and totally self-taught, Federico explores various techniques and digital tools, combining them with conventional art in order to rework both the past and present and with them build the future. His art is never the same, as he loves to experiment, reinvent, rediscover, and, above all, to push the envelope, tackle political, historical, and social issues with a strong surrealist bent, question the status quo, and rail against the unbridled capitalism and narcissism dominating the present through a crazy dance of powerful and well-known past and present personalities such as Donald Trump, Elon Musk, Kim Kardashian, Christopher Columbus, George Washington, Napoleon, Mark Zuckerberg, Oprah Winfrey, Warren Buffett, Abraham Lincoln, and Montezuma.

"I try to offer a far more explicit and disillusioned reading of history, present and past, by questioning those figures who have been its protagonists, sad to say. I want to ridicule them by portraying them as clowns covered in medals that in reality they've never done anything to merit," he says.

Federico admits that he arrived at digital art practically by accident, driven by his own creativity and, above all, by his insatiable curiosity, as well as by his visionary spirit. "I was born in Bologna into a family of shopkeepers. There weren't a whole lot of books circulating in our house; my parents worked at the Mercato delle Erbe in Bologna, and I would not have had an opportunity to acquaint myself with art had it not been for my personal interest. I got a degree in accounting, and I was the only one in my family to graduate from university. When my father died, however, I had to work in the family business—while my schoolmates went on to university—until my sister turned eighteen . . . ," he recounts.

By that point, Federico already had clear ideas about his destiny: "I knew I could never be happy if I didn't become an artist. I spent a week in Paris and didn't like it, so I decided to go to New York, and was captivated by it . . . to the point that I never came back home. I was twenty-five years old, had no training in art, and didn't speak English. After carefully observing the art world, I came to understand that, in its own way, Bologna had provided me with a background of sorts." Federico began studying literature, philosophy, and art on his own, and soon realized that masters like Annibale Carracci and Giorgio Morandi moved him deeply and had become key figures, great models from which he could draw inspiration.

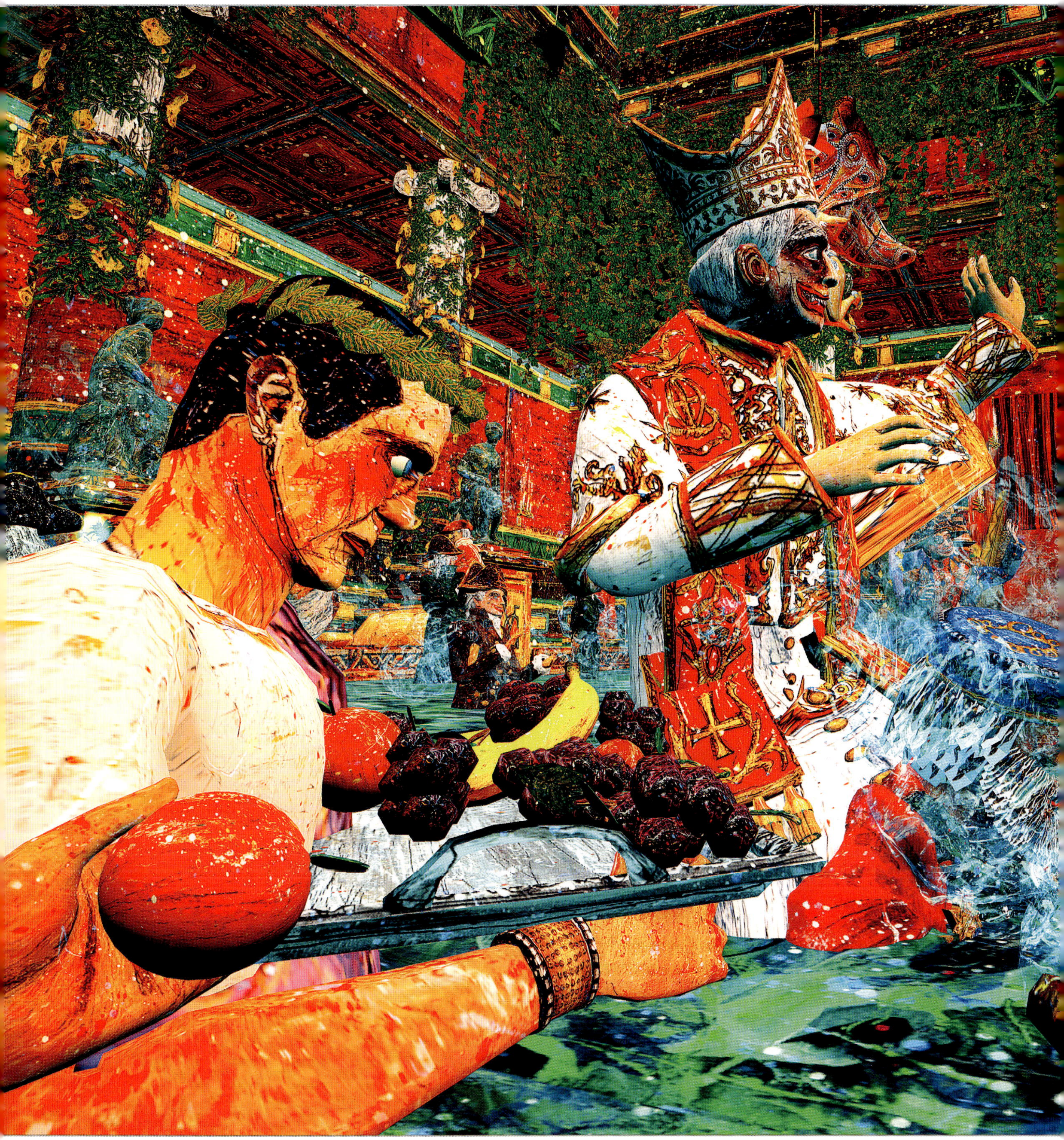

THE BACCHANALIAN ONES, 2021

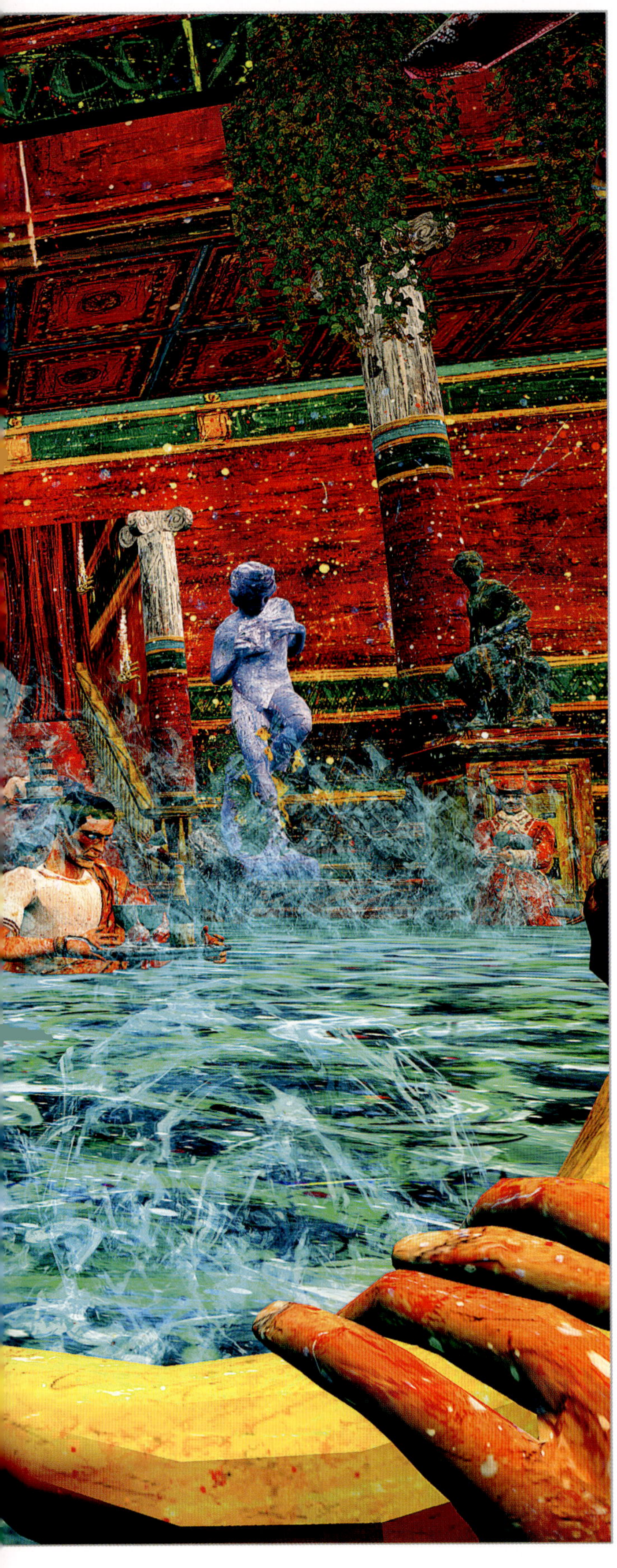

"I strolled around Dumbo, a neighborhood in Brooklyn situated right below the Brooklyn Bridge, which was at its artistic peak at the time. I soon became part of that community and began exhibiting my works at avant-garde galleries. Little by little, I managed to grow and achieve success as an artist. In 2009, I was awarded the John Simon Guggenheim Memorial Fellowship by the Guggenheim Foundation in New York, and from 2016 to 2022 I taught in the Visual Arts Department at Yale University . . . without even holding a degree," he recalls. Convinced that he had something to say and refusing to give up, Federico had a real passion for art and was driven by an enthusiasm that won people over. "In 2002, I began exploring the digital world. Although I wasn't a fan of video games, I was fascinated by their graphics. Unlike many artists who were convinced that video games could not serve as sources of inspiration or spark new ideas, I wanted to transform their graphics into narrative images on which to devise my own characters and stories. I thus converted my paintings and drawings into digital images, joining two different worlds . . . I came across the Grand Theft Auto (GTA) video game series during a difficult moment for that market, just as many people began holding it as somehow responsible for inciting violence in youth. I started by transposing the frames of the game into drawings, then building digital worlds and transforming them into paintings, and vice versa," he recollects. His work is characterized by a complex and extraordinary chromatic quality, a succession and superimposition of intense and jarring colors that dazzle the eye in a nearly breathtaking way: "This exacerbated expression of color arises precisely from my desire to involve all the senses of the spectator on a deep level . . .

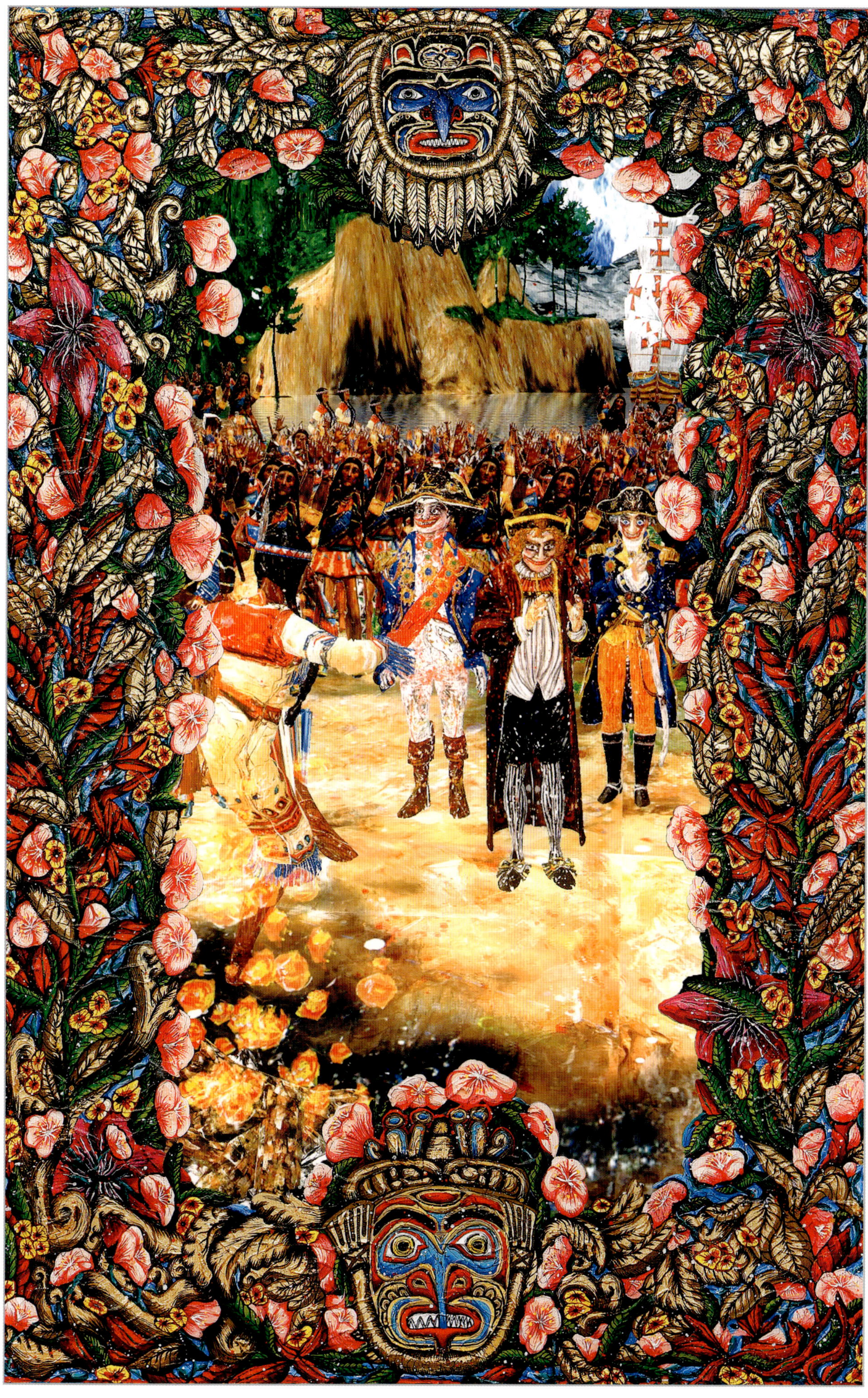

Here I recognize the influence on me of great works of the past, for instance Giotto's *Scrovegni Chapel* in Padua with its saturated colors, Goya's grotesque figures, and the Sicilian pottery of Caltagirone, as well as the paintings of my favorite period, which falls, paradoxically, in the 1400s, with Piero della Francesca, Paolo Uccello, and the other 'imperfect artists,' as I like to call them, who differ from the unsurpassed artists of the Renaissance such as Michelangelo, Leonardo da Vinci, and Raphael: artists that I also love but feel less connected to," he says.

History and the art of the past are an important source of inspiration for him, but the present too plays a fundamental role in his work: "I've always been interested in the social contexts in which we live. After settling in the United States, I read in depth about American history and learned about the dark side of U.S. colonialism and how, over time, North America 'strangled' the development of Latin America." All of Federico's works are meant to highlight the injustices and disparities inherent in our society and underscore the presumptuousness and frequent ineptitude of the ruling elite: "My worlds are organized by algorithms and software, but I've learned to tame these with drawing, painting, animation, video editing, and virtual reality . . . I felt a need to add humanity and organicity to the digital world, which is extremely fascinating but often dehumanized. I, by contrast, want to make my work accessible to the broadest possible audience. That's also why I love designing art for the public squares of the world, where human contact is immediate and real."

In addition, Federico believes in the absolute freedom of the artist and criticizes academia in which talent is often in danger of being obscured by a teaching system anchored in the past. "All too often, contemporary art is detached from the issues confronting the people, and tends to become the heritage of an elite group. This is why I've always been fascinated by the great Mexican muralists like Diego Rivera, José Clemente Orozco, David Alfaro Siqueiros, who produced social art with a clear message," he points out, stressing the equal importance he places on diversity and originality.

THE GREAT EXPEDITION, 2017

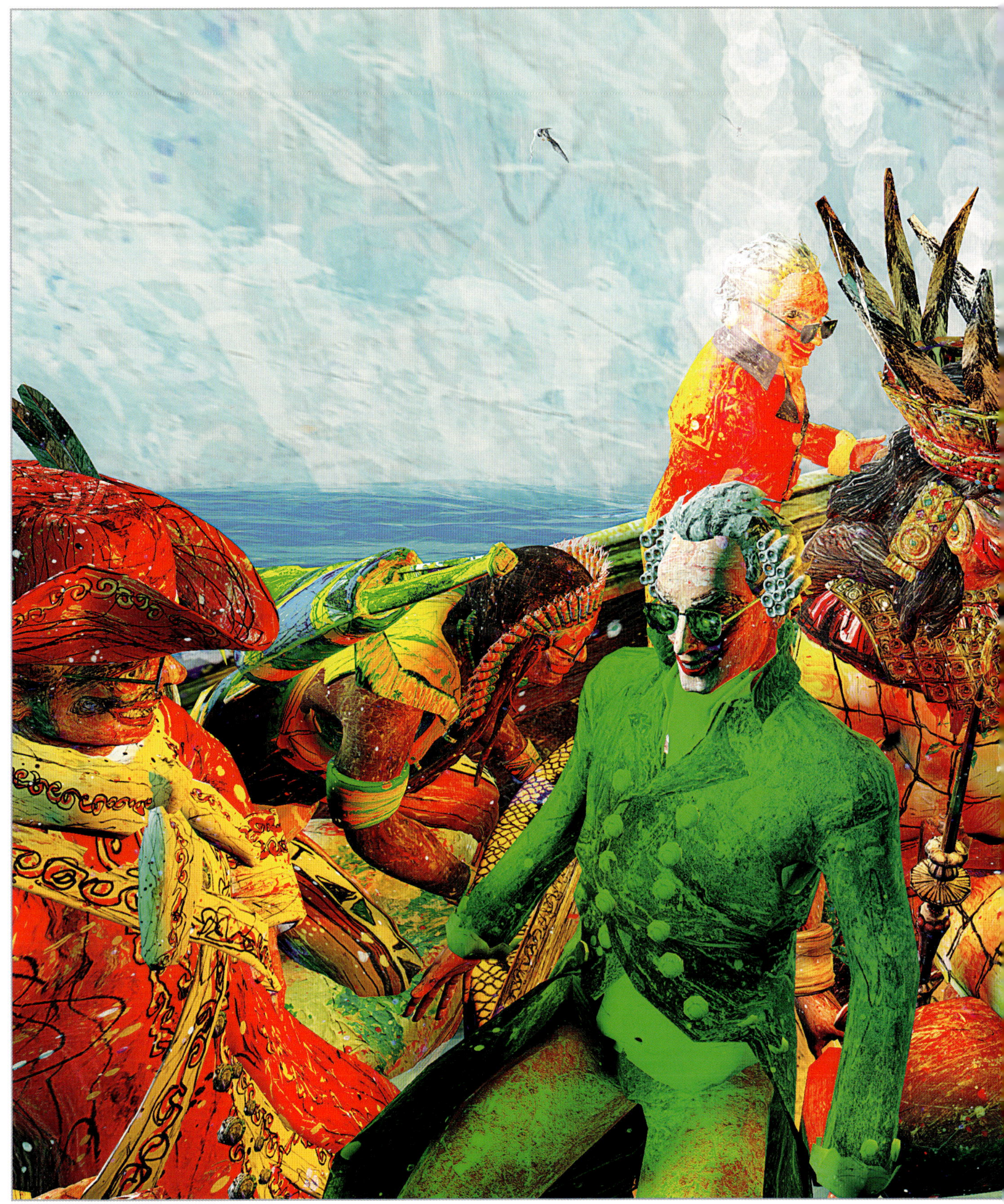

"Artists often tend to repeat themselves; I, on the contrary, always want to invent something new, to stimulate my imagination, to keep myself up-to-date on a technical and pictorial level, to experiment with all the means at my disposal. I'm not afraid of technology, because I'm convinced that culture will never disappear or be forgotten, and will instead integrate itself perfectly into the world of tomorrow," he concludes.

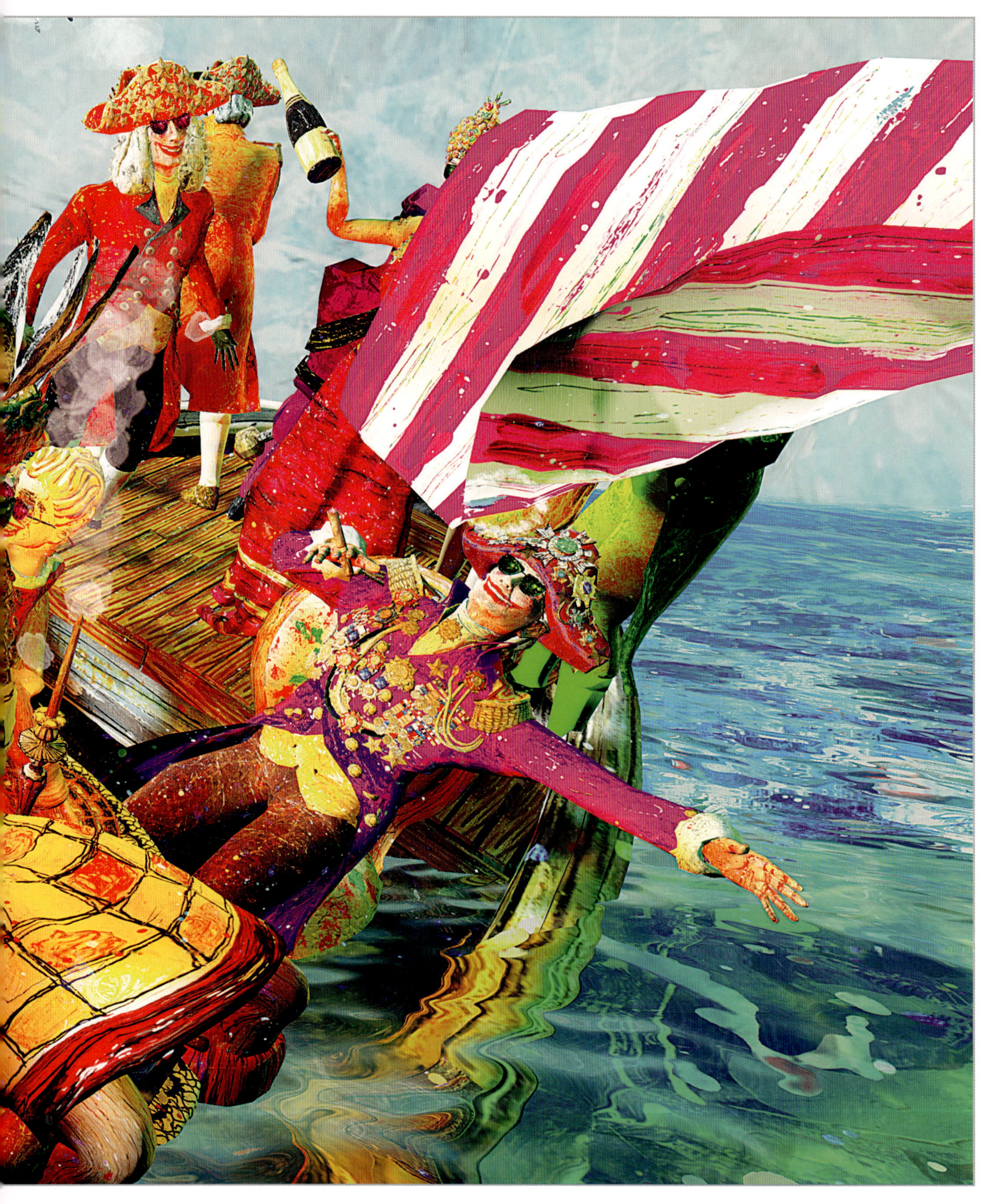

THE PLASTERED FATHERS, 2020

207

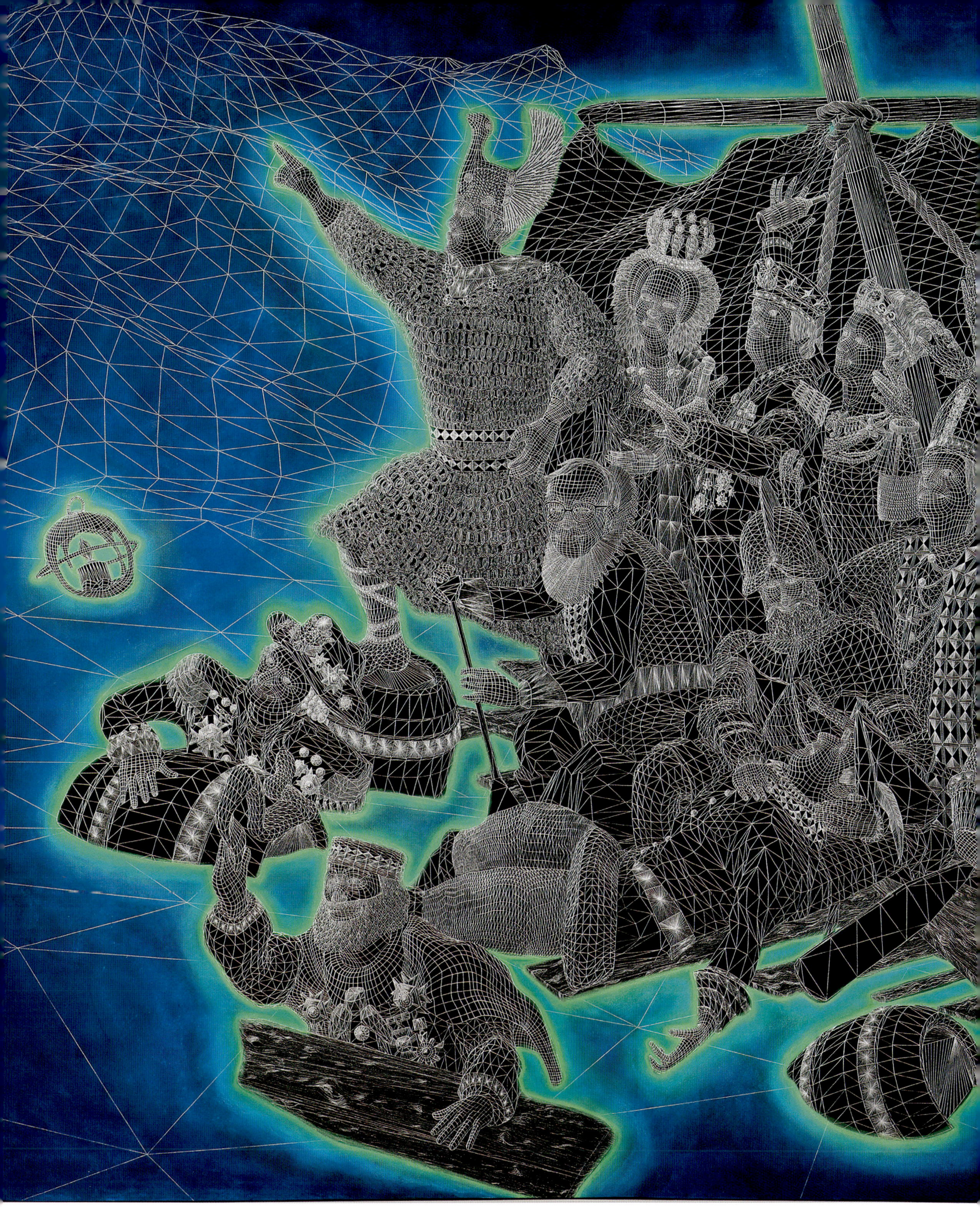

THE SHIP OF FOOLS, 2024

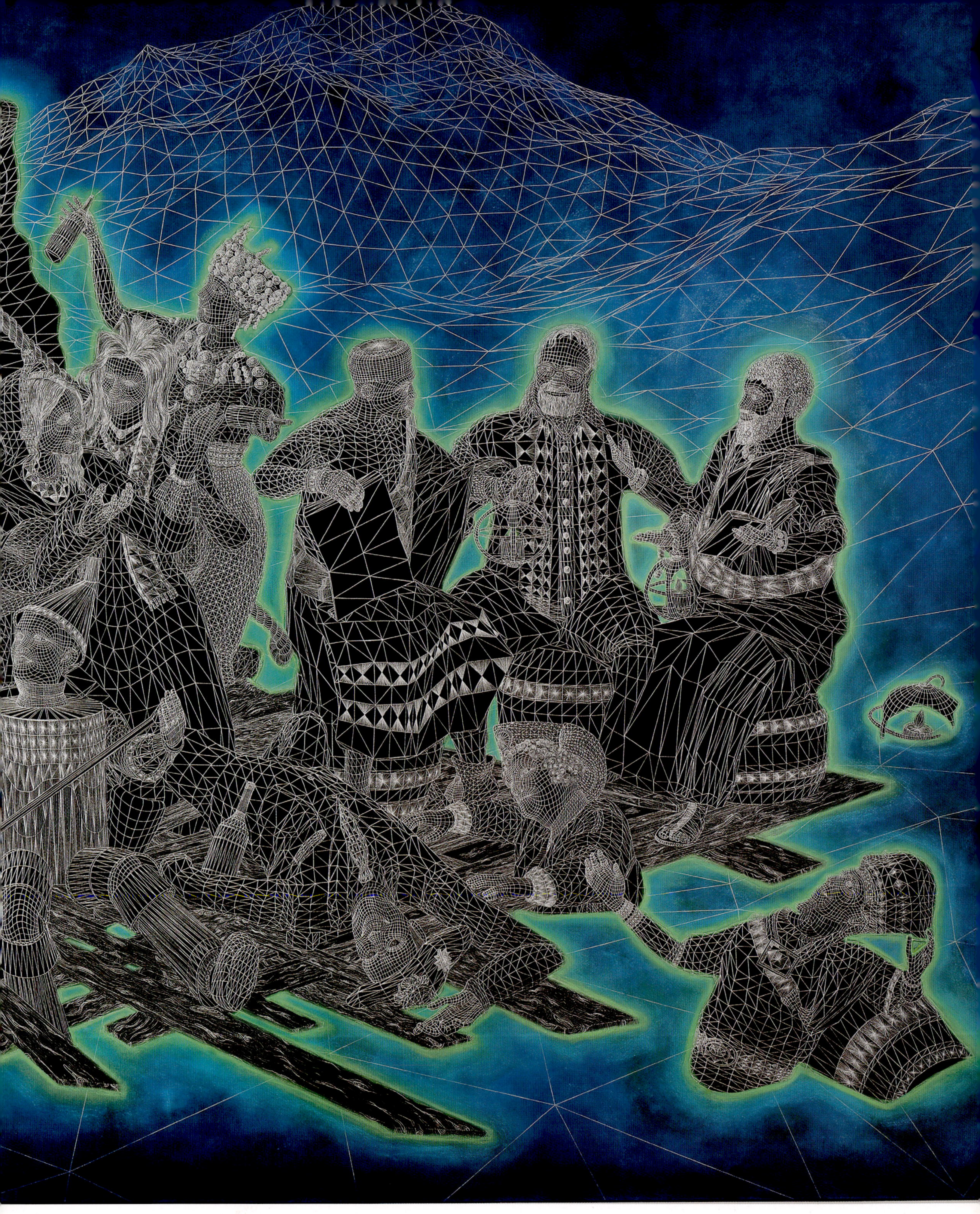

ANNE SPALTER

WHEN TECHNOLOGY MEETS TRANSFORMATION

**"I MUST CONFESS THAT I'M OBSESSED WITH AI.
I'VE BEEN USING IT IN MY WORK SINCE LATE 2020.
FOR ME, IT'S LIKE MAGIC, AND I'M ADDICTED."**

Anne Spalter is truly an innovator who pushes the frontiers of digital art. She loves to explore the landscapes and intricate paths of the contemporary world, and is adept at playing around with and reworking them, granting them a new identity, and transforming them into something sublime. Through her vision she explores infinite oceans, endless roads with no precise destination, microcosms of intense emotion and sensation, and more . . . There is also color, strong and vibrant, powerful and intoxicating. Anne Spalter is a visionary. Her mission as an artist is to focus on the potency of transformation, on understanding contemporary society and collective problems with the hope of coming up with concrete solutions and a possible—not merely imaginary—future. In her quest to find joy and happiness, the celebration of life, the connection between beings, she pushes herself to the limits of a world bordering on delirium.

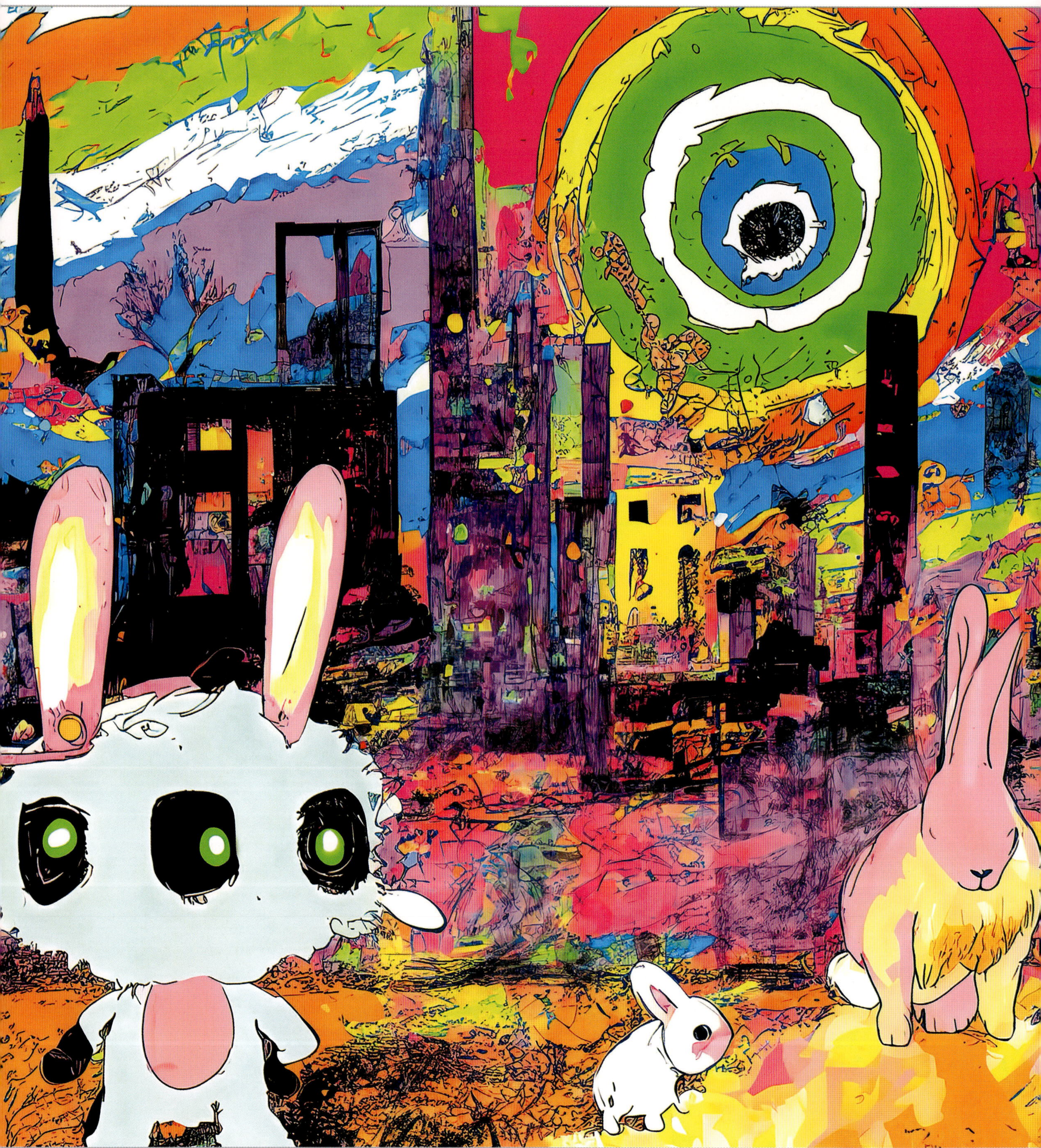
ZELDA 2022

Anne Spalter never tires of exploring the "contemporary landscape": while traveling, she draws, takes photographs, and creates videos, combining traditional art techniques with those offered by new media without being afraid to venture into recent, more modern technologies. "I remember my parents dragging me to museums when I was a little girl. At the time, I protested vociferously . . . Only after I entered high school did I begin developing some interest in art, though it remained at the margins of my world . . . At that time, I was obsessed with the Rolling Stones and constantly drew images of Keith Richards that I discovered while leafing through magazines. I used one of these drawings for an engraving, and was amazed and fascinated by how simple lines could create something that looked so alive . . . I had the good fortune to find a teacher who knew how to use this interest of mine to push me to learn and delve deeper into more conventional art techniques," she relates.

From the outset, the concept of art assumed a very particular meaning for Anne. "In graduate school, I was given the following photo-journalist assignment: 'Collect images that you consider sublime.' It got me excited, and I've continued doing it ever since," she says. "Initially, I wasn't all that attracted to technology and, in fact, preferred manual crafts. It was only after graduating that I began appreciating computers' extraordinary power to expand one's own creative abilities. And, since there were no specialized electives on the subject, I decided to delve deeper into the subject on my own. Later, I was actually asked to teach an in-depth course on the subject, which led me to write a book, *The Computer in the Visual Arts*, and create and collect early examples of computer art," she recalls.

Anne began discovering the frontiers of digital art in the late 1980s at Brown University, where she majored in mathematics and the visual arts, and continued this exploration in the 1990s, at the Rhode Island School of Design. Her book, *The Com-*

puter in the Visual Arts, published in 1999, established her as a pioneer in the field as well as a profound source of inspiration for other artists. In collaboration with Michael Spalter, former chair of the board of the Rhode Island School of Design, she founded the Anne and Michael Spalter Digital Art Collection ("Spalter Digital"), one of the largest private collections of digital art, whose works are frequently exhibited at MOMA in New York and LACMA in Los Angeles. In the meantime, Anne established herself as one of the foremost contemporary artists in the field. One of the best-known and most innovative of her numerous works is *The Bell Machine*, acquired by the Buffalo AKG Museum. "The program with which I create a work of art depends on the project and the location for which it is intended, but my style, my intention, and my mission essentially remain the same," she notes.

For a while now, Anne has split her time between Providence, Rhode Island, Williamsburg in Brooklyn (New York), and Brattleboro, Vermont. "I could say I'm a 'digital nomad,' though the place in which I spend the most time is definitely Brooklyn," she explains. Basically, however, she doesn't care where she is: what's essential is that she be able to dedicate herself entirely to her art, a kind—digital—that never ceases to amaze her. "I still find it strange and really fascinating that typing a few commands in a program can generate an unbelievably interesting image. It's incredible, if you think about it . . . All the same, I feel it necessary to emphasize that the art I create with artificial intelligence is not substantially different, especially in terms of intention or purpose, from the kind I made in the conventional manner," she says emphatically. "I know there's still a certain skepticism about the use of AI in creative fields, but I believe that ultimately it will prove itself a force for good. Over the past few decades, our world has grown ever more visual, and I'm convinced that artificial intelligence will help people express themselves visually in a far more effective and immediate manner than is possible at present," says Anne with confidence.

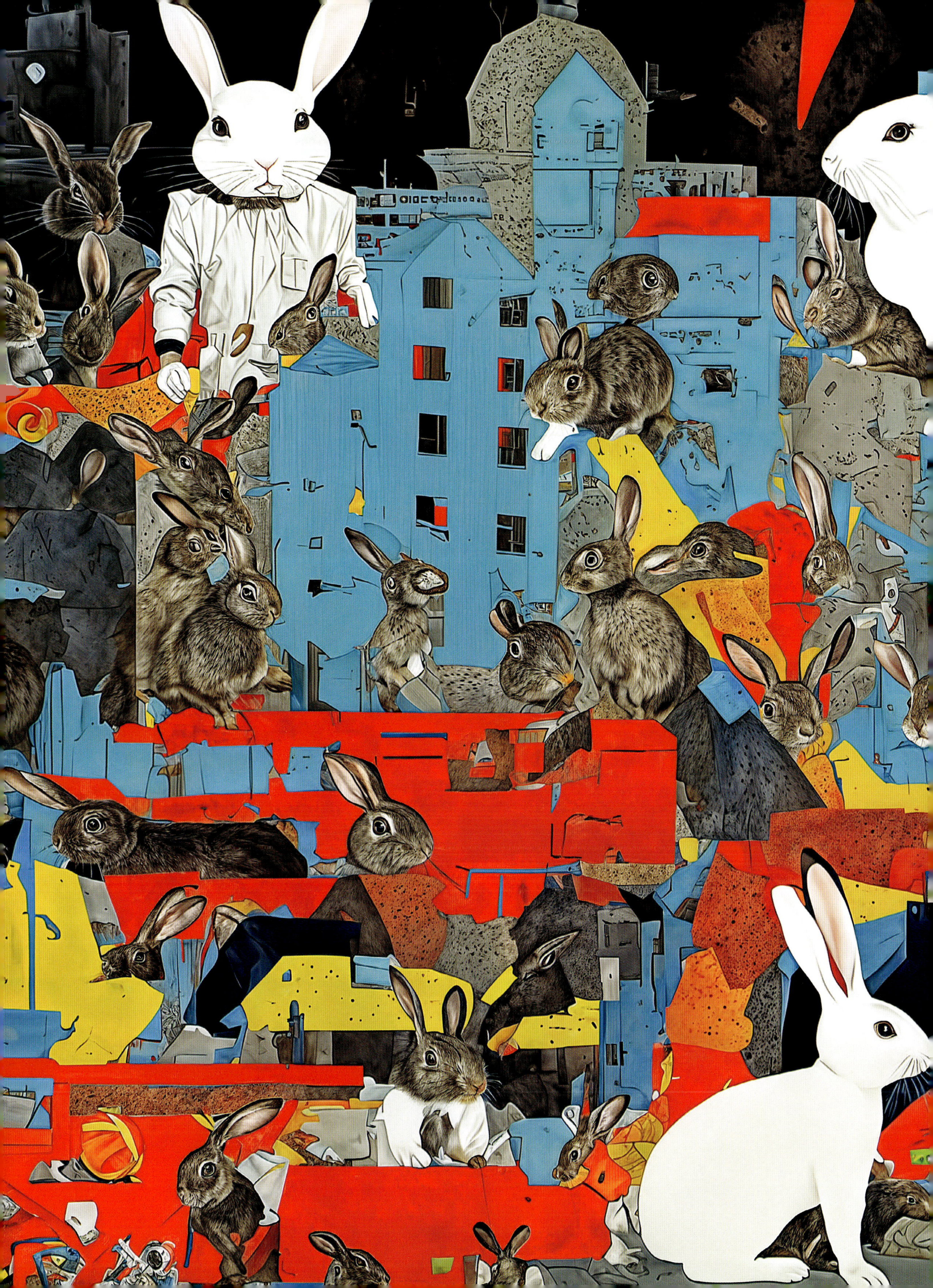

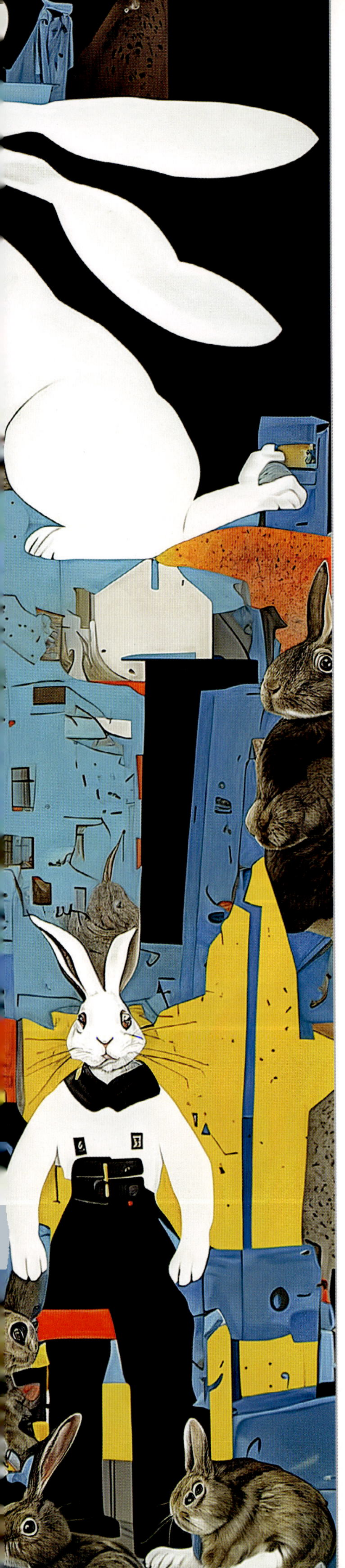

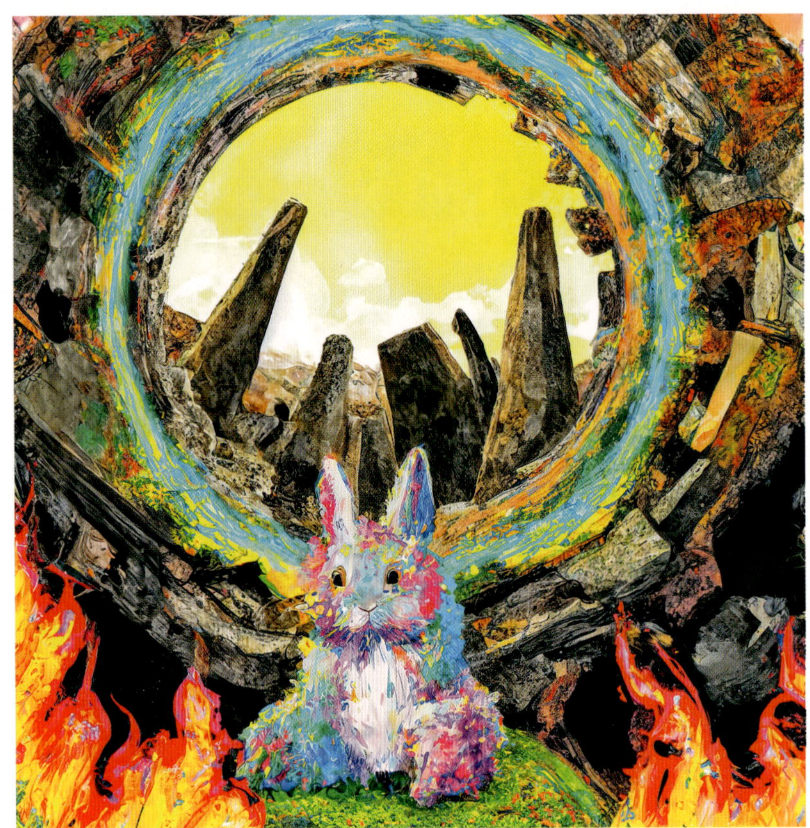

CHRYSANTHEMUM 2022 ⟶

"Right now I'm using artificial intelligence to explore post-apoca-lyptic landscapes, and I'm inspired by the interaction of destruc-tion and rebirth, by the resilience of nature and the human spirit. This fusion of technology and creative vision enables me to delve into issues related to the ever-more-pressing problem of our surviv-al on this planet—issues like the reconstruction of cities, the pro-tection of nature, and, in a more philosophical sense, the future of humanity. Artificial intelligence grants us the ability to plunge into an endlessly fascinating investigation of possible scenarios that lie beyond the end of the world as we know it," claims Anne, with ever greater conviction that AI will take her toward previously inconceivable horizons.

⟵ **QUIVER AND CREW 2022**

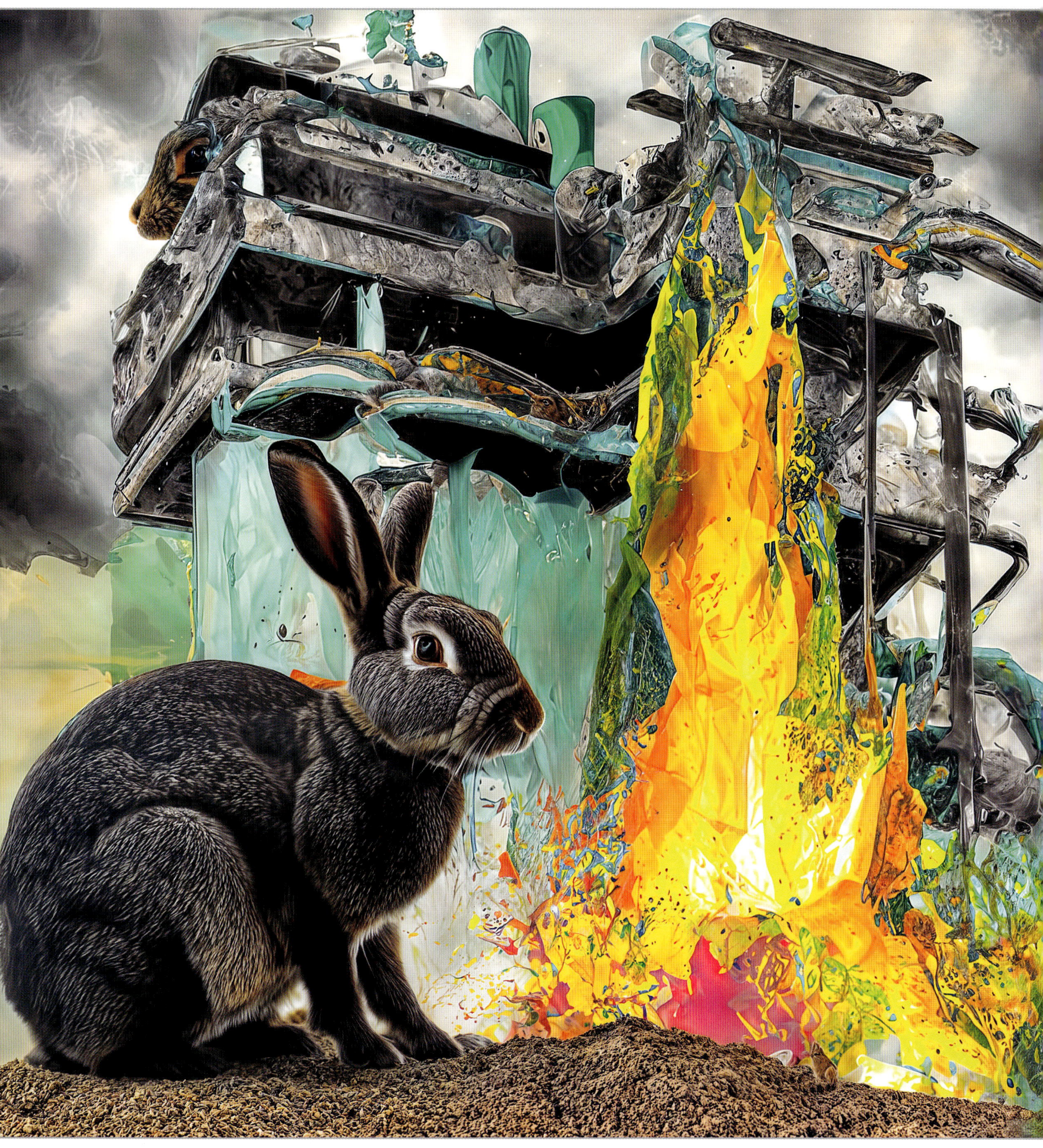

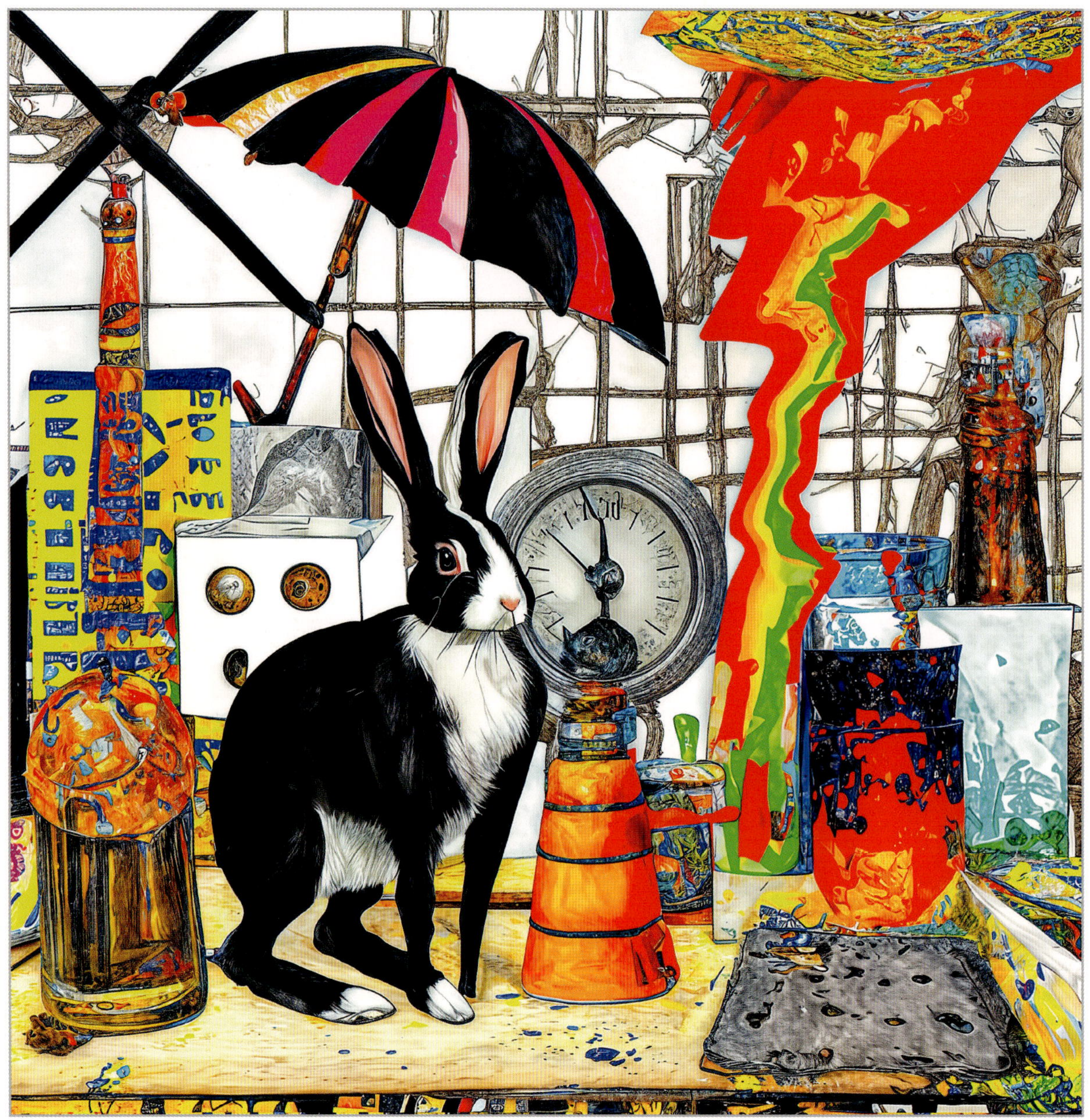

The common thread in Anne's personal and artistic development is her passion for color, one that leads to a perfect connection between the past, present, and future. "I think Chagall got it right when he said 'Color is everything. When the color is right, the form is right. Color is everything; like music, color is vibration; everything is vibration.' I've studied color theory a great deal and love artists like Chagall, Hans Hoffman, Stanley Whitney, Howard Hodgkins, Pierre Bonnard . . . These were all masters of color. It's difficult to foresee and plan chromatic effects; but when they're right, you can feel it, you can clearly perceive it," she notes.

As for the future, Anne wants to continue her journey through the world of technology, forever experimenting with something new, of course—something that allows her to push the boundaries of her fervid imagination even further.

FIRE CASTLE 2022

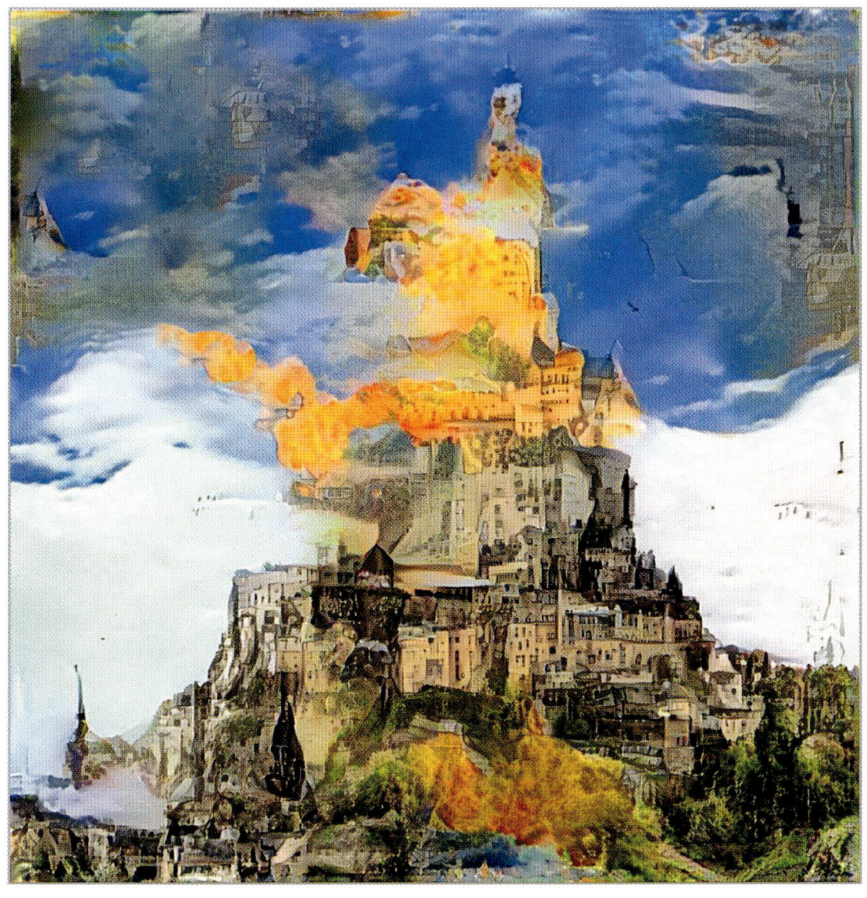

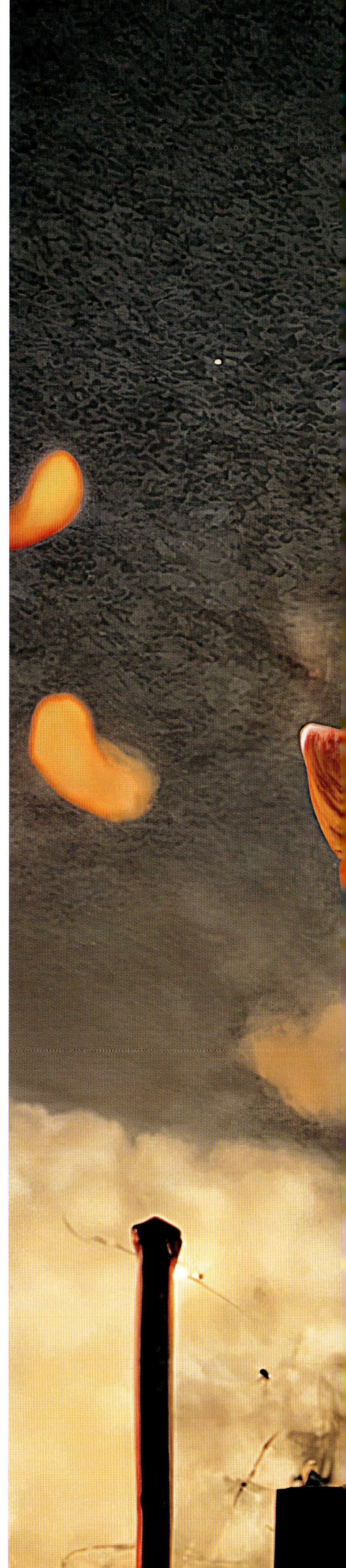

FACTORY BLOOMING 2022

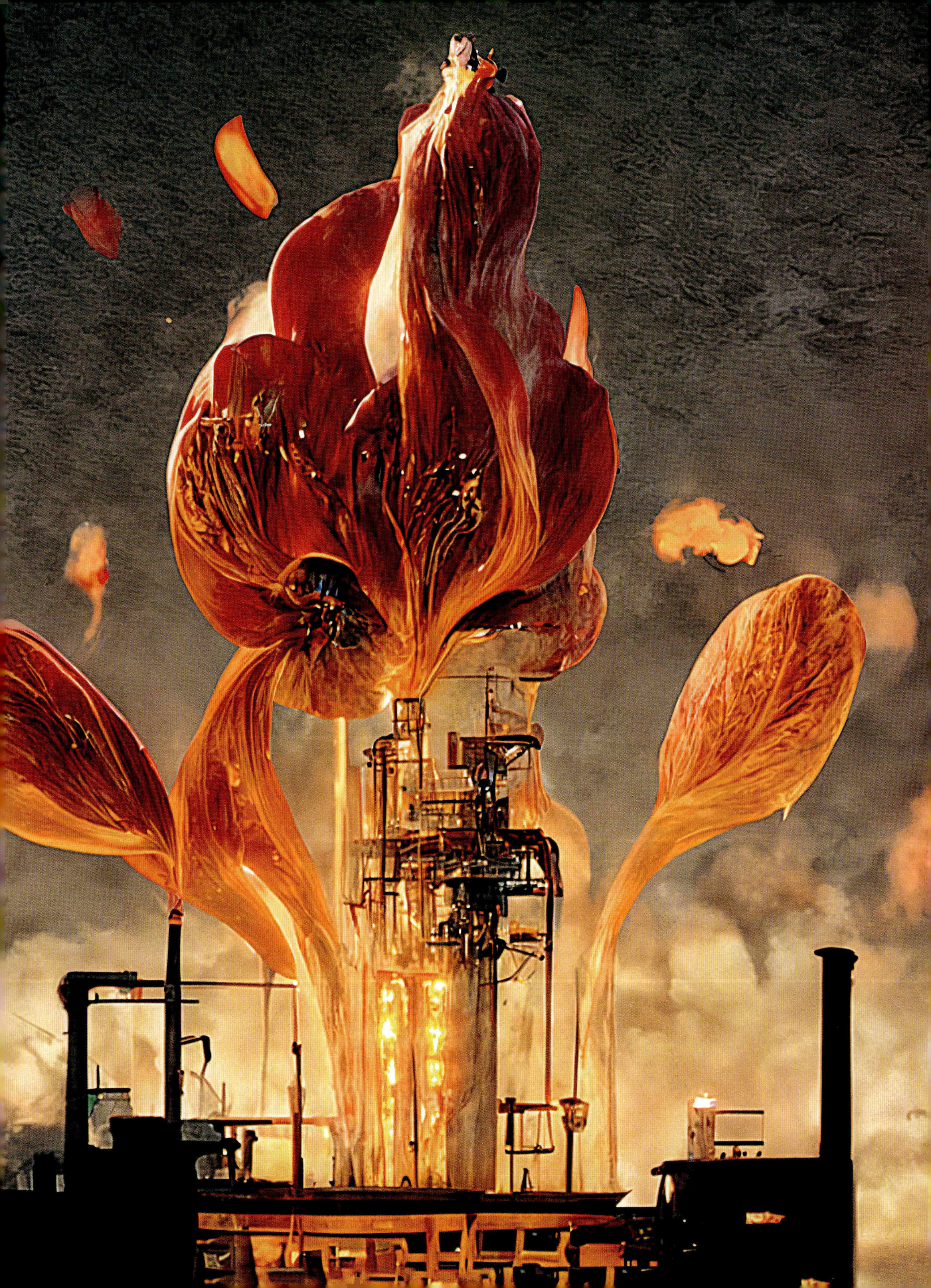

ORI TOOR

*WHEN IMAGINARY WORLDS TURN
INTO IDEAL HOMES*

"IN GENERAL," SAYS ORI TOOR, "I DON'T LIKE BEING SURROUNDED BY CHAOS. WORKING DIGITALLY FREES ME FROM THE NEED OF AN ENORMOUS SPACE, FROM WORRYING ABOUT RUNNING OUT OF MATERIALS OR SHIPPING PHYSICAL ARTWORKS AROUND THE WORLD. AS ONE DELVES A BIT DEEPER, TECHNOLOGY BECOMES TRULY STIMULATING AT EVERY STAGE: FROM THE DESIGN PROCESS AND PRODUCT ENGINEERING TO THE STUDY OF GRAPHIC INTERFACES."

Ori designs new, diverse, and colorful worlds for living in or being devoured by so that we can lose ourselves in them and their ephemeral existence. He never has a specific plan, a system, a consolidated group of sketches that gradually become more and more concrete . . . His greatest talent lies in improvisation. His works are always as inventive and creative as he is.

Ori Toor is definitely one of today's most eclectic and original artists. His images appear to be a playful mix of pop art and sophisticated cartoons, hinting at the infinite nuance of color and light. He admits that among his favorite artists are Souther Salazar, Paul Klee, the Fleischer Studios brothers, Jim Woodring, and Jon Burgerman, and that Hayao Miyazaki, the master of Japanese animation, whose movies serve him as an essential source, is one of his greatest heroes . . . The influence of this great Japanese artist is, in fact, perceptible in all of Ori's work, even if he's managed to develop a style of his own—poetic and engaging, complex and intricate, intense and entrancing.

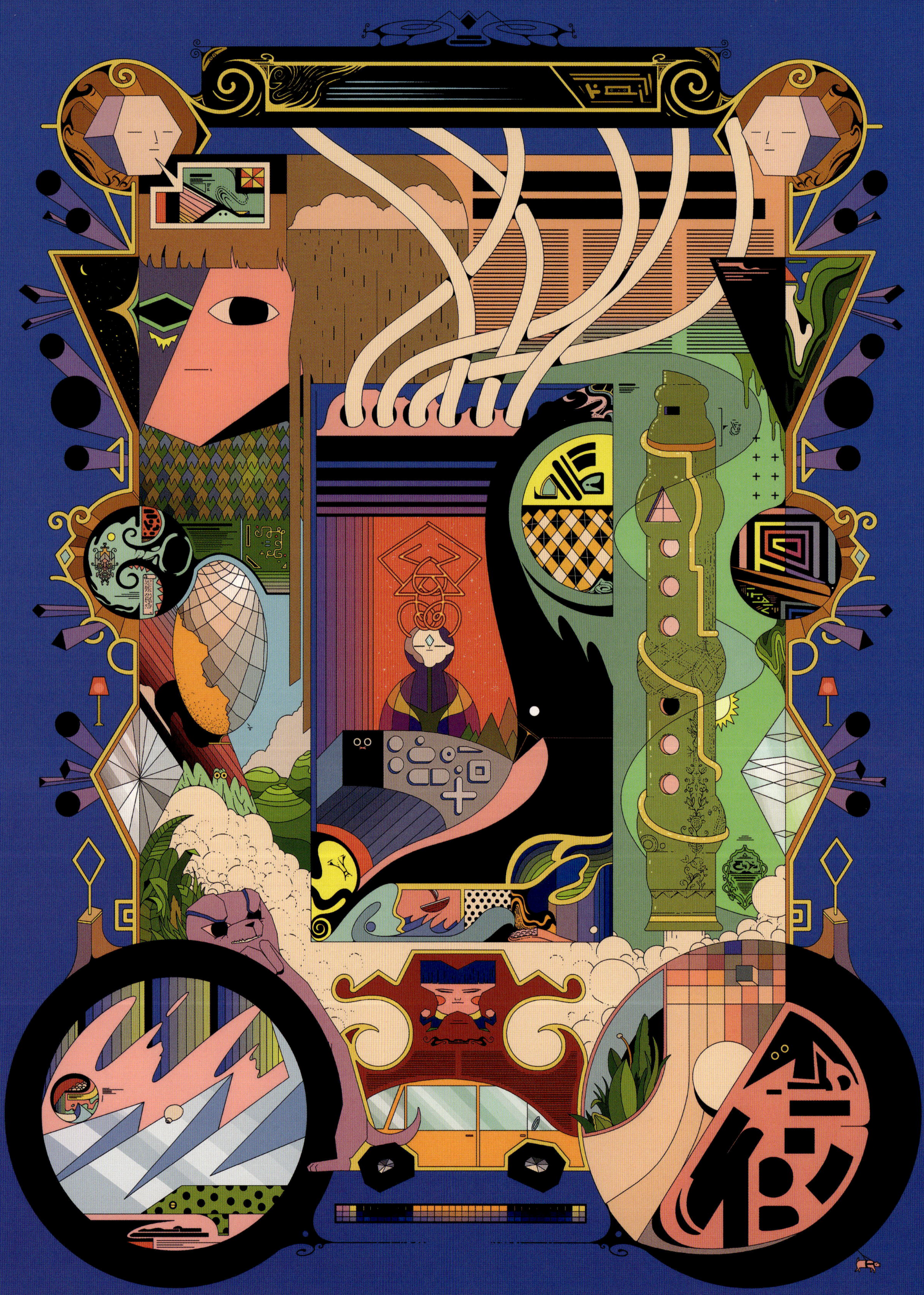

Ori fell in love with art early in life, first as an illustrator, and afterwards as he grew ever more enraptured by the magic of technology and the infinite opportunities it offered. "I became interested in art at an early age. My mother was a textile designer, and I recall that I loved watching her as she used watercolors to capture the texture of carpets. Sometimes I joined her, and we made them together . . . Art was always present in the house in which I grew up, but my interest was sparked above all by watching cartoons, especially those featuring Wily the Coyote, Beep Beep, and Bugs Bunny. It was then that I realized that the ability to create images out of nothing was a kind of superpower that enables the construction of new worlds," Ori recalls. "At home, where I was surrounded by art books, I was obsessed with the Surrealists, especially René Magritte. I was equally fascinated by cartoons and the wizardry of Disney animators, by the technological tools that allowed them to sketch characters perfectly with lightning speed," he adds.

Ori feels that he's genetically predisposed to technology and that this has sealed his destiny. "I've been fascinated by technology ever since childhood. There's something incredibly interesting and engrossing about computers and interfaces—as well as about science, for that matter. I'm not a hundred percent sure why, but I think it's due mostly to the way in which man-made creations differ from the natural world. Although in nature you can find circles and recurring patterns, it's difficult to find a square. What I find surprising is that prior to man, there were no rectangles in nature. Everything we do stands in sharp opposition to nature, and I just love this contrast," he observes. "Although I'm not a 3D artist, my current obsession is 3D technology," he states.

With time, Ori has developed a deeply philosophical and existentialist view of his art. "My vision of art is the opposite of what one might expect. I grasp the meaning of my work only after I've completed it. The act of making is in itself

a voyage marked by exploration and discovery. I think my general objective is to create welcoming spaces populated by kind, friendly characters, a version of reality in which I feel at ease. There are always surprises along the way—some ambiguous, some amusing. It's becoming ever harder for me to remain surprised at my art, but that's one of the things that fascinates me most. Naturally, I also seek beauty and equilibrium in chaos . . . More precisely, I generate a bit of 'visual' chaos, then work on bringing about a new harmony among the elements . . . ," he notes. Ori does not limit himself to the artificial world of the Internet; he lets his creativity be influenced by everything that revolves around him, that affects him, or that he observes and absorbs like a sponge. Ori admits that everything can begin with some sketches drawn by hand on a sheet of paper—even he doesn't know how these "free" lines will end up and what they'll constitute: ultimately, it's a bit like working, like experimenting with the computer . . . He describes himself as an expressionist with the soul of an illustrator. "My inspiration comes from all that's around me; even the most banal and boring things can contain interesting ideas, stimulate points of departure. I simply have an irrepressible—I might say 'automatic'—need to make art. I don't even know where it comes from. Perhaps it's a need to please and be appreciated—all that is certainly part of my creative process—but basically I'm fine with not knowing everything. I enjoy and find it stimulating not to be fully aware of what I'm doing. It's the only aspect of my life that seems a bit mystical, transcendent. And this generally applies to my existence as a whole. I get distracted if things are explained too much. The truth about the reality around us is that we don't know enough about it, and I like the truth," he says with conviction. From a distance, Ori's works resemble a large conglomeration of elements in which everything meshes perfectly; but as one draws closer, one notices contrasts, clashes, motion, action, and a liveliness that is purely existential,

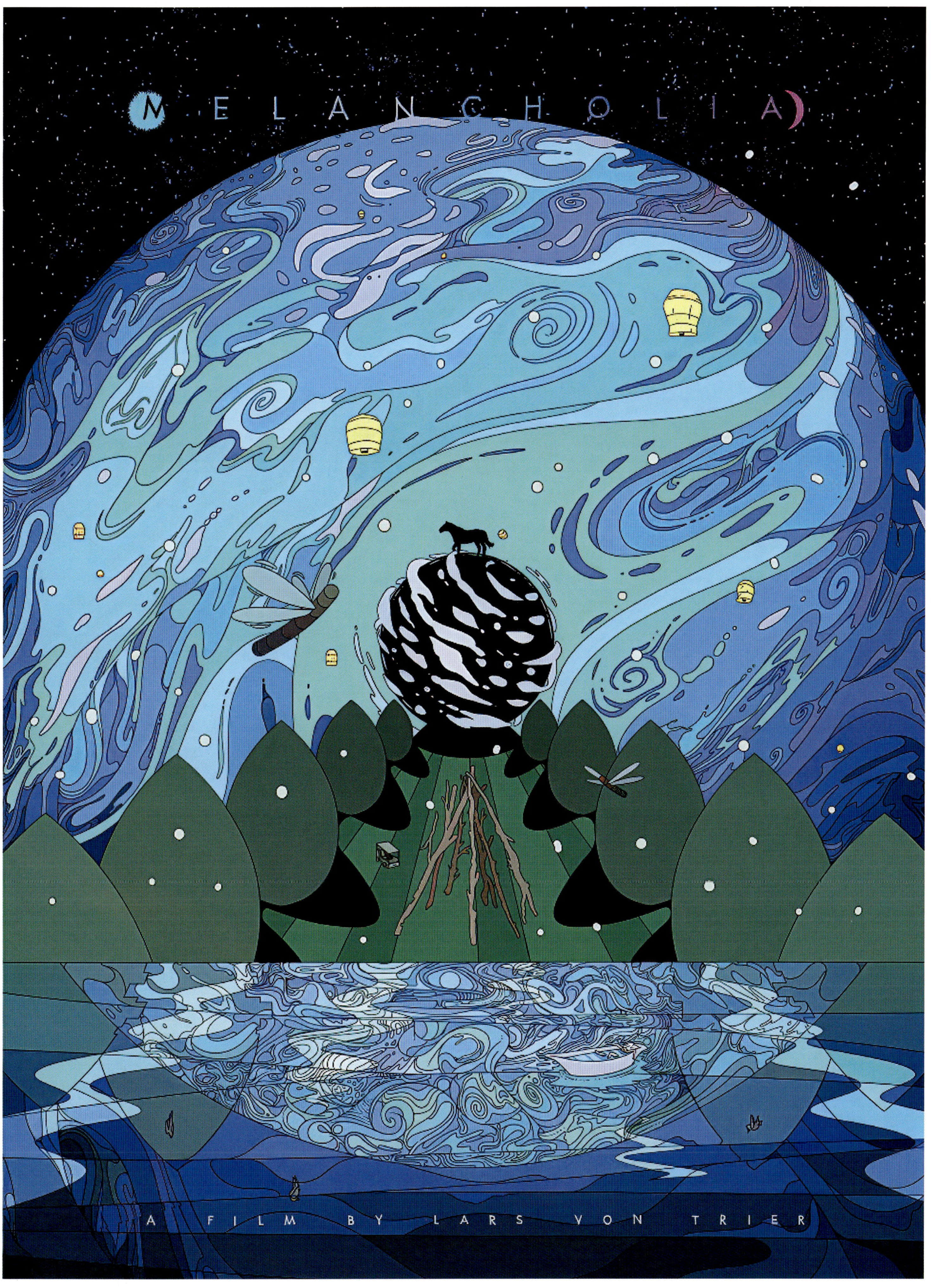
MELANCHOLIA)
A FILM BY LARS VON TRIER

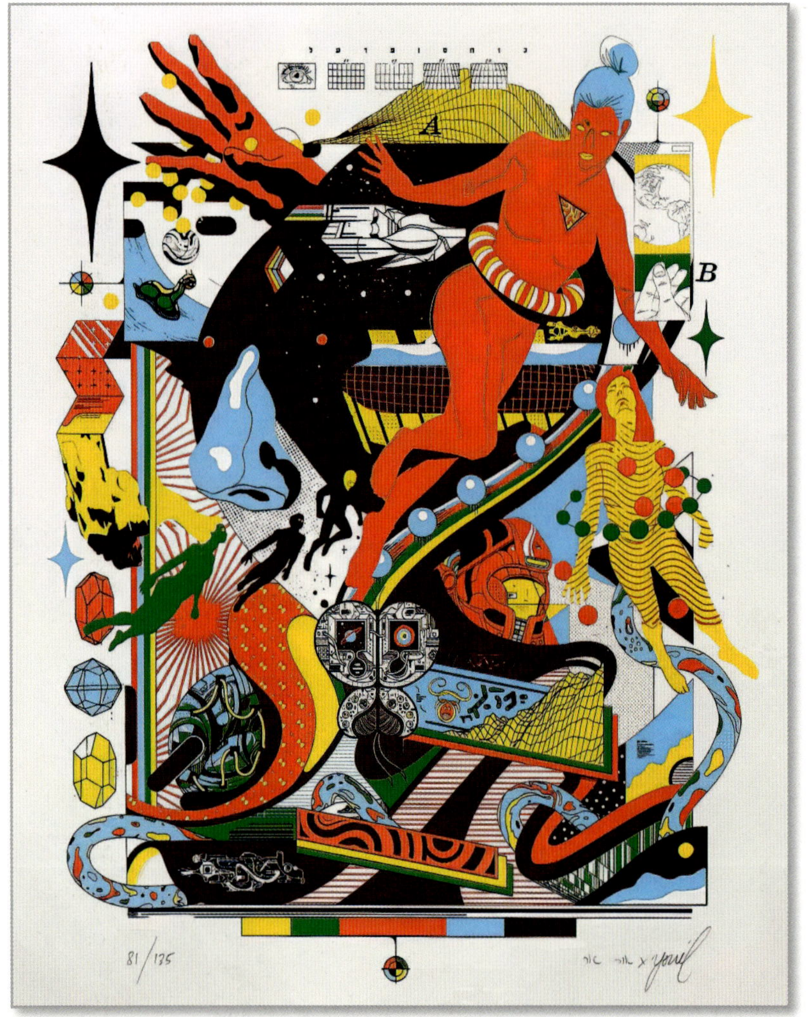

that continuously evolves and changes. A certain more accentuated realism can be read in his works, particularly when he limits himself to black and white. Ori is bluntly honest when revealing anything about himself as an artist: "At times I wish I could work exclusively in black and white. The real reason I use so much color is because people are more attracted to it, and I want to keep on working. It's not that I dislike colors: I adore them; but most of the time my approach to color isn't about the color itself, but rather about light and the way it bounces around, creating reflections and shadows. That seems strange, because in my work, which is so graphic, colors seem flat," he notes. All these elements, hues, lights and shadows, the running lines turn into extraordinary characters and play a part in his fantastical worlds. But does Ori envision an ideal world just as the ancient masters did? "My earliest memory of something approaching this comes from the Disney movie *Fantasia*. I recall being literally mesmerized by the fairies who flew among the leaves at night. Like them, I too wanted to flutter between the leaves and branches of a tree, flying around the tiny homes of my friends.

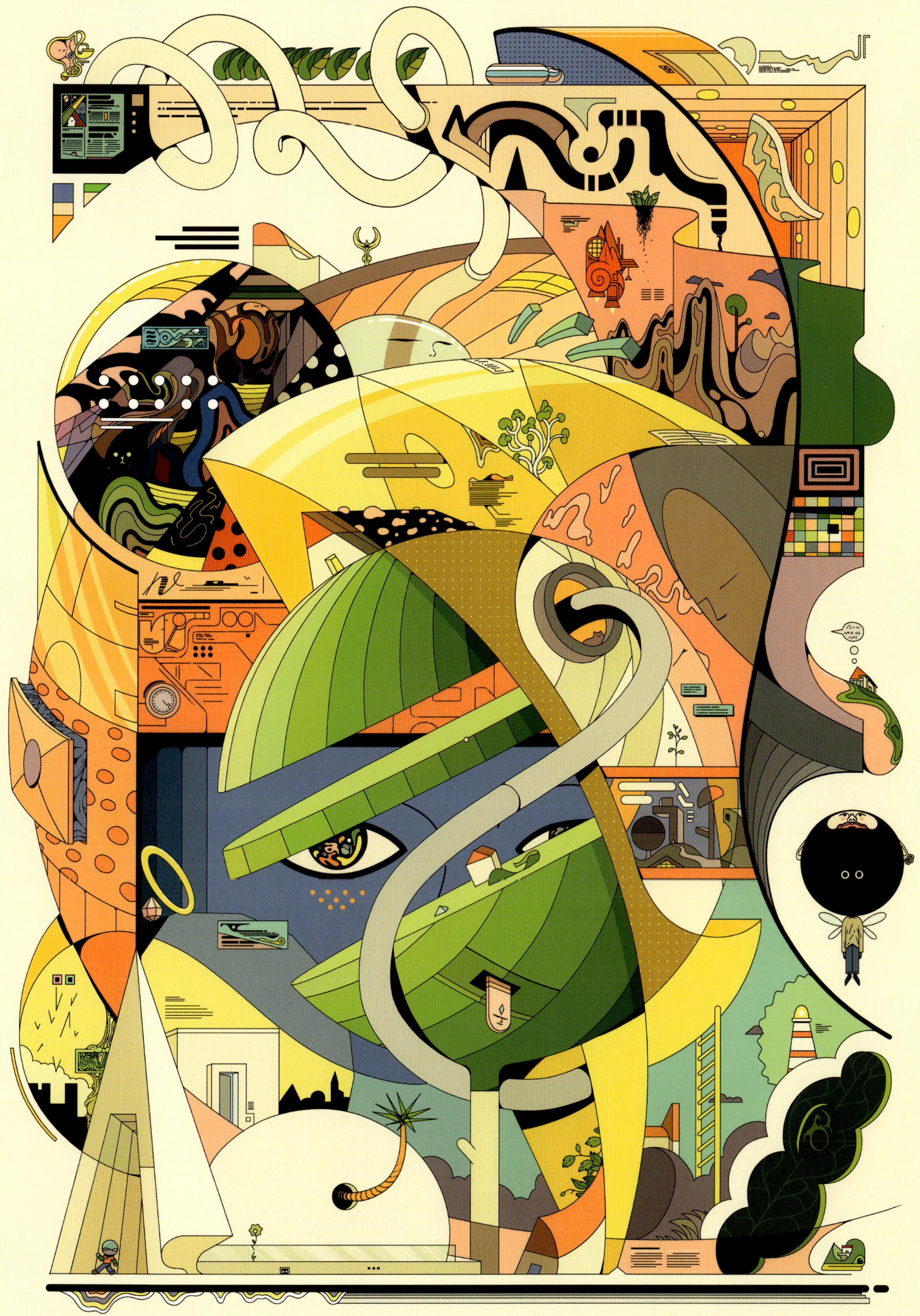

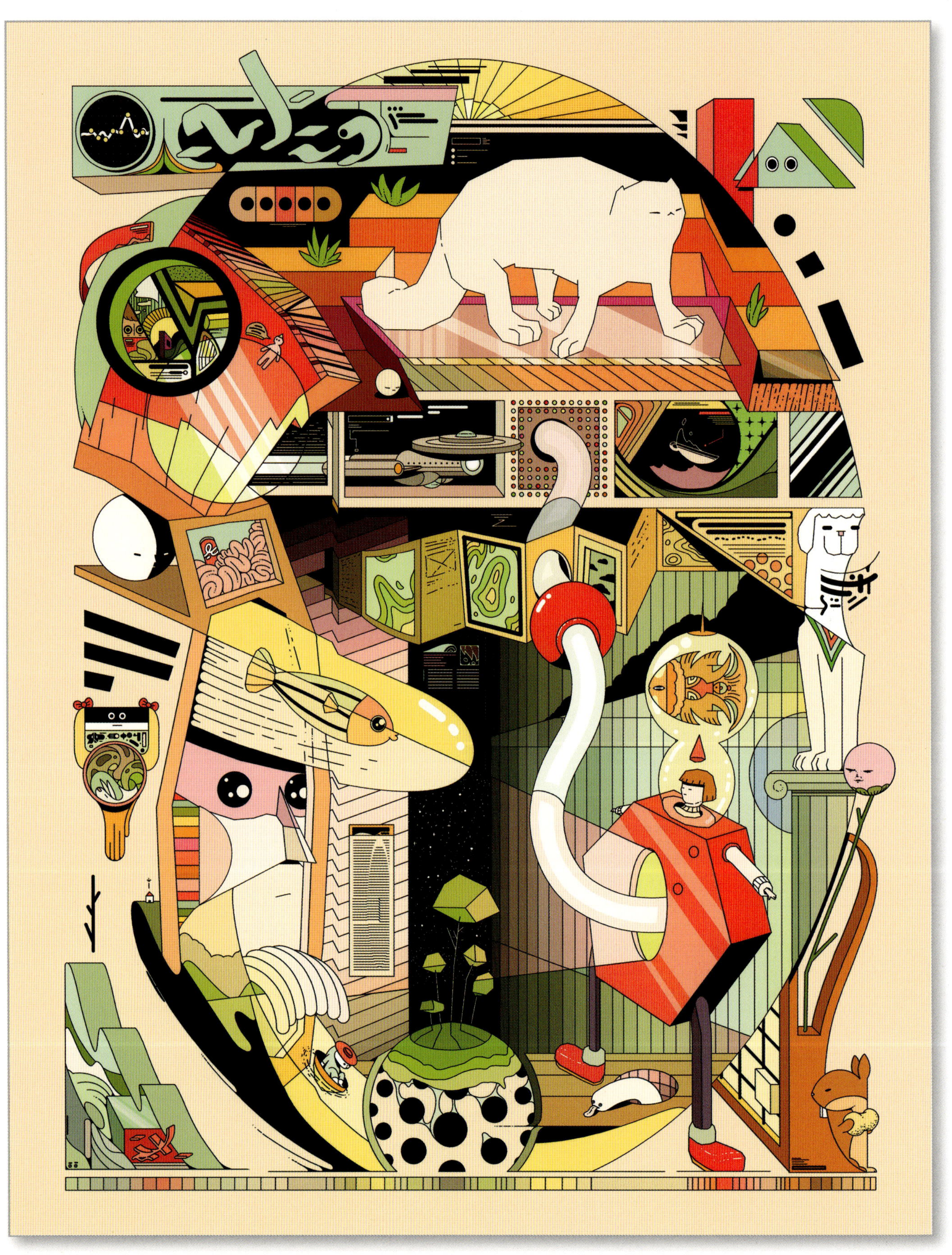

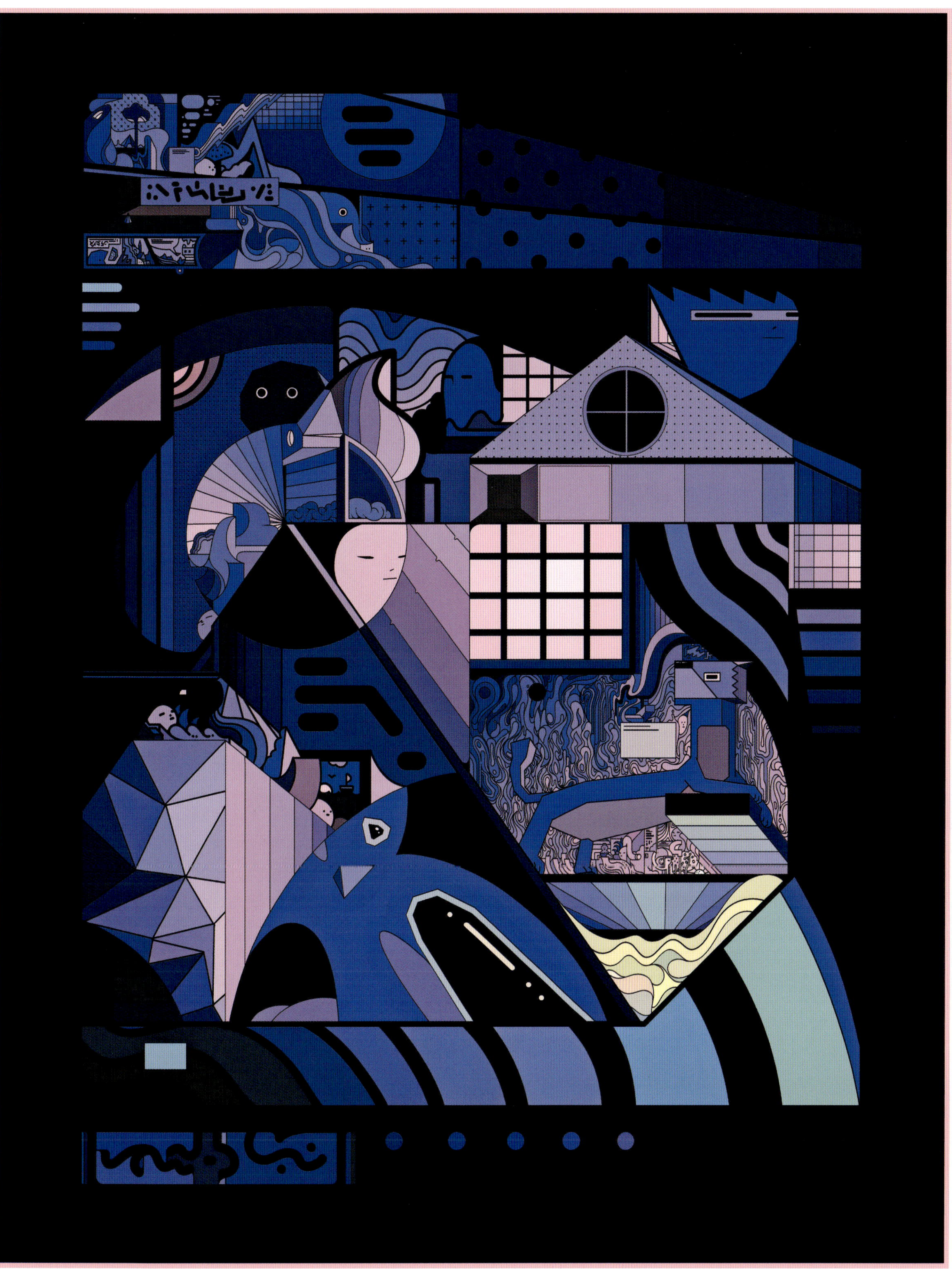

UPODOPO

This dream filled me with a sense of well-being: I felt at ease and welcome . . . ," he replies.

"In my art, I try to create a magical world, an imaginary one that opposes the real one in which everyone can feel safe. Because I'm an introvert, slightly agoraphobic, with a history of depression, I want to build a space for myself that combines my craving for wonder with a sense of security," he openly confesses without hypocrisy. It's precisely this deep honesty that characterizes his art. Ori is equally direct when revealing his values as a human being. "I'm gay and grew up as the only child of a single mother in Israeli society, which is still highly chauvinistic. I always felt at home with my mother and friends, but I never felt part of my country. However, I can't go live elsewhere because I'm deeply bound to my partner and family, so art serves as my escape in every respect. For me, art is like a home in which I seek that sense of belonging that I lack," he reveals with emotion. Ori experiences a certain unease when he thinks about how his art may change and mature in the future . . . "I really appreciate artists who have an easy time evolving. I think it's an important aspect of art in general, but I lack the ability even to imagine how my art will develop in the future. I've gone through various phases in the past, but in recent years change has really slowed down. I'm not even sure whether it's happening at all, and this scares me a bit. Thanks to art, I've already suffered several mental breakdowns and have also experienced boredom. That's a terrible and difficult thing to deal with when it affects one's principal source of livelihood. If I ever get bored making art again, I wish with all my heart that it'll only be a temporary phase that ultimately propels me to explore new avenues . . . ," he reflects.

PINDAR VAN ARMAN

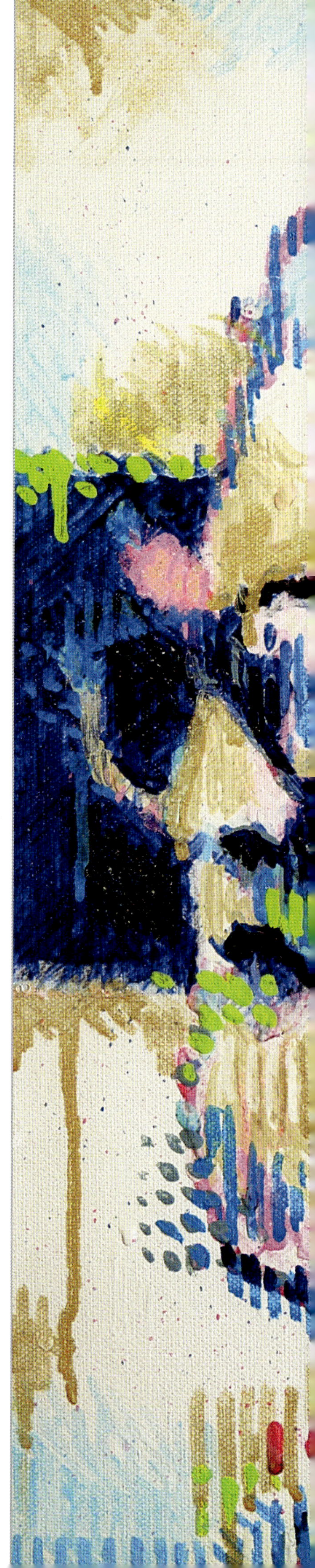

WHEN MAN BEWITCHES ROBOTS

"I'VE ALWAYS BEEN ATTRACTED TO TECHNOLOGY;
FOR ME IT WAS SOMETHING INCREDIBLE
AND NECESSARY. FOR A LONG TIME,
I DID BOTH PHYSICAL AND DIGITAL ART . . .
UNTIL I DISCOVERED ROBOTS . . .
SINCE THEN, I'VE GONE TOTALLY DIGITAL."

PAST PRESENT AND FUTURE

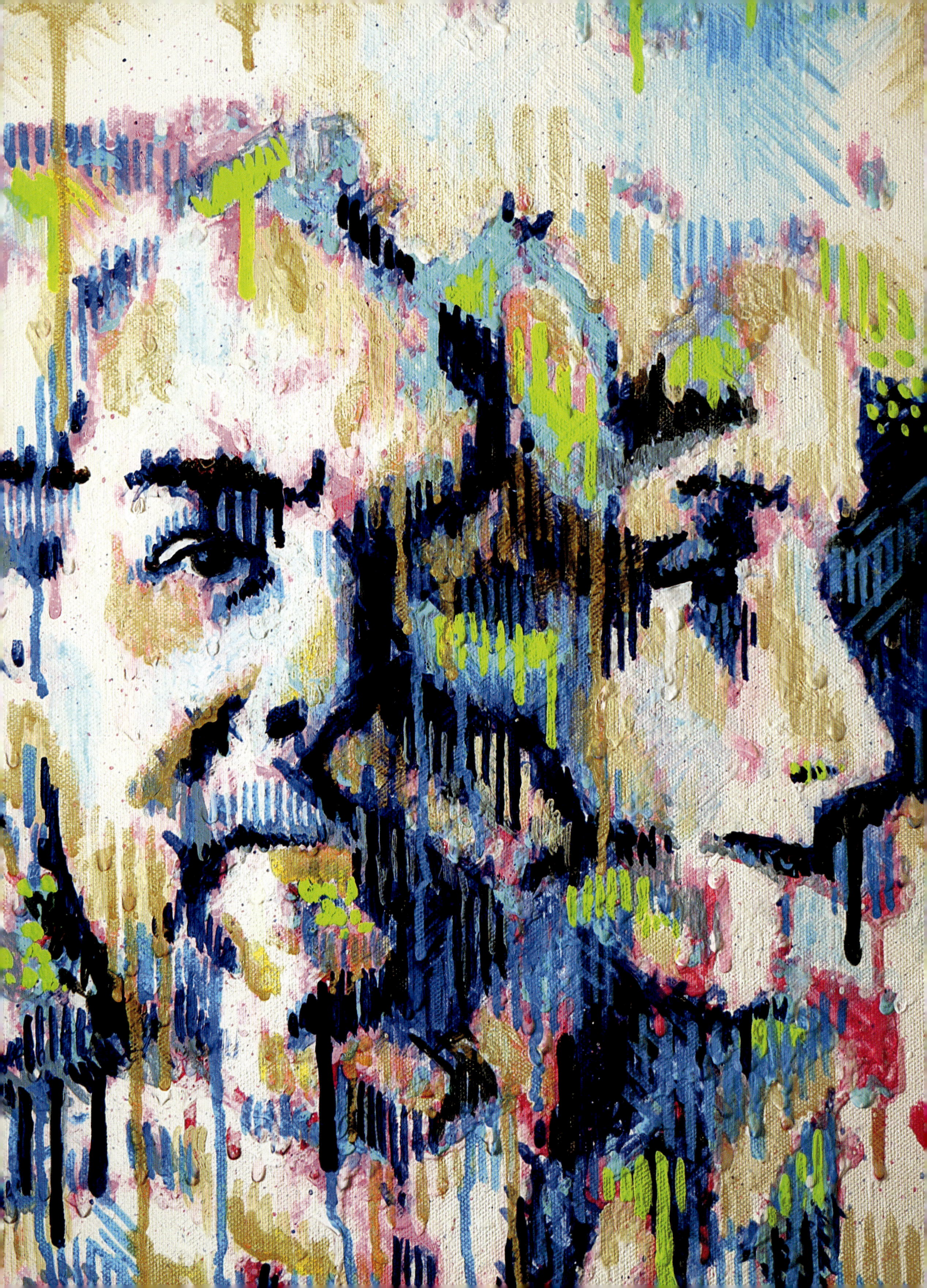

Pindar Van Arman bewitches robots with the power of a snake charmer. He is fascinated by AI as an instrument for exploring the secrets and mechanisms of the human mind. "When I work with a robot, whatever I 'teach' it refers back to me, to my way of acting and feeling. I study its behavior in order to comprehend my own; I analyze its reactions to understand mine," he explains. As he himself points out, he may be the only artist in the world to work in this manner. "I teach robots to paint in my own style. First, they leave a stain, a mark, on the canvas. So I interrupt the work and ask them to take a photograph: I want them to see what they've done, to reflect on it before continuing . . . I called this project *Reflection* because it's meant to be a process of reflecting—almost like a mirror—of the human mind," he says.

Pindar's aim is to analyze the differences between human and artificial creativity. Usually his robots paint with a brush on canvas, but recently they've begun exploring new creative horizons, even demonstrating that they're able to make their own decisions. Are robots capable of free will as well? "By now, the artificial intelligence of robots has nearly reached the level of the human brain, and it's developing ever more quickly . . . I'm generally the one who tells the robots what to do. I try not to assign them names. I treat them as though they were my tools, like the tip of a brush, and instruct them on what they need to do . . . But sometimes it happens that one of them decides on its own what it wants to do . . . ," Pindar openly admits, not hiding a somewhat disturbing aspect of these new characters on the art scene. But actually Pindar loves his robots almost as though they were his children. "When I'm standing before my robots explaining to them what they need to do, I feel as though I'm in front of my own children . . . I have four children; and one of them, in particular, fills up every blank page that ends up in his hands with blobs of color, reminding me exactly of the methods used by my robots. In fact, the algorithms I use for programming are all inspired by the way I try to teach my children . . . My family and many of my friends often tell me that I relate

better to robots than to people . . . ," he confesses. His path hasn't been easy: "I was born and raised in Washington, D.C., but no one there or around there ever really appreciated my art. By contrast, outside my own country my works have aroused a great deal of interest, and I've been invited all over the world to speak about my art projects: in Paris, where I 'met' several robots who were capable of feeling emotions and knew how to be more empathetic than some human beings; and later in Berlin, in Korea, in Australia . . . Digital art is a great opportunity to make oneself known everywhere, beyond physical borders . . ." In 2018, one of the works he created with the CloudPainter robot and the use of artificial intelligence won first prize at Robot Art, an annual robotic art competition; the prize was based on the following rationale: "CloudPainter was able to paint evocative portraits with various degrees of abstraction."

"I've been using this technology for quite some time: my first robot artist dates back to 2005–2006. The reason behind it? I had a family, children, and wanted to find more time to spend with them. I've always created both physical and digital art and often found myself working on a painting for ten hours . . . I painted a lot, without taking a break. Then I hit upon the idea that if I were to have someone who could start the painting for me, I could finish the piece after putting my children to bed . . . And so, since I was already spending many hours before the screen and the world of computers definitely fascinated me, I decided to find collaborators in the field who could help me realize the project of my life," he explains.

Pindar, therefore, initially turned to technology for a basically practical reason: he needed to support his family and dedicate the right amount of time to it, but at the same time he had to find a way of making his art: this would never have been possible without AI. After graduating from Ohio Wesleyan University in 1996 and earning a master's degree from the Corcoran School of the Arts and Design at George Washington University in 2010, Pindar found himself looking for

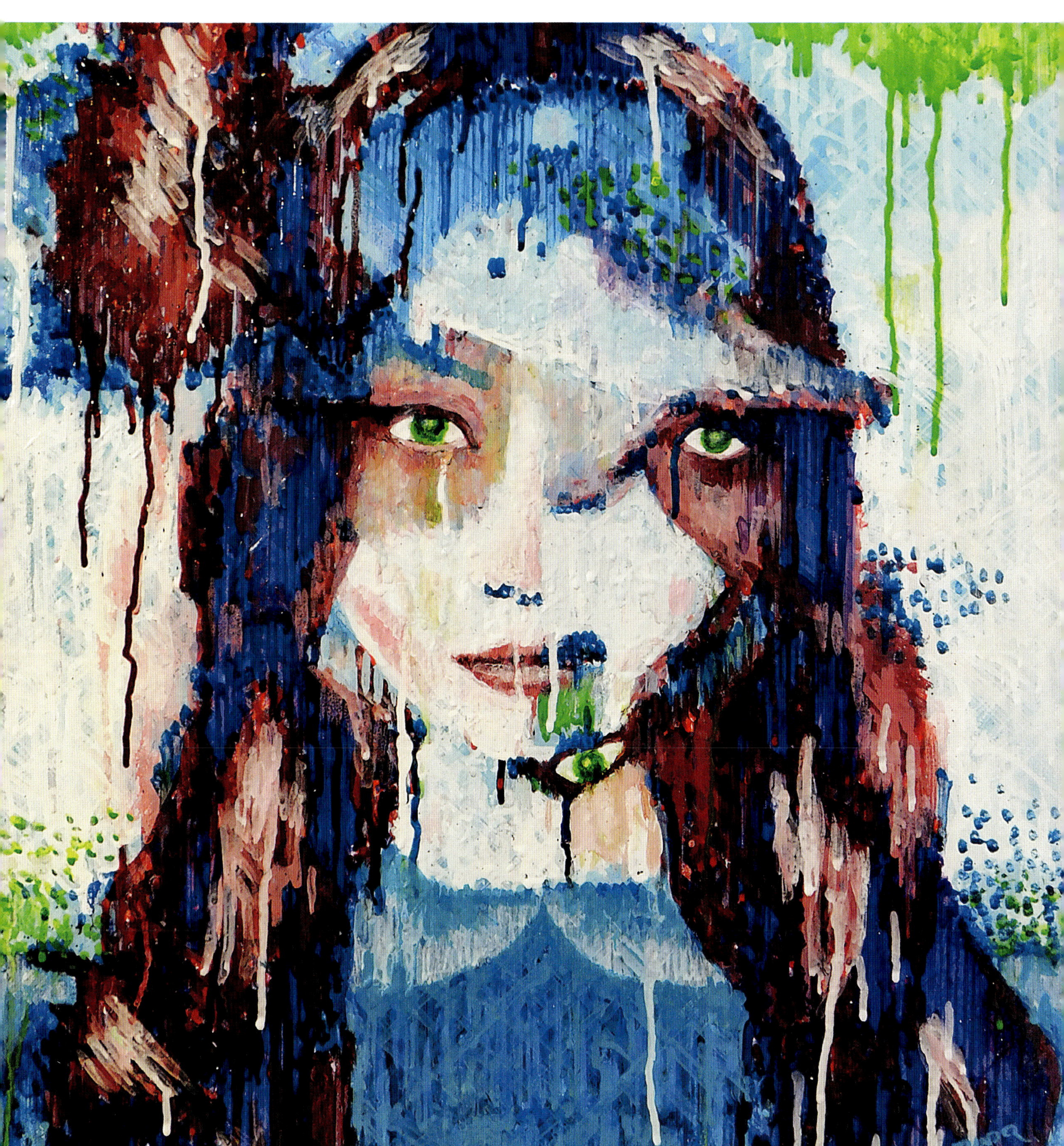

ANITA IMAGINED BY NEURAL NETS
AND PAINTED BY ROBOTS 2018

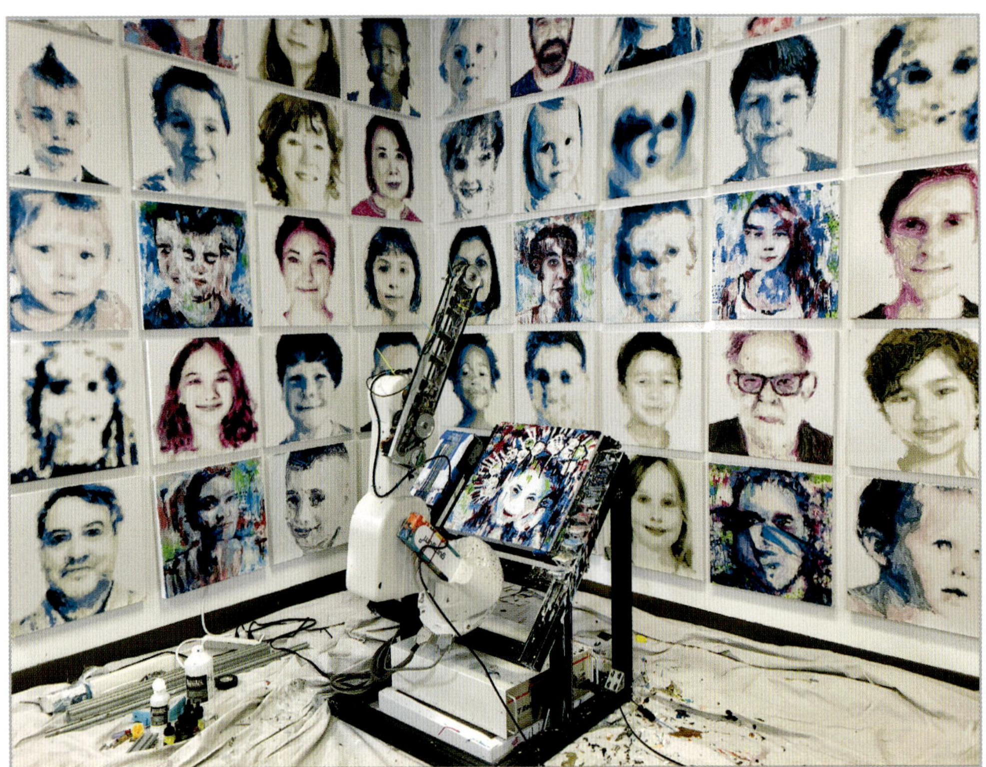

employment. "I needed a permanent job: I had bills and invoices to pay; I couldn't afford to experiment. So I began working as a graphic designer at a company that specialized in designing websites, where they advised me to focus on programming to earn a bit of extra money. I instantly found it a fantastic universe, full of possibilities," he recounts.

It was here that his great "collaboration" with robots began—one that still leads him to pry into the most secret corners of his mind and marvel at their depth and complexity. "Working with robots is a collaborative process. I call it 'synthetic incarnation,' as I am the one who decides the subject, though sometimes the robots, who have their own vision, modify it. In most cases, we work together until I get the result I want. When the robots paint their first blob, photograph it, then reflect on how to proceed, they have at their disposal twenty-four algorithms that I created to determine the next step," he points out.

The result? His art works are often portraits that seem to move between two parallel universes; sometimes they're nearly evanescent, sometimes they're colorful or deformed as if hiding multiple personalities that melt into and mix with each other into a whole. "I've focused on portraits because I think they're more interesting. Nearly all robots are capable of making marks with colors; but with portraits, it's different—they truly have to draw. I was inspired by my wife, my children, people I know. My objective? Painting better, and even better," he says with conviction.

"Robots provide me with an ever-better understanding of the human brain; their very existence grew out of philosophical questions, ones that I've constantly asked myself and to which I've tried to find answers by taking specialized courses . . . What does it mean to 'be human'? Am I conscious? What is free will? Why do I think? Working with robots, I've also tried to discover why I had that inescapable urge to make art . . ."

For Pindar, it all began in childhood. "My mother was an artist, and I would draw and paint, trying to impress her. I also enjoyed working on art because she let me work by myself, and I've always liked being alone. In high school, I decided to pursue a career as a professional artist. I went to a conservative Catholic school: with my long hair and rebellious and introverted nature, I was an outsider. Nonetheless, everyone loved my art, and this made me feel important," he admits.

His vision for art? "Exploration: I explore my mind and my creativity. I'm trying to understand what creativity is and how it can be encapsulated in a machine. My mission is to show people how complex AI is becoming, and how comparable it is to the human mind," he explains. His enthusiasm makes one think of the explosive colors of his works. "In both my physical and digital art, color has always been important. I like bright green, I love magenta, cyan, primary colors, and the kind of green one often finds in computers and that exists only there and cannot be replicated in the physical world," he states. Pindar's future is well mapped out: "I want to concentrate my efforts even more on AI and robots. That's my path, and I can't wait to discover where it'll take me on the voyage of discovery that life is."

GUM GUM

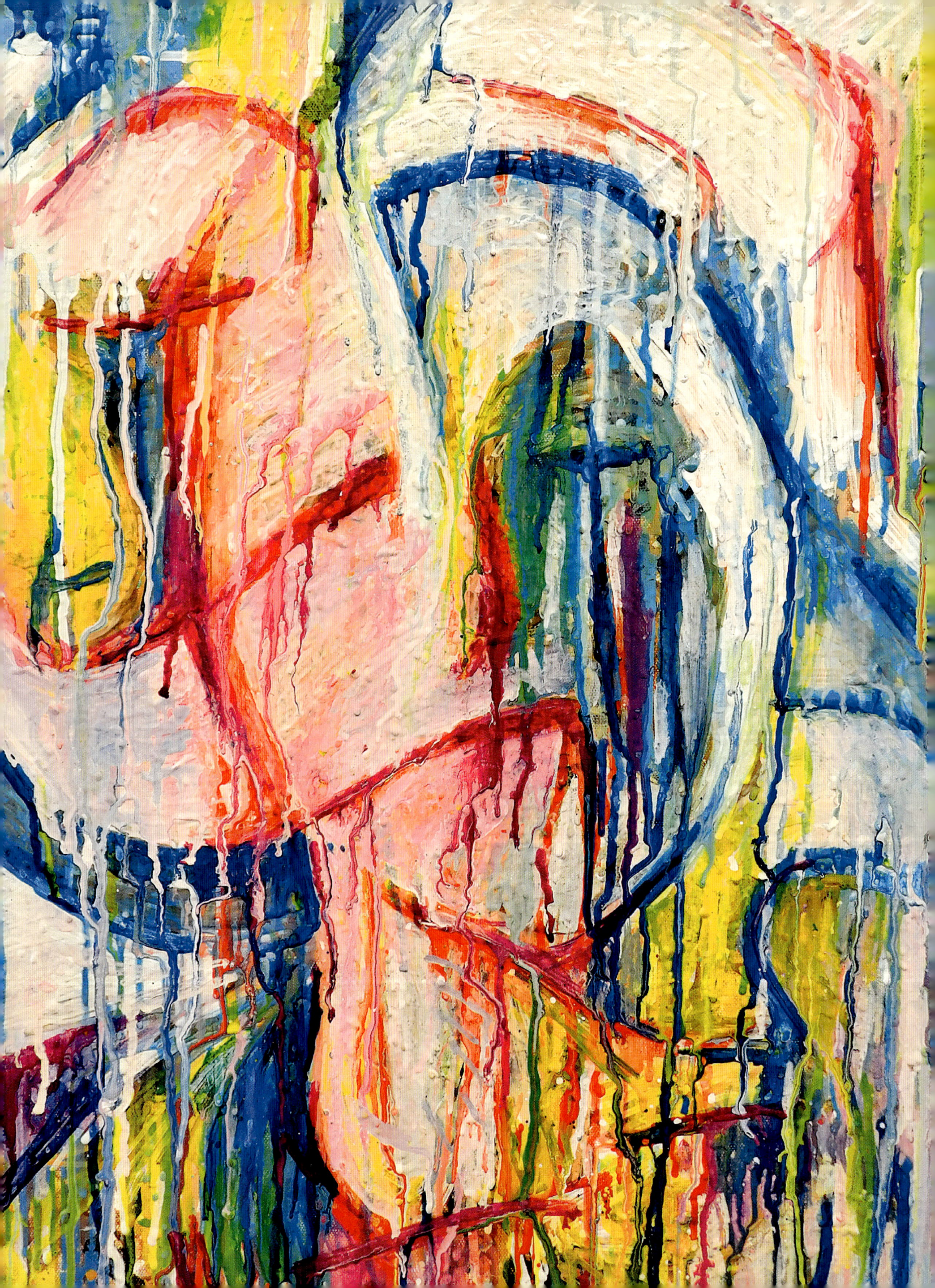

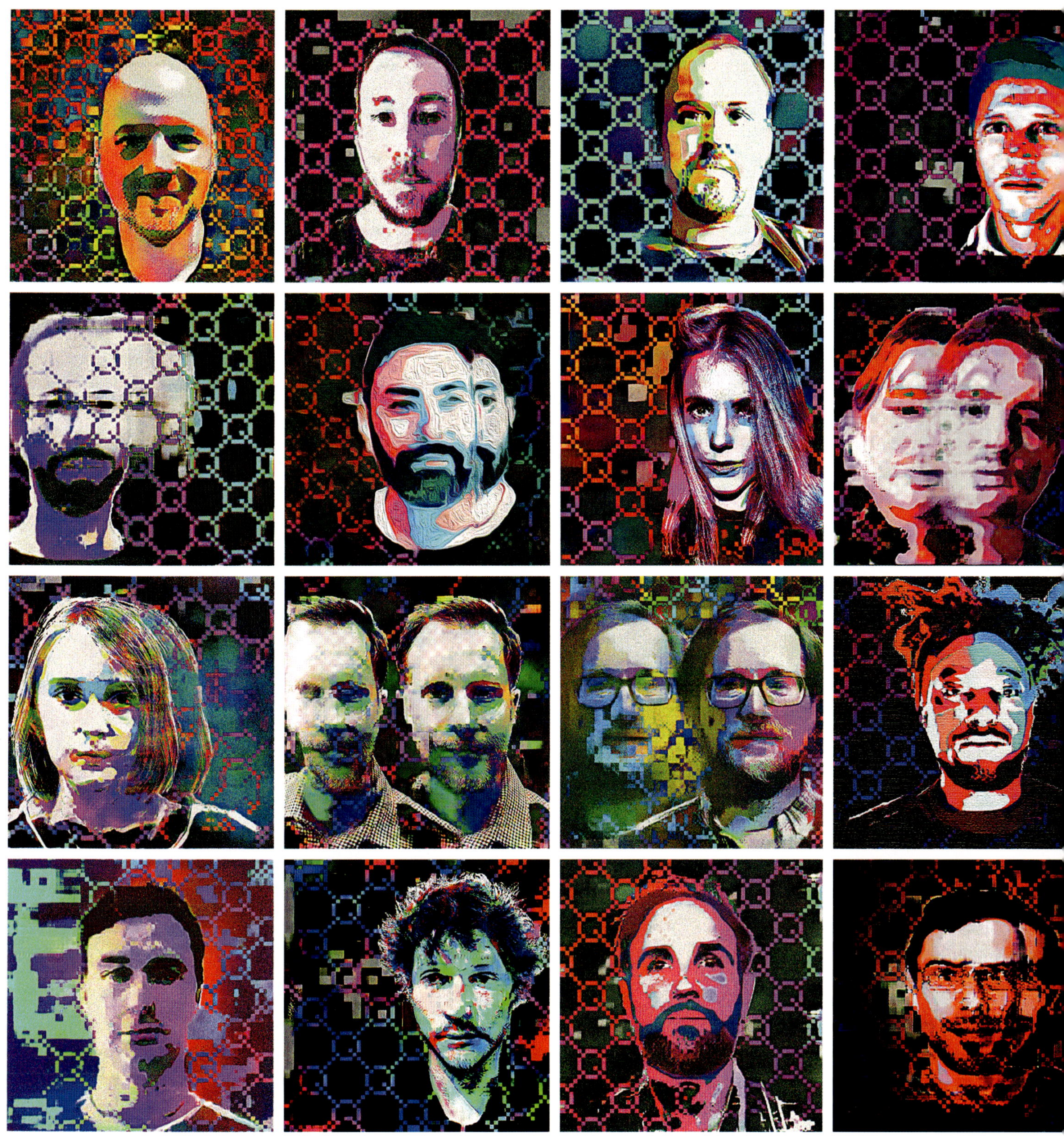

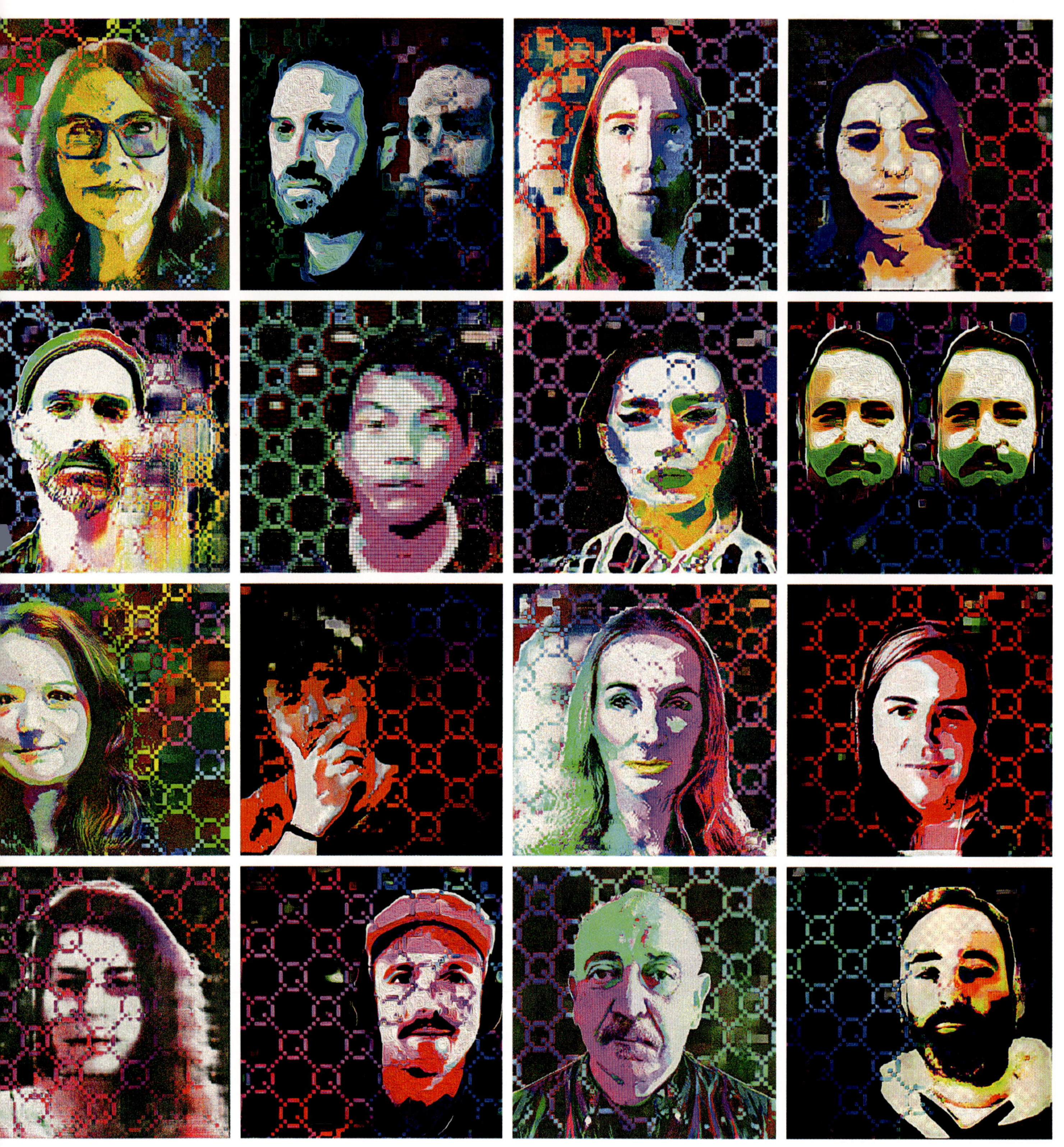

QUANTUM PORTRAITS

ALESSANDRA MATTANZA, award-winning author, journalist, screenwriter, fine art photographer, and multimedia artist, divides her time between Munich, New York, San Francisco, Los Angeles, and Paris. She is a contributor and writer for several magazines, including *Forbes, Vanity Fair, Elle, Cosmopolitan, How to Spend It, Icon, F Magazine,* and *Natural Style.*
She has also penned novels and murder mysteries for various publishing houses. Mattanza has received many awards and prizes, and her articles and books are regular award-winners in the National Arts & Entertainment Journalism Awards and the So Cal Journalism Awards, both held in Los Angeles.
Of them, it is worth noting her first place wins in the nonfiction category with *C215 #christianguemy, Stencil Art* and with *Banksy,* and in 2023, with *Street Art is Female,* and in third place with *Street Art. Famous Artists Talk About Their Vision.*
As a writer and a multimedia artist, she created the *New York Black and White* (www.newyorkblackandwhite.org), a project exhibited at KUNSTLABOR 2, the contemporary art museum and cultural center connected to the MUCA Museum in Munich, Germany, and *A Better Planet, A Better World* (www.abetterplanetabetterworld.com), which was presented in a major show at the United Nations Headquarters in New York in 2023 and which is still on display until 2025 at the Permanent Mission of Italy at the UN in New York. The latter project is focused on the environment and was inspired by the book *SOS Planet Earth. Voices for a Better World,* published by National Geographic and White Star.

SERENA TABACCHI is the Director and Co-founder of MoCDA, Museum of Contemporary Digital Art. She works as an independent digital art curator and is currently curating a web3 art program at Rifugio Digitale in Florence. Serena previously worked at TATE and curated some of the first international NFT exhibitions, events and fairs (NFT London, CADAF Miami, CI Bloom Istanbul). She is currently researching possible DAO governances for art institutions and is part of the SuperRare DAO Council. She curated digital art exhibitions for museums and foundations (MAXXI l'Aquila, Fondazione Palazzo Strozzi, Fondazione Terzo Pilastro, Palazzo Cipolla, Museo della Permanente DART, Dynamic art Museum) and curated the first NFT art auction in Italy with CAMBI auction house. She is part of the BGA board (Blockchain Game Alliance) and works as partnership manager at The Sandbox metaverse and Cinello, DAW® (Digital Artwork).

|||||||||||||||||||||||||||||||||||||||||||||||||||||||||||||||||||||||||||||||||||||||||||||||||||||||||||||

Except where expressly indicated, all images have been provided by courtesy of the artists themselves.
The QR codes on the pages direct to multimedia content provided by the artists and are active at the time the book goes to print.

|||||||||||||||||||||||||||||||||||||||||||||||||||||||||||||||||||||||||||||||||||||||||||||||||||||||||||||

PROJECT EDITOR
VALERIA MANFERTO/CONSULTING D&D

EDITORIAL ASSISTANT
GIORGIO FERRERO

GRAPHIC DESIGN
MARIA CUCCHI

Published by Schiffer Publishing, Ltd.

4880 Lower Valley Road
Atglen, PA 19310
Phone: (610) 593-1777; Fax: (610) 593-2002
Email: info@schifferbooks.com
Web: www.schifferbooks.com

The scanning, uploading, and distribution of this book or any part thereof via the Internet or any other means without the permission of the publisher is illegal and punishable by law. Please purchase only authorized editions and do not participate in or encourage the electronic piracy of copyrighted materials.

All factual information has been researched to the best of our knowledge and with the greatest possible care. However, the editors and publisher cannot guarantee the accuracy and completeness of the information. The publisher welcomes any comments and suggestions for improvements.

"Schiffer," "Schiffer Publishing, Ltd.," and the pen and inkwell logo are registered trademarks of Schiffer Publishing, Ltd.

WS whitestar™ is a trademark property of White Star s.r.l.

© 2025 White Star s.r.l.
Piazzale Luigi Cadorna, 6 - 20123 Milano, Italy
www.whitestar.it

Translation: Irina T. Oryshkevich - Editing: Phillip Gaskill

ISBN 978-0-7643-6890-5
Library of Congress Control Number: 2024950005

Printed in China

Cover Art By: Other World
Back Cover Art By: Greg Mike
Cover Design By: Molly Shields